Measuring Sky
Without Ground

D1192686

Measuring Sky
Without Ground

**Essays on the Goddess Kali,
Sri Ramakrishna and Human Potential
with Selections from
Remaining Texts in the Series**

Richard Chambers Prescott

First Published
By Grascott Publishing
Seattle, Washington

It is said that Ramakrishna would not lose his intention, identity
or direction even in a dream.

Divine Mother, I offer this cerebral stone at your feet. Smash it
into a trillion bits so it may return into the Infinite!
Clearly sever with Your sword of Clarity
this dream mind's imagination
from what is Real Self Being
at every single moment
of my continuing delusion!
It is a small task for you,
Wondrous Divine Mother!

ISBN: 1-58721-866-6

1stBooks – rev. 06/14/00

About the Book

"The Mirage and the Mirror: Thoughts on the Nature of Anomalies in Consciousness" and "The Goddess and the Godman: An Explorative Study of the Intimate Relationship of the Goddess Kali with Sri Ramakrishna of Dakshineswar" have already been published as one book by 1st Books. This text, "Measuring Sky Without Ground: Essays on the Goddess Kali, Sri Ramakrishna and Human Potential" is the compilation of the remaining six texts in that series. Please see "The Mirage and the Mirror" for a description of the eight texts. The topics of this present book on Tantra and Vedanta are as follows. Kalee and the Sacred Feminine: An Initial Blessing of Her Direct Reality. Groundwork for New Edition of "Measuring Sky Without Ground" is on the Self as Atma and the Divine Mother. The Goddess' Primordial Formula is on the Primal Principles of the Waking, Dreaming, Deep Sleep, Self Paradigm. Clear Consciousness is on Waveless Thought. The Creatrix Kalee. The Goddess' Tantra. Kalee Kunda. Kalee Bhava I: The Heroic Moods of Friendship, Wisdom and Oneness in the Goddess Kali. What Ego Might Be (A Quick Journey of Discovery). The Source of All Ideas (On Bhavamukha: The Divine Mood of The Goddess Kali). The Unqualified Power of The Divine Mother as Pure Being (On the Apparent Dualism Of Bhavamukha and Nirvikalpa). Measuring Sky Without Ground (A Pragmatic Psychology Of Non-Duality). The Lucid and the Elucidation (The Non-Dualism of Light and Emanation in the Three States of Consciousness). Inextinguishable Feeling: Goddess Centered Poetics On Love As The Central Emotion. Defining the Groundwork On The Skills of Kalee. Clearing Consciousness and Creating an Opening to Happiness. Absolute Self Bliss is Primordial Power. Kalee Bhava IV: The Causeless Jewel Of Happiness. Rendering the Indefinable: Primary Emotion and Its Conscious Connection in Spiritual Feeling. The Deathless Self and the Dramatics of the Psyche is on Consciousness as Just Consciousness, Kali's Image and Kali's

Play, Kali's Nose Ring and Her Symbols, Kali as Kha, Kali as Kama, Kali as Radha and Krishna, and Kali as Her Self Uniquely Free, Ishta: The Chosen Ideal and the Revolution or Turnabout in One's Own Consciousness, Imagination and Reality, and The Threshold of Response. Because of Atma is on being nourished, staked out, caused, and fulfilled in the Self as expressed in waking, dreaming, deep sleep and the Transcendent. Soaring Thoughts: A Reconveyance of Non-Dual Goddess Consciousness. Sahaja Sakti: Immediate Power in the Direct State of the Goddess Purely Unfettered by the Four Conditions of Consciousness. Wisdom, Self Balance and the Great Sentiment: Vijnana Bhava: A Particle of Bhavamukha. Ignorance, Knowledge and Perfect Wisdom. Fear, Love and the Great Sentiment. Phenomena, Noumenon and Self Balance. Existence, Pure Existence and Self Existence. Nitya Mukha and Lila Bhava. Neti Neti, Brahmajnana and Iti Iti. Wisdom, Self Balance and the Great Sentiment. Sublime Emotion and the Face of the Goddess. The Day and Night of Kali (The Lila, the Nitya and Vijnana). Turiya Bhava: In The Mood Of The Fourth State. Her Footprints Through Time: The Old Goddess Tradition in the Far East, origins, the ten Wisdom Goddesses, the Goddess and Narada and the Transcendent Function. Goddesses of the Rigveda: A Questioning of Origins comparing Tantra and Veda. Bursting the Sharp Mid Point of the World Mind Cultus: On the Subject of the Cultic Mind Set. The Guru Problem: Spiritual Trauma and Abuse in the Causal Dynamic of the Guru Dilemma. Spiritual Solutions to Psychological Equations. Spiritual Moments in High Sakti and the Problem of Return to Complex Cognition. Living Sakti: Attempting Quick Knowing in Perpetual Perception and Continuous Becoming. Living Sakti Within Physics, Psychology, and Spirituality. Kali: The Allayer of Sorrows: On the Spontaneous Experience of Innate Non-Dualistic Subjective Consciousness. The Empress Kali: The Pure Power of Her Sakti In Independent Natural Spirituality. Moving, Feeling, Being with the Mystic Sage of Kali's Dakshineswar. The Radical View of Kali: A Study in Religious Distortion. Great Delight: On the Primary Emotion of Love and Its Paradoxical Relation to Our Spiritual and Sexual Nature. Defining The Groundwork for Kalee Kunda: The Goddess' Flower (Poetics On Rapture And Ecstasy In Goddess Consciousness, Within The Symbols Of The Sacred Feminine). Free Thoughts: Tremendous Love, Kalee Lovers, Primary Spirituality, Consciousness and Neural Activity, Ineffability.

COLLECTED TITLES

The Sage
Moonstar
Neuf Songes
The Carouse of Soma
Lions and Kings
Allah Wake Up
Night Reaper
Dragon Tales
Dragon Dreams
Dragon Prayers
Dragon Songs
Dragon Maker
Dragon Thoughts
Dragon Sight
Kings and Sages
Three Waves
The Imperishable
The Dark Deitess
Years of Wonder
Dream Appearances
Remembrance Recognition and Return
Spare Advice
Tales of Recognition
Racopa and the Rooms of Light
Hanging Baskets
Writer's Block and Other Gray Matters
The Resurrection of Quantum Joe
The Horse and The Carriage
Disturbing Delights: Waves of The Great Goddess
Kalee Bhava: The Goddess and Her Moods
Because of Atma
The Skills of Kalee
Measuring Sky Without Ground
Kalee: The Allayer of Sorrows

The Goddess and the God Man
Living Sakti
The Mirage and the Mirror
Inherent Solutions To Spiritual Obscurations
The Ancient Method

Kalee and the Sacred Feminine
An Initial Blessing of Her Direct Reality

The Celts called Her Kele, the prehistoric Tantrikas called Her Kali, I cherish the name Kalee as a more universal invocation. For She was never confined to any one culture, place or people. The Sacred Divine Feminine is present everywhere, though the path has been suppressed by the hardness and fear of the dominator mind. But things are changing in an uphill battle of idealism at the level of spiritual education. .

To separate the mind from the heart makes for a one sided person. To divide the masculine and the feminine does an even worse thing to the human spirit. It robs the soul of it's full inheritance. That is why the essential duality of the male and female must be brought together into One Unity, for this breaking of the two halves is the wound of the world.

The Sacred Feminine is the most cherishable in the world, the essential primal sentiment of all living beings. This is the first Great Emotion that we learn when we enter this world of life. That is why the restoration of the Great Sentiment is so important to becoming a spiritually alive and a real human being. The denial of the Profound Sentiment is the root cause of so much suffering, individually and universally.

Kalee is my Disturbing Delight. Disturbing because She puts asunder the agitations of our crowded concrete conceptions of what we perceive this relative life to be. She is Delight because She is greatly pleasant to know. She is Delight because She is the Fearless Loving Untrammeled Unconditioned Light which is such a Great Delight to welcome and invite into the Sense of the Great Self.

Sri Ramakrishna of 19th century Dakshineswar saw Her as a Living Being. She would stand on the balcony of the Temple and watch the night lights of Calcutta reflecting over the waters of the Ganges. He would commune with Her, talk with Her, become One with Her in Samadhi (an ecstatic spiritual state). He was moved, guided, taught, comforted, enlightened by the Divine Mother Kali. What are mere human relationships compared to this? A living relationship with the Transcendent Infinite Goddess. It was She who brought him into the theater of the world stage and She who withdrew him back to the Infinite when the play was done.

What can we say? The Goddess Principle of Sheer Identity in Consciousness is called by many names. These precious names are too many to number. So I will dwell on and within Kalee. She is Kha, the Pure Space of Ineffable Consciousness, the True Self_ and She is Li, from lila, the wondrous cosmic play that is spread out before you, the universal tragic comedy drama we see in front of our eyes.

She is the Breather (Infinite Formless Brahmanic God Consciousness) and She is the Breath expelled as the Finite manifesting as your four states of self consciousness, none other than the waking-dream-sleep-Self paradigm. Our entire self conception is within the parameter of this paradigm which is but an emanation of Her Universal Immensity. So what is this thing we call who, you, me?

She is Two-ness, She is Not Two-ness and She is the Resolution of Reality in the Threshold Between. She is Identity in the Sheer Force of Consciousness so much more than the feminine-masculine limitations of embodied awareness. She is union and unity, birth, death, rebirth, transcendence and cycle, celebration, tragedy, joy and freedom. Every word invokes Her. Every thought rises out of Her. Every feeling dark or light emerges out from Her Infinite Sentiment.

Her Jewelries are the catholicity of the Waking States. Her Garments are the universality of the Dream States. Her Fragrances are the empyrean cosmic canopy of the Depth of Dreamless Sleep States. Her Self is the Self Conclusive! Kalee is passion, mysticism, Deitess and Essence.

The Mood Tone of Facing Her in Every Direction and in the Directionless Free Transcendent Above the Highest Point of the Spiritual Horizon are words trapped by finiteness hopelessly speaking of the Unspeakable Goddess. She is the Moment of Rapture when all this is realized and She is the Coming Back to the realm of what we refer to as world, life, death, relativity. O Mother Goddess Kalee, remove from my mind this last barrier!

My flesh and blood is the Fluid of Your Mind O Best Kalee. My dreaming consciousness is the Fluid of Your Heart Sentiment. The original and final idea of what I call me is a wave thought on the Fluid of Your Sea of Dreamlessness. O Kalee, You are right in front of my eyes and The One who is seeing through my eyes and all the eyes of the mortal realm of generation, intensity, magnitude, the Spring Tide that sweeps the scope of Boundless Void and Ample Sphere from Indus to Pole, from China to Peru.

Description of the Eight Texts

Kalee Bhava: The Goddess and Her Moods, was born out of torment and love crashing together like lightning hitting the Earth to ignite life into existence. It is nothing but passion for the spiritual. This book was the work of Healing Sakti in my life. I began to heal what has seemed to be a never ending torrent of wounds, everything from the wounds of Jesus, to the wounds of inability to attain Advaita (non-dual transcendence) permanently. The distorted imprint of this world leaves us with many delusions, scars, and schisms: sexual, psychological, and religious. My healing began as I began to embrace the Image of Kali as my Ishta Sakti, the Chosen Ideal of Spiritual Power.

Because of Atma: Essays on Self and Empathy was the work of Vedanta Sakti coming back to me. It is my inquiry into the Pure Atma, true self as What is Behind and yet Within the Curtain of Enchantment. But I must confess my own non-originality. If Ashtavakra describes the Atma as "glory" and thousands of years later Swami Abhcdananda describes Atma as "glory" and then perhaps a decade or two after that someone else uses the very same word, well, who is then original? No one person is the holder of Truth, it is Truth that is the Holder of every individual. The Lamp of the Turiya was translated into Dutch and republished in the journal Vedanta. Spiritual Solutions to Psychological Equations was republished in The New Times. Bursting the Sharp Midpoint of the World Mind Cultus was republished in Prabuddha Bharata and The New Times.

The Skills of Kalee came later as a process of autonomous self arrival. As it is with almost all writing and poetic efforts, some of it is a scholarly construct and some is spontaneous creativity. As it is, I think the feeling within each sentence speaks for itself. This manuscript was the work of Loving Sakti in my life. The text is an exercise in the practice and application of learning to love and to use my own mind as an instrument for loving the Goddess.

Measuring Sky Without Ground: Essays on the Goddess Kali, Sri Ramakrishna and Human Potential came out of thinking upon Turiya Sakti, that is Mother's Advaita returned from the waking, dreaming, and deep sleep states back into the fourth state (turiya), at least, in a cerebral perspective, but expressed with powerful feeling. For me it was like the dawn of spiritual life inside my heart. The title essay, Measuring Sky Without Ground: A Pragmatic Psychology of Non-Duality was republished in The New Times and Prabuddha Bharata.

Kalee: The Allayer of Sorrows is a return address to some important historical and spiritual subjects which for me are a salute to Tantra Sakti and how She has expressed Herself in my life. From this text, The Radical View of Kali: A Study in Religious Distortion was republished in the journal Matriarch's Way. The Guru Problem: Spiritual Trauma and Abuse in the Causal Dynamic of the Guru Dilemma was republished in The New Times.

The Goddess and the God Man: An Explorative Study of the Intimate Relationship of the Goddess Kali with Sri Ramakrishna of Dakshineswar was my greatest pleasure and joyful labor, being in itself a work on pure Kali Sakti. It is a probing search, and an unworthy attempt to fathom the depth of his spiritual experience, written at the borderline where the absolute transcendent Goddess expressed Herself in the person of Sri Ramakrishna of Dakshineswar (1836-1886).

Living Sakti: Attempting Quick Knowing in Perpetual Perception and Continuous Becoming, I prayed, was to be my culmination, after thirty years of writing, perhaps that I now might live in Peace. To enjoy what has been discovered in Sakti and to live what has been uncovered by Sakti.

But Mother would not let me rest and just live in Her Sakti. She once again forced me to continue writing and so the eighth text was born from my mind womb wherein She could not resist impregnating me with more thoughts on Her. So *The Mirage and the Mirror: Thoughts on the Nature of Anomalies in Consciousness* was born. It was written from the Perspective of the Witness Consciousness (The Mirror). All else is the Mirage.

xvi

As to whether or not, in the Final Conclusion, the anomalies within the Mirage are considered to be real or unreal, is up to you, as both the Tantric and Vedantic views are given. Either view, is still only a consideration within that Consciousness, the Mirror. It is the work of Clear and Lucid Advaita Sakti.

These eight texts are what I see as eight parts/stages of one book which is the embodiment of my devotion to the Goddess. The overall title of these eight book/stages is Advaita Sakti: A Poet's Journey To The Goddess. Advaita, of course, is Non-Duality. Sakti is the Immeasurable Power or Energy of the Divine Mother as Pure Consciousness and Pure Love.

I am simply a poet who loves the Goddess. I am just one seeker of Truth who has written down his thoughts as so many of us have done. I am no one special and knowing that this is so, is one of the most healing emotions I have ever experienced. The emotions we entertain become the moods we live in and for me, the Sweet Current of Love is the mood in which I would wish to spend as much time as may be. While working on these texts, Advaita Sakti, the most excellent thing that I learned in the process, is that it is for the Sake of Her, not I. You may taste these thoughts, you may swallow these words, or, as you choose, you may spit them out. I lay no claim to these works. Ego is a massive cloud that consumes the body idea, the content of feelings, and the mind's addressing of one's life, so with that I try not to identify. May She protect and inspire the emerging of the Love that is within you.

The Mirage and the Mirror, including *The Goddess and the God Man*, with *The Lamp of the Turiya* is published by 1st Books under the title *The Mirage and the Mirror*, and is available through Ingram Book Company's Lightning Print or Print On Demand. *Inherent Solutions to Spiritual Obscurations* with *The Ancient Method* is also available. And hopefully *Disturbing Delights: Waves of the Great Goddess* will also be available.

SUBJECTS

Kalee and the Sacred Feminine
An Initial Blessing of Her Direct Reality

Description of the Eight Texts

Foreword
Preface
Introduction

Groundwork for New Edition of
Measuring Sky Without Ground

The Goddess' Primordial Formula
Clear Consciousness
The Creatrix Kalee
The Goddess' Tantra
Kalee Kunda
Kalee Bhava I

WHAT EGO MIGHT BE
(A Quick Journey of Discovery)

THE SOURCE OF ALL IDEAS
(On Bhavamukha: The Divine
Mood of The Goddess Kali)

THE UNQUALIFIED POWER
OF THE DIVINE MOTHER AS PURE BEING
(On the Apparent Dualism
Of Bhavamukha and Nirvikalpa)

MEASURING SKY WITHOUT GROUND
(A Pragmatic Psychology Of Non-Duality)

A Particle of Bhavamukha

TURIYA BHAVA
In The Mood Of The Fourth State

HER FOOTPRINTS THROUGH TIME
The Old Goddess Tradition in the Far East

GODDESSES OF THE RIGVEDA
A Questioning of Origins

**BURSTING THE SHARP
MID-POINT OF THE WORLD
MIND CULTUS**

THE GURU PROBLEM
Spiritual Trauma and Abuse in the
Causal Dynamic of the Guru Dilemma

**SPIRITUAL SOLUTIONS TO PSYCHOLOGICAL
EQUATIONS**

**SPIRITUAL MOMENTS IN HIGH SAKTI
AND THE PROBLEM OF RETURN
TO COMPLEX COGNITION**

LIVING SAKTI

**Attempting Quick Knowing
in Perpetual Perception
and Continuous Becoming**

**Living Sakti Within Physics
Living Sakti Within Psychology
Living Sakti Within Spirituality**

KALI: THE ALLAYER OF SORROWS

On the Spontaneous Experience of Innate
Non-Dualistic Subjective Consciousness

THE EMPRESS KALI
The Pure Power of Her Sakti
In Independent Natural Spirituality

**MOVING, FEELING, BEING WITH THE MYSTIC SAGE
OF KALI'S DAKSHINESWAR**

THE RADICAL VIEW OF KALI
A Study in Religious Distortion

GREAT DELIGHT
On the Primary Emotion of Love
and Its Paradoxical Relation to Our
Spiritual and Sexual Nature

Defining The Groundwork for
KALEE KUNDA
The Goddess' Flower (Poetics On Rapture And Ecstasy In
Goddess Consciousness, Within
The Symbols Of The Sacred Feminine)

FREE THOUGHTS

Foreword

People are victims of their conditioning. That is the reason why people of the East and people of the West sometimes think differently. Richard Chambers Prescott has grown up in the West. He has had Western conditioning. Yet his inquiring mind has taken him to the shores of Eastern knowledge - particularly the knowledge of Hindu philosophy and religion. He is one of the few Western friends I know who have tried to explore the wealth of Hindu wisdom with the mind of an ardent and admiring student, and not that of a chance traveler or a supercilious surface-taster. The articles contained in this book clearly reflect his open-mindedness, impartial self-examination, and mental enrichment attained through the exploration of both Eastern and Western wisdom. Rudyard Kipling once said, "Oh, East is East, and West is West, and ne're the twain shall meet." Mr. Prescott has proved him wrong. In him the wisdom of the East and the wisdom of the West seem to have blended together in perfect harmony.

Swami Bhaskarananda

The Vedanta Society of Western Washington

Preface

The nature of this text may be summed up entirely, by a few quotations from Swami Vivekananda's lecture entitled The Atman, delivered in Brooklyn, New York on February 2, 1896. "Any new thought, especially of a high kind, creates a disturbance, try to make a new channel, as it were, in the brain matter, and that unhinges the system, throws men off their balance. They are used to certain surroundings and have to overcome a formidable mass of superstitions - ancestral superstition, class superstition, city superstition, country superstition - and above all, the innate superstition which makes men forget their divine nature. Yet there are a few brave souls who dare to conceive the truth, who dare to take it up, and who dare to follow it to the end." "I am omnipresent, eternal. Where can I go? Where am I not already? I am reading this book of nature. Page after page I am finishing and turning over, and one dream of life after another goes away. Another page of life is turned over, another dream of life comes, and it goes away, rolling and rolling. And when I have finished my reading I let it all go and stand aside; I throw away the book, and the whole thing is finished."

"Thus man, after this vain search for various gods outside himself, completes the circle and comes back to the point from which he started - the human soul; and he finds that the God whom he was searching for over hill and dale, whom he was seeking in every brook, in every temple, in every church, the God whom he was even imagining as sitting in heaven and ruling the world, is his own Self. I am He, and He is I. None but I was God; this little I never existed." And finally, Swami states with the greatest eloquence and power of the truth sayer, "We know that very few in this world can come to the last, or even dare believe in it, and fewer still dare to act according to it." To those brave and daring people, that we all will become, I dedicate this work, *Measuring Sky Without Ground.*

Introduction

If there is any need of an introduction to this text it is simply one of stating purpose and intention. In a word, that intended purpose is accessibility. I make no personal claim to realization or liberation. I am a student of Truth, and as Truth is the Great Property of one and all, no one holds special authorship on Its Immensity, regardless of the names we place on this Principle, this Reality, this Defining Existence.

As Swami Vivekananda, has strikingly stated in his text, Raja Yoga, "Samadhi is the property of every human being- nay, of every animal. From the lowest animal to the highest angel, some time or other each one will have to come to that state; and then, and then alone will real religion begin for him." What an astounding validation of our potential. The potential of samadhi, which briefly defined is the equilibrium of consciousness in that which is most commonly referred to as God, either with the idea of cognitive forms or free of those forms, that is formless consciousness which knows that Nameless Wonder of God, Self, Truth, Reality. 'Sama' means peace or sameness. 'Dhi' means force, power, attention and focus of an absolute sort. So, you may gather your own meaning on what samadhi, God Consciousness, is to you. Again, 'dhi' means to satisfy or gladden, as well as, thought conception, insight, understanding. The word is divinely pregnant with highest human potential.

Through most of the years of my life it has been the tendency of my mind to think of Brahman, the great non dual infinite, as Timeless. But Ramakrishna has given us a much more accessible and illuminating definition. "That which is the Real is also called Brahman. It has another name: Kala, Time. There is a saying, 'O brother, how many things come into being in Time and disappear in Time!' This is an absolutely beautiful definition as it makes the inaccessible Timeless Eternal the very most accessible Time in which we all are living, being, thinking and feeling. The transcendent definition becomes the immanently real direct and immediate state of our being. Not a far off and distant idea.

Ramakrishna gives us even more insight into the potential for spiritual peace. "That which sports with Kala is called Kali. She is the Primal Energy. Kala and Kali, Brahman and Sakti, are indivisible." They are identical. They are the same. They are not two principles. That is the import of non dualism and the beauty of it is that everyone experiences Primal Energy. It is the Mother stuff of what we are made. It is what we taste, eat, think, dream. It is the stuff of the vast universe and the sweet feeling of peace in the heart. It is the stuff of Time and as Time is this Kala, this Brahman, then by the loving abundance of Mother Kali, we all being but the stuff of Her primal energy, well then, the distant non dual realization becomes most highly accessible, if not even more so as the most demanding and imploring absolute, entreating us to spiritual accessibility, that one might conceive.

Time as Kala is Tantric in its taste. Time as Brahman is Vedantic in flavor. Ramakrishna completely accomplished both traditions, as he did almost all of the world's great religions, proving to himself and the world that they all do arrive at the same divine destination. Yet for him, the Goddess Kali was his special favorite. To him, She was Allah, She was Brahman, She was Christ, She was Krishna. There is no comparison in the spiritual history of the world, as to the nature of Ramakrishna's consciousness and the universal accessible spiritual potential expressed by him.

Going beyond the dualistic context of a personal deity or an impersonal reality, the Goddess Kali, is none other than this Primordial Power Undifferentiated, as and being, the Primordial Absolute Itself. She is Sakti, Pure Spiritual Power and She is Kundalini when this Sakti is coiled up, wrapped up or circled up into the phenomena of our measured experience as the waking, dreaming and deep sleep states which inherently and innately contain the Reality of Pure Consciousness which is none but Her Power.

Swami Vivekananda, Ramakrishna's beloved emissary of the Vedanta, states in the article, The Psychic Prana, "Wherever there has been any manifestation of what is ordinarily called supernatural power or wisdom, there a little current of the Kundalini must have found its way into the Sushumna. Only, in the vast majority of such cases, the people had ignorantly stumbled on some practice which set free a minute portion of the coiled-up Kundalini. All worship, consciously or unconsciously, leads to this end. The man who thinks he is receiving a response to his prayers does not know that the fulfillment comes from his own nature, that he has succeeded, by the mental attitude of prayer, in waking up a bit of this infinite power which is coiled up within himself. Thus what men ignorantly worship under various names, through fear and tribulation, the yogi declares to the world to be the real power coiled up in every being, the Mother of eternal happiness."

Sushumna literally means, the very gracious. In the physical sense it is thought of as the central nerve canal wherein electric and chemical impulses move. In the more subtle definition it is the psychic gate and in the higher sense it is the spiritual opening to the loving non dual consciousness. The current of Mother's eternal happiness is ever moving within the Sushumna, ever present as Her potential within each person. The blessed Sushumna is not unlike the central or single primary vein within an individual leaf. If one thinks of Mother as the tree and all these many leafs as humanity then one may picture Her very gracious Power moving universally as the nourishing spiritual current of happiness.

As it is, in his beautiful clarity, Vivekananda has defined that religion is what you are, not merely a system in which one believes. To this, those systems which in not knowing what real spiritual power genuinely is in fact, through ignorance have declared some misleading or rather more lengthy and difficult courses to what is the most simple and pure power of Mother.

If the mind is rubbed by trouble and crushed by distress, to wit, tribulation, and out of fear, tinged with that anxious sense of apprehension, those systems of the mind, may in the end have been less clearly of any help than they could have been, if they had more clarity on what this authentic spiritual power is in reality. We cannot feel Her, or carry Her within ourselves if we carry or are burdened by distorting superstitions which fragment consciousness into dualistic opposing forces, within or without. Nor can the peace of Mother's happiness find us if we are obsessed with rod-like guilt or defined by a morality which speaks of anything but the law of divine Love. How can it be, how may the Mother's power come into one's life, sweetly and simply, when the mind is distorted with the antagonism of secondary cognitions which strip you of your primary spiritual dignity.

Those systems which instruct or teach of an outside factor that controls, dominates or observes you, as it were, can only be, in the end, destructive to the sense of primary being in your own spiritual dignity. Once again, the heroic emissary of fearless Vedanta speaks, "What is the proof of the Christs and Buddhas of the world? That you and I feel like them. That is how you and I understand that they were true." The key here is in feeling what they felt, not in a delusive thinking that you are them. It is this wonderful potential of spiritual feeling that I have always sought to express.

Finally, Ramakrishna goes far beyond all that I, both laboriously and spontaneously, have written, with his splendid remarks pertaining to the Divine Mother Kali, "Who can ever know God? I don't even try. I only call on Him as Mother. Let Mother do whatever She likes. I shall know Her if it is Her will; but I shall be happy to remain ignorant if She wills otherwise." And to this, what greater or more obvious evidence could there be of the Wonderful Power of Mother Kali, than that Her loving devotee ever intoxicated with that Wonder of Her, could in a single day attain the highest human potential of nirvikalpa samadhi, the absolutely free formless non dual consciousness. Whereas his instructor in the method of nirvikalpa samadhi, who at the time was not a Kali man, took forty years to uncover within himself this exquisite state of human potential. May the

Mother guide our minds to that liberated state and ever keep us free from worry.

Richard Chambers Prescott

Groundwork for New Edition of Measuring Sky Without Ground

"Your Own Atma Is The Divine Mother."
Swami Aseshananda
1899 - 1996

Divine Mother! Lift Your Maya from my mind, thought and feeling, in this very Moment, so I may see My Own Atma as Thee! Oh Kali! Goddess! Sakti!

I write to cool down my mind and to serve the purpose of the Goddess as I am nothing but the lowest dust under the feet of the least of Her lovers. I even prayed to the Divine Mother to kill that feeling of wanting to be celebrated, appreciated or respected. If any of these writings touch only one or two persons and raise in them that moment of communion, contact, insight and oneness, then Mother has been successful in Her play! Sakti, just make these books easily available if they are desired and not shrouded by the arrogance of secrecy.

How can I express Humility, the foremost spiritual gift, next to Surrender and Love? I bow to the Goddess Alone in hidden dual worship, where other's dual worship is seen by all and non-duality is seen by none, being beyond the eyes and all their visions or perceptions. Goddess! I prayed for many things like Humility, Surrender, Purpose, a Reason to Be, then I realized I am too stupid to know what I should even pray for! Goddess give me what You see fit, or not, just connect my feeble mind into the Immensity!

Sakti, keep my mind from descending into the conceptual circles of worry, or of fear, or worst of all, hateful resenting! Are we not all just straw puppets moved by the strings of Your Sakti? So why should I worry! There is no doubt I have learned well that every worry is a waste of energy. But still I have not learned the mystery of worry. Giving in to one inch of it releases a thousand miles of it! Mother keep my mind in Your

1

Womb of Peace, do not let it disturb me by sinking into the world of worry. Let me perceive things and people from the Vast Expanse of Your Consciousness!

By the Grace of Sakti I am more comfortable with disappointment, with sorrow, achievement or failure! None of these shock me like they once did. I am not denying these, but now knowing these in the primary sense as adjuncts or distractions of the soul! If I shield myself from feeling then how shall Life, the Great Teacher, teach me! How else shall I become Humble!

Is the ego that seeks to please itself even something that I may say is "my ego?" The Goddess has made it, as She Herself has also created the impulse of the consciousness of "I"! I give this energy of Her's (the "I" impulse) back to Her - with both arms raised! Only from Here, this sacred moment, can I understand what Love Is (as Pure Mind) and so know what any relation (with lover, friend, teacher, parent, child, enemy, self or otherwise) may mean! Even as self, in the form of friend to itself, enemy to itself, lover to itself, parent to itself, child to itself or teacher to itself! The Universe has always been just fine, only the ego's "I" impulse, its fake ideas of what would satisfy it, got in the way of the View!

Why does ego think that it should or even could create something perfect? It is vanity. My hope of success blinded my Peace. Free of that hope, let me just serve You, Goddess, without hope or expectation, accepting Whatever Arises As Your Grace! I offer, I give, I let go, I surrender my energy to the Goddess without containment, in no limitation, with no dream in the mind, no hope (of heaven, the perfect), no fear (of hell, the imperfect) and no expectation (of the world)!

Goddess give me that Divine Blissful Indifference to those circle conceptions of worry and fear where mind may be captured by the vapor of nothingness! Give me indifference to sense pleasures and make me the true angel of your spiritual lust. Make me indifferent to business affairs, social relations, achieving imagined perfection or equally imagined failure as imperfection, internal psychological and emotional currents, even to the passage of life and death, but not to Love, nor to the Knowing of You as Atma, appearing in the Waking State, arising into the Dream State, and restful as the Deep Sleep State and the fully alert and consciously awake in the Wide Open Expanse of Your Turiya! Divine Mother, keep this mind in the Infinite, fill the three conditions with the Infinite!

The "mind" of Ramakrishna was a human mind knowing the Atma as Kali! Yet his was a mind in Bhavamukha. A mind in Absolute Oneness without conceptual ideas in or over Experience, Consciousness and Love (Nirvikalpa). And at the same time his mind was in the Mood (Bhava) of Facing (Mukha) out from Here! Imaging his mind creates the making of contact, communion, and oneness with the Deep Self, the human mind's potential that goes further and deeper than the surface self or ego. Ramakrishna's wondrous remark about this conveys the entire possibility within the grasp of every person in one sweep, "Sometimes I say to myself in the Kali temple, 'O Mother, the mind is nothing but Yourself.' Therefore Pure Mind, Pure Buddhi, and Pure Atman are one and the same thing." This "same thing" is the same thing for everyone who lives and breathes or who passes as a spirit loosened from the body being the potential of Peace for every soul and the destiny which should be regarded at the arrival to it and in the expectation of that arrival of realizing it.

The real Ramakrishna is Pure Mind, not the personality born in 1836 and dying in 1886. That Pure Mind is Satchidananda, the Divine Mother as Pure Experience, Consciousness and Love and it is the same with you in your own Real Essence of Self, of Soul, of True Spirit! I am not waiting to become Consciousness for I am Consciousness! I am not waiting to become Existence as Experience for I already Exist and Experience Existence! Nor do I wait to become Love, for I am Love, in the Love that I know! Peace.

We experience Atma without knowing that we experience Atma! So come now in the moment to the Knowing in the Divine Mother! Divine Mistress of this Pure Sudden Instant, lightning like with thundering sound, when Pure Mind, Pure

3

Intellect, and Pure Self are One in You, is there anything else you would have me sing? She who plays with Ramakrishna said by him, "It is the Divine Mother who exists in the form of the universe and pervades everything as Consciousness." Everything is said here for this "form of the universe" is you as Atma, and all the rest of creation too!

In the ultimate spiritual sense Ramakrishna's ultimate spiritual experiences were guided by the Divine Mother alone! "The Divine Mother would put me in such a state that sometimes my mind would come down from the Nitya to the Lila, and sometimes go up from the Lila to the Nitya." It is the Divine Mother who moves Ramakrishna's mind from the Infinite Eternal (Nitya) to the relative finite current of consciousness playing as the form of the universe (Lila). No other is doing this. Peace is uncovered as it has always been present, when you realize or discover for yourself, what Ramakrishna says as, "these are two aspects of the Same Reality" which is the Non-Dual Atma of the Divine Mother which somehow remains as the Absolute Eternal Oneness (Nitya) and yet displays itself simultaneously and spontaneously as the wondrous display of the universe (Lila). This is truly the most amazing miracle of all and yet it is quite natural and just is what is. The Divine Mother is Humble for She wraps us in the most wondrous and amazing wrapping and we generally remain quite numb to it, when we should be perpetually astounded by it! What greater Humility could there be? This glorious creation made by Her so rarely noticed by anyone except in peak moments of life and then even just as particles of this wonder, and that the wondrous (lila) and the source of the wonder itself (nitya) remain as the Same Reality which is the Atma of the Divine Mother. Even here where we are soaring high on the current of the Divine Mother's thought the eloquence of words is stifled by this poet's numbness and stupidity.

We experience Atma without knowing that we experience Atma! So come now in the Moment to the Knowing in the Divine Mother! After "Felt Awareness" (an expression Swami Aseshananda used to describe spiritual experience) in the

4

Moment of this Knowing Feeling of Atma as the Divine Mother, there is often the tendency to rebuild the layers of ego identity in the returning context as a lesser identity complex, easier to hold in mind, until mind is more comfortable with the familiar feeling of Divine Mother as Atma! Ramakrishna would say from the Highest Height, "Sometimes I say to myself in the Kali temple, 'O Mother, the mind is nothing but Yourself.' Therefore Pure Mind, Pure Buddhi, and Pure Atman are one and the same thing." This "same thing" is the Divine Mother! And this is exactly what Swami Aseshananda said, "Your own Atma is the Divine Mother." Yet here Ramakrishna is not only saying that Pure Atman (Self) is the Divine Mother, but that the Pure Mind is the Divine Mother. The Pure Buddhi (Intellect) is also nothing but the Divine Mother and if we are to take the translation which says "the mind is nothing but Yourself" as referring to the ordinary mind then that too is the Divine Mother! How wonderful!

This is the profound point and the epiphany of spiritual feeling that must be emphasized over and over until the accustomed feeling of this "felt awareness" becomes absolutely natural as once was the awareness of the perishable body or bodies, gross, subtle or causal. The body, gross, subtle or causal, is only an idea, a concept, a condition existing in mind and mind itself is but a body of thought. Death is a delusion! In a dream the Divine Mother was guiding me in death practice. I could see my corpse on the ground below and I amazingly said to myself, "I am not that corpse. I am not that body. Nor am I this subtle body that I feel and perceive surrounding myself at this moment which I am using to look at that dead body." Then for a split fraction of a second in the dreamtime I felt the Divine Mother as a comforting Loving Light. Atma is What You are! "Your own Atma is the Divine Mother." The condition of one's conditions around this as life experience does not change the Reality, the Truth of this, no matter what those conditions are!

And that this person, with "felt awareness" can have fear, worry and even psychological distress (even as Ramakrishna did at times) but still be able to work up their self into Ecstatic

5

Moment States of Goddess Awareness and Feeling, Knowing their own Atma as the Divine Mother - living as a natural person, humble, without pretense, self glory, exhibition, or the demand of self worship - even unnoticed and unknown - a spiritual friend to each one they meet without distinction as to what that friendship is. Then you don't have to strap yourself into the hell pit of trying to be a perfect being, or believing such a one exists. Awareness is a journey that never ends and we become humble before that Awareness. In that humility we are progressing. Perfectionism is the sickness that chooses to not accept that the ego has faults. This obsession comes out in diverse patterns usually not addressing the primary problem. Ego! The curing comfort comes in Humility. If you are obsessed with perfectionism how can you see the naturalness of Mother's Atma? Perfectionism freezes Creativity which is Life, even if one's creativity is never seen, existing only as the flowing of spontaneous and encompassing thought. Thought that knows that that thought is the Atma of the Divine Mother! Perfectionism is externalized insanity because only the Divine Mother as true Atma is Perfect, in total full Self Experience! And in Humor, that is, in the moment of Humor, the mind sweeps clear of the three states and there is Atma, the Divine Mother!

That I must question how we all got here floating in this Milky Way galaxy and that I see and must believe that it is a Spiritual phenomena. Psychic forms are empty until one puts an emotion into them. I hang in the Vastness, waiting for the world to catch up! If we can test, challenge, and question Ramakrishna, as he has invited us to do and still find his Sense of Reality true, then we shall know Something Extraordinary! Ramakrishna is a (the) Sakti of Kali and so are you, in essence as what is your own Atma! Perhaps mere human beings have mythologized and divinized a handful of extraordinary human beings, making them Incarnations of Spiritual Power (Sakti), as it is nevertheless, we say God or Goddess has assumed human form. Is it really so? Or is it the Extraordinary Power of the Divine Mother (Sakti) which is within each mere human being -

divested of illusions - no hope for heaven as the perfect, no fear of hell as the imperfect, no expectation of the world itself, so sweetly and lovingly at Peace in Spiritual Sameness!

If I question spiritual phenomena such as Kali or Mary in visions and astounding events that cross over the high ascendant of the natural world, then perhaps, you too will question and not just believe, and by doing so then your thoughts might eventually find True Spiritual Reality. I am hoping for you that this will be Love!

In One Sweeping Glance!, comprehend the sweet Simplicity, Love, which Knows All that is worth the Knowing! Love is the Sought and thought is the seeker. In one sweeping glance find Atma in the Divine Mother and know Love. May all beings on the precious blue pearl of this mother Earth that is floating within the mother of the Milky Way galaxy - Realize Their Own Atma as the Divine Mother themselves!

Ramakrishna's whole life was pervaded by the Divine Mother. It was She who taught him everything and it was She who was the Power in that Mood of "Felt Awareness" Who Taught through him. In his own words, "Mother, I do not know at all what I should do; I'll learn what Thou Thyself wilt teach me." He admonishes the Goddess to teach him personally, "Mother! if Thou dost not teach me, who else will? For, there is no refuge for me except Thee!" (Quoted from Swami Saradananda's records) The Swami states, "What may be called the "I" of the Divine Mother manifested itself through him as the spiritual teacher..." The "I" is the Atma, the real "I." It was not he as a mere man (even as he was considered to have been the great Rama and the magnificent Krishna in former lives before). This is the true significance! Look beyond the person to the Power! Feel It as You! Your own Atma! This is most high and pure Advaita! That mood of "felt awareness" knows with Knowing Feeling, that this is this, Atma is the Divine Mother! Know that no matter what the condition of conditions may be, that this Power of the Divine Mother as the Atma remains active in you. Be absolutely sure of this!

7

The presence or absence of such auspicious signs and characteristics like the quality of the eyes, or the weight of the forearm, the condition of conditions, whereby Ramakrishna would determine spiritual levels of development in people, does not really matter at this level of the Atma as the Divine Mother. She, here overrides all condition of conditions. Even if one were to have all the auspicious signs of an enlightened Buddha upon one's body and in one's surroundings and yet something more powerful than those signs held you back, the Divine Mother would override that obstruction and show Herself as the true Atma! This is Her unique doctrine which frees anyone who embraces it.

It is Sky only! No ground! No dual reference. As it is in Gaudapada's Height, the poet of Advaita who gives no quarter, no space, no ground for duality! My personal spiritual requirement is that nothing less will do. All dual mind ground ceases. Below that everything is still Maya, the Measuring of the Sky to Ground relation, or duality.

Divine Mother, please help me to be clear enough to explain to myself some more of these important points of Your most unique and novel doctrine which is lovingly liberal to any and to all! Mother, may I rejoice in Your Blissful Knowledge and this knowing feeling as imperfect as it is in me.

"The figure of a young Sannyasin looking like me used to come out again and again from within me and instruct me on all matters; when he emerged, sometimes I had a little outer consciousness and, at other times, lost it altogether and lay inert, only seeing and hearing his actions and words, I regained full external consciousness only when he entered the gross body again. The Brahmani, Tota Puri and others came and taught me afterwards what I had heard from him previously--they taught me what I had already known." Ramakrishna.

This is truly a most extraordinary statement of Ramakrishna's spiritual experience. It is possibly quite puzzling to even the most thoughtful spiritual seekers. One thing is that the figure who looks like a Shiva sadhu (dhu means to shake off and sa means the true Atma of the Divine Mother but also sad

8

means Pure Existence, a sadhu is a person who has shaken off everything that is not the True) in the form of a young sannyasin appears just like himself. That is, this subtle image looks just like Ramakrishna. Psychologists could have great fun with theories of projection from the subconscious of a self- image on the screen of the conscious, or even without external consciousness in a dreamlike condition. But the sweet simplicity of this is that this is Ramakrishna's own pure mind acting as the teacher of himself; his own mind is his guru. There is great wisdom in this, for is not our mind always with us? However, a physical human guru is not always there, and so one might become deeply dependent upon the presence or absence of such a teacher. The light (ru) of his own mind is what lifted and removed the darkness (gu). This is fantastically beautiful. And if one remembers that Ramakrishna saw his own mind as ultimately nothing but the Goddess Herself, then what is this saying? Could it be that, like all things, She indeed appeared to him in the figure of this young Shiva - like sadhu and taught him everything that was later to be redundantly defined by the Brahmani, Totapuri, and the rest? If Ramakrishna says that he learned everything then and there from the self-figure of the sadhu, then it is so. The Brahmani was a woman Tantric teacher. Totapuri was a Vedanta teacher. With Jatadhari, he practiced the worship of Ramlala, and Govinda Ray was a Moslem Sufi with whom he practiced that course. But you see, they did not teach him anything new. It was Ramakrishna's Goddess as the current of his own mind that taught him everything originally. The Sakti of Tantra, the Nirvikalpa of Vedanta, the subtle plane experiences of devotional contact with the Chosen Ideal in the form of the baby Rama, and the depth consciousness of the formless Allah Ideal were already absolutely known by him previously. So, the arrival and the engaging with teachers was for some reason performed, though completely unnecessary for him. Perhaps it is more for us that, to some extent, we should recognize a degree of spiritual education but that, in the final degree, it is none other than the Goddess appearing as our own mind that is the one and only one

9

who shows us Truth, Reality, and Love as pure Sakti Experience. This again is a type of manifestation of the Chosen Ideal expressing the Greater Reality, but in some certain spiritual perspectives, as that of non dual Vedanta, the Chosen Ideal, even so, is thought to be ultimately illusory, since it emerges out of the mind content; and only Reality is Real. So what can mind teach to the mind? We come then to a realization of the Sakti Consciousness as the one process of revelation into the Real! (from "The Goddess and the God Man")

In defense of the guru system and the necessity of this mind map, many have quoted from the example of Ramakrishna and Tota Puri, who showed him the absolutely free state of consciousness (nirvikalpa samadhi). Those who cite this episode have not completely comprehended the life of Ramakrishna. Ramakrishna had already come to that state of consciousness on his own, by himself, as is clearly illuminated in this comment, "The Brahmani, Tota Puri and others came and taught me afterwards what I had heard from him previously-- they taught me what I had already known." The "him" that is referred to here was an aspect of Sri Ramakrishna's own consciousness which appeared out of the Power of Chitrini to him in the cognitive form of a young sadhu (seeker) who looked just like himself. What could be more wondrous and beautiful? The Pure Power of his own Self manifested to his outstretched consciousness and taught him everything, as it was already known to his Self. I cannot address with as much power as I would like, the importance and the value of this pure spiritual insight as it answers what I have called the final anomaly! (from "The Mirage and The Mirror")

I call this Self mind form of Ramakrishna the Shiva Sadhu because in "The Life of Ramakrishna" he is described as holding a trident, dressed in ochre robes and having a calm expression on his face. Of course it is most important to never forget that this "young Sannyasin" looks just like Ramakrishna. This sadhu is an Atma Sakti Rupa (Spiritual Power Form of the True Self) of the Divine Mother. Keeping all his spiritual acquisition in context you must remember what Ramakrishna says, speaking of the Divine Mother, "Yes, She has taught me everything." And telling us of his knowledge of Tantra doctrine, of the depth experience in the Vedantic nirvikalpa samadhi and of all other spiritual awareness he acquired, he states, "One by one She has revealed all these to me." He again divulges the Source of all spiritual learning, "The Divine Mother has revealed to me the essence of the Vedanta." And what is this essence of the Vedanta but the knowledge of Atma as the Divine Mother!

In the purest perception of Reality, we can say that the Divine Mother, through Ramakrishna, taught the four teachers that came to him much more than they originally knew, in fact. The Brahmani Bhairavi, though a most excellent Mistress of Tantra, was very possessive of Ramakrishna and she felt he belonged to her alone and to no one else. She learned not to hold or try to possesses Ramakrishna's form of personality but to love him in Reality. Totapuri was strictly nirvikalpa minded and believed only in the formless aspect of Reality, where all else is illusion. When he tried to take his life due to the pain of an illness, the Divine Mother revealed to him Her Consciousnesses not just in the formless but in form as well. He saw Her in the trees, the stars, the river where he tried to drown his body, the shore, the air, the sky, everywhere. His heart was changed. On the other hand, Jatadhari, who was so attached to form in the statue of the baby Rama and to subtle plane experiences with the child Rama, had to learn of formless Love. Something like Brahmani Bhairavi's lesson. He left the small statue at Dakshineswar and so too, he left behind his single mindedness on subtle plane experiences and soared on deeper into the formlessness of Divine Love. With Govinda Rai, the Sufi, we can only suspect that he learned to expand his acceptance of wider religious and spiritual paths beyond Moslem Sufi Ideology by his company with Ramakrishna, but who can say.

The young sadhu manifesting out of the Pure Mind of Ramakrishna is the greatest evidence of the Truth of Pure Mind as one's Supreme Teacher. Remember emphatically, that Ramakrishna says that when the human beings who came along later in his life as teachers to teach him, they taught him what he had already known! The Tantra, the deepest experience of Advaita in Nirvikalpa and all the rest. And because he had already been taught by the young Sannyasin of his own Pure Mind he was in fact never kowtowish to any of those teachers, the Brahmani, Totapuri, Jatadhari, Govinda Rai or even the earlier Kenaram Bhattacharya who gave him the Goddess mantra and was shocked by Ramakrishna's instantaneous Bhava in the Divine Mother's mantra!

Of great importance is what Swami Saradananda writes in "The Great Master," that the vision of this young sannyasin appeared "within his body, like the image in a mirror" even so from almost the beginning of his spiritual practice and that Ramakrishna gradually became "accustomed to be guided by his advice." Well, who is not mystified by this? Yet it can be explained. Is it so different from our own inspired dream states filled with spiritual content? Like a dream Ramakrishna would sometimes be unconscious of the external world while listening to and conversing with this young sadhu (his own pure inner mind), until reentering the consciousness of the waking body as he states in the quotation about the "figure of a young Sannyasin." But with us it does not have to be as spiritually dramatic as it was with Ramakrishna. Whatever brings you Peace (of or to the mind) will do in this wondrous process of self reflection upon the Self (the Atma of the Divine Mother)!

A Dzogchen counterpart to this process is Garab Dorje's subtle mind reflection reflected within his consciousness deified as a deity in Vajrasattva who taught him Dzogchen. And with King Janaka in his pleasure garden, who was taught by what I feel was the same spiritual process as that of Ramakrishna's young sadhu, of course, when the discarnate Siddhas appeared to Janaka's mind and taught him the knowledge of the Atma as expressed in the "Siddha Gita." Both of these events can be found in great detail in the book, "Inherent Solutions To Spiritual Obscurations."

As important as it is there is not a lot written about this mind "figure" which emerged or appeared in the consciousness of

12

Ramakrishna to teach him as he did. The most of it is found in "The Great Master," the chapter about the first four years of sadhana, section 24, written by Swami Saradananda who Swami Aseshananda assisted for quite a few years, by the way. But let us turn to "The Gospel of Sri Ramakrishna" where we will find the "figure" mentioned a few times. "Another time, in an ecstatic mood, I saw that a sannyasi was leading me by the hand. We entered a temple and I had a vision of Annapurna made of gold." This sannyasi could in fact only be Ramakrishna's own mind sadhu. Annapurna is one form of the Goddess, the Divine Mother! The mind form of Ramakrishna reveals to Ramakrishna the vision or awareness experience of the Goddess! The figure is not self serving, the figure leads him by the symbolic hand, as it seems, in his own consciousness to see the Goddess who is made of gold, that is priceless or incomparable!

Now, an "ecstatic mood" is one where one's consciousness gets out of the confinement of the physical body. It may even be rightly compared to a near death experience where consciousness is released from the physical context and Self Images come up out of the recently released Pure Mind and teach or guide, reveal or advise the ordinary phenomenal mind of the former waking, dreaming and deep sleep consciousness that was contained in that pre-death condition. I think this is a very similar process if not exactly so!

But what is imagination in the waking state? Or dreaming in the streams or currents of the dream state? Or just the dullness of deep sleep when unrecognized as the bliss of non-duality? Such conditions should not be confused here, for you see it is described, "Whenever a desire arose in the Master's mind to worship a divine image at a distant place or attend a chanting of the Lord's glories at functions held in places far away, he found this same young Sannyasin coming out of his body in an effulgent form similar to his own and traveling to those places along a luminous path and returning along the same path to his gross body." This may be confusing to some, but not so if you will remember that many people report the phenomena of remote viewing which happens during almost every near death experience recorded. It is most common when consciousness is released from the ordinary body mind contained complex. I think this is in common to what Ramakrishna would experience in those ecstatic moods where his consciousness was no longer confined to the body mind container (waking, dreaming and deep sleep).

Also here we find the figure of the sadhu described as "effulgent" and as moving on a "luminous path" going and returning by this path, which only enhances the awareness of the pure quality of light in the Pure Mind itself. Even so, the dream state is said to be Taijasa, which is literally the Bright, like fire reflected in a mirror, which is again like the image in a mirror reflected in the body (or mind) of Ramakrishna. Effulgent and Luminous is the Pure Mind and its reflection in ordinary phenomenal mind. Even as it was with Garab Dorje's subtle reflection of the luminous deity, Vajrasattva. Or with Janaka's bright and luminous mind reflections of the disembodied siddhas!

You see, Ramakrishna's own mind became his teacher in all things spiritual! The Pure Mind or the Goddess assumed a form out of his own consciousness, emerged from his mind and appeared before that mind encouraging him "to go forward." Anyone who has ever had a single moment of artistic, creative or spiritual inspiration would realize that that is the same process when that moment of blissful awareness as to what it means and where it is to go onward and forward, dawns with clarity! It is the same process!

And, in the most dramatic, dynamic and wondrously beautiful way we may see clearly how this effulgent figure on the luminous path of Ramakrishna's own mind, consciousness or Self perfectly embodies the saying of the Buddha Sakyamuni, "Atma Deepo Bhava." Be a Light onto Your Self! Even though at the highest level this is meant not in the context of mind phenomena or dualistic mind play of Self watching the activity of any figure or event in the stream of consciousness. All is Peace in that Light of the Self or Bhava (Mood) of Atma! Nevertheless we have an effulgent or luminous demonstration

14

here of that Light to the Self in the play of the Pure Mind teaching or uncovering the deepest and most profound depths of Spiritual Reality. There and only there, does This take place!

Pure Mind or the Atma of the Divine Mother teaches non-duality to itself through duality and non-duality, yet ever remains beyond both! It is astounding! Very few have realized who and what this figure of the young sannyasin was for Ramakrishna. This sadhu who licked with his tongue the innermost self essences of the seven chakras within Ramakrishna causing these to awaken! This sadhu figure who stood with trident in hand to keep his "mind" alert! This luminous figure who he himself says taught him everything even before the historical arrival of various teachers! Who was in fact the Divine Mother of his own mind, as his own mind! "O Mother, the mind is nothing but Yourself!"

Now let us examine the duality and the non-duality in this most sacred mind teaching image of Ramakrishna's. For one, there is the more well known account of how the Pure Mind appeared in the form of the young sadhu with his trident in hand, who then slayed, that is killed Ramakrishna's ego form which appeared as the wild man of untamed emotion. This was a very intense action of the Pure Mind on the ego mind.

This sadhu mind figure has a voice of his own, which is astonishing really, but in the apparent visionary dimension, not uncommon. He speaks to Ramakrishna in this example of one out of how many we cannot know for sure, but there must have been a tremendous amount of communication for all the Tantra, the Nirvikalpa of Vedanta and all the rest to be communicated. With trident in hand the cognitive mind form of the sadhu speaks, "If you do not fully give up all other thoughts and meditate wholeheartedly on your chosen Ideal, I'll pierce your heart with this trident." The chosen Ideal of course is the Atma of the Divine Mother! And if you would remember how Totapuri put the piece of glass to Ramakrishna's forehead prior to his mind merging in the infinite formless depth of the nirvikalpa samadhi state, you may see how this experience is so similar to that one and yet more intense by far because the depth

15

of nirvikalpa is being revealed to Ramakrishna from the mind reflection in the depth of his own mind to himself. Astounding. Wonderful! Excellent and Perfect! This is the Atma of the Divine Mother within him working Her wonder at the core of his very soul and pure being! Both examples being not unlike the Divine Mother Kali's sword of knowledge severing off the head of ego (dualistic obstructions)!

We see the other example of the Divine Mother of his own consciousness manifesting Herself in the cognitive figure of the young sannyasin mentioned as coming in the form or mirror like condition of self resemblance, looking exactly like Ramakrishna himself as he in his own words describes some of these amazing visions. "I distinctly perceived the communion of Atman. A person exactly resembling me entered my body and began to commune with each one of the six lotuses. The petals of these lotuses had been closed; but as each of them experienced the communion, the drooping flower bloomed and turned itself upward. Thus blossomed forth the lotuses at the centers of Muladhara, (Svadhisthana), Manipura, Anahata, Visuddha, Ajna and Sahasrara. The drooping flowers turned upward. I perceived all these things directly." And from where but the Atma of the Divine Mother can this be perceived!

Elsewhere, but also from "The Gospel of Sri Ramakrishna" the same experience is described but instead of a communion with the Atman a different expression is given with the Sushumna being described as it is the innermost nerve of non-duality wherein the Atma is said to dwell in the human body. More of this is described in "The Mirage and The Mirror" as well as the power of spiritual cognition as it is in producing such experiences. Nevertheless, "This is a very secret experience. I saw a boy twenty-two or twenty-three years old, exactly resembling me, enter the Sushumna nerve and commune with the lotuses, touching them with his tongue." He goes on to explain how each lotus center and its petals of consciousness became awakened where before they had been drooping. "At his touch they stood erect."

16

A third description of this Tantric awakening or higher and higher expansion of consciousness into the plane of Infinite Consciousness is given in the licking of the chakras to awaken or become alive and erect with divine awareness. But here, instead of a communion with Atman in the self reflection of the young sadhu or of that same cognitive figure actually entering the Sushumna we find the young sannyasin coming to shake the spiritual nerves to awaken. "When I attained this state of God-Consciousness, a person exactly resembling myself thoroughly shook my Ida, Pingala, and Sushumna nerves. He licked with his tongue each of the lotuses of the six centers, and those drooping lotuses at once turned their faces upward. And at last the Sahasrara lotus became full blown." Indeed, there is divine symbolism. Is it not merely turning the face of Consciousness, confined by the three states, to look upward to itself in Pure Consciousness, the Atma of the Divine Mother. And he attains God-Consciousness with the act of this mind sadhu coming forth from the content of his own mind!

You can see how the first description is uniquely Vedantic in its feeling or revealing of nirvikalpa and how these three are specifically Tantric in essence. The drooping petals on the six or seven chakras are centers or aspects of consciousness and knowledge, feeling and awareness yet to be awakened. Like a mother lion licking the wounds of her cub to heal them, so are the lotuses licked by none other than the Divine Mother who is licking his own Atma to Awaken!

We embrace the duality of this mind image, as it is, something like a dream or a strange image of the Self which teaches non-duality through duality. You have the tough and the tender images. On the one hand the Divine Mother appears in the form of consciousness as the young sadhu with trident in hand who is saying he will kill Ramakrishna, that he will indeed die (even so as we are indeed dead nevertheless until we have awakened) if his thoughts deviate from his chosen Ideal of the Atma in the Divine Mother. Then on the other hand we find the Divine Mother in the conscious form of the sadhu licking with Her tongue his innermost essences as drooping centers of consciousness to awaken these to the full on alert in the state of Atma. One is tough. One is tender. One is hard and fierce. One is gentle and soft. Is it not the way of mind in the waking condition as it is also in the whirling interplay of self reflecting images in our dream state? Yes.

Even though there is so little given about this there is always more about this for the Spiritual is like that. "Do you know my attitude? As for myself, I eat, drink, and live happily. The rest the Divine Mother knows. Indeed, there are three words that prick my flesh: 'guru', 'master', and 'father'." Ramakrishna most boldly and fearlessly states in a very non-traditional manner. His allegiance, all and all, was only to the Divine Mother. Take note, he never refers to the image of the young sannyasin as guru, master or father and so there is no pricking whatsoever, no spiritual irritation from this, no dualistic stress because this image is his own Pure Mind, Atma, the Divine Mother, at play for him! The sweet solution to the teacher stress and the teaching and taught dual stress tension is found here in this thought that has been conveyed.

You see, a guru is one who thinks they are a teacher and usually they demand to be worshiped by others. A master is one who controls others. And a father or patriarch is one who dominates others. So it is easy to see how these three ignorant states of identity would prick the flesh of Ramakrishna. This pricking is the stress and distress of dual identity tension. Indeed. As the poet says, it is really the Divine Mother alone who is the Teacher of all beings and the only One who is worthy of worship. It is She alone who controls the Entire Universe. And it is She alone who has dominion over all that is within Non-Duality and all beings who move in the identity of duality. None other. Yet, as the poet says, "And men call it theirs." Astounding. And why does it irritate the flesh of Ramakrishna, because, when it is All the Divine Mother, yet then men say, "'I am the master, father, and teacher' - all these ideas are begotten of ignorance." That is the insight of Ramakrishna! Those misconceptions are born or begotten out of ignorance or stupidity so it is a very pricking or stressful state of mind to observe in others.

Again what is the attitude then of Ramakrishna? To live happily knowing and trusting that the Divine Mother knows all the rest. It is the attitude of abandonment to the Goddess. It is joyful simplicity and blissful trust in the Goddess. It is a child's sweetness in the sweetest Love of the Divine Mother and it is a carefree felicity of mind in the knowing feeling of the Divine Mother as the true Atma! "Your own Atma is the Divine Mother." And She, the Goddess overpowers every teacher, person, place or thing! She is what inebriates them, you, and me with Love. The Divine Mother is nothing but Love, yet you cannot understand that "felt awareness" by mind fixation on conceptual obsessions!

What is said by Ramakrishna? "Atman cannot be realized through this mind. Atman is realized through Atman alone. Pure Mind, Pure Buddhi, Pure Atman - all these are one and the same." And that is nothing less than the Divine Mother! But what is "this mind" which was at least the playground for the sadhu image if not the source itself of the sadhu's cognitive form which had communion with the Atman for Ramakrishna. He tells a simple story to communicate the thought. A bird is sitting on the mast of a great ship. The bird flies out over the ocean very far, searching for land and not finding it, returns to the mast of the great ship. There the bird has no more worry nor restlessness. So you see the mast of the great ship is Pure Mind. The bird is ordinary mind. The bird in its searching over the ocean is this ordinary mind going or flying out, seeking somewhere else for Reality other than the Pure Mind, but when it returns to the Mast there is no more worry. The Atma of the Divine Mother is the Sought and once there, there is no more worry or flight of the mind away from This!

This awareness of Atma is the state of the jnani, the knower, the sage. It is a simple state. Ramakrishna says of the jnani, "He doesn't utter the mantras, nor does he observe the rituals." This is because he has known the Atma. But there are problems associated with this simple redundant state of the jnani.

19

"Formerly, I had the state of mind of a jnani. I couldn't enjoy the company of men. I would hear that a jnani or a bhakta lived in a certain place, then, a few days later, I would learn that he was dead. Everything seemed to me impermanent; so I couldn't enjoy people's company. Later the Mother brought my mind down to a lower plane; She so changed my mind that I could enjoy love of God and His devotees." You see, it was the Mother who gave him the state of the jnani and it was She who changed his mind so he could enjoy Love. It was all Her! That is the wonderful point of the illustration. It is all within the Divine Mother at the foremost level!

It is called Analocana, the cessation (Nirodha) of ordinary mind, where Amanibhava is experienced as the Atma of the Divine Mother. This Amanibhava is the "Felt Awareness" of the Divine Mother, which is an Awareness without the concept of an ordinary mind, that is the actual meaning of A-mani, then bhava is the feeling, the mood of it. Analocana is where Amanibhava is happening or is experienced as ever present all the time for every being. The word analocana means non-observation, where there is no thought or feeling object for Atma to observe as witness, that is, of ordinary mind, thought, feeling, experience. Yet it is more commonly described as the gap or space or opening between two thoughts where the Atma of the Divine Mother is experienced. It is "where" there is no thought (amani), before thought comes back. That is it and that is happening all the time as one thought ceases (nirodha) and before the next thought comes up again, in this consciousness, consciousness is in the Pure Mind. It also occurs as one feeling dissolves, then Loves appears, before another feeling comes back. Even so, at Death, before another life arises. The same gap or opening is true between any experience or event, in particular the Atma of the Divine Mother appears in this opening between the waking and dreaming states from either direction. And again She shines as the Atma in the blissful happy peace of non-duality experienced in the deep sleep state where all ordinary mind activity of the waking or dreaming condition has ceased (nirodha) and there She is as the Atma. This is the

20

Moment of Amanibhava when Atma as Mother is known in this ever expanding Felt Awareness. The practice is to stretch, widen, lengthen and expand this moment of opening into the Divine Mother and that is the real meaning of Tantra which is to expand consciousness to the endless and undisturbed awareness of the Atma as the Divine Mother. This is Prajna or true wisdom as the all consuming source of deep sleep, and this is the place from where all is created in the waking and dreaming states and to where it goes back again. This is the overpowering Consciousness of Sakti, the Goddess. After this samadhi (felt awareness) true spiritual life begins. Before that, what was mind? It was the same stuff and bliss of the Goddess even as it was now and then known in deep sleep, for it is to see in deep sleep the cloudless Sky of Atma where what was the darkness of non-duality in this deep sleep is now the bright shining space opening itself to the Atma of the Divine Mother. These methods may be found in the Tantric text, the "Vijnana Bhairava."

It is really the quality of one's own samadhi, which is simply for mind to be absorbed, dispersed or unified into the Peace of Atma, in the Divine Mother, as insight, feeling, light and understanding of "Your own Atma is the Divine Mother." It is not necessarily complete cessation of the ordinary mind in nirvikalpa samadhi even though the dear Swami Aseshananda said, "Absolutely," to its possibility in the Divine Mother guiding one's mind there! Even thoughts just stirring here may be rightly considered as first level samadhi - but this samadhi can go into the depths of the Infinite Itself, which is none but the Divine Mother as Atma.

It is simply to become more accustomed to the Felt Awareness of Sakti, the Power of the Divine Mother as Atma, "At" meaning moving and "Ma" being Mother, the divine meaning so beautifully embedded within the word itself, than to the feeling awareness of being so familiar with a gross or subtle body and mind as waking and dreaming. If truth be told, Enlightenment in the Atma of the Divine Mother is discovering What You Always Have Been, not becoming something you never were not! It is the Core Self that has always been with

You as You are the Atma. You are never without the Atma. But how deep is your idea of the Core? And what is this strange human need for validation in the Atma which can only be given by the Divine Mother Herself? And why is it there in the human mind at all? What you think of as Atma might simply be a conscious concept and not the Depth Within!, where there are no more layers to penetrate. Nevertheless, that Depth Within is always within and so the Divine Mother is unfailing and that is why She is Divine in the first place! But somehow and in an infinite variety of ways that validation comes by the grace of the Divine Mother. Exalted, yet accessible, confident and yet humble I have found the Ramakrishna monk Swami Swahananda to be. An excellent example of the Ramakrishna experience. It indeed gave me a validating joy to hear him say, "Once the mind settles down, the Mind itself becomes the Supreme Teacher." That settling down just naturally happens within the analocana which, without effort, reveals Amanibhava and actually more so, the Mind here is in fact the Supreme Reality Itself where no teacher is needed at all! Ramakrishna says, "It is the mind that becomes at last the spiritual teacher and acts as such," but was this not always so no matter what the mind was processing as words, as persons, or experiences.

Bhava is the Mood of Felt Awareness when the mind settles down or becomes amani, that is no mind. Here the Atma of the Divine Mother shines clearly as Reality and as the Guide to Reality. Very simple. Could this happen naturally, just you by yourself, yes, for mind is nothing but the Divine Mother at this plane so clearly known. And Ramakrishna was alone by himself (before any of the teachers arrived) in the Kali temple when this felt awareness of Pure Consciousness as Atma dawned upon his mind. "The Divine Mother revealed to me in the Kali temple that it was She who had become everything. She showed me that everything is full of Consciousness. The Image was Consciousness, the altar was Consciousness, the water-vessels were Consciousness, the door-sill was Consciousness, the marble floor was Consciousness - all was Consciousness." Only the Divine Mother was present with him. So it could be the

22

same for you since Ramakrishna portrays the potential and the possibility!

To this potential and this possibility Kashmir Shaivism offers an explanation of its own. In Direct Grace, the first, highest and most primary relation of contact is between Shiva and Sadasiva. Shiva is the Pure Is-ness of the Innermost Self of Atma. Sadasiva is Pure This-ness as the All Pervasive Self even in past and future, not just the present. Sada means Always. This is the pratibha principle which is that Truth is Reflected Everywhere at all times or Shiva as the innermost Atma is reflected in consciousness everywhere, always and all pervasive. Here, Sadasiva as the only "object" of teaching or of Reflection melts away into the Perception of Shiva in Shiva, like Ramakrishna's, "Atman is realized through Atman alone." It is the highest direct grace, even higher than sambhava (mood) or sakti (direct power) or anavo (practices) upayas or methods. What Ramakrishna describes in seeing the Divine Mother as Consciousness everywhere is justly so and directly shown to us as this principle of Atma reflected as the pratibha, so perfectly described in his own words.

So in direct grace which comes only from the innermost Self (Shiva), strictly through the power of one's own reflection (pratibha) immediate liberation (nirvana) is gained. In this first and highest contact one drops the body almost immediately, like Ramakrishna saying that if one gets this state one leaves the body in twenty one days. In the second stage of this contact with grace one retains the body and lives on. In the third, human contact with a teacher is involved. The next stages are partial liberation. Full liberation comes only and finally with the higher stages. In the next down there is human contact but not full satisfaction until after death. In the next, again human contact, when one dies there are pleasures fulfilled in heaven/paradise then liberation becomes satisfied from that after death dimension. This is certainly a reminder of the power of spiritual reflection in this dimension of mind not being blurred by body. Remember Garab Dorje's mind reflection of Vajrasattva and Janaka's mind reflection of the disembodied Siddhas, even so

23

Ramakrishna's Shiva sadhu. In the next stage down, human contact with a teaching takes place, after death there are pleasures in heaven yet then one returns to the mortal coil, and here lives a short life before Liberation is Satisfied. The last stages down are less partial liberation or realization which have degrees of deeper enmeshment within unsatisfied spiritual and human pleasures before the objective ego and the subjective soul come to Liberated Satisfaction in the Atma of the Divine Mother. The point of all this is to think over the highest of these potentials! Swami Aseshananda would sum up these three potentials quite simply, "Nirvana, Heaven, or Return." Keep the highest point of contact with spiritual grace in mind, that is, the Innermost Self teaching the reflection of the All Pervasive Mind. Then going down from there the all pervasive mind teaches a cognised deity form. Then that deity form teaches a half divine half human form. Then that half and half teaches a human. Then humans teach humans. It is a nice illustration that makes the point of what is the highest Spirituality.

As is greeting a friend, embracing one's beloved or listening to an educator, so is greeting, embracing and listening to the Inner Guide, the True Teacher of the mind, the Divine Mother! Swami Prabuddhananda thrilled me when he said, "Go as quickly as you can to the Inner Guru!" And is this not the Divine Mother, felt and known in analocana where Amanibhava is ever present? This swami shared his pure delight by further affirming this truth, "It is only a change in psychological perspective." And that makes it so clear, where once the psychological motion was to go outward to seek the Answer, is now but changed in perspective to know the Answer given by the Inner Guide who is none but the Divine Mother shining as one's own Atma! This Truth is thrilling to know in its liberation from all confining circumstances or conditions in which one has formerly thought that knowledge was conveyed!

This Bhava of the Inner Mood of the Divine Mother could be said to be Exalted Emotion, that which feels in contact, God, Truth, Reality, the Goddess and the Self (Atma)! In this exalted emotion of Atma as the Divine Mother, She is the Birther and

24

the Birthing of the Atma in Felt Awareness, She is the Giver and the Giving of the Atma in this Felt Awareness. Clarifying this process of feeling we start at the base of emotions. Next comes the refinement of those emotions which leads one to penetrate or cross over and through the numerous layers of feeling and emotion. One comes to the point of arousal in feeling which turns into those Epiphanic Peaks of Love. Love lengthens in its extension. This becomes Love as the familiar journey. The journey ends or perhaps truly just begins when Love is knowingly felt in its own comfort and ease!

This comes to us over and over in every way. The Divine Mother is ever at Play (lila) with us, ever abiding with us, never leaving us! Yet, the Divine Mother as the Atma ever remains unaffected by the play! We all experience waking objects in the waking state. We also experience dream objects in the dream state. These are both mind manifestations in the examination of the experience as consciousness in its purest sense. There would be no waking or dreaming objects if there were no Consciousness. So it is Consciousness that matters here. So, Consciousness is here the Cause of Mind, and when mind rests in Consciousness cleared out of the content of waking and dreaming objects that is known as deep sleep. Deep sleep is where mind is in its cause, Consciousness. Now when this unique awareness starts to become clarified, (even as exalted emotion or bhava) those clarified moments may be called Atma states or even so samadhi states (without all the dramatic ideas about attaining samadhi). This potential rests within every living creature, for do we not all wake, and dream and rest in the cause of mind as deep sleep, while the fourth state of the Turiya (or Atma) of the Divine Mother remains ever unaffected! These three conditions of consciousness which are ever within the fourth (turiya) as the Pure Consciousness of the Divine Mother are just naturally or innately given or embedded within us as states or practices that are being experienced or put into effect all the time. Are you not a waking, and dreaming and sleeping being, in the Atma, Just So! This is AUM itself, going on all the time as A, the waking state, U, the dream state and M, the deep sleep state. And the entire unified meaning of Aum is in a constant state of awareness of itself, feeling its own Reality. You are never without it. (This is also what Sadasiva is as Nada, the perpetual always present divine sound within the ether of time and space.)

So the question could be how much intensity do you have for the Goddess? As that intensity itself becomes the level of intensity one feels. To intensity would be added passion, method, control and discipline of mind and feeling in the direction of the Goddess. My mind and feelings wander away to so many places, even so, regardless of the condition or state of conditions, my Atma remains forever Her Own! These feelings or states are always with us to one degree or another. So, spiritual practices are just naturally here within us. Do you need a practice to be taught to you, to teach you that you are your own Soul which is Atma, itself the result attained by all practice? Are you not yourself the Soul? And are you not as the three states in passage, naturally, as the Aum in Unity experience, in Awareness that feels Atma as the Divine Mother Ever Present? Do you really need an external something or someone to teach you this?

As spiritual practice, all this, everything is already built into the natural system. The Goddess' way is the natural way. She has already birthed, or given all practice or spiritual skill to you in a natural way. Have no doubt. Like dreaming itself equates with visions and visualizing. The practice of mantric thought is there as the voice and thought process itself, for all words and thoughts are mantras of the things or states they describe to the mind and feelings. And posture is as being, as you are just so. The layers of simply Life, like the natural elements of earth, water, fire, air, ether, the sun and the heavens (or star fields) are so often mystified, esotericised, eulogized, ritualized or religiously doctrinized into the exclusive ownership of special systems, when all of it, especially the most spiritual part of it, the Atma, is just naturally yours. You will somehow find that one thought that opens the way of feeling and then that thought itself melts into Consciousness as the Atma of the Divine Mother, and then experiences!

The only darkness, spiritually speaking, is doubt! The Inner Process of the Inner Guide is so simple! Divine Mother! Why can I not be Happy just accepting what is, like a natural person? Let me please have the Happiness of Your Own Atma! The Light in me writes to the dark in me, the doubt! This has always been the motive for it! But look here to the inner process of light to dark and dark to light ever moving as a single current in the Consciousness of the Divine Mother! One has doubt (gu) about any reality, especially so, the Atma of the Divine Mother. That doubt is nothing but darkness. That doubt becomes worry. That worry is nothing but wasted energy! Wasted of energy, the mind becomes fixated on the object of doubt. Because it exhausts the mind's energy, resentment arises. In resentment the mind becomes angry. In anger arises self hatred which denies the Atma. From there comes the loss of Self (Atma). And that loss saps Joy from your Atma. That is the deep most inner process going into the dark of doubt, the gu of guru. Ru is the Light, reversing the process just described in the direction of the Light of Self (the Atma) is moving in the direction of being guided toward the Divine Mother. This process may go in either direction, this matters not, what matters is that you know and feel that the process is going on all the while within the Divine Mother. So then you should have no fear, for fear is the off shoot of anger, and both lead to self hatred. And there is no reason for that! It is waste. Life itself is the study of this dark/light, light/dark process and it is the Divine Mother who is showing us this all the time! So, when She is Here, what need is there for searching?

Depression comes when you give away your Power, your Freedom, your Atma, to any other but Her! And here I especially mean depression in the spiritual search, that anguish which arises when you give your power away to any external person or thing, and so experience that feeling of the loss of Self (Atma). That power and freedom of the Atma is your own true self identity, to give this to another, psychologically or project this upon another, can only bring about a stress and anxiety that is an emotional imagination that feels it has lost the Atma. But it is never so for the Divine Mother is never separate or dualistic from you as Atma!

The True Teacher is the Divine Mother in the shape of your own Atma. The false teacher is anyone or anything else. For you see, the human mind has the strange tendency to project a superimposition of a personality out of the memory content, upon the Primary Light of Truth, as the One Principle, doing this projection out of fear. A fear that is based upon the need for dependence upon another, and not being bold in the Divine Mother as a non-dependent being!

The Divine Mother is no less, what Gaudapada describes in his final conclusion as Tayi, the All Light State, and this is no less the Divine Mother, for in Her there is no darkness, no doubt, no duality. Ramakrishna tells of two types of spiritual people, one non-dependent and the other dependent. The Shakta says, "What! I have felt the Atma of the Divine Mother, so what shall I fear!" Where the Vaishnava cries to Krishna or to some personality or human person, "Oh this. Oh that. And whines and whimpers." I have paraphrased Ramakrishna's actual quotation to make the point in context, but the integrity of what he said is here. And so, why would you go back to any other view or feeling after you have even the smallest inkling of the Divine Mother as Tayi and that as your own Atma! It is not a question, it is a statement!

Gaudapada's View is the Tayi which is the All Light view where there is no duality at all, nor was there ever any duality existing whatsoever. He does not even bring the Divine Mother into this. But Tayi can only be the Divine Mother from this side where there is duality in the mind. Tayi is Gaudapada's final analysis, his ultimate solution. For him and for me, nothing less will do! Is this the Divine Mother? Or the Atma? It is the Divine Mother as Atma! And that is Tayi, finally and ultimately! "The Absolute alone is the Primordial Energy," these are Ramakrishna's own words. Is this not the Divine Mother (Ma) Moving (At) as the Atma! Gaudapada's conclusion is expounded upon in greater depth in the text "Inherent Solutions to Spiritual Obscurations."

Contemplating a non-dual idea dualistically, can only create spiritual stress. Though I have the deepest and most sincere endearment, love and respect for the Ramakrishna swamis, especially Aseshananda, Bhashyananda, Bhaskarananda, all so many of them really and above them, even more so, Sri Ramakrishna himself as the great spiritual prototype of what is potential and possible for all of us, but not during the non-dual Moment itself. Not during that Moment of Measuring Sky Without Ground, for no ground reference will do and any such reference only creates dual stress. This is because any addition to the non-dual experience of your own Atma in the Divine Mother, is just that, an addition into the oneness and that is stressing the pure experience of your own inner reality or utterly Simple Bliss with the Divine Mother. It is She alone, in the display going forth towards the All Pervasive! We are all humbled.

It is the Divine Mother alone who causes in the mind the attraction toward Advaita. This is said in the "Avadhuta Gita," but in terms of "Isvara Karunam" or God's Grace, but we are not so narrow to divide the two ideas of God and the Divine Mother as different. This text also says, "Na tvam, na me, na guru, na sishya, na mahatmo..." (no you, no me, no guru, no disciple, no great soul) only the spontaneous Principle of Pure Mind is Real. This is the Divine Mother, this is the Truth, this is the Reality!

One must be very bold in the spiritual assertion of the Goddess. One's Nerves, one's Breath, one's Concepts, all must be applied with a unified strengthening of the three forces into one single mass of Consciousness. Then hold the Atma of Kali There! This is the attitude of the Bhairavi, the Fearless Goddess! In this the Heat of Pure Spirit lights up with a warmth that melts the gross, subtle and causal concepts, which correspond to the nerves, breath and conceptual points by which the mind holds to some texture of identity. In the Sakti, or the Kundalini of Kali, free your subtle body, which is just mind, at its deepest Cause. In death, one lets go of this body composition in terms of its three parts as we have mentioned, the gross, the subtle and mind at its cause, but for now, use it as the Bhairavi Goddess Herself.

Perhaps one should assume the permanent assertion of the Fearless and Angry Bhairavi, in the Atma of Kali's fortunate servant and blessed slave, through the nerves, the breath, and the concepts within the causal source of Mind! Indeed, why anger? Why any of the emotions? They are all turned to the Atma. One's anger is at the illusion which bars the mind from knowing Atma. One's fear is only the fear of not being one in this Atma. One's desire is the desire to know, no, the loving lust to know and feel the Atma. One's pride of ego is in the ego's mask being ripped off by the knowing of Atma! One's jealousy is only a jealousy of one's own limited self which appears to not know enough of the Atma as one might wish.

With the stance or posture of Atma Sakti, the Power of the Goddess in the Self, one's mind may view points of thought or concepts and then have the fluid skill to drop them immediately. It must be, for we want the Primordial, Undiluted, Pure Non-Conceptual Experience of the Divine Mother within one's own Atma! Even an undisputed King of the entire Earth, of the Northern and Southern Hemispheres and of all the lands of the Eastern and Western Continents together, is nothing in feeling, compared to this energetic Loving Power of the Goddess within the ecstasy of one's own Atma!

Swami Aseshananda's one statement to my ears has had so much influence on me, little by little, through these years. "Your own Atma is the Divine Mother." It is to say that your own Atma is Kali. I came to interpret the four great sayings of the Upanishads in the Light of the Divine Mother. Aham Kali Asmi, I am Kali. Tvam Kali Asmi, Thou Art Kali. Prajnanam Kali, Consciousness Is Kali. Atma Ca Kali, the Self Is Kali. What is so often forgotten by students and even by teachers themselves is that Teachers are here on this Earth, have come here, are raised here and so forth, to Serve theirs Students. Ramakrishna's example demonstrates the truth of this truth. "As for me, I consider myself as a speck of the dust of the devotee's feet." In Aseshananda one would find this attitude of the "one" who served the devotees. When asked if he would go back to India he would say, "No, I am here to serve the Americans." What a rare person he was!

You see, Swami Aseshananda did not create this Truth, he only stated what this Truth is, "Your own Atma is the Divine Mother." But if I think of Aseshananda while contemplating this Truth thus stated it gives me stress, and not the non-dual Peace in the Divine Mother, for She Herself overrides all else and the experience of the Atma in Her must be just within Her. You may get one thing here or there, but where do you get the Real Thing? The Divine Mother! Yet what was said in this statement of Reality is the Maha Karana instruction, the Great Cause instruction. Ramakrishna clarifies the thought I am having, "That which is the Pure Atman is the Great Cause, the Cause of the cause." He gives further clarity, "And what is the chitta (mind stuff)? It is the 'I-consciousness' that says, 'Aha!'" The mind stuff of the I consciousness which says Aha is the cause, but the Great Cause is the Atma of the Divine Mother, it is She who brings about the Felt Awareness of this Great Cause which has Caused the cause which is the mind that turns around to know at its base or core, the very nature of Her Great Cause within it! All doubts disappear when She in Her Own Light is realized as this Great Cause.

But This cannot be successfully contemplated dualistically in terms of where it was heard. It is not a dualistic idea, not a dualistic conveyance. I had a dream, and is it not like Ramakrishna's own Sadhu speaking to him, yet in my dream mind of course. Why not? For what indeed are we speaking of and trying to convey if not your own Truth in the Atma of the Divine Mother? Part of my dream mind was in confrontation and question with itself. Yet a stronger part of my dream mind responded assertively. "The Self Path or the guru path!" This dualistic idea arose in my dream mind and answered itself. Janaka says, "There are both!" Yet in the Final Analysis it must be the Self! "Your own Atma is the Divine Mother!"

Swami Shantarupananda admitted that the Vedantic scriptures actually contradict themselves on this. On one hand they state that Truth is realized only by reliance or dependence on Self alone. But on the other hand they say a teacher is needed. "It is a contradiction." But what of a teacher like Ramakrishna's Sadhu? That is no contradiction. It is reliance on Self and Self helping the self! It is the Best of all! And again, there is never a contradiction in Love! All the three layers of waking, dreaming and deep sleep melt away there in Love. The guru or teacher idea is two movements which are still duality and so cause stress. The gu is Darkness (doubt) which is in attraction to the Light. And ru is the Light which is attracted to remove the Dark. This dual movement or process is a form of communication that takes place at either or all of the three layers. In the waking state words are heard and they sink into the mind's texture. In the dream state, self images arise, come up or appear from the deepest depth of the Core Self and speak to the surface self of the ego trying to explain to it exactly what it is in its own Reality. Yet then equated with deep sleep is the very Cause of the the mind itself which jumps forth with self image in the dream state and listens to words in the waking state. But remember Ramakrishna's young sannyasin, his Sadhu was both seen and heard, in the waking and dreaming state as the pure Cause of his own mind coming forth as the Inner Teacher in divine and wondrous display conveying all knowledge of Vedanta's nirvikalpa and Tantra's doctrine and all else. There was no other teacher that was "necessary" for him as the scriptures state and so he broke through the scriptural barrier into a deeper and more transcendent and divine experience of his very own. It was all the "Self Path" for him really!

Love is the Key, the Path, the Result. Swami Vivekananda describes Love as a triangle with three points. "Love knows no fear." The meaning of which can only be obvious in that there is no room to feel fear when there is Love! "Love knows no bargaining." Love does not say to itself if you give me this or that then I shall love you. Love only Loves without making any bargain for return. "Love knows no rival." Which means there is nothing in contest or in competition to this feeling of Love which overrides all other feelings, and to who or to what may one indeed have such a feeling, but the Divine Mother. Is any human relation comparable?

Love is the Unity of Felt Awareness in the Atma as the Divine Mother! As Ramakrishna says, this Consciousness of Atma in the Divine Mother is, "realizable by means of spiritual mood (Bhava) alone... 'As is one's mood, so is one's gain; it is faith that is at the root. It is through mood alone that Love sprouts.'" So when I asked Swami Aseshananda what was the quickest way to get rid of the ego, he laughed a most wonderful laugh and then seriously said, "Love of God." "What is Love of God?" Swami came forth, "Attraction to the Ultimate Reality, like a needle to the Magnet." Of course, the Ultimate Reality, the Magnet itself is nothing else than the Atma of the Divine Mother! Is it not? I asked him, "Must Love be Unconditional?" And Swami responded, "Yes, Total, Pure, Free of Worldliness." And what is such a Love I tell you, free of body, free of mind, free of anything that comes forth from or arises out of the waking state, the dream state or the deep sleep state, for that is what worldliness is. It is a Love More Than any of this! Love of the Atma in the Divine Mother which overrides all worldliness in any relation to those three states. Total in Her. Pure in Her. Free in Her!

It is the level, amount and intensity of Love that you feel for others, in any regard and regardless of whoever or whatever they are, teachers or tyrants, loved ones to one's own self, that really and truly teaches you. Love is the Divine Mother. Love is the One Guide. Love is the Result as the Reality found when guided to. Yet Love, even as the Divine Mother, is more than the Guide there and the Reality once Found. More than both, More than either. Love is the Entire Truth. Love is the Sought!

Love comes, easy and natural, like the lover's effortless "attraction" to the Beautiful within their lover adored. The needle is pulled to the Magnet. Love may be a Choice to take in the path. And so its opposite, hate, also may be a choice in that it is a decision to react from a self conception grounded in ego which is insulted in many ways in the course of life. So hate is to react to this insult, but life is going to insult the ego; aging, illness, disappointment, many ways, then life in its aspect of death naturally does so by ripping the mask of ego away. Try to have Love and so too, Compassion for those things, people and events that obstruct one's selfish designs, for they shake up, rock and imbalance the ego, unknowingly, and so, are good teachers, also unknowingly, but that is only to the degree of Love that is there.

It is the Atma of the Divine Mother which is the Sought. As "embodiments of the Divine Mother" the sacred feminine is described by Ramakrishna as "Bliss Giving and Nourishing." Then what is the masculine but for the seeking. Then bring together both as One. One Atma as the Divine Mother. Is it not what is sought from our most recent death, to most recent birth, and from long before those? To be Given Rest in the Nourishment of Bliss is what is Sought! The Sought, is it not what drives all Arts, all Music, all Poetry, all Achievements, and all Spiritual searching and seeking! It is the power which fuels the engine and the destiny that this engine seeks!

In this light the Divine Feminine is the Sought and so the masculine is what seeks. Thus the Goddess is Ultimate as What May Indeed Be Sought! Is this "Attraction" what we most often think of as Love? Or is Love Itself the Absolute Oneness that is there behind everything, every being, Luminous, as What Makes the "Attraction" happen! When this Bliss Giving Atma, as Absolute Oneness in Love, as the Sought Itself, is found, then woman is seen without lust, then you see her as an embodiment of the Goddess, the Sought through the Sought is realized, in the same way of seeing Atma through Atma alone and not through the mind. Women are known then as Goddesses, it is desire that blinds, by wanting, chasing the display as otherness, in that dual stress we have been talking about, rather than knowing well, the Sought (Atma) just As You Are! So Be It!

As a Dualist, I softly and gently worship and adore the sweet Beauty of the Goddess. As a Non-Dualist, She rips hard this ego apart with Her fine formless Bliss. As Radha so much Loved

Krishna!, with all my Love and spiritual lust turned up, I adore Kali the Goddess, becoming She who devours all flesh in space and time (the waking state), all mind (the dream state) and its cause (in deep sleep). If Ramakrishna could mind manifest the trident carrying and lotus licking Sadhu, then why not anyone their own Self Form! This Beautiful Bhava is the worship of the Goddess Within, the Sought Itself, as She is Love! Non-dual on the outside. Goddess worship inside. Whose combination is this? What combination is yours?

What can I, this helpless fool of a poet, say of Her who is Love Itself! "Kalee, are we all not but a speck of dust and You the Laughing Dust Enhancer delighting in this dance of straw dolls who must finally realize that the one needful and true thing is Love." (from Kalee: The Causeless Jewel of Happiness) "Kalee, can I say that You are a presence and not a process, both, something more or none of this, all of this, as You Are, never defined nor marked by the assayer's sifting mind. Kali!" (from Kalee Bhava II Simplifying Complexity: Jarring Consciousness Out Of Esoteric Difficulty) "Kalee, She, illustrated by Oneness which kowtows to none nor knocks the head with unknowing kinetic motion inside the little helpless knuckle trying to figure out its clues to that which has no figure, to this undoubted, obvious, evident, unpretentious kernel and ken of bliss alert, aware, ever lingering as itself in a life lucky to be the fullness of insight... inward, immediate, always with result, interpenetrating all that is dualistic by Her total envelopment of the ever unbroken never dual. Kali! Kali! Kali!

Kalee, now that all is finished, what shall be done with this thing, this body compounded of material atomic elements, this blessed, one of a kind, this altar tool of loving Kalee, used and then discarded like a dried up flower once used for your worship. It is but a leaf on your wind that lists and lusts as you please. Kali!" (from Kalee Bhava III Equipollence: The Exquisite Emotion) "I got away from all that, put it all outside and behind. Then I worshiped Sakti and nothing else. She made me a Skillful Sky Poet with the Sight of Her! She pulled all

35

ground phenomena out from under me and made me Trust only the Sky Experience of Her Pure Sakti!" (from The Empress Kalee: The Pure Power of Her Sakti in Independent Natural Spirituality)

This fool says the Divine Mother gives real Peace! The Soul (the Atma Self) apparently wanders into the body and mind here on this Earth world and we think this dimension is real or permanent. It is the same delusion with hell or heaven. For some, Earth is hell, for others it is heaven, for some it is a mix. So those conditions are a matter of perception and experience. This Soul is Atma. May it come to Rest in Bliss, when it knows it is the Divine Mother!

In after world conditions I suppose anything is possible, but this is where I go! Heaven, well if it is what you want. Nirvana, well eventually perhaps. Paradise, or back further, before these were conceived in the Texture of Consciousness! Aseshananda would say, "All poets and philosophers Love Death." Because it is the Ultimate Question, but truly, so is Life the Ultimate Question. Yet, Death wipes out the struggle of poets and philosophers and so by its conclusive power they are fond of it, not afraid of it. And because Kali, is the Mystery behind the act of death or if it gives you more peace of mind say the dream of death or the phenomena of death. Aseshananda also would say, "Death tears off the mask." The mask is but the ego's feeling awareness of the body and mind as a contact experience with the surface self, rather than the innate and blissful Deep Self. It is the Divine Mother here that tears off the mask of the surface self and so She is the Most Natural Revealer of what is There in the Deep Core Self of Atma! An interesting thought is that Ramakrishna in the Kali temple and Totapuri at the river were both ready to tear off the mask, before the Divine Mother appeared to them in all Her Luminosity as Blissful Pure Consciousness pervading everything. Perhaps one must be ready to sacrifice (let go) and surrender (give over) everything most precious as the life of the body and mind contact, before the Divine Mother will Show Her True Self to you. It makes sense because otherwise you are holding on like a tight fist

36

instead of opening your hands. And what at all can you see like that so gripped in the tight grip of fear.

On this side of death some of these thoughts may be terrifying, but once the deathlessness of the Atma is known and deeply felt, these things, one and all, for once and for all, now lose their horror! Mother Kali! When my death comes please just kill this body outright so that the encasing of Your devotee's Soul as Atma does not have to wander the Earth helpless and crippled by partial death, if it is Your Desire and Goddess thank You for reminding me this day, not to hold on to this life that much! Let this "I" as Atma the Soul simply, and freely separate from the twenty four cosmic principles, In Pure Death, Asparsa Death where there is No Contact! Atma is not mind, intellect, ego or the undifferentiated unmanifest (Prakriti) upon the surface of which the memory rests! Atma is not the instruments of the five senses. Atma is not the five sense experiences. Atma is not the instruments of the five organs of action. And Atma is not the five subtle elements which turn and become the five physical elements. Atma is not these twenty four cosmic principles and yet as the Divine Mother, the Atma is everything! So who really understands at all!

Kashmir Shaivism offers thirty six principles. It may be evident that the Shiva Shakti religion existed, was indigenous to that part of the world now called India, prior to the Indo Aryan invasion as shown by the Shiva seal from Mohenjo Daro. And these Shaivites claim a lineage going back long before and then coming down into Sanatkumara and Durvasa who are found in the Vedic and the Upanishadic times. Also, the twenty four principles of Samkhya are consumed in the thirty six principles of the Shaivites. Samkhya is also not a Vedic doctrine. At any rate, the thirty six principles are as follows. The five physical elements, earth, water, fire, air, and ether which could be called atomics. Then their five subtle sensory or quantum counterparts which correspond and yet are of a finer dimension. Then the five senses which we all know. And the five instruments of activity; hands and feet, sex and anus, and then the mouth that talks. The next five are the mind, the intellect, the ego as the

37

outward soul, then prakriti as the undifferentiated mass of consciousness not unlike individual or universal deep sleep where all memory and mind stuff (chitta) is contained in its unmanifest form. Then is purusha or the inward soul. Next, the five bindings which create a sense of bounded, limited and finite self conception. These are time, space, limited knowledge and limited power, and then desire as in the chasing outward for waking or dream objects, instead of resting in happiness. These are held by the bewitching dream of Maya, which is lifted by Vidya (Knowledge or Wisdom). This brings the Sight of Isvara (God) as Perceiver (the Witness). Extending this out toward all the universe or expanding that sight outward everywhere is Sadasiva. Then the last two principles are Shiva and Shakti, the God and the Goddess. Different schools of thought emphasize one more than the other. The truth is that when properly understood they are the same Reality, as Ramakrishna so often did say. There is also the thought that Shiva (Pure Is-ness as nothing but Atma) is a sleeping white corpse without the Goddess. Consider this, that if all the universe and everyone in it were wiped out by Shiva's all destructive power and there was nothing left but just Self, isolated, alone and purely independent with no relation as if in a void where there is nothing but just that sense of Self alone, well then, would it not be similar to a lifeless corpse in some metaphorical way. So let the Goddess dance on You, bringing the lifeless to Life! For She alone is not any of these principles and yet is all these principles. And She, the Goddess, is most unique as She is both the Pure Power of All Is-ness and All This-ness!

The idea of karma as reward or consequence is there, with good acts being rewarded with a resultant Spirit life in heaven and selfish acts suffering the consequence of hell. But Siberian and Native American people also have the belief that it is what one does in the Spirit world that determines the nature of their vacation or holiday on Earth. Very interesting. Does the human become spiritual or does the spiritual become human? One system turns the karmic belief system on its head or gives us both a spiritual karma and an earth karma. Even so removing

38

the karmic weight as an idea. Atma as the Divine Mother, here, You are Atma, you have come here to consider Atma in these conditions which are a temporary realm, a momentary dimension of thought and contemplation, even as karma (cause and effect), maya (cognitive dream like illusion) and anava (the incomplete individual sense yet to emerge as the Atma, or the conceptual self limiting concept where you still think of your own Self as anything else which is not the Atma of the Divine Mother)!

It seems though from the Pure Mind viewpoint or as it is the Atma in the Divine Mother, that all survival or continuance in the next world or Spirit world is all in the Mind, the Pure Mind, all encounters, all worlds, everything, even as that consciousness supports or gives a sustaining reality to the causal body, or the subtle body as it did to the physical body. Yet, all that is in the Mind! Ramakrishna told his wife, Holy Mother Saradadevi (of who Aseshananda would most delightfully remark, "For I have seen her!") after his death, as she saw him in her mind as a vision, "I have only passed from one room to another." Is that not moving further and deeper into the Atma of the Divine Mother, that next room, and so is no death at all! And does it not provide for us such continuance of Consciousness!

So, when the time came for Swami Aseshananda to drop the dry leaf of his old body, lying on his back both his arms went up straight into the air, his hands grasping what I can only believe was Ramakrishna or Saradadevi, or the Divine Mother Herself saying, "Okay. Okay. Not yet. Not yet." He did this a few times and then when the right moment came he let go of his own sakti into the depth of the Great Sakti of the Divine Mother! Om, Divine Mother! Hring, Advaita! Now the Sudden Lightning Like End of Misery! It is a blessing to anyone who hears of this to know of such a beautiful letting go. May yours, may my Let Go be a Good One in Her, even if the mind is at its most denigrated level at that moment!

Mother Kali, and here with Her, it is not the worshiping of death, do not be mistaken, but living in its heightened awareness where the "mask" is ripped off... please kill in me the wish to worry over how unworthy and imperfect is my offering to You,

39

even though it is a high point of life for me it is only a small thing in the world. And destroy the wish of the ego to be appreciated for this! Let me let go and offer my energy, my worry, my passion to You, Kali, my hope, fear, and expectation to You, my arms also opened and raised! Mother Kali, let me choose the alternative of Love, rather than the human tendency to go back and forth from acceptance to impatience! And if You in the shape of death come too soon for me it is well that I may know that what has been written is out there, even in its small way, and yet the letters sent to me are the proof of the most special feeling a writer seeks.

Why can you not just be in your own Atma! As You are nevertheless. Independent! Loving! Open! So often spiritual teachers negate you and cause just the opposite making their students grossly dependent on the teacher, filled with neurotic love toward that one and narrow in their outlook and love of others. Why can't you just be in your own Atma I ask? What is this strange need for validation? One feels clear in their own Reality and then they turn around needing reassurance. Walt Whitman discovered spiritual practices and realities to the Self puzzle, in his Self discovery without ever once relying on a teacher. From where does this validation of the Atma come? From everywhere, from everything, for it all sings the song of the Atma. The stars! The floating Earth! Flesh, Dream, Mind and Soul! Even in that you may doubt the Atma in itself validates the Atma! For who but Atma, watches the current of doubt?

You see, these teachers who generate neurotic love, dependence and narrowness are not wholesome. They cause you to fall from Truth into the distortion of guru worship and as Swami Prapannananda said, this in turn is the cause of cult fanaticism which on a larger scale is religious fanaticism, which is the reason for numerous wars. You see, Knowledge conveyed from one to another within the form of natural human heritage is a wholesome thing, but the fanaticism of guru worship is not.

Truth is and certainly should be a spontaneous experience. I have read a young woman's description of spiritual experience while walking on the beach at Puget Sound and to me it embodied more true spirituality than did Larry's description of his Spiritual experience in "The Razor's Edge." Philippine Christians have themselves actually crucified during Easter ritual. One man has consecutively been crucified seventeen times. Aghoras collect the parts of dead bodies discarded in the Ganges river, cook those parts and in imitation of the all devouring Goddess will take a bite of the cooked flesh in order to overcome repulsion and learn a Love which knows no fear. It is not cannibalism for its own sake. Shamans let their minds dance the wild dance of mystic journey following the mind wherever it goes. While Buddhists will sit making the mind tranquil and calm. And Dzogchenist practice the art of sudden realization. It is not these things in themselves it is the intensity behind them. The intensity of the people engaged therein! With all this why not the adoration of the beautiful Goddess which when done culminates in the Advaita which knows and feels the Atma of the Divine Mother!

Realization may indeed be but a massive release or vacation from all fears, worries and dualistic stress engaging. All worries were never needed and everything has always been okay. It was all a matter of one's mental energy, as to where it was and where it is now. Perhaps the problem simply was the suppressing of one's own Truth as to one's being the Atma of the Divine Mother! "Worry never changed any misery." Something said by Swami Bhashyananda. Good words, though the saying still prognosticates misery. Don't worry! Over and over, the Divine Mother shows me all worries were wasted energy, in the particulars especially, losing the Universal Feeling and Vanity (Ego) the Trickiest of Mistakes!

Aseshananda's answer was so perfect and profound that I could not even remember the question for years, it did not come back to me, which is what a powerful spiritual Answer should do. Eliminate the problem embodied in the question. "Does the Divine Mother Guide us to Realize the Atma?" The question did come back to me. His answer has never left me. "Your own Atma is the Divine Mother."

And when I asked him, "Can we just taste the Sugar or can we become the Sugar?" His answer was, "Absolutely, Pray to the Divine Mother. She will Guide you." To that high question. Yes, absolutely, you are the Sugar. Sugar being a poetry for the Infinite Itself. And the Divine Mother will guide you there! Not just taste. Who shall explain the Taste to you, if not Your Self, your own Atma, which is the Sugar!

As Swami Vivekananda put it, "We are forced to admit, as a last conclusion, one teacher who is not limited by time; and that One Teacher of infinite knowledge, without beginning or end, is called God." And this comes from one who was so close to Ramakrishna and still this is his felt awareness of spiritual Truth! I had asked Swami Brahmarupananda about the teacher, he said, "In the Final analysis, Satchidananda alone is the only Teacher." I reflected what he had said to Swami Bhashyananda who then added to this going even deeper, "In the Final Analysis, Satchidananda is All There Is!" Is this not Love itself as the Atma of the Divine Mother, who is none but Satchidananda, Existence, Consciousness and Bliss. As the Tayi, the All Light of Gaudapada! Even so reducing what guides us to Reality as being secondary to Reality, and what, if not Love itself, may reality be secondary to! Love reigns supreme in the realm of spiritual Truth.

The last words of blessing Swami Aseshananda said to me in this realm of the world were, "Sakti! Sakti! Everything will be All Right!" All of Aseshananda's words, about the Atma, about the Divine Mother, about Unconditional Love, and about everything being all right have come true because of the Divine Mother, because these were Truths about Her and not just some truth about Aseshananda as a human being. He blessed me with a living faith in Her. He prayed that She would keep me under the object of Her Shining Grace! Blessed is that, no doubt!

Aseshananda was such a humble swami. When we would eat he would stand partly behind the door of the dining room and chant from the Gita. With other teachers you serve them, but Aseshananda showed the humility of Ramakrishna. At the worst time of my life he helped me and made me feel the Best of my life, that is, worthy of Truth in spite of all my suffering. I was like a dark crucified angel as I fell down on the wooden floor and said to him, "I am a fool." He looked at me with nothing but Love and Empathy as to my pain. Yet other spiritual teachers seem to have gone out of their way to make me feel the worst they could during the best times of life, and the result of being with such teachers is their students would consequently speak with back biting and insults to each other and of all who were not in their narrow little world. Is that not so far away from the Truth we seek! Yet Swami Aseshananda taught me to handle the worst events life can dish out and remain Spiritual throughout. Bless him. There were those here and there who seemed to be somewhat afraid of Aseshananda. I asked Swami Bhashyananda about this and he said, "He is like a great elephant. Outside there are tusks. Inside he chews the sugar cane." So for me he was one of the Giants of God!

Even as we, in our own lives, will come to know that the images in the dream mind are just images and not the Pure Mind, or that these images in dream consciousness are not the Consciousness of Atma as the Divine Mother, so too this blessed spiritual example of Ramakrishna came to know that the image of the young sannyasin was indeed just an image and that what was indeed the true nature of his own mind was the Pure Mind, the Atma of the Divine Mother as demonstrated in previous quotes such as, "O Mother, the mind is nothing but Yourself." So too we must learn to let go and soar on from our identities with the dream mind, or the names and forms which appear or arise in the consciousness of the dream mind. This consciousness is nothing but Pure Consciousness once one has determined this Luminosity as a Self-Right without the limiting designations of dream images, names, or forms. Those are all conjuring and not the Conjurer, except of course in the non-dual sense of it where what appears to arise is not different from the Source from which it arose.

While working this groundwork for "Measuring Sky Without Ground" I have made dream notes of eighteen dreams which I remembered, to have contained spiritual images.

Though all of them were pleasant, precious and uplifting dreams, the truth is that none of these dreams show what Mind really Is! No dream does. It only shows an image. When the bewitching dreams of maya (the measuring out of all these relative forms in time and space) stops, Spiritual life begins when you simply, without show or sham, realize, "All This is my Mind." All this, all that we have been talking about, the Atma, the Divine Mother, and everything else we have discussed. Pure Consciousness, the Atma, is not ever affected by any dream state! Or waking state, or deep sleep state! For Pure Consciousness is the witness of these states when they are happening. (See more about this in "The Mirage and the Mirror")

My point is, are not these dreams of ours like Ramakrishna's young sannyasin, yet lesser in intensity of course, yet appropriate and worthy to our own consciousness at whatever level that consciousness may be beheld! Of course, our dream states are related in their quality to the condition of our nerves, to psychological persuasions, and suggestions, attitudes and sentiments. Also, the lucid or the non-lucid ambiguous conditions of neural effects in the organic level of the the mind as functioning in the brain. Yet, even with all this you will realize this Consciousness is beyond and free of any dream, as Mind without dream, then you are There, Awake, in the Atma of the Divine Mother.

One cannot compare the Immensity of the Divine Mother with the human mind's archetype of a physical body birth giver mother for that will cloud the picture with preexisting emotional personality concepts and colorings. No human being conveys Her Being! It is the same problem with teachers and all relationships, that we use our preexisting set of concepts as determinations of what we think Immensity or Spirituality must be, even as the conceptual projections of the idea of incarnations and what we think these are or should be in our minds. No comparative archetypes describe by memory's relation. You must find a New Meaning for the Divine Mother, Goddess, Sakti, Kali or the Wild Dakini!

Simple psychological equations or the mind's formulas are not There in the Divine Mother, or they do not successfully reach the state of mind that is meant to be portrayed in what She is as Pure Consciousness itself. The Atma! But you see, bringing down the Atma of the Divine Mother into the psychological mind or the ordinary mind, gives a Living Spirituality to life and not just a sense of Inner Transcendence! We might be capable of defining thought processes, but not the Gap or Opening (analocana) where the Divine Mother as the Atma of Pure Consciousness is Ever and Forever Experienced!

In truth, we think, or see within our thoughts, only in representations or symbols of what we actually experience in the psyche or streams of consciousness generally called mind, until we see Consciousness Pure as Atma. For example, if a say a word indicating a certain object, your mind brings as a referential representation or symbol of what that word means to you and most likely it is a different reference than what I mean by the word. Even internally, our thoughts as they are, that is as Self or Atma, are not seen for That, but we tend to see thoughts more like we see dreams or symbolic references. Even so, admittedly, scientists say that Consciousness (which as Atma is the Divine Mother) ever remains something that cannot be defined by the scientists of the brain and mind themselves. But for one to get a "felt awareness" of this Consciousness it seems at first one must clearly separate not only all dream or thought images, but all the emotions, except Love, recognizing them immediately as they come up, as mere chemical or neural currents in the physical body, as well as getting out from under all genetic personality traits and characteristics. As you are the Atma of the Divine Mother, then what do you have to do with all that in the final analysis of what you are!

Of those eighteen dreams I mentioned earlier I would tell you of one or two. I saw the Universe as a circle within which was a densely packed particle field. Yet then, Love came as an actual living and physical Energy and filled the entire circle of the Universe, at that Moment all the particles within the circle disappeared as they were over shined by the Presence of this

Divine Energy of Love. This dream left me with an especially good feeling. I had a dream also, where for a moment, for one sweet beautiful moment, Ramakrishna's eye's felt as if they were looking out at the world around me through my own eyes. I felt his hands had become my own hands, his face my face and all the rest of his blessed being, even so, the feeling of his nirvikalpa state, the Light of it, just for a moment, I dreamt this.

Well, one or two more. I dreamed of a lama who showed me a hidden altar in my own living room, who said, "I want to show you something." Above the altar was a turning ball of joyful luminosity which was the soul or spirit of an even older lama. I said, "Thank you, for showing me this." In another dream I dreamt of "Souls of Light" who were just that, nothing but Light! All right, I will tell you one more dream as their meanings have always been an obsession of mine. Five or six swamis were initiating my wife and I with Tantric bija mantras. She was first, then I. The ceremony was very powerful as it opened up dream memories of past life reviews. There were panoramic views of cities and temples and other places I had never seen. I was going over these many places as if I were flying. I saw us being married in different lives. Then as it seemed we were somewhere during World War I or II, and together we died in a plane crash. I saw our two children from that time, a girl and a boy. I held their hands and danced with them. Many yogic purifications occurred (kriyas). So many tears. Such high feelings.

I do not know if the dream is actually what it appears to be or if it is a fabrication of my mind. What is important with such dreams is that we somehow see the Atma of the Divine Mother brought down into the relative play (lila) of the dream mind and the waking mind. An inner meaning or a Sense of the Atma is given to the mind's psychology and to the experience one has with the life that one is living. It is an abundant meaning, more than a mere psychological interpretation of the mind's individual formula. Dreams are the mind's images in luminous conversation of Atma with the phenomenal experiencer of the waking and dreaming states. Even of how that mind interprets

46

the nature of deep sleep, where Atma is felt as Bliss, to itself, when back in the phenomenal dreaming and waking conditions.

Have no dualistic thoughts which create stress. Advaita (non-duality) throughout. That is how it should be felt and seen with your Atma and the Divine Mother. A Single Mass of Consciousness transcendent? Or Atma's Identity through all as the All? My own Consciousness in every perceivable shape and then at the same time without any shape whatsoever? Atma is the Divine Mother throughout all diversity and as the Divine Mass of Unity! Knowing this is the "end of misery!"

In the Advaita the knowledge of Aum is there. In the Tantra the knowledge of Hring is given. The Mandukyo Upanishad gives spiritual meanings to the four states of Consciousness which Consciousness assumes, (while remaining Non-Dual) which every single living being experiences, and I think too, so do the disembodied. H which represents the universal waking state experienced by one and all is Apti, the All Pervasive. This is the A of Aum. R is the same universal experience in regard to the dream state which is called Utkarsat, the All Exalted, because dream is a little above and more luminous than the waking state as a more immediate or direct reflection of consciousness. This is the U of Aum. The I of Hring represents the universal deep sleep state which is called Esah Yoni, the Divine Womb, the All One Womb where the whole universe returns and from where it emerged. The meaning is the One Source of All. This is the M of Aum. It is Miti, the Measure of All. Waking and Dreaming are the Ground. Atma is the Sky. As the finality of description in what is the Atma of the Divine Mother you have the Ng of Hring, meaning the end of misery, completeness, oneness and fulfillment. And the same meaning in designation is the unified Om of Aum. This state of consciousness is said to be Prapanco Saman, which means a condition of All Divine Sameness being reached when the composition and substance of the five great elements (prapanco) of earth, water, fire, air and ether are realized as being just the stuff of Consciousness. This again, is nothing but the Divine Mother! And of course, this applies to the "seven limbs and the

47

nineteen mouths" as much so to the thirty-six principles of the Shakti Shaivite system. Reality is not merely seeing four states as waking, dreaming, deep sleep and turiya. It is an All One Experience in the Atma of the Divine Mother. No division or break from Her, no matter what appearance of what state seems to come up. It is All Her. No duality!

The Mandukyo Upanishad describes a universal and individual experience of the waking state and the dream state in reference to images in Consciousness, of "seven limbs and nineteen mouths." I have some thoughts on this but there has been much more written about this subject in "Inherent Solutions to Spiritual Obscuration" in the part titled "The Ancient Method." Nevertheless let us engage our thoughts on the seven limbs. It is a description of Cosmic Deity or Deitess encompassing the Entire Universe of the Waking State. The Heavens are said to be the Head. Now this word, heavens, could indeed be the spiritual worlds or dimensions that the word so commonly indicates. Yet also it could very well mean the Star Fields around the mother Earth that ancient peoples so often thought about. But now days our comprehension of the Star fields and the "heavens" has expanded so much it is absolutely amazing. We have this Milky Way galaxy with four spiraling arms turning around the luminous core of the galaxy. Mother Earth is on the outskirts of the third arm. Within this Milky Way is every imaginable stage and type of star and planet at every multitudinous and inconceivable level of evolution one could imagine. The stellar and planetary diversity of energy, luminosity and most surely, life, within this single mass of the Milky Way galaxy is astounding. And even more astounding is the universal fact that the Milky Way is just one of so many galaxies expanding, living, being born and dying, in every direction infinite (most likely). Our Milky Way galaxy is but one among an unknown number of galaxies that have formed in our universe in clusters and superclusters going out into the Uncountable! Now within our galaxy alone there are estimated to be two hundred to two hundred and fifty billion stars it seems. Considering all these at all their stages of formation, life and death, it is thought that perhaps ten billion of these stars have Earth like life bearing planets. If ten percent of these indeed have peaked on an evolutionary time scale as our own and are not too distant, that is in our own stellar neighborhood, and not on the other side or a different arm of the galaxy, and they have evolved a communicable intelligence such as our own, well, even then considering the synchronized timing of the peak of another civilization with our own, it would still be extremely difficult to communicate. Yet it does not mean the galaxy is not filled with life even if there are only one billion or less, life potential planets it is still quite a lot. And now think of this as the "heavens" that are indicated to be the "head" of the universal waking state and you will certainly be filled with Beauty! Think of all this and every galaxy existing as the Ground, and now, Measure the Sky!

Next in order of these limbs is the Sun, our medium sized yellow middle aged star, which is said to be the eyes of the waking state. Fire is the mouth of the waking form. Air is of course, the Breath of this universal waking being. Akasa (time and space) is the middle part (the chest and breast) of the body of the universal waking condition. Water is said to be the kidneys. And earth is the feet. These are the seven limbs.

Now the nineteen mouths. These are described as mouths because by these nineteen mouths the experience of the three states of waking, dreaming and deep sleep are experienced, tasted or devoured. If one goes to the single mass of consciousness, that is deep sleep, one tastes or devours Consciousness itself and may well see the heightened and deeply indicated meaning. But you see, you have the five senses which are thought of as mouths that eat sense experiences. They eat the consciousness of these experiences. Then the five organs of action; hands and feet, sex and anus, and the mouth that speaks. These too are thought of as mouths that experience the waking state, and with the five senses, also the dream state, yet as reflections in Consciousness, as mind only in dream. Then are the five pranas or the five energy currents within the human physical body but also the subtle body of the dream state. These

49

seven limbs and nineteen mouths refer both to waking and dreaming conditions or physical and subtle experiences. These experiences are experienced through the four inner mouths that are the mind or manas, the intellect or buddhi, the ego or ahamkara and memory or chitta (or prakriti as the undifferentiated primordial mass of energy and consciousness, again, is this not deep sleep) which as consciousness contains the actual experiences of the waking and dreaming states or the memory of these conditions.

This system gives us a wonderful and beautiful picture of our psychological and spiritual experience. Yet remember, no dualistic thought throughout! Universally, it is the Mind as Bhavamukha, no less. Thinking upon Bhava Mukha, the supreme mind state of Ramakrishna, which was the Goddess' command instruction to him, my ego's perception cannot but be blind to what that Mind state is, for there is no ego there and the consciousness of Consciousness facing (mukha) Consciousness in felt awareness (bhava) is ever expanding as is our own knowledge and feeling awareness of the universe is ever increasing and expanding.

Atma (your True Self) was never separate from the Divine Mother and is not this Bhava Mukha Her Own!, with the Atma as a mere idea floating within Bhava Mukha, which is filled with infinite conditions and immeasurable possibilities! When I think of Aseshananda, Bhashyananda or Bhaskarananda, are they not all in my Mind! Like Ramakrishna's luminous divine sadhu, are they not all just experienced in me as through this Mind! Which is Ever Existing and even so, Non-Dual! Love holds us all! Even this concept idea of a "myself" or an idea of Aseshananda, Bhashyananda, or Bhaskarananda, or Anyone, or Anything, is Held there by Love! Even as Mind Alone previously, before the idea of "I" or them or those ever existed! Is it not All and has it not ever been Anything, but the Atma, the Pure Mind of the Divine Mother!

So, by Maya (the Measuring), the Atma identifies solely with the body and mind in the waking and dreaming states, thinking, and then believing it, as ego is the controller. From this mistaken position, the Atma then believes in itself as the Karmic "I" and by the power of this belief identifies with cause and effect (impulse and the consequence), resulting in reward and suffering, heaven and hell, success and failure, etc. Atma has yet to realize that the Divine Mother set up the preexisting conditions that became one's impulses and results thus appearing to become causes and effects. The Karmic "I" identifies with this basis of temporal conjunctions in cause and effect. When the Divine Mother begins to Shine in Her Causeless Mercy, the Atma realizes that not a single leaf falls from the tree, nor a wave comes upon the shore, nor a star turns within the deep without the Will of the Divine Mother. This is a higher view than karma. This is Rta, the Harmony of All, seen in Spiritual Seeing. It is the Way of Heaven where the Divine Mother is seen in all things. It is Divine Order where not a leaf falls unless the Divine Mother wishes it to be so, then whatever arises is seen as Her and so then whatever happens is just fine. This is a spiritual view. Now Atma Knows the Divine Mother does, has done and will do everything: spiritual, cognitive, emotional, quantum, atomic, elemental and organic. None but Her is this spiritual mood (bhava). With this, Atma now Knows the Divine Mother in Her Lila, the Play of Her Divine Drama or Comedy and knows it was all always Her. This becomes the melting of the mind's attitude trapped by the idea of cause and effect into the spiritual free state of High Sakti. With this, Atma Realizes that everything was always (including itself) in Nitya Kali, the Eternal Infinite Divine Mother. Swami Aseshananda thought of the Ocean as a symbol of the Divine Mother. Now, feeling that thought, consider Swami Vivekananda's saying, "The wave was nothing but water." Ego never was. "Your own Atma is the Divine Mother." She Alone (even as Atma) is and has always been the Immensity. This is Bhuma, the Super Abundance in Sakti Experience. Bhu is the Everything, the Anything, the Aggregate or Sum Total of all that is, that can be found anywhere in Super Abundance as the arising, the proceeding, the coming forth from, the producing of, the becoming of whatever and whenever, from Ma, the Divine

Mother, as Pure Abundance never exhausted by producing Super Abundance! Bhuma is this Immensity, the Unlimited, the Infinite Joy, and as Atma it is one's own power, identical with the Divine Mother, but not as ego or as obscured by ego. Bhuma is Brahman, it is Absolute Consciousness, the high goal of life, where the Atma is known truly as it is, as the Self (Atma) which contains Everything. Atma is recalled by Atma alone (one's own power) within the Divine Mother, for as far into the past as the past can go, you have been the Atma! The Atma as your own True Soul is your Birthright in the Divine Mother. Her Abundance is present within the large as much as the small. Human individuality is like a streak of lightning. Here and then gone. While this Super Abundance ever becoming, ever proceeding from the Divine Mother, remains. Have you seen Her Face! Have you Measured Her Sky Without Ground!

March 2000

Richard Chambers Prescott

52

THE GODDESS' PRIMORDIAL FORMULA
(The Primal Principles of The Waking-Dream-Sleep-Self Paradigm)

What is Love? A little story tells us something of it. A man was given a mantra and told that its power would liberate anyone in an instant, but that if he revealed the mantra to anyone else he would go to hell. He asked, "Will it free anyone?" "Most certainly." So he went to the roof tops everywhere he could and sang the mantra so all could hear. Like this, many traditional bindings can hold us back from the greater and larger experience of Love, Luminosity and True Existence.

In the Blessed Tantra, the Mantra of the Great Goddess, the Divine Lady, the Mother of the Universe, the One With A Beautiful Powerful Face is given. This is Hring. There are some meanings to these asomatous letters which have a special and unique potency in the process of spiritual cognition. Hring is the Bell that Awakens!

The letter "H" is the equation of the Waking Condition. The letter "R" is the equation for the Dreaming Condition. The letter "I" is the equation for Dreamless Sleep. And "NG" equates with the Resolution of the Three States into Turiya (The Fourth) which is Clear Consciousness, Clear Love, Clear Self.

By this Primordial Mystic Formula of the Great Goddess, one dissolves each letter and condition into the next. This is done both in the Unique Sense and in the Universal Immensity. It is the Return Movement to Wavelessness without movement. H, the waking material body gets merged into R, the finer bright body, which is the central nerve of the sushumna cave where there is no noise of distracting cerebrations. Then R is merged into I, the very refined causal spiritual body of the soul. The final stage resolution is Clear Consciousness, NG, giving the complete formula of Goddess Consciousness, Hring. This is Luminous Self-Effulgence, when all the limiting cognitions are left behind.

53

One other very beautiful interpretation of the Primal Hring Formula is that "H" is the Eternal Absolute Self and "R" is the Relative Fire of Cognitive Consciousness. "I" is the Goddess Herself who consumes both these two within the Immensity of Her Loving Force. "NG" completes Hring, which is the Nectar of the Moon of Undividedness, the End of Misery in Blissfulness, the Ultimate and most Courageous Assertion of the True Self as Clear Consciousness.

There is another very nice way to look at this Blessed Formula, these mystic sacred and secret syllables which have come down from prehistoric eras within the Tantric Tradition of the Goddess. Existence Consciousness Bliss is an extremely old expression indicating what is the Nature of True Spiritual Reality. Please consider for a moment that the characteristic of Existence may be in fact attributed to the nature of the sense of being as it is in the waking realm of experience (H). So then the finer characteristic of Consciousness may be an attribute of the Dream Realm (R), wherein the activity of consciousness itself has free flowing and internally reflective capacity to express itself without the confining logical dimensions of the waking state. This leaves us with the very Blissful characteristic of Dreamless Sleep (I), where even the Function of the Witness Self has melted away into the Non Dualism of object free Awareness. Here even the subjective musings of the Witness Subject have ceased, for consciousness has slowed down to the very peaceful point of turning within itself as what is called a mass of bliss-consciousness entire. This is described as Bliss, for here one reaches a Carefree Felicity because all the disturbing and delightful vagaries of phenomenal manifesting consciousness have stopped. Consciousness has become Wavelessness (Nirvritti). This is the Ultimate Resolution of the Fourth Principle (NG). So here the three spiritual indications, Existence-Consciousness-Bliss, have gone into Something Wonderful and Indescribable, and are no longer needed as supports for the imagination to picture what Reality might be. This is nothing less than the Resolution of the Nectar Moon of Undividedness, the Loving Happiness of the Great Goddess.

CLEAR CONSCIOUSNESS
(Unconditioned Conditioning)

What would it be like to experience the Vertiginous Height of Clear Consciousness with no disturbances from gyrating cerebrations? What indeed, would it be like to live or even momentarily know Consciousness cleared of every sort of cognitive distortion imaginable? Traditions say that this is possible, innate within every human being.

We might call this Waveless Consciousness. Or we might think of this as Scious Wavelessness, Living Awareness freed of any otherness, any sense of consciousness with (con) another subject or object before it's field of perception. In Tantra there is the insight into Chitti and Vritti. Chitti is a feminine word denoting the Consciousness of the Goddess in a pure and unperturbed state, like absolutely still water. Then comes the flux, the waves (vrittis) of thought and ideation creating this waking and dreaming world realm. This is surely the Power of the Goddess. Yet the idea is to also see Her in the Wavelessness of Chitti, the Primary Absolute Undivided Scious Bliss. This is Nirvritti, "without waves," Wavelessness. But even the idea of this being a her or a he, is a wave-idea, a thought form which comes out of the secondary stirring of consciousness in the metaphorical expression of waves (vrittis).

In order to clear out the obstruction of apparently limiting spiritual cognitions, let us first take a peak at the Ancient Paradigm of Waking-Dream-Sleep-Self. For it is the principle of differentiation and distinction in wave consciousness that deliberates Clear Consciousness into the four folded paradigm. Our idea is to have Waveless Clear Consciousness as the Ubiquitous Experience. Waveless Waking, Waveless Dream, Waveless Sleep and Waveless Self, this is what is presented. It is a giddy thought no doubt, yet one that we may become aware of by the simple sentiment of fondest attention.

The Waking State is designated the Realm of Forms. Here the optic nerves perceive a diversity of forms, differences and distinctions, of course, the other senses too. Yet, when the melting lines disperse, we get the Sense of the Continuum of Wavelessness in the Waking State. A sweet wondrous Universal Expansion occurs in consciousness. It is as if the entire field of the waking continuum begins to appear as one great massive book, instead of all these different books by different people with different stories, on and on. Another metaphor would be that your personal soul's discernment of the waking condition is like a tree. Yet the forest, with all so many trees within it, is one assemblage. You may even go further with this metaphor and realize that all the trees in the forest are just Wood, one single substance, the Sum Total.

The Dream State is exactly the same in this sense, even though it is a more refined energy field. Thought waves, more or less, are disengaged from the material nature of the waking conditioning. In some ways the Dream State is the Realm of Ideas or Words in their finer meanings. For we reflect on these meanings symbolically while we are dreaming. That is what rapid eye movement is when one observes a person who is dreaming. What is Wavelessness here? Consider that your soul's personal dream state is as a wave. Yet all dream states together are as the Ocean. Very nice, and the Expansion of Wavelessness comes here when one recognizes that the Wave and the Ocean, yes, of course, are One Substance, Water. Differentiation goes! Waveless Consciousness enters a welcomed arrival.

In the light of the Dreamless Sleep State, the same such principles of metaphor may be practiced. This slow wave sleep where no dream reflection manifests is the Throb of Consciousness undivided, unbroken and very blissful, for no disturbance of the cognitive sculptings of dreams ever appear at all during dreamlessness. No subtle visionary subjects or objects appear, no distinctions, divisions, differentiations are there in the sheer consciousness without dream waves. All the determining lines that tell us what is what have here melted away. This is Deep Sleep. We enter it every night at least for a time or so, when we cease the function of tossing up before our inward attention all those images of the dream conditioning.

Again the metaphor, your soul's personal dreamless sleep may be thought of as a particle of light. The entire field of dreamlessness would then be as the complete spectrum of electromagnetism. But of course, a particle of light or the whole spectrum of light are nothing but the One Substance of Light itself.

The idea is to get rid of all these limiting distinguishing cognitive emanations that apparently materialize a sense of keeping you back from the Emergence of Clear Consciousness, the True Self, the Final Fold of the Ancient Paradigm we are observing with the wish to penetrate it's secret. Whether Clear Consciousness is there as an always existing Background Witness of the phenomenal panorama or whether this Principle actually emerges in one's consciousness is another question. I think both are true facts of spiritual physics answering the eternal and relative sentiments of human nature. Since one definition of the soul is a wave on the sea, or of the sea, we must address both aspects. But when our thought waves slow down into stillness and we feel the deep peacefulness of Dreamless Sleep, then these dichotomizing questions do not haggard or perplex us at all. For there we feel without knowing, the Depth of the Real Self. Yet, when we re-enter the thought waves of dreaming and waking cognitions with all their noisy cerebrations, we forget the Vertiginous Self Joy we glimpsed in the Unbroken Blissful Moment.

It is the Self Universal and the Self Personal, wherein the melting lines of differentiation have completely gone into the Wondrous Wavelessness in the Consciousness of the Great Goddess, speaking through the voice of the Oldest Era of the Tantra. It is the Principle, the Pinnacle, the Turning Point, the Culmination and the Hurricane Height. All barriers as distinctions of myself, yourself and so forth have been transcended by Greater Consciousness, the Entirity of the Marvel of Self Being, the Awesome Sense of the Surprising Continuum of Astonishing Amazed-ness.

And what is This really, simply, but Love cleared of all emotional distortions. Clear Love if I may say so. For Clear

Love is the Singular Substratum of all feelings, emotions, wants and needs. It is the reason we hurt, hate, destroy, fear, manipulate or become enraged, when this Primal Sentiment of Self Reality is distorted within the moods of the heart. It is the reason we cherish, adore, defend, sacrifice, serve, give and forgive by letting go, crave, desire, nourish, nurture, pray, beg of the beloved or romantically worship the worthy-ship of the loved one. Clear Love is what makes us feel like entire people, otherwise one is empty, even if you possess encyclopedic knowledge of all religions, philosophies, sciences and galactic phenomena unending.

Clear Love is the Waveless Unchanging Sentiment, the Ultimate Background of every emotion. Take the example of the word, Young. No matter if you say this word in Chinese, Spanish, Bengali, English or Greek, no matter what the sound of the vocal chords make, the meaning behind the sound is that one is 'young', not very many years in age. The Sentiment of Love is the Same. As it is the Great Emotion, all other emotions and sentiments come forth from it, by it, of it, in some way or another. Love is always there in some form or fashion, as the single Causal Background in the spectrum of diverse affections, personal or universal. Love is God. God is Love. Love is Truth. Love is Reality. Really speaking, it is so simple.

The Creatrix Kalee

Kalee! Goddess! Give me the Heart of Tantra. Give me the Intellect of Buddha and the Mind of Tao. Give me the Self of Advaita and the Soul of Kindness. Give me the Body of Humanity and the Love of the Christ. Goddess give me the Untrammeled Freedom of Your Own Great Sentiment. Give me Tao without the thought of Tao. Give me Christ's Love without all the mania over Jesus. Give me the Waveless Tatha Gata Garbha without the idolization of Buddha.

Kalee is the Creatrix free to create as She wills. She Creates, not me, not you, not others. Everything is done by the

Force of Her Self. Nothing is done by others. This is the concept of Ritam in Tantra and Vedanta. Ritam is the understanding that whatever happens happens because it is meant to. Not even a leaf falls from a tree without the Decree of the Goddess Kalee. Everything is within Her Matrix and is merely spreading out through Spacetime, like a fabric being unfolded. To be in Tune with Tao is called Wu Wei, which means "Doing Without Doing". That is to say in another way, that Everything is Being Done by the Tao. Or in other words to be in Harmony With the Will of Heaven.

It takes Unconditioned Conditioning to Feel this Balance. All of us are otherwise so conditioned to think and feel on the psychosomatic level only. This is the fixation of body-identity out of which the persona arises and assumes that it is a dividuated separate agent differentiated from the Greater Entirety. Thus, the persona has the sense of dancing out from the Unity. Character or the true human spirit self arises and emerges out of the Soul, the Atma, the Self. It is the resolution of the mistaken identity of the Soul, that is the great mystery of life.

The Goddess' Tantra

The Blessed Tantra of the Great Mother Goddess gives some very clear definitions of the Stages of Clarity and Sentiment. These are most true and real whether one may find oneself alive while living in the body or in after-life when one has discarded the costume of the material body. In the Great Cycle of the Sacred Goddess, life, birth, death, rebirth are one and all but parts of Her Wondrous Continuum.

Untrammeled Loving Liberation and Freedom whether in this world or the after-death plane may be said to be of five kinds. First: Salokaya. Here the Soul Shares the Same Plane, Realm, Region, Dimension, World or Place of Spiritual Habitation with the Goddess Herself. Second: Saristya. Here the Soul Shares in blessed similarity, the Same Powers and Divine Magnificence as the Goddess. Third: Sarupaya. Here

59

the Soul Shares the Same Form as the Goddess, in the Spiritual Sense. Fourth: Samipya. This is the attainment of Nearness, Closeness, Proximity or Parallax with the Great Goddess Herself. Fifth: Sayujya. Here, the Soul has Contact or Union with the Self of the Divine Goddess. The differentiation of I and Thou melts into the Eternal Thou. Her Supreme Self Shines. All sense of otherness melts into Unique Universal Identity. This is the Freedom of Kalee, the Clear Self, the Clear Love, the Clear Consciousness. Yet, one may even go a step further into the Pure Absolute Kaivalya or Ultimate Singular Unity and Aloneness with the Goddess where even the idea of the Goddess Herself melts into the Wavelessness of Nirvritti. This is Standing in the Self Without Support, a Stateless State that many souls might fear because It is Absolute Unconditional Love Itself! This is a Love that consumes the Relative Circle, the Eternal Circle and the Threshold Borderline of the Crescent Moon Facing the Two Which Have Always Been The One.

The Freedom of Kalee's Clear Consciousness is the Reality of the Loving Self, imperceptible and perceptible. She is Lucid Intelligibility. She is Perspicuity Itself. Yet in order to See Her as Luminous Clear Consciousness one must let go of even Kalee's Personal Form, Features and Figure.

Now no longer to see Her dancing the potent dance of life and death, creation and destruction over the Impotent White Corpse of the Absolute. Now no longer to hear the mystic sounds of sacred syllables tinkling by the movements of Her Girdle Belt, Necklace, Armlets, Bracelets, Thighlets or Anklets. Now no longer to smell the sweet scent of Her Flowing Black Hair caressing the Galactic Clusters with Living Energy. Now no longer to taste the Taste of Sameness, Her Delicious Essence of Oneness. Now no longer to feel the Tenderness of Her Flower Soft Feet painted Red and Black, signifying the Relative and the Eternal. Now no longer to Dream Contemplate Her Mystic Symbol or the Secret Meaning of the Asomatous Letters of Her Sacred Secret Name. No longer to watch Her waving Her two left arms making Disturbing Signs, the upper one swinging the sword of Deathless Nirvritti Consciousness, the lower one holding before one and all, the Head of the Ego Obstruction. Nor to witness, nor view the wonder of Her two right arms making the Delightful Signs which signal to us the Great Sentiment, the upper one saying "Fear Nothing," for fear subtracts from the Loving Bliss, and the lower one gesturing with Undeniable Certainty, "I will Give you Everything, all Boons and Blessings and Untrammeled Freedom Itself." No longer will the Fragrant Breath of Her Lovely Nose blow Living Energy into the Sentient World Realm. No longer will the Dazzling Pleasurableness of Her Mouth Devour with Lusty Licking the Taste of phenomenal Food as the Body of the Universe brimming with Animate Living-ness within Spacetime. No more will the Tender Bloom of Her Delicate Skin arouse, excite and awaken in me the Most Loving Spiritual Mood. No longer will Her Elegant Graceful Ears Listen to the symmetry of my thought nor hear my precious emotions.

No longer will the Splendors of Her Senses Face My Own. Nor will my two eyes look into the Radiance of Her Two Charming And Sublime Eyes Viewing with a Flattering Look this Immanent Universe and the Transcendent Soul. Nor will I gaze into Her Magnificent Mystic Eye Between Her Exquisite Brows Behind Which She is Observing this Infinite Expansive Matrix. For Now, Her Consciousness no longer Faces My Consciousness, since Our Two Faces Have Melted into One Another, Leaving Only One Clear Consciousness. Kalee!

From "Kalee Kunda:
Poetics On Rapture and Ecstasy
in Goddess Consciousness"

Kalee... You have driven me like a sweating fast horse to put poetry down here.... these are no childish words simple as they may be... nor is this word weavings, painting the feelings we see... their boundaries, their latitudes, their dimensionless cheer past the mind's measurement.... Take Note and Keep Well with the Feeling, when Formless Feeling is Felt, every shape outside touches what is Perfect, coming Out of the Center. Yet in the gap, the missing, the sinking... a moment of voidness is felt in the heart... then, Charge your self-sentiment again with what Love Kalee Be... ever pleased with Her Self and thus ever pleasing others in a way that simple pleasure as a self to be experienced can never be described by the entangled confinement of word-thoughts, dream-thoughts or concepts of Unbounded Bliss.........

Kalee... as this Formless Feeling, having no requirement nor need, is as She Is, a Stance in the Emotion... from the Highest Flight, to the muscle flexed between the thighs... Felt, not described, Fantastic, without figure-ment... the Living End! The Divine is simply the Excellence of the Highest Infinite... the Truth said by the Sayer Poet.... that is the genuine import from the country of the divine... My Kalee is Divine! Release in me everything my mind says to consciousness that does not Release Your Loving Joy in Me...!

Kalee... I am tired of the present state of knowledge... it is boxed, not free... unsatisfying... there is not enough free knowledge that frees the heart... Kalee... the Blessed Kunda, the Red Pearl Petals, the Fountain... the Source of Life... the Sacred Triangle of Bliss... a Step past Happiness... Virgin Independent in Her Self, Mother Creatrix of Joy, Crone in Wisdom Steeped... this is not the symbol of death worshiped by those hypocrites of Love....

Kalee... in all honesty scorching my own soul to which I sometimes lie to myself I myself may be the greatest hypocrite

63

on one hand singing Your magnificence and on the other indulging in gossip, compromise, flip flop feelings over what is blessed singular love and what is just the chimera of lust. This generates shame in me, Kalee, what shall I do? Just cease,... easily enough said. No, it is the permanent contact with Your happy spiritual power that makes all negative down pulling emotions disperse all together. When shall it be permanent for me?

Kalee... my life lasts only seven days... Monday I'm ten, Tuesday I'm twenty, Wednesday I'm thirty, Thursday I'm forty, Friday fifty, Saturday sixty, Sunday seventy... Kalee, maybe one extra Monday or Tuesday... Shall I dance or dream this time away, shall I be up with my life or just think about my being alive? There is no knowledge greater than Happiness, Kalee, not the happiness as a reflex of the sorrowful, but Happiness where emotional dualities melt in the complete resolution of what is called majestically, Bliss... what shall I do? When Goddess, shall I see the Divine Feminine as the great poetess Sappho did, so clearly perceiving Your Wonder as Joyful Radiance, the Silvery Moonlight of the Goddess, bathing everything in undivided ecstasy?

Kalee, Kalee, Kalee, ... She is Love, Love that cannot be forced... Love that cannot be stopped... All anyone wants is to be affirmed by this Love, the Healing Curative Power of Life... the blessed affirmation of worth, releasing all that resentment, moving past the recognition of fault... This is the mystery of Love's Attraction... masculine to feminine, feminine to masculine, divine to human, human to divine, excellence to fault, missing to reaching, loss to having. Its simple hold on us is Love... the most self trusted feeling in this world... This is no fantasy, no daydream, nor dream state... I no longer feel, nor think over those single, same, dual or dual-dual sentiments... my feeling is all for Kalee, while all the excitement inside my soul turns toward Her...

Kalee, Kalee, Kalee, ... my hands cross over my breasts rising to touch my throat, they are Yours... Your hands touch the pits of my arms sliding to the length of my wrists, they are

Yours... my eyes, my tongue, they are Yours... Your name rings out like thunder claps in the silence of the nightless night... it must be You who is speaking, Kalee, for it is not me... Kalee, what is this Feeling Formless and yet so Full of the Form of You? Such is this Gratification, craving the moment to be physically and mentally one with You, but even more is the craving that You would be one with me... and more and more are You, pure absolute Satisfaction, giving me all that I crave... every desire for unbroken mood in You fulfilled. Yes...

Your affirming agreeable non dual mood springs up in my heart... Happiness free of opposite sentiment! ... gratifying, satisfying my non dual desire, the relief from that former pain of multiplicity. You are my Comfort, releasing me from annoying dualities, warming me by the Fireside of Your Never Dual Illumined Love... I can no longer speak or think of You as a mere Principle, such as the Endlessly Beautiful, for You have become my Living Reality, not ever to be lost, standing above even the vacuum void of death... so commonly feared and uniquely respected by each in their special way...

You are my Sole Enjoyment, Kalee, definitely and consciously ever I discover only Delight in You, my own Kalee... You are the vivid, arousing, intensely agreeable Pleasure of non dual emotion raising my faculties to the melting point... You are my only Worthy Pleasure never in the past, ever remaining as Tranquil, always remaining Satisfaction, for the instrument once known as me, then demanded in my craving for non duality, the Agreeable Consciousness of having this completed. Not a passing mental state of momentary gratification, You have become the ever abiding great importance of Satisfaction, continually verging on Happiness. And I am now no longer living so often in the lower order of sensibilities called intellect... that poor and unworthy feeble tool which can never tame my Kalee Jewel, She who is Happiness without a connected reason...

My automatic Mirth, my spontaneous Cheer, my instinct of Merriment, my intuition of Contentment, my Blessed Kalee, my Uplifting Dear, never failing to leave my heart inebriated.

Blessed Be Her Blissful Bliss, free of differentiating expectations, leaving far behind the congested concept of heaven, ... a place where we go? What is that when one is Free Now Standing in such Bliss as This... Blessedness Itself... the once and forever sense of it all beyond the state of created things to be reached.... True Triumph! Rejoicing now as Immediate Direct Joy... what is that narrow human perspective of which I am so tired, that delusive waiting for this to arrive?, ... even the philosophical thought of Felicity is cold like ice compared to this... She is Pure Gladness overflowing in the happy and joyous countenance, the voice, the manners and actions. She is that Intense Joy, this deeper Happiness, more noble, more enduring than the necessities of transient pleasures of which there are many, numerous, diverse, but Happiness is Singular... there are no such things as happinesses, we beings never speak of counting happinesses, we calculate our pleasures as the trivial demonstration of what is superficial... shallow, merely on the surface.... She endures... for Her Nature, Her Natural Secret of Attraction is that She is Timelessness, to use that old expression, Eternal Love, if you like, whatever should bring you to Delight, vivid, intense, overflowing joyous Happiness in the fountain of utterance, in the festivity of Her celebration melting your face into Hers... the state of extreme delight, extravagantly bold emotion bursting all conceptual weight in the mind.

This Delight is Ecstasy... I am beside myself with Joy coming out of the One Affection for Kalee... the Full Sense of Happiness, mental, spiritual, both, the Result of Absolute Satisfaction... She has pulled out of me those vicious numb pleasures of the dull and dumb... Her Happiness is never vicious, never transient, not passing through the temporal... our perception of it may be so, but not Her Reality, the Constant Spectrum of Love... She is the Rapture, the Serene, the Exalted, the Enduring, I am Carried Away with Her Love, I am Seized by Her Eternal Emotion, the Divine Feminine, transported past the simple mind... She has consumed the three states!,... conscious, finely conscious, superbly conscious... the border is gone, and I... I am Ecstatic while looking at the Face of Kalee... this same

'I', designated by the name 'Me', is Rapturous, Being in the Mood of Oneness with Her Eternal.....

She has swallowed me... into the Sacred Moon Drop of Indescribability... where no longer may the three conditions perplex... there never was a cosmic illusion, for everything is but measured out by Mother Kali... She is the Cognitive Thunder of Lightning Consciousness creating... Yet, She has ever Remained ... the Eternal Space filled with Pleasure Bliss, Her Self pouring out the dark rain cloud of numerous forms..... Kalee... Kalee.... Kalee....

Kalee... as all noises, words, concepts, cognates and thought waves finally go into the Silent Depth... As the years, months, days, hours, minutes and seconds are swallowed by Time... so is all life and matter, all affairs and connections, all memory and emotion, all elements of waking, all bright luminous dreaming and all the voidness of transcendent sleep swallowed by Kalee Kunda....

My Kalee guides every little thing... for all things are little to Her... I find a word or a thought only when She wants me to... or a thing or event happens only when and as She wishes! So can you say that I have a life among others?

In the Womb, Being Sweet and Happy... of Dreamless Consciousness... the Child/Consort/Friend of Waking and Dreaming... are One with the Goddess... Yet Turiya, the fourth, Existence Consciousness Bliss Unconditioned is the Kunda even of that Dreamlessness... Being the Sheer Bliss of Consciousness without any association.... This is Maha Kunda, the Great Kunda, that Naturally Sucks Up the Entire Universe into Her Self, ever consistently and without any hesitation, freely and spontaneously happening within each conscious being.... grossly thick, finely woven in the subtle or supremely unconditioned and free.... O Kalee Kunda, Kunda, Kunda.....

Kalee... O, You have made me causelessly cool and sober and crystal fine joyously beautiful in this new born life and now so inebriated in this Jar of Joy, this Beautiful Simplicity of Kunda Bliss, In Kalee Ineffable..... Kalee Kunda!

I do not live in anyone's world but my own... I set my own standard of what things mean to me... Yet, since I see everything as Goddess, how can you understand me? Truth, is to hide nothing, not even a dream as it is all swallowed within the Joy of Her Kunda...

Was it once, that the disturbance of thought as forgetting, was a portent of movement at the front of activity... I then dreamt of an enlightened being, woke up, read their words, it was enlightening, so simple, yes, but what does it mean... the song was forgotten, now I am learning to listen to the Goddess... in the Timeless Time of my own time... the sheer simplicity without secret so seldom said... I am Who and What She Is... as all meaning is finally measured out as it is in Her Kunda.

Now the Goddess pulls me to Her, as other things once pulled me to them... the great difference is now I am Joyous...! Yes, Joyous... between the reflexed vagaries of emotion and the Pure Flex of Love, between the Altered and Unaltered, between the Changing and Unchanging, between Shapes and No Shape, There you may find Me, within Kalee's Kunda.

My Very Real Goddess Kalee has given me the True Freedom to draw the illustration of my own self in deep, powerful, confident lines... Because She is Standing next to Me... Beside Me, Before Me, Behind Me, Above Me, even Under Me........ Do not call me by my name anymore, there will be no response for I am Gone... She is now here... as it has become with other Kali poets, no longer themselves... reborn, quick and new in Her, perfectly perfumed, amazingly adorned, bejeweled causeless and ever more, She lingering Lovingly Luminous in them as Kunda Consciousness!

Kalee... with all this Love in my heart I have no fear of rousing my blessed insanity for You, how else will I get out of the truly insane sanity of logic, which makes no sense at all, once gone into Kalee's Kunda Well of Bliss...!

Kalee, I am now still and silent as deep water, making no more new karmic waves forms, nor do I need returning to the mother source, nor the joyful experience of cosmic conjugal ecstasy, nor do I contain those dualistic thought bundles now that Your Kunda Bliss has covered me!

Kalee, now that the lotus stalk of my ego consciousness no longer feels any distinction from the Red Pearl Petals of Your Divine Joy, I realize that it is You, Goddess, Who are the Experiencer, no one else is there, as this must be the reality of non dualism and this is so, in every misery or any single joy, if they may be defined as those feelings.

Kalee, everything that was once me, or that I held dear, is now in the state of renunciation for the sake of realization of Your Kunda Bliss. God Absolute! This is nothing more than complete letting go of the surface of all life, the show of life, the bundles of Your dualistic playfulness, simply for the Sake of Peace. I think and live and feel only for the level of Your Joy. Nothing else matters. The first and the spontaneous thought or emotion is the true one. I do not involve myself in secondary circles of feeling or such philosophies that knot up the mind.

Kalee, I know that You are the Absolute Kunda of all things made, and yet You are infilling every other single mood of making with nothing but Your Bliss, as a spiritual well quenching the ancient thirst of the soul! You have made shadow and light mix in wondrous play showing me my deepest fear of letting go of all support and my highest joy in knowing that it is higher to cherish helping and the returning to life and the staying in life, for the sake of others, rather than simply melting away into the infinite and the purely unbounded existence. What is the use of that when such extreme and beautiful empathy may be practiced?

Kalee, finally, now that this ego has subsided somewhat into the Well of Love, the One Feeling I have been seeking with great effort all this life, now identified with the Cause of Bliss, Your Divine Kunda, I have become capable of learning the great lesson. Out of fear, that fear takes the form of anger and that anger takes the form of resenting. Yet before I resent someone or something, even a thought, a speculation, an opinion, I ask myself without egoism or fear, with humbled earth centered honesty, how many times have I made jest, or criticized or denied someone else's thought, speculation or opinion? This lifts the sense of egotistic righteousness and self importance off of me. This brings back the sense of balance in self, this equalizes those feelings and makes Your empathy alive in me, who has become no longer so serious, for now I know that each dualistic darkness has the counterpoint of light connected with it in the life lessons of Your Play, ever happening by the pure bliss of the excellent Kunda Power and that I will see this connection if I wait and watch, even if need be, for a thousand years. So strange it is that we human creatures always feel better when we all realize that we all share imperfections and that none of us are special....

Kalee... the Goddess, has Lovingly Shown Me through the Gladness of Her Inebriating Love, in the Sweetest Company of Her Lovers, by Arousing to the Peak, these Blessed Emotions of Harmonious Tendencies Toward the Divine, ascending up from the Well of Weeping, the Tear-Bliss caused by the conjunction of separation and union during the Exquisite Sentiment... Coming Up from the Primordial Kalee Kunda, here ever making forth the Universal World! So that no one should ever have any fear... not of the heart seizing up nor the breastplate cracking open, nor of the Earth falling out from under your feet, nor of lightning, cosmic rocks or balls of stardust descending from the sky-space, nor of water surrounding and drowning the body thing. These are nothing, for my Goddess has forced me to feel a million sentiments of bliss from a dozen universes combined with the pain of thirteen thousand scorpions biting... an emotion caused by identity and separation felt together, yet still only a single raindrop compared to the beautiful dark storm cloud of Her Bliss, Incomparable Happiness, free of the unborn, though appearing as a born amusing dualism... the Kalee Kunda, where all these descriptions of Her Natural Wonders emerge, dance and return... Once Kalee is lovingly realized, there is felt no more dual danger and what is known from this is that a loveless soul who seeks to create fear in others, is the one disappointment in all the universe...

Kalee Bhava I
The Heroic Moods of Friendship, Wisdom and Oneness in the Goddess Kali

On the Full Midnight Moon of Kalee, Something Happens. It is as if Her Light takes Over. My Body Mind held together by the promiscuous rascal identity, who, as ego, knows its true worthy esteem and cannot be gotten rid of except in the Never Dual, is now Hers, a beloving servant and She is My Soul... It is Clear in the Head, Feeling Good in the Heart, Knowing Now why the Absolute Principle of "I" is always Staring, ever looking, eternally recognizing and constantly remembering Kalee who is the Absolute Principle of "I" ... Kali.

Under Her Feet is the Ultimate, the Inaccessible made Accessible by Her, She Being Even More! The Oneness of the Ultimate is Erect with Mystic Passion for Her Above, even though this one Sleeps the White Corpse Death Dream! Without Her, that is what it is. Kali.

Her Anklets tinkle the Sound of Consciousness moving up Her open legs, past Her blessed thighlets making music that alerts to the Altar of Bliss wherein Her Never Dual Ecstasy is Felt beyond the function of knowing or reason, that which maintains the conjunction of body thoughts with Consciousness creating ego making multiplicity, diversity and variety... Kali.

Her Hips are adorned with the arms of karma, Her Girdle belt where all Cause and Effect ceases deep within Her Womb of Reality... Rising up Her Breasts, Nipples Intensely Erect with Excitement I Know that Indescribable Surpassing Sentiment, newborn with eyes in Absolute Trust of Mother.... Realizing no effort is needed... as Her Blissful Necklace of Skulls have most Happy Faces... fearlessly deathlessly... One, Never Dual with Her, resting as they are, around Her Neck and Breasts, She having cut away the little nuisance of their Ego Circles... Kali.

The Four Arms of my own Goddess Warrioress sway Gently with Vigorous Compassion employing the night of fear as metaphor for what the human heart fears but has no need to fear... For She is Loving Consciousness behind, the Background of the dream idea of death which is no death, only movement and stillness, amazed by its own paradox... the dualism of Terror and Bliss... which inhabit the dream phenomena, made conscious by Her Conscious Encompassing... Kali.

Since the only Real Celebration is the Celebration of ego death, Her upper left arm swings the Divine Flaying Sword of Undivided Non Dualistic Wisdom Sentiment... the Beginning of the Unique Knowledge of Eternal Self Consciousness encompassing all that is Relative Mind as the Same Substance of Itself, the "I" Sentiment Sublime. For in Time is death and Time is Relative, so making death the same... this being no death in Eternity... but an imagined make believe, not Truth, from Her Point of View as Her Sword continually sweeps clear, cleaning the house of the mind.... welcome it... Kalee, flay me out of my mind box body ego obsession keeping me Awake to Your Divine Directions... Kali.

Since She has Freed the Head of Ego from the circle of ego, She holds this objective thing once ago identified with things not itself... not total, universal nor complete... now blissfully relaxed in the grasp, the Graceful Grip of Mother's lower left hand. Fear cannot get you into the Blissful Sentiment, nor mere Desire cannot make it come, nor Anger at your self ego trap won't force you to Change You Permanently nor Brilliantly... Only Kalee's Permanent Brightness Changes You... Kali.

Open, with Endless Benevolence... Her upper right hand signs, palm heartfully wide, expansive to the Truth that there can be no fear for the Eternal Self of Kalee never dual ever free living not just within, but As all things. It is fear that paralyzes your conscious mind from liberated consciousness. So Kalee says, "Have no fear, have no anxiety, not even of nothingness, for I, Kalee, am there, as I am All things, thing-less and the thing in itself, Eternal, Relative... Non Dualistic, Dualistic or In Between.... Kali.

Palm Down, Her lower right hand expresses the Continuing Kind Empathic Gift ever descending from Her as wish fulfilling wants fulfilled, "I grant you Everything ever granted freely given with Love Never Dual, ever released of any whim for return...

Sublime Emotion I grant to my heroic feminine focused friends... Consciousness in relative and eternal I grant to those in Unique Wisdom apart and separate from the sense of exclusive isolated liberation... and High Mood Sentiment Unbroken I bestow on those who are in the Mood of Me, Kalee Infinite Unbound Free. My three gifts." ... Kali.

She, the Utterly Most Alluring Cosmic Woman Goddess whose Skin is the Touch of Rapture Blissful, drawing me into the Radiant Brightness, the Non Dual Never Two Primal Darkness of Her Great Night, wherein all things of two-ness involved revolve back into their ever present real and original nature... Ah, that is such a Light so Luminous no otherness ever appears, may arise, or can emerge... Kali. Kali. Kali.

The Depth of Her deepest mystic Eyes ever perceive and see simultaneously, inconceivable dualisms within the vast incomprehensible non dualism... Eyes of such Primal Depth, that gently gaze upon that most Primary Wondrous Beautiful Emotion that is There exceeding and before the extent of Time or Timelessness, Comprehending all Cause and Effect... Kali.

The Gale Force of Her nose breathes the flow of the two forces that pound the very gracious singular central nerve, emitting a Fragrance of Generated Joy that ceases all pounding... Her Fragrance of Eternity's Oneness... To touch Her mouth, or Her Mouth touch yours, is the Taste of Samarasa (Tasting Oneness, Sameness)... the Sweet Flavor of Non Duality, the Taste of Atma Liberated, ten millions times more the Pleasure than natural human pleasure... to Be Sure, The Self Free... As it is in fact, in True Evidence by Real Consciousness, Her Ears Hear the Perpetual Poetry of Pure Free Unbroken Consciousness and the Indescribable Silence of dream-free cognition and the singular sweet music in dream consciousness, where mind just speaks in whispers to mind itself... and She is Here Hearing all the sounds, chords, noises, resonances, percussions and repercussions by two things striking one another producing vibration and audiology in that place of waking consciousness where the Subject of Self becomes identified with the Self as Object. Ah... my Kalee, You Alone as True Self; See, Hear,

Feel, Taste and Smell Non Duality, Original, Free, Eternal as Kalee... Joyful Hands extend to the Sky and over the Eight petaled Heart, ecstatic with three fingers upright and two folded down, pointing out Your Sacred Secrets... Kali.

Your Red Tongue Long Extended is covered with Mystic Tantric Syllables... Hring! Shring! Kring! You Lick up the Lotus Chakra Jungle Swallowing this divine emanation, for individual and universal beings, back into Your Final yet Unending Devouring Bliss and then for Bliss' Sake You extend this curious Tree back out again. each tender flower of divine locations, gods and goddesses, powers, forces, elements, energies, categories of the psyche, letters and symbols, being licked, sucked, kissed and caressed by Kalee's Tongue Trickling a Thousand Honey Drops of Sublime Emotion Continuously Generated... Kali.

In Your Nose Ring is contained all finer particles of every self, as if all souls as diamonds, gems or pearls with brilliant, passionate or slow natures were there threaded through, Ever Connected to You, no matter what precious thing they may being seem... The Undoubted Unwavering Beauty of You Inebriates Me... Like a Teardrop Within a Teardrop, on the Bridge of Her Nose, there this Dream Consciousness within Waking Consciousness as one Field of Experience within the Other, O Kalee... Both Are But You... As is the Spot, the Little Circle of Relative Consciousness, between Your Bewitching Brows, where Imagination Divine Begins as a Small Stirring within Dreamless Cognition... Your Imagination, Your Reality, Your Joy Generating Play of Sublime Emotion... Above that Sacred Spot is Your Threshold Borderline Meeting Ground, the Blissful Crescent Moon of Kalee's Luminous Consciousness where Bhavamukha and never dual vijnana bhava manifest the Sport of the Self...

Hers is Nitya Bhava, the Eternal (nitya) Mood (bhava) of Sublime Consciousness, the 'Ka' of Kali... Hers is Lila Mukha, the Playful Sublime Emotion of Facing the Foremost Face of the Goddess Kali Facing Herself in all Relative (lila) Facing (mukha), the 'Li' of Kali... It is Here that my blessed Chosen

74

Ideal of Kalee makes the Turnabout, the Divine Revolution in Consciousness, my own such consciousness... A Revolution where She frees the revolution of consciousness by even transcending Her Own Goddess Ideal, becoming as Always Was... but the "I" Independent of any conception, always Non Dual, Never Dual... Oh Blessed Kalee... This is Your Eternal Eye, dead centered in Your Forehead... what more can be said, when thought stops, leaving only Divine Feeling to Continue in Kalee Bhava, even after twenty one days, if the body drops like a dead leaf... in Kalee Bhava... Kali.

Goddess, the Aura of Your Untrammeled Black Hair in Waving Liberated Tresses of Freedom blows the frightful dualisms away as a Radiant Bright White Blessed Light Emits Itself in the Background of Your Stance. Yet even this Bright Whiteness is Surrounded, Encompassed By Kalee's More Radiant Shadowless Hues of Non Dualism, Oneness Never Two and Wonders Beyond as She Dances in this Beautiful Universal Cremation Ground Enjoying the Blissful Conjugal Union of Consorts... while surrounded by lowly yet worthy creatures, such as me, who once thought that we were simply just mere ego and who like me and perhaps you, are outcast by other traditions and systems of spiritual embrace, that perhaps are lacking in that most divine sentiment of empathy in which is seen without resentment, that all systems and structures of the Infinite, are Real. It is only that Her Method has returned me to the Great Pleasure wherein I can see, feel and be What I Am... Kali. Kali. Ah Kalika......

As I am but Humus, Humble before my Kalee... Her Sacred Heart Diagram being drawn on the Earth below Her Two Delicious Fragrant and Beautifully Seductive Feet... The Corners of which are the Vast extent of Creation, the Eight Heart Petals within being Mind, Intellect, Ego, the Ether of Spacetime, Air, Fire, Water and Earth. The five triangles of fifteen corners being the Five Senses, the Five Moving Functions and the Five Forces of Life Giving Power. The Innermost Primal, Perpetual and Finishing Triangle being the Waking Object, the Dreaming Subject and Dreamless Free

75

Cognition, appearing as three yet Whose Substance of Consciousness Is the Same as Kalee... All these, all these principles in sacred mystic formula are not merely equations of Kalee but Kalee Herself Never Dual... The Ultimate Self Mystery, the Final Dot, the Center Point of Her Sacred Heart Diagram, the most mystic Tantric Syllables, the Inebriating Spiritual Wine Drop... just enough to Completely Overwhelm the dry delusion of distorted dualism, Remains as Sublime Perpetual Kalee Emotion... Peaking during the Conjugal Bliss of Never Dual Realization... Kali!

I Go Into This Primal Mind Becoming One With Kalee... If I Respond To The Responses Of Others, Then How Shall I Respond To Kalee.... Kali.

What Ego Might Be

A Quick Journey Of Discovery

After twenty years of writing, finishing one project and then beginning another with hardly any break, I decided to give myself two months writer's vacation. Being the obsessive writer that I am and finding myself with an abundance of mental energy, I decided to send my ego to the shop for repairs and fine tuning. I hope I am not practicing the art of self deception in sharing some of my discoveries with you.

As I learned to direct the writer's energy into the deep dynamic of self work I started to understand the apparent psychology of my own brain, it seems. The first thing I discovered is that the ego is more sensitive than the inner ear. The gentle side of ego is so easily hurt, as hurt is to ram or impact, and how many wounds my ego had been carrying around. With this thought I began to understand that as ego identifies with painful memories the associated emotion comes with the memory. But strangely a new development came as I stopped resisting the painful emotions, I started to accept the surfacing of memories without emotion. There is the memory and there is the emotion and I could distinguish the two and deal with the memories on their own ground without emotional distortion. This was good for me.

I took a deep look at my obsessive need for perfection and realized that when my ego sought the perfect I was then disappointed. For what or who is perfect? Peace came when I accepted my own imperfections, but more, the imperfections of others. My expectation for the perfect made my ego focus quite tense, by letting go and moving through the surface of that concept, suddenly my ego began to relax. At this point I started to think about the associations that go with the ego. How often I was not dealing with the right now, but with things, associations, imprints and impressions which had nothing to do with the 'right now'. It was like having a dialogue with someone and not really listening to what they are saying right now, but thinking about what they used to say or trying to inwardly predict what they were going to say. So often my ego associated with things that had nothing to do with the living moment. This, then realized, stopped being such a distraction to the conscious sense of self.

The all too obvious and funny thought came to me that everyone has got one, an ego. So why do I need to figure it out? Because when one ego jumps on, insults, another ego then problems come up. But where is the ego and why, for there are great parts of me that no one can jump on. The much older word for ego is Igo. I am wherever I go and there is really no limit to this except the thought of limit. My ego and your ego can and should be identified with so much more than the point of insult.

Since I may honestly say that my ego is a connoisseur of appreciation and affirmation from others, it came as a difficult challenge to my ego when I realized, that at the lack of appreciation or respect, resentment, which is just nothing but anger, comes up when one feels that their self is a victim, a victim of this or a victim of that, it matters not. And with un-confronted anger remaining contained in the victim thought, that emotion recycles into the form of basic depression. A place where my ego has often been lost, where the 'Igo' had a hard time seeing where to go. This vulnerable side of the ego is a challenge to face, but I felt better after accepting the reality of these facts, even though the need for external affirmation is said to be a symptom of low self esteem.

I reached a plateau on my ego work, a kind of answer and question which was hard to penetrate and unite. What my ego wants is Love, it wants Love coming at it, it wants to be able to send Love out from it and it wants to be Love. So if Love is what ego really wants, what does it matter what ego is or if the ego is there or not. As I began to focus on Love as Self instead of self as ego, some feelings began to come to me. A real gratitude for every good and bad thing that brought me to this point of life. A humility that could tear me down to the ground, but I, could still stand up. An acceptance of others for just what they are, whether they were consistently the same or fluctuating in their nature. A letting go of anger and resentment by letting go of the thought of my ego as a victim, I am just in life as everyone else. The capacity to forgive and release myself and others or the thoughts I hold at others or myself came to me. It is not so hard just to move through the surface of life and arrive at Love. I do not know if this was a spiritual awakening or a human awakening, or if there is any difference, but I certainly feel better about life.

On the other side of my self work was the dream work. I had six or seven recalled dreams during this period that I turned over, thought about and it seems found some meaning for myself in regard to my ego. One dream was of star systems and planets, listening to my dream mind, the thought came that the sense of spacetime on planets is due to the influence of gravity. How does this apply to my ego? Certainly, the sense quality of my perception is due to the quality of gravity in my ego. I dreamed of a great library, immense, with many rooms and every manner of book within and many people. I thought because ego is the experiencer, perhaps ego has a greater knowledge of life than I presume. Again, I had a dream of Ramakrishna, the 19th century East Indian sage, who was saying that when the ego goes what one becomes is.... a teacher. I ran from this dream thought, this teacher idea, even Ramakrishna disliked the words, father, teacher, master. The concept itself is a great obstruction to pure free spiritual life. A concept of dependence which ruins people, keeping them under the dominance of an authority instead of being their own authority. This is not what my ego wanted, nor I, even if it was to be gone for a moment in a dream.

Again, I saw written in a dream, that the ego is a subtle object in the mind of consciousness. Yes, it seemed true, the ego is a something that is thought about and who is the thinker of this thought of ego, this subtle object. I found myself dreaming in a valley, my friends and I were joyfully riding up and down the hillsides of this valley in wheel barrels. Great clouds formed over the valley and let out their voice and power saying, "The thunder and lightning will guide you." There is sense to it, the ego is like a wheel barrel rolling up and down

79

with friends side by side, but there is a greater something than the ego which guides us like the power of thunder and lightning within. Another dream found me reading poetry to people in a park in front of a large building, it felt good and when I was done they applauded me. Yes, no doubt, my ego, like everyone's, needs appreciation, for some reason, and an acceptance where in Love may grow. But I also had dreams of jumping from high trees into deep dark waters and of being pulled into the depths of watery darkness where I would cry out in the night and awaken my sleeping wife who was by my side. What does it mean? There are parts of the ego deep and primal, that when we face, we are facing the old fear of letting go of all previous concepts once held dear to us. This could perhaps be the most important dream, for in this ego exploration one must be ready to let loose of former conceptual attitudes that prevent the progress of deeper expanding viewpoints. Must I enter the dark waters of unknowing before I might become knowing?

Interestingly, present modern scientific observations of the human brain, state that the neural activity of human consciousness, consisting of billions of transmitting neurons, nerve impulses, synapses, dendrites, axons and their terminals, is constantly and continually, whether in waking awareness or dream consciousness, identifying and re-identifying what the ego or self idea is at any given moment, based on past information in reference to a future context of self identity. But because of lack of data within the physics of the material field, cannot state what pure consciousness is, nor what love is, nor spirit, nor any of this beautiful divine stuff. What is it when ego touches the timeless moment of being cognition or what is the acute identity of ego in peak experiences or within the states of plateau consciousness? We have many scientific, cognitive and spiritual definitions, all of which may be simultaneously right and wrong, or rather limiting and expanding at the same time.

Talking to an elderly Norwegian friend, a man who I feel has a great amount of inner wisdom, he stated that if you get rid of the ego, there is a vacuum, and that something must be replaced there, otherwise that ungrounded vacuum might cause a kind of insanity. He was talking about the true inner reality replacing the ego. Beautiful I thought, but even so, that might again be a form of the ego, though more noble and spiritual in its context. Certainly, we all seek the true Core Self, the Self of Love without question, unperplexed by dualism and self doubt. This is the process of Self Making, the discovery of greater realities within.

My friend's ideas were quite good. There should be no ego structure forms nor authority constructs in cognition over the Self, especially at the subconscious level where subtle inputs from the external world of religious or dogmatic suggestions, such as extreme renunciation of natural human feelings fill the mind with unattainable conditions. Such as, the hypocritical challenge of unconditional love which demands a set of conditions one must surrender to, before unconditional love may be received. We are all too familiar with such religious requirements. This old man's spiritual practice is to get up in the morning and see God in everything around him, in everywhere, including his self, without need of any intermediary deity concept, as he says, "before my ego wakes up..." And for him this works well, he has peace, free of metaphysical distortions.

During this period of time I may have experienced this vacuum and the filling of it, of which my sagely Norwegian friend spoke. As the emotional intensity of my ego examination increased, questioning this self to ego question, seemingly answer-less, I found myself at the point of exhaustion experiencing a breakdown over the ineffectual instrument of my mind to resolve what seemed to be without answer. I began to cry with genuine tears, not just mere sentimental feelings, praying to my chosen ideal of the Greater Reality, to please just take this ego away. After the release of tears, something happened, nothing great, nor nothing profound, but it was peaceful, deeply peaceful. I felt an ego connection had melted within me. I felt closer to Love. When I expressed this to some people, this idea of getting rid of the idea of ego contents and of a spiritual setting in, some nodded with affirming sighs, but some laughed saying this could never be done. Perhaps they are right. I am open to both sides.

After this release, I had two feelings that came to me. One feeling came at four a. m. while looking over the treetops at the moon, beautiful massive dark clouds passing before the cherished orb. I felt for just a short sweet moment, that my chosen ideal of the Greater Reality, the Goddess, was there in what I was seeing as much as She was there within me. Later, another feeling came, the thought of 'I', my ego sensation and of Her, as an infinite, immense and unlimited Being, seemed to gently shift, in a manner of speaking. I think perhaps my ego was starting to loosen. I do not think of these feelings as enlightenment, I don't care for the idea of enlightenment, nor nirvana, nor heaven, nor any such impossible ideas, high thoughts that make in the mind a reality to high to reach for common beings such as myself. I care for a useful Reality usable right now. One that I can feel.

Words, may or may not carry the heavy weight a writer imagines them to, but if you will have a little patience with my ego, I would like to continue with my story, hoping there will be some weight to it for you. Looking into this curious subject-object of self assertion, ego, I went to see a friend, Swami Bhaskarananda, at the Vedanta Society of Western Washington, who shared some brilliant thoughts on the nature of this mysterious subjective influence over all of us. In the field of Indian thinking there are the three forces or qualities, which pertaining to ego complex, influence it as such. In the ego, tamas is the force that negates, here, the ego is lethargic, lazy, asleep, closed minded, narrow, resentful, angry, etc. Again, rajas is the force that distorts, making for an ego which when insulted wishes to punish and when praised or flattered wishes to reward and protect. Quite contradictory and reactive. Then, sattva is the force that reflects the wondrous principle which somehow never mixes with ego. This force makes for an ego which is all loving, all forgiving, comprehensive, non-violent, harmonious with others and with self, etc. For me, these were very helpful thoughts, these faces and forces of the ego.

From the heights of the Vedanta viewpoint, Pure Self, Pure Consciousness never has the problem of ego. How could that be, for this is absolutely godlike, if not the essence of this principle itself. Nor does the problem of ego exist during the deep sleep state, for there one can find no otherness, no sense of a second entity of consciousness, no dualism. No egoism is there, for that condition is only the Deep, where no conscious image has yet to appear. Ego would then actually begin within the state of dreaming consciousness, the dream ego, which may as we all know so well appear as anything one might project into the dream contents. It is in the waking field of consciousness that the idea of ego becomes more or less fixed, the daily identity of who one is and the consciousness of that identity. This sense of identity is also consistently present in the dream state no matter what appearance dreams may take, for waking and dreaming have a cause and effect relationship. I may have had a glimpse of this while sitting in the Temple at the Vedanta Society of Portland. Others were immersed in absolutely still meditation, but I could not help swaying a little to the powerful peaceful currents of spirituality in the room. Then, perhaps it was the voice of my higher intuitive self that whispered to me, "Before you go into Deep Sleep without Dream, Stay Alert, Stay Aware." Whatever it was, I was happy to be charged with something new.

The swami's thought is that basically, the ego is a mental illusion, the sense of separateness. It is the illusive sense of separation not only from the infinite transcendent god self, but also the sense of division in the immanent, the material physics of this phenomenal world. Ego is what makes me feel that my body and mind are uniquely different, when in reality we are all connected, if not one, even as the entire realm of physics comes from one primary substance out of which the 'mental illusion' of diversity is created. Most interesting, very lofty.

Two thoughts on ego in the stratosphere of Indian thought are asmita and ahamkara. The first is more refined than the second. Asmita is just pure acute identity with the cosmic mind, the universal mind or identity. It is ego just in the pure

83

reflective sattvic condition, not just simply identifying with a single body and mind, but an expansive identity, pervasive and inclusive of the totality of bodies and minds, yet aloof from this same totality. Ahamkara is the individual sense of the ego identified with one's own unique body and mind. Curiously, the word individual means divided-dual, the sense of being apart or separated. Ahamkara is the I-maker which makes us feel we are the only thing going on, the sole enjoyer, the only doer of all that is done by the identified body and mind, when really there is a greater power which is guiding, doing, enjoying and making in every body and every mind.

Meeting another swami from England, I asked a question, "Can an ordinary soul like myself become the Sugar or just taste the Sugar?" He replied that it must be so, that it is our destiny. Sugar is Ramakrishna's metaphor for the Sweet Reality of Self. To 'become' the Sugar is absolute identity with the Infinite Sweet Self. To 'taste' the Sugar is to have moods of connection or glimpses of oneness with this Unlimited Immense Self. The same swami expressed the idea that dharma, the right path or direction is that which leads one to Self Centeredness, something more than just doing the right thing as we often think of dharma. And adharma, the not right direction is that which leads to self annihilation. What leads us to become one with the Sweet Self in the Timeless moment of Joy and what leads to the ego self as confined to time and space, either material or subtle with all its restrictions? As there is some dualistic sentiment expressed with these directions, and I seek one non dual answer to this question of ego, I feel that both directions are really one direction, the flow of life, where our self annihilating mistakes are blessings that teach us, leading us to the understanding of ego and self in a more genuinely expansive centered way. It reminded me of healing the schism in the psyche or the unifying of the divided self in modern psychology.

I find the discoveries and documentation on the mystery of human nature by Carl Gustav Jung, inebriating. For one, he felt that the method of active imagination is much more suitable for the Western mind than the Eastern technique of suppression of thought. When I read this it helped me understand myself a little better for when I practiced the technique of the East, often more than none, forbidden thoughts as we call them would come like a torrent. By not fighting those thoughts, but by just letting them surface from the unconscious, not denying, but accepting them as what they are and as a part of what I am, my psyche began to heal from that schism of self divided fear.

Most of us are familiar with his thoughts on the conscious and the unconscious and the meeting of these two within the psyche as the ever continuing life process of personal individuation. Defining this as the need to experience one's own inner being, " he thus acquires an inner stability and a new trust in himself," or herself certainly, as, "an inwardly stable and self confident person."   Jung exquisitely states, "During this centering process what we call the ego appears to take up a peripheral position." This heightens our feeling for the flow of life, when ego moves to the outer edge of the circle of consciousness. One learns that the experience of consciousness is different from the ego and the symbolic life of the psyche. "The investigator of the psyche must not confuse it with his consciousness, ... how different it is from consciousness,... for which reason we cannot take psychic reality to be commensurable with conscious reality." That is they are not of equal measure, but on the surface Jung felt we could not get rid of ego consciousness, for who would be there to know this, "for his ego now appears as the object of that which works within him,... he strives to catch this interior agent, only to discover in the end that it is eternally unknown and alien, the hidden foundation of psychic life." To you, I must honestly admit that sometimes I feel powerfully stable with the beautiful flow of life and sometimes I don't, as when I have not had enough psychic release in the dreamtime or when I am in need of nourishment or disturbed by external relational connections. Then I feel like the world is a meaningless pile of dust. This is not a bipolar, manic depressive state, this is being human.

Abraham H. Maslow is perhaps one of the most brilliant psychologists and thinkers we have yet to see in the Western stratosphere of thought. He was more concerned with peak experiences than with neurosis, ego or things like that. In peak experiences one feels godlike or one with the highest, self-actualized, real, whole, complete, alive, good, beautiful, unique, effortless, playful, joyful, exuberant, autonomous, independent, at ease, not striving and not interchangeable with others, that is that one does not practice the habit of psychic transference of other people's idea of self onto one's own self conception. These farthest reaches of human nature come to us when we no longer imitate nor follow other people or their ideas, we become our true self, so if you must have a mentor for the self let that mentor be your true self and no other.

Peak experiences also come by being cognition, the fulfillment of basic human needs which are, most simply put; survival (food, sleep, sex), safety and security, the sense of belonging, self esteem and self value for others, as well as the higher human experiences of truth, happiness, spirituality, love, reality, and the sense of being all there. His thought is that it is the deficiency cognition of these basic essentials that cause problems; neurosis, psychosis, ego confusion, ego distortions and the aimlessness that we sometimes experience.

Maslow describes peak experiences as, "a fusion of ego, id, super-ego and ego-ideal, of conscious, preconscious and unconscious, of primary and secondary processes, a synthesizing of pleasure principle with reality principle, a healthy regression without fear in the service of the great maturity, a true integration of the person at all levels." A beautiful statement on the human mystery. One thing that stands out for me is the 'preconscious', still in the womb, prior to ego shaping, as what we are before all those effects in the psyche are shaped in us, by parents, belief systems, relational connections, the personal trauma of being born and living in this crazy upside down world and all that. Again he gives us the strong insight into the 'primary' or what is essentially the real self at play, this primary emotion, primary creativity, etc., as opposed to all the secondary layering that we all do. Really, genuine happy human living is solely when we are at play and the rest is a put on, a throw up, a mask.   What is the perfect acceptance of life as Maslow expresses it, "In the first sense, every living human being is perfect; in the second sense, no person is perfect, nor ever can be." Universally we are great, and yet standing alone we are flawed.

Alfred Adler's theory was really simple, but often very practical.   Essentially, all our parents have, knowingly as in abuse or unknowingly with good intention, beat the hell out of our self esteem. So the rest of life is mostly wasted, expended in our attempts at self assertion, in order to compensate the instilled sense of inferiority. It is a waste of energy because in reality none of us are inferior, we are just tricked into thinking it is so. We all have rage at this and the depression of recycled anger because of this. It arises when we feel we are the victim of life. Then comes the vanity of guilt over our cherished pain which is not unique, whether physical, psychic or spiritual.

The pain of life is pain for one and all, yet with different measures perhaps, external events vary, but inside it is the same pain, whether we have been raped by drugs and alcohol, had our souls kidnapped by crusty old belief systems, or our self value was murdered by the people around us or if we were just generally beaten up by life itself. It is like an auto (self) accident (mishap or fall) where we are not in control over what others are doing. All we may hopefully control is our own attitude and a spiritual one at that, as an esteem which permeates our psychic environment and goes beyond it at the same moment, dissolving the psyche's insecurity, named ego.

Carl Rogers theory is the same as Adler's really, with just substituting the need for love with the need for esteem. He felt that we as children want so desperately to be loved and accepted by our mothers and fathers, people who in their psychic history, themselves, never felt what it is to be loved, that children will do anything with the hope of getting that love. And what they do is to fundamentally learn to suppress their true self, deny their real core of being, in the hope that they will become someone the parents will love. How drastic! What a catastrophe for the small yet to be shaped ego, which becomes left with the legacy

87

of not knowing how to love. For like it or not, you cannot love unless you are in your true innermost and real self. I have felt all these things and for me this is why the ego is so sensitive to criticism and builds so many useless mechanisms of defense against what is critical toward it.

Toward the end of my journey I went to Portland to see the ninety six year old Swami Aseshananda. I didn't go there looking for self knowledge, I went out of my fondness for the old soul. He is the last living swami initiated by Saradamani, the wife of Ramakrishna. I wanted to talk with him so I asked some questions. He said, "Richard, yes, Richard." It made my ego feel good that he knew my name. I asked, "Swami, what is the quickest way to get rid of the ego?" This made him laugh so I was delighted. But then he seriously replied, "Love of God." The next question was obvious, "What is Love of God?" "Attraction to the Ultimate Reality," replied Swami, "like a needle to the magnet." I thought to myself, attraction is to delight in something and a magnet pulls the thing to it without effort on the thing's part. "That is the best answer I ever heard."

I asked,"Swami, does it matter if ego is there or not if Love is there? Must Love be unconditional?" His nearly blind eyes opened widely, "Yes, total, pure, free of worldliness." "Is the removal of the ego the play of Love?" "Part self effort, part Divine Will." "Can an ordinary soul become the Sugar or just taste the Sugar?" "Absolutely, pray to the Divine Mother, She will guide you."

One evening during the daily readings from The Gospel of Ramakrishna there came the description of death as being like a sword being pulled from its sheath. I watched Aseshananda, his head gently went back with a smile on his old, incredibly featured face. I learned something at that moment. I have always learned from watching our elders. Every night this beautifully sweet lady would stand at the stairs as Swami would slowly go up. She would say, "Swami, I love you." And he would just say, "Ok, Ok." I suppose he knew somehow that Love cannot be expressed with words. A few years before I was born as this ego that I am so heavily identified with, Swami had a dream he told us of when the Divine Mother told him that it was better to die young. But he added, "But only if your wish is the Divine Mother's wish." To everyone that visits, this old swami says, "May the Divine Mother bless you." But the last thing he said to me was a bit different, "Sakti, Sakti (The Name of the Goddess as the Power of Life). Everything will be all right."

I came to eventually realize a new respect for life, this most precious and very fragile experience, though it is not permanent. It was to this greater power of all Life that I became dedicated, rather than to individuals. It was a quite and peaceful acceptance, an overwhelming sense that life is just life and that is why its called life. Yes. I may freely love human beings for what they are but I do not expect a great deal out of them. The resounding song of myself is that if you go looking for your own light in the light of another, that just may be a fool's darkness. Life is my teacher. Life is my guide. There is no other structure form over Self. I must confess, I don't know much about people, they always seem to be fluxing on a spiral. I just say, "Ah," and look into my own inner blue sky. Ego is the just a pivot point of perception, that is all, so what does it matter what your perception is of me or me of you. The real question, the one that has an answer, is Love. It might always remain a question. What my ego wants, has always wanted, needed and searched for is Life. Life is Love and it is to this immense universal great power of life that I give myself.

The real meaning of spiritual is to feel spirit. Spirit is Love. Religions are just belief systems, hopefully mere passages to a place beyond them. If what I say makes you feel good, well thats okay, but if it irritates you and makes you itch, thats better. For me it was to accept that I had wounds before I could heal them. To me, ego is the wound. Ramakrishna has has said from the farthest height, "When the ego is taken away, what remains over is one undivided ocean of Existence, Consciousness and Bliss." For me it is when the wound is taken away what remains is Love. Love is the one mood that goes there to that universal feeling, the true face of us all, that playfully borders the finite psyche and the infinity of consciousness by the immense power of life.

When I expressed the idea of getting rid of the ego to some people, one woman honestly replied that if she were to get rid of the ego she would never be able to get anything done. I thought to myself, who doesn't feel that way, so perhaps one should not worry nor hurry and just be happy with a little of the ego "I" consciousness. But then it came to me, that with that thought I was then still hastily gripping on to something other than trust in this immense and universal power of life which in truth is doing all that is done, free of the idea of the enjoyment of whose ego is mixed up with it. The limited sense of myself must indeed have a greater sense of power behind it, otherwise, how could I maintain a thought or even write a single word... Some say Love accepts the wound as a gift. Others say that Consciousness actually never feels the pain of the wound since it is simply pure awareness. But I say that Love is Consciousness and that you yourself must answer only to your self what ego might be.

The Source Of All Ideas

On Bhavamukha: The Divine Mood
Of The Goddess Kali

It finally struck me with a fresh new clarity, what this bhavamukha might be, at least for a small mind as my own. In my feeling this is one of the greatest gifts of what spirituality is that Ramakrishna gave to the world. He bestowed a precious treasure to human beings by actually demonstrating what might well be the highest human potential of experience. If one human being can, in the divine, consciously live in the source of all ideas touching God and one with God, then others also might possibly do the same. He was indeed a king in the realm of ideas.

Bhavamukha is Sakti Herself. Sakti (Pure Power of the Divine Mother) and Brahman (Infinite God Consciousness) are One. This is Advaita, non dualism, pure and simple. In bhava is the cognitive power of all moods, being and ideas. Moods are ananda related. Being is sat related. Ideas are chid related. Any fair student of Vedanta knows well that sat-chid-ananda is the ultimate expression of highest reality. In mukha is the source. Bhavamukha is as the after effect state coming out of purest non dual realization. Nirvikalpa samadhi. This is the source of all in the mood of being one with that source.

As Sakti in not any different than Brahman, so this wonder of bhavamukha is not any different from the exalted state of non dualism. It is conscious non dualism. It is living in conscious contact with the absolute non dual, the final condition of God. It is more than connection with God as the source of every mood feeling, being in existence and idea in consciousness. It is the very living state of that Principle, not different from the Principle. All moods, ideas and being are indescribably known and felt as they are nothing but the absolute being of that Principle. This bhavamukha is the immense universal mind of the unlimited 'I' of God, as the true self of all.

The beauty of this is most difficult to describe. It is the mood consciousness of being one with God, for lack of a better word and as this One Being, so commonly known. A state too high to comprehend, what is known by God is known by the mind in bhavamukha or perhaps more accurately, as to human potential, it is to tap into the God Mind as source of all. Or to realize the Universal I-ness of one and all without a break in consciousness. Or to know that Sakti is all that is out there.

Bhavamukha is simply the mood being of consciousness at one with the source of all, that is Sakti, God. One may have to allow oneself the thought that in bhavamukha there may be a little trace of the 'I' consciousness of a human being. Only for the practical purpose of understanding or to have something to consciously grasp in the imagination. But really, how could the ego mind thought as we know it be there at all? In nirvikalpa samadhi, it is said to be the final absolute extinguishment of all 'I' consciousness in the absolute eternal beyond all words, or moods, ideas or cognition of being. It is the incomprehensible complete death of the ego. But in reality it is something further and deeper than death itself. Death is a reflex of life, a duality, nirvikalpa samadhi is the final extinguishment of all dualism, the complete and total finishing of all conscious projection from the screen of the mind. Where mind goes and what is left cannot be described, for an ego is needed to effect a description. That nirvikalpa is simply without (nir) the play of the mind or the cycles of the mind stuff (vikalpa), one, is one in God Consciousness (samadhi), yet without even the idea of One. No duality.

So, who is actually there is bhavamukha, encased in a human body or even divested of the human body, without body, disembodied, if one may entertain that most liberated thought without fear. "Whole-hearted, intense love, we have only for this ego of ours and for this lump of flesh called the body. That is why we entertain in our mind so much fear of death or of any radical change. But the Master had indeed none of it." (from Sri Ramakrishna: The Great Master. by Swami Saradananda).

How could there be any trace of the absurd effort for ego maintenance in bhavamukha? It is conscious living in the complete effortlessness of the Divine Mother's Power. It is nothing but Her, nothing is there but Her. There is no you in bhavamukha, nor thought of me, all are but particles of emanations as the Divine Mother's Power. It is effortless living in Her, knowing, feeling, being, in, as and one with the Deep, deeper than the furthest reaches of death and yet at the same time, may I even say time, knowing, feeling, being consciously one with all the violence and beauty of this creative life or that which is created, projected or out there. Cosmologically, one might say that it is the source awareness of everything. All thought, all feeling, all minds, all egos, all memories, intellects, bodies gross, subtle or causal, all the past, all the future and everything in the present, how each person, place or thing relates and interrelates by cause and effect throughout and the destiny of all, where they came from, where they are now, where they are going and even when they might realize God, Self, Sakti. You might think this is like psychic phenomena, but really, what is psychic phenomena compared to this. Phenomena like that is only a brief tapping on the God Mind, the Sakti Mind, and may or may not be genuine. This is the God Mind, the Sakti Mind itself.

If, for a moment, we were to use some expressions from the Western field of psychological and spiritual thought, that of Carl Jung's discoveries, one might possibly say that this bhavamukha is the ultimate bringing to the border of all consciousness, the total awareness of the entire collective unconscious into a personal conscious reality, where the totality of all psyches and the personalities of these are known clearly as indeed God or the Great Self knows them. It is incomprehensible really, by the limited ego mind which seeks with effort to attain a concept. It is purest conceptual-less being with God, Sakti, as the only moment there is. It is difference within non difference and non difference in difference completely inconceivable by dualistic mentality. So it is Self alone going and gone beyond all difference yet completely and effortlessly at play with every

93

difference. But who understands what play is even in this so very serious world held in earnest by the ego mind. Playfulness is a lost concept for most of us, something only children do, but even children become so committed to play that they also lose sight of what play actually is. Sad, because we are only truly human when at play and play is spontaneity without thought or concern for outcome in regard to what has passed into the past or what will come in the future. Play is or should be pure joy and absolutely carefree. Play is God's, Sakti's bhavamukha where the creativity or termination of all universal and cosmic phenomena has no fear about it's outcome, for it is totally without the fearful consciousness of the ego self identity.

"Remain in bhavamukha." This was the Divine Mother's, the Divine Goddess Kali's command to Ramakrishna after he spent six months immersed in the absolute deep of nirvikalpa samadhi. In other words, She told him not to melt all trace of the 'I' consciousness into the Great Absolute, but live as the Great Absolute, the Source of All, expressing nothing but the Playfulness of the Great Absolute in all mood, being and idea. In reality we are all particles of this. By imagination and cognitive meditation we may benefit by thinking, feeling and being in our own mood of what bhavamukha is. We may feel consciously connected as parts of what is bhavamukha. Yet if I were to say I have attained bhavamukha that is nothing but an egotistical exclamation. But to say that I am not within bhavamukha is a lie to oneself, for even if we are not connected with the source of all ideas, we are indeed in reality, ideas from the source of all. Bhavamukha is to live as the Great Absolute expressing the mood, the being and the idea of the Great Absolute as the playfulness and the eternal freedom of the immense and unlimited universal 'I'. Though in no way may I say that this is mine, I may certainly say that all my life, being, moods and feelings, thoughts, ideas and cognitions are a part of and exist within bhavamukha.

This cognitive mood being at the source of all ideas may be thought of as not rubricizing anything, but of seeing and feeling everything as God, Sakti. Or one might think of this blessed state as rubricizing everything as God, Sakti, within one's innermost self, including oneself. From our point of perception we might inwardly label this as God or Sakti, but from pure bhavamukha there is no labeling on itself as these two ideas, as a dualism. That highly beautiful absolutely loving consciousness does not in itself designate the dual dividing of a masculine and feminine, of an animus or anima. Those dividing lines exist only inside the cognitive psyche of the human mind. A young sage named Suka had in his thought nothing but "I am the Self of all the universe," so when he came upon a group of beautiful bathing damsels, they felt no shame in front him for his consciousness registered no differentiation. But when Vyasa came along, they quickly put on their clothes being filled with the emotion of embarrassment, for the old sage's psyche still maintained the limited distinctions of the masculine and feminine dualism. In the spiritual quiet and peaceful serenity of bhavamukha, those distorted efforts of masculine power struggles and those noble efforts of and for feminine liberated emergence finally come to rest.

The unlimited universal immense 'I' feels all moods, all emotions, all sentiments, attitudes and cognitions. The intensity of the totality of all the great feelings combined cannot be imagined by ordinary individuals. Just the mere emotional power of bhavamukha could not be handled by most of us. Consider the five or six basic mood feelings or the background flavors of emotional taste coming at you, all at the same time. That is the great mood. One feels the serenity of God, Sakti's presence, one feels the master or the mistress to servant emotion, one feels the friendship connection, one feels the child parent combination, one feels love even for one's antagonists, as well as the lover beloved connection in all its bliss and power exploding. Yet, on top of this all these emotions circulate through various profound stages; the awakening of love bright as sunrise, the spontaneous dedication of all feelings of love, the feelings of refusing the beloved's love toward oneself because the emotion is too powerful, the wondrous feelings of being wounded and hurt by love but still loving the source of the

95

wounds and the inexpressible pain of separation from what is loved, caused by the utter illusion of emotional separation from what is loved. Can you imagine feeling all this for one's self and yet for others, universally, as all these emotions are going on. The idea forces my head to bow to this great wonderment.

Whose mind sentiments could climb the height of bhavamukha wherein all the violence and beauty of universal play is comprehended in the purest reason for it. Inwardly one would not even cognise the violent beautiful dualism but outwardly one would feel it all, yet knowing why it is there. In a lower plane of the mind we are always asking ourselves this question. If indeed everything was beautiful always, this world itself would be paradise, but it is yet to be that and may never be that. If there were no violence or no disturbing forces would we ever awaken from the sleep of phenomena, would we ever question our existence, our feelings, our thoughts. Would we ever ask for an answer to the mystery of ego consciousness as an 'I' force of identity ever involved in the investigation of who, what, when, where and why. Embracing the significant forces of life brings one to an acceptance of life and life if I may say, is what is occurring in bhavamukha.

In the technology of yogic mysticism, at the level of individual personal phenomena, bhavamukha may be described as the spontaneous and simultaneous awareness of the sixth and seventh centers of consciousness. The meeting ground, the border, the place between yet at one with both. But that is only an intellectual description and mere intellect may never comprehend what bhavamukha is. For one thing in regard to mystical yogic technology, bhavamukha is not individualistic awareness, it is non dual universal awareness, the immense universal 'I'. So the idea of the state being between the sixth and seventh center would have to expand to the total collective of all frontal conscious centers (the third eye as it is known) as an awareness coming out of the absolute oneness in the seventh center, which is pure consciousness itself. Completely one. Completely free of duality. So this bhavamukha awareness cannot even be said to be of a 'between' or 'border' type since it is the non dual experience of all in one moment without distinction or differentiation. There is no God, or Sakti thought there, nor thought of ego, individual or collective. It is the total universal immensity felt without any figuring over its nature. Could it be the knowing feeling of ceaseless universal creativity in consciousness ceased of all duality. It is the source of all eloquence, but all eloquence fails to describe the source from where it came.

From the height of bhavamukha, the dweller therein views, feels and experiences Eternal Consciousness and all Relative Phenomena as the 'One'. In imagining what this state is like we must remember that what is there is the Immense 'I' and nothing else. The one who returns from the Height and Depth of the Infinite, who reclaims a trace of 'I' consciousness only apparently has regained an ego connection. In reality, the ego has become purely, totally transparent and is filled only with the Immense 'I', the Universal I-ness, the Consciousness of the Divine Mother. So, who is really there in bhavamukha. Is it God? Is it Sakti? Is it the Great Reality? Words may only touch the edge of the Deep.

The fourth state of consciousness is called turiya, the pure Self, existence, consciousness and bliss. Deep dreamless sleep is the condition where no dream appears, no internal psychic activity of dualistic projection. Since there is no dualism here, this state, though unique, is one and the same for each individual. A universal condition free of dualism, where only the sense of being in unbroken peace is experienced. The diversity of individuality only comes with the variegated activity of the projecting psyche on the screen of the ego mind's contents within the reflective and internalized condition of subtle dreaming consciousness. The waking state reaches the end of the material output of universal phenomena as the individual physical body identity, senses, connections, relations and so forth. So this bhavamukha might be slightly understood by realizing that it is the mood of oneness free of the dual sense of a between-ness, at 'One' in the turiya and the other three states. But with bhavamukha, remember it is the Immense 'I', not the individual ego perceiving only it's own three states. In bhavamukha the mental illusion of separation in waking bodies may not exist. In the non dual wonder of bhavamukha that strange sense of the divided ego self idea may not exist in relation to the total content of all dream minds universally. All bodies are but ideas, all dream minds are the same and all these are seen as a great oneness rising up, surging along and merging back into the Greater Reality of which we have been speaking.

"The Mother showed me that there exists only One, and not two." Ramakrishna. That is it. As words may take us only to the edge of the wordless, it is said that this nirvikalpa samadhi is the absolute cessation of all dualism in the Self, existence, consciousness and bliss absolute, pure and infinite. Yet this bhavamukha is the mood of being in the consciousness of the same, 'there exists only One,' and so it is not two different states. The question as to whether the Great Reality is formless or full of forms is then no such question being answered by the 'One'.

Many people have such various opinions about what Kundalini is, but most simple, She is Power. The Power of Bliss, the Power of Consciousness, the Power of this Pure Existence itself. She is Primordial Power, One in, as and with that Primordial Absolute. She is the Goddess Kali, the Divine Mother. She does and moves everything at the quantum, atomic, elemental and organic level. It is really She who is performing all cognitive, psychic, intellectual and egoic functions which appear as the property of an individual. She is the blessed power of spirituality, the essence of what makes the Divine, something that is divine and the boundlessness of what is infinite. It is She who is the ecstatic feeling of love in the devoted soul, the wisdom knowledge of the sage, the concentrated serenity of the contemplative and the ego-less activity of the ones engaged in empathic works. It is She who causes that waking state. She is the only one projecting all dream contents. She is the peaceful rest in deep sleep. And She is the Bliss of the fourth.

It is She who raises consciousness to the edge, then into the Deep. We do nothing, even if we think it is so. She is the universal power of the Immense 'I' and the Immense 'I' itself. What is bhavamukha, comprehends what She is. She is the sweet mood of love that unites our consciousness with the Absolute. Every soul's individual kundalini is but Her one universal power. The ego self cannot raise Her, She raises Herself. Then feeling comes to the source. With this, how can one continue as an ego? Ego is but a thin temporal idea in the oceanic oneness of this bhavamukha. And that is the playfulness the Goddess has played with you.

A person who reaches the depth of nirvikalpa samadhi drops the body after twenty one days (Ramakrishna broke all rules of spiritual physics by staying in nirvikalpa for six entire months) in that final state, never to return again to dualism, unless the Divine Mother has a purpose in store for them. In this case they dwell in bhavamukha. But it is also possible that they would come back down to the realm of the ego personality like Totapuri, the naked one, Ramakrishna's Vedanta teacher and instructor in the technique of nirvikalpa samadhi. He had not yet realized who and what Kali, the Divine Mother is and yet this came to pass through his connection with Ramakrishna. Who knows, after Tota's realization of Kali while standing in the river during an attempt at drowning himself, he may also have dwelt thereafter in the wonder of the Divine Mother's bhavamukha as an actuality for himself.

A gentle idea entered this mind the other day. A sweet mood of cherishing understanding came with it. What if the person of that Hindu prince who experienced the one Buddha principle and the person of that Hebrew rabbi who experienced the one Christ principle, simply expended great effort at first, then became exhausted, only in the end, to both accept Love and Compassion, Pure Conscious Living Empathy as their reality. What if that is so in the simplest explanation, as a thing, that is happening and will happen to one and all of us within this human existence, ever as it is, and eventually to be so.

For in truth, everyone in this world expends great energy in speaking, thinking and feeling over the love of their own ego. And ego is but Self in another shape. Therefore, by the evidence of this, it would seem that Self is of the greatest importance in this world. The ruling factor. We think it is one thing when really it is something none of us comprehend. As the comprehension of it is not our own. It is the possession of the Immense 'I', none other. Ego is but a plaything in the play of bhavamukha. By ego we feel special. We feel alone, but we are not. Finally, we become exhausted with that. Then acceptance comes. Love. And Love is to realize that all our feelings are moved by Her and that She is the Divine Power of Absolute Spiritual Attorney to which we give ourselves.

The Unqualified Power Of The Divine Mother As Pure Being

On The Apparent Dualism Of Bhavamukha And Nirvikalpa

She it was who showed him the forms and She who showed him the formless and it was She who showed Herself to him once again as both, one and beyond. It was She, Kali, who showed him all that was within the personal and universal consciousness, the outside, and it was She, the Divine Mother, who showed him the deepest innermost reality, absolute oneness, and it was She again who brought him back to the outside, filled with love and compassion for humanity. She showed him the confusion of dualism, the peace of oneness and back again to the confusion of humanity, yet now filled with Her Divine Power. She took him from the inscrutable play of mind, to the wonder of inscrutable oneness and back to the play of the mind wherein poor souls like me having been dwelling so long without peace. This is how we explain to ourselves the spiritual wonder of the unqualified power of the Divine Mother as pure absolute being, from the point of view of dualism.

From the divine lap of Her Power, to Pure Being, to the lap of Her Power, a non dual movement, pure spiritual wonder. It is as simple as that. "After Love is felt, how could ego stand there as it once did before, where it once did before... it would not be enough." Someone told this to another in a dream of mine and this dream helped me to understand some of these things. Indeed, after the experience of non dualism is felt how could one return to dualism really. The non dual experience is nirvikalpa (consciousness absolutely without any mental duality present in that consciousness), the Pure Being of the Divine Mother. But even as the one who has gone into nirvikalpa comes out of nirvikalpa, isn't their experience of return to the universal immense consciousness of bhavamukha (the divine mood of facing the source of all that is), that of the divine mood of non

101

dualism. For then, what is bhavamukha is but nirvikalpa turned outward. The utterly absolute pure being of this exalted nirvikalpa is but the unqualified power of the Divine Mother turned outward in bhavamukha.

"By his own tremendous efforts, under the guidance of the ever - wakeful Teacher concealed in the hearts of all, Sri Ramakrishna had achieved the apparently impossible feat of transcending all the limitations of finite existence, and uncovering his true relationship with the One Existence - Consciousness - Bliss, in the compass of a few short years." (Life of Ramakrishna) This was because his primary reliance was on the Divine Mother. But in order for Her to bless the world with Her universal liberal doctrine that all paths and practices lead to the Great Reality, She brought to Ramakrishna a variety of secondary teachers for the purpose of the divine universal drama of breaking up the restrictive archetypes of a consciousness which holds to barrier thinking in spirituality.

There were many unsolicited instructors, major and minor, but four essential ones. The lady Bhairavi Brahmani represented Tantra, Totapuri, the Vedanta, Jatadhari, the worship of Rama, and Govinda Ray was there representing the Sufi path. Now, when Ramakrishna was engaging the technique of nirvikalpa samadhi in the tutelage of Tota, he there came to the point where the one form in his mind which held him at the border line, the edge of absolute indistinguishable pure consciousness in utterly complete non duality, was that of the Divine Mother. It is said that he then had to take up the psyche's symbol of the sword of discernment and sever the form of the Mother, to then dive, completely immersed, in the eternal consciousness of nirvikalpa where the relative phenomena of dualism was totality extinguished. This is a metaphor for a process, a movement in consciousness.

But the very nature of the metaphor sometimes seems to bring a misunderstanding in its wake. The Mother is not a lesser form that needs destroying and this was not a form of aggressivity toward Mother that I sometimes detect in the subtle tones of people's voices when they speak of the sword of this psychic discrimination. Some take this as if She were purposefully limiting him from nirvikalpa consciousness, no!, Her image took him to the edge of the Wordless, the blessed form of his chosen ideal, that of Mother Kali, on into the Ideal of the formless. She, as Absolute, is formless, and She is form. She is beyond dualism and this, that She is, is not rigid stillness, another common misconception. "Knowledge, knower and known dissolve in the menstruum of One Eternal Consciousness, " as described in the Life of Ramakrishna. More so, it is entering the Unqualified Divine Power Flow of the Divine Mother as Pure Being, which by its infinite immensity appears still compared to universal motion. The final throbbing of 'I' consciousness stops and what is there cannot be described.

There are comparisons to this spiritual phenomena of Deep diving. For example, the universal cosmic form of Krishna makes the puny ego idea of self seem so insignificant that one eventually lets go and experiences something so great it cannot be put into words. The throbbing of the little self dies and something greater than that sets in. Krishna's cosmic form is nothing but God turned outward, but even that outward phenomena must be crossed or severed in order to get a sense of the innermost reality which is clearly designated as something completely different from that outwardness, yet paradoxically, absolutely non dual and completely one with it. Wondrously, bhavamukha then dissolves in nirvikalpa and so does the universal Krishna dissolve in self realization. The immense 'I', the ripe 'I' of bhavamukha is free of the confined, unripe and limited 'I' concept. Even the bhava (the mood) of the immense 'I' dissolves into the nirguna (unqualified) aspect of the Divine Mother. So it is non dualism, not two-ism.

Another example is the Buddha who said please don't worship me, if you worship my form you are missing the point entirely. I am the tatha-gata-garbha, the reality thus gone to the other shore, the womb of suchness. If you worship this body complex what good will that do for you because the body complex terminates, not a lasting reality, so why be dependent on an un-lasting thing. Be purely self actualized, independent and free in yourself. And of course, the words of this writer are catching the meaning but are not the direct quotation. It is a funny and strange thing that some great souls visit history, pure and simple, but then complex psychological situations are built up around them when they leave. I heard Dr. Clarissa Pinkola Estes say, "God gave spirituality to humanity as a gift, but then the devil came along and said, 'Let me organize it for You.'" That says it all, doesn't it.

One must be almost constantly awake and alert to the inflow of dualistic conceptualization into the natural inner state of consciousness in oneness. All that spiritual power comes from this consciousness of oneness ever generating meaning for the silly and wonderful play of life. In other words, all spiritual power comes from the epiphany of total and purely non dual nirvikalpa consciousness, the pure power of this unqualified being of the Divine Mother. Then it comes down to the world like honey. Sadly, people are truly so desperate for this sweetness that they tend to mistake the bee for the honey. The honey is the Divine Power of Mother's bhavamukha. The bee is but a simple instrument of Her workings. As Swami Saradananda writes in 'The Great Master' about Ramakrishna, when anyone would address him as a spiritual teacher, a father, a master or patriarch, his flesh would sting because of this utterly wrong concept, then he would exclaim, "I am the lowliest of the lowly, the servant of servants,.... And saying so, he would immediately take the dust of your feet and place it on his own head! Has anyone witnessed a more humble attitude? And it is this very person whom they are making into a spiritual Teacher and God... which he was not!" Absolutely, most emphatically!

Again, the dualistic mind will prevent, by the strange sense of getting stuck in the mind, an understanding of what is this bhavamukha power. It is said that an ordinary human being has an aura which extends or radiates three feet in each and every direction and it is said that the Buddha's aura extended three miles in every direction. Stay with me, I am making a point. The expression of the state called vijnana is what an individual ordinary soul's comprehension of bhavamukha may be, but since we are not a total God person we cannot partake of bhavamukha in a total way. Fine, but am I not a part of what is divinely bhavamukha anyway. I was created out of this one divine power of bhavamukha and so were you, so then, are we not non separate and non dual in bhavamukha, enjoying the honey, even though we may not be that great of a bee, or such a master of the skills of collecting honey. Those most excellent honey collectors have auras that emanate a great distance, encompassing like bhavamukha itself, but is not my aura within that one and one with it. The discerning line between the consciousness of bhavamukha and the consciousness of vijnana is a dual limitation. The vijnani sees that the personal centered view of relative and the absolute are one and the same. The 'one' who exists in the divine continuum of bhavamukha sees and feels that the entire field of universal consciousness and the absolute consciousness are just that, one and the same. If there appears to be a difference it is one of degrees, not inner content. One of quantity and perhaps, who knows, not quality. The pure substance of an aura's energy is one and same, if it extends three inches, three feet or even three miles and across the universe. A strange comparison perhaps for some of you, but I am just trying to get this non dual idea across to you.

Now, let us please consider those four classical states of consciousness, the waking state, the dreaming state, the deep sleep state and the fourth state, that of pure absolute consciousness, but with a new fresh paradigm shift in our consciousness and feeling toward these conditions. A shift in the paradigm of our mood which is free of all those former associations of the divisional ego concept and those thought processes triggering the mechanics of one thought touching another and another thought and another thought and another thought in the cause and effect reductional process of the psyche. A memory concept triggers another memory concept and we hold to those as reality and are put into a hypnotic sleep that these are reality. Let us go deep diving into an associationless thought where consciousness once associated with the ego paradigm now shifts to a consciousness greater,

105

more sublime and more powerfully free than that former condition. The world system at times may appear dry as a bone and yet at other times filled with creative bliss. In truth, we may direct our thoughts to the deep, toward the consciousness which is filled with the mood of creative bliss. Then suddenly a paradigm shift occurs there in that consciousness and what appears there is now a fully alive living reality.

The tendency of the human mind is to cognise these four states as a kind of theoretical outline of something in front of you, when in reality these four conditions are a divine cognition of what we are in fact, as the great fact itself inward and real. Another tendency of mind is to place in consciousness, these four conditions, as structured steps of a hierarchal arrangement, when they are more like a fully circular continuum. Spirituality is round not square, and it is full not partial. Yet at one moment we are only conscious of one state and unconscious of the others. This is a great key.

In the waking state the ego strongly identifies with the body moving through the time state of that condition, with the illusive conscious contact of memory with that body. The point will be made, for example, the body is in one position, you get up and move through time to a new position. Now, what is the memory of that movement. Is it a reality to you or just a tracer of mental illusion in the reference of the new position. Certainly, the memory retains the illusion of the body through time and after so many memories condition the deep conscious mind, one becomes habituated to think in the pattern of this as a reality. It is memory that retains the illusion of the body, of course, in reference to time past. It is the phenomena of the conscious memory of the now former illusion of once moving through time, when in real fact it means nothing really as to the new position of the body in the time state of waking consciousness. But we hold on to it as a reality and that is what keeps us from going forward spiritually. This applies to all memories.

When the consciousness of the dream state sets in, one becomes totally unconscious of that time oriented ego identity with the body of the waking state. One was then unconscious of

106

the dream state and is now conscious of this condition and unconscious of the waking condition. The beauty and simplicity of it is that it takes no effort on your part, consciousness in just naturally pulled away from the time perceptions of the waking condition. The conscious connection with the waking condition simply and just naturally sinks away and dissolves. And yet so often, we find people engaging their ego in making great and noble spiritual efforts to raise their minds into higher states, when it just happens by the very nature of the way we are made and it takes no effort.

But, in the dream state, the ego consciousness of the psyche is still deeply engaged in the dualistic excogitation over the nature, result and outcome of itself, the ego, in the relational connection of the past with the future. The sense of self rarely rests in the pure present where non duality may be experienced, but engages itself with the duality of psychic dream activity ever referring this dream ego identity with what are past causes and future effects on what this ego consciousness is. The dream state is consciousness ever exploring consciousness, while so trying to find the unique form of expression in the dream contents which bridges the gap of dualism between what one is conscious of at that moment and also unconscious of at that same moment. That is, the condition, the nature and the reality of the other states of this circular continuum.

The deep sleep state is a spiritual gift to us from the Great Reality wherein we are one with the peaceful power of pure being, as the great fact of our true existence smiles upon us as we lay unconscious. One is no longer conscious of the dualistic activity of the psyche as it was in the dream state or the waking state. That dualism has dissolved, it has sunk away and there we have naturally been pulled by the Great Reality into this dream and waking free condition of consciousness, at one with the ineffable fact, for then no dualistic psychic activity is generating a sense of the ego mind's separation. But deep sleep is still sleep and it is still unconscious, not only of the dream and waking psyche, but it is unconscious of the great fact, the profound and true spiritual evidence of the fourth state. But here

107

we experience the bliss of the immediate present, absolutely free of cognitive phenomena engaged in the figuring of past causes with future effects. The sense of the present self is real to us now as a direct experience of that self full of power, being and joy, yet still unconscious. There is absolutely no spatial dual producing excogitation in a psyche which has crossed the melting line into deep sleep.

But think just now for this moment and let the mind make a crossing through a paradigm shift. The removal of sleep from Deep sleep is the Deep. And the Deep is this one pure being, the power, the reality. I have heard from those who are familiar with these things that the way into nirvikalpa is through deep sleep and others say no. Perhaps, yes, and perhaps no, but this is still dualistic opinions on the nature of who you are in the great fact. If deep sleep is a negative state due to its unconscious nature, then it may be turned to the positive state of being conscious of pure power and being by the removal of the unconscious sleep aspect. As far as approaching pure reality one has already gotten rid of the dualistic phenomena of the habituated psyche and ego so deeply involved in the dualism of waking and of dreaming. One has gone a long way here and without effort, one is in the oneness of pure being, and all that needs doing is to bring the unconscious to consciousness.

This would be the fourth state of the circle, the self as pure being totally in its own power. Perhaps it is divine power alone that may arouse the unconsciousness of deep sleep to the full consciousness of itself. Somehow this does happen, the unconscious melts into consciousness, but no one can speak of the peak of ineffability that is then experienced, because for the simplest reason that this is too beautiful to describe. Words stop at the Edge of the Wordless and that is the Deep which is never asleep or unconscious. That is why nirvikalpa is a gate to what we are, a spiritual state, a window to what is beyond the window. Nirvikalpa is as such, absolutely free of the play or cycles of the mind, totally immersed in non dualism. The deep unconscious sleep quality in the continuum of the Deep, is part of the play or cycles of the mind. To say more may be to say too much. One may either feel that it is self effort or divine will or a combination of these two that eventually awakens the unconscious sleep to a new view of life and self, but these are still words steeped with inability to express the Wordless.

Perhaps it is simply a cognitive reconditioning of what is the unconscious, purely, in a new familiarity with what is our spiritual potential. Isn't that what mantra, prayer, all our mediations and spiritual practices, listening, thinking, self work and all that, are in fact. All simply deep diving. Remember to be alert to the subtleties of dual thinking. You want to make efforts to reach the divine gate, when you are already on the other side of the gate as the unqualified power of pure being. You want to practice being what you truly are in the great fact of what you are. How can one practice being, the effort to reach the effortless is still a dualism. The non duality of nirvikalpa comes when all effort stops. Then it shines. Reality smiles. Even divine will stops, this is absolute oneness and that is true power. Can you say it is divine rest, no, for that implies that there is something in you that is not at rest, a dualism, and that thought leads away from non dualism back into all those dualistic efforts.

For example, if your practice is an Eastern practice, you might recite the mantra "aum". With 'a' as the symbol of waking consciousness. With 'u' as the symbol of dreaming consciousness. With 'm' as the symbol of deep and dream free sleep consciousness. Then the fourth state, the pure self, is the unified consciousness of the three in one. Very good, but you want to move ever forward with the powerful cognitive enhancement of practicing the intensely divine Tantric mantras such as hring, shring and kring. Your cognition and emotion increases like a tidal wave over the pool of your mind and then as if it were in state of dream consciousness, the chosen ideal of the Great Fact begins to arises in that consciousness. Finally, you begin to see far behind the chosen ideal into the formless and unqualified nirguna aspect of the Divine Mother. You are thinking in terms of the unqualified nirguna and the qualified saguna polarity, here is nirguna as pure being and here is saguna

109

as pure power, but that my friend is still dualism and you, like me, have yet to realize what the Divine Mother is in Her own Great Fact.

One can get all this in a second, like when a single detail of a dream is remembered and then suddenly every single complete detail of the dream is recalled. But what is recalled is the Great Fact, not just a simple dream with all its contents and phenomenal associations. Some folks of wisdom have thought that very young children simply feel spontaneously and know their true self quite clearly, but as they grow, the world tells them this cannot be so and because of various reasons such as wanting people to love them they bury their true self in order to please those around them. Perhaps we all have repressed our true self unaware of what we were doing to ourselves or perhaps we have suppressed our true self quite aware of what we were doing in order to fit the world's paradigm idea of what we should be. Ramakrishna, even as a grown man always referred to himself as a child of the Divine Mother, he never lost touch with his own inner reality.

We approached the four conditions of our consciousness through the theory of illusion and psychic duality, so now let us approach the same states, through the idea of reality, not illusion as before. So then, the fourth state is sheer consciousness, unshaped, formless, the great fact of absolute oneness. It is also named or rubricized by the human mind as super-consciousness and sometimes the super sensuous state, which implies that it is highly enjoyable, blissful, not dry, fully alive with the creative bliss of the Divine Mother. This is the pure unqualified power of Her and the one source of all great loving feelings, of all knowledge, of all concentrated and serene understanding of the mind's workings and of all actions done by the empathic free self for the sake of others. It is the great reality and the source of all great things.

Moving, stirring from there, somehow, that deep reality of the Divine Mother becomes the unconditioned and the unslated void depth of the unconscious, which is our deep sleep state. Though, the word void indicates more the non presence or absence of psychic activity. This deep sleep is real, it is consciousness free of all sense activity. The senses are not just the five organs that manifest in the waking state or the internalized essence of the same that are projected in the consciousness of the dream state. Mental activity is also a type of sense instrument by which consciousness is outwardly aware. Intellectual activity, a more refined part of the mind, is a sense instrument as well. The ego is also considered a sense by and through which consciousness works. Beautiful. Memory also is a sense instrument of consciousness.

In deep sleep there is only one consciousness of peaceful being, no senses are at work there and since this is so, no dualism in that consciousness manifests. This is such a beautiful idea to me and I know all this is real. I say that the unconscious state of deep sleep is unslated. There is nothing planed there, so one is fully present, no record is being kept on the past or future. No dualism has been slated in the mind. Nor is the sense of the mind there, mind functions in the dream activity of consciousness. But here in deep sleep, consciousness is there just as one pure being and because of this freedom from that consciousness of all dual activity, it is blissful, peaceful, not in wanting, not in craving and not in need of dualistic otherness, that which generates the dual reality of something that wants, needs and craves something other than absolute oneness, a secondary existence. This could be the desire for dreamless sleep by the unconscious itself, and why we are all not awakened right now.

Somehow, divine need, divine want, divine craving kicks in and we enter the subconscious reality of the dream psyche, the dream ego. It begins to get interesting as we would say, quite colorful as our dreams are, full of radiant meaning, diversity and all that. For me, I find it a most fascinating potential that one may experience a paradigm shift in the activity of the dream condition. It is the sense of ego division that puts a boundary on what you think is your dream mind. Why should there be boundaries? They themselves are but dream concepts within the circular continuum of the subconscious dream reality, made so

111

as a personal reality and distinguished only by the sense of ego idea. And that ego idea is a very vaporous thought concept especially in the dream state. All the time, people dream that they are someone other than who they are in the conscious waking reality. So why not expand on this principle of the dream psyche's consciousness and extend the reality of the dream subconscious further and then far beyond the individual fixation of the ego into a paradigm shift toward the universal and cosmic subconscious dream mind, which is free and without the personal ego's divisional lines.

Carrying this beautiful self discovery over into the waking state of individual conscious reality, the same principle of a universal conscious reality comes as a very genuinely true experience when the divisional ego lines between our ego concept of the individual body mind complex identity melts the feeling of separation into a reality which has none. The boundary of identity becomes cosmic. This is the basis for so much phenomenal mystical experience. It is this paradigm shift from the limited and isolated idea of self to the immense 'I' generated through the cognition of the bhavamukha reality, the universal reality, out of which then comes real empathy. True love then fills the heart and compassion is generated in the universal conscious mind reality as universal love. Of who does this remind you? That thought itself is then the beginning of this wonderful and real cognition, which is to be reborn or refreshed spiritually.

A drop or two of the Divine Mother's unqualified power makes an ordinary soul great, more than a drop or two creates a world teacher. When those world teachers die, religions spring up around the memory of them, which are but human beings trying to explain the phenomena of this divine power to themselves. But by the problematic nature of definitions, religions often become a limitation in themselves due to human inadequacy in explaining the divine power of bhavamukha. But remember carefully that the idea of the ordinary and the great is a perplexing dualism and that this bhavamukha cannot be understood from the point of view of dualism. It is the one ubiquitous universal divine power, not confined by anything, any system, any ego, any human personality. Religions simply pertain to re-linking or rejoining with something divine. I am writing here about something so absolutely spiritual and at one with itself, that it is never involved with the confusion of dualisms which need to attain something.

On a more practical note, for I know you are asking why all this, when I begin to understand the workings of my own mind, its functions, its responses, its processes of associations, identity, feelings and so forth, then I, without effort and automatically begin to understand your mind, feelings and so forth. If I can comprehend the circulation of emotions through my own limbic system, then I also by that knowledge may then understand the sameness of your circulations of feeling. By knowing the nature of one grain of sand, one knows the nature of all grains of sand. This is the cosmic knowledge of other's states, moods and positions that is felt at the super sensuous level of blessed universal mood in bhavamukha. So it is actually very practical as well as mystical, spiritual and blessedly loving. In other words, by comprehending my own worldliness, which is nothing more than the substance and the content of the waking and the dreaming states, I then comprehend the substance and content of universal worldliness without the idea of egotistical dualism getting in the way. By fully facing the nature of my own psyche, not pretending it is something else, that also shows me the nature of yours.

As long as the bond of love persists, all our quirks, all our dual mind behaviors, our obsessions and promptings of the psyche toward the interpersonal yet independent identity with others, all that makes us tense and fearful, and all that stresses us into divisional thinking and feeling then matters very little if at all. It is this bond of love that is our connection with the spiritual power of oneness in this bhavamukha. The psychologist Abraham Maslow who did deep studies into the nature of peak experiences, the best moments of human life, put it this way in the thorough documentation of his discoveries. Some people in peak experience reported this sense of perfection, "In the first sense, every living human being is perfect; in the second sense, no person is perfect, nor ever can be." The line of dualism melts between what is perfect and imperfect. Each person is both at the same moment, how can that be. It is because of the very dualistic nature of language trying to express something which is not dualistic, but nevertheless felt in the heart during peak experiences. Maslow made excellent records of numerous insights, wisdom states, ecstatic conditions and so forth, of people who had these beautiful moments of what is best in being human. Peak experiences may be simply the conscious total acceptance of what is most real in us.

It is said that Ramakrishna was so often in the divine mood of bhavamukha that it was sometimes difficult to tell if he was there or in his usual self, the humble aspirant, the child of the Divine Mother, completely charming, full of sweetness and utter humanity for humanity. But I ask you is this not the dualism of one's mind projecting upon the oneness of the immense "I" in bhavamukha. Where is the division line really. When he assumed the loving mood of bhavamukha he was the instrument of that divine power and when he was in the so called usual self he would often respond to inquiries by simply saying, "Ask Mother and She will tell you." It seems to me there was no division at all but just a degree of intensity at the mood of the moment which is purely human. We are human, but that is no good reason to hold to the illusive sense of separation from the great fact of our real existence and of what we truly are. Again, duality does not penetrate the mysterious reality of our eternal non dual nature.

The great fact of this non duality is that we are all holding on to the Unheld which holds us all eternally. But it is this holding that creates the dual sense of separation in the mind. The Immovable moves and we are moved by it as we are one with it, while the divine Unheld is the only Consistent in this world of every other thing inconsistent. Everything else is absolutely insignificant to the Unheld which is holding us at one. And we dualistically take everything so seriously and earnestly, forgetting that we are at play, and even more so, how to play at one with the Unheld. Letting go into the Unheld is like waking up from a dream. One does not hold on to the content of every dream detail, only the essence, the essential mood of the dream.

I know what Love feels like, everyone does. But no matter how much I write I could never describe the feeling. No matter how much concentrated loving knowledge self work my writing expresses or if I write now just for the sake of myself, my purpose, my sense of being closer to the great fact or in some way that it serves the purpose of bringing another self closer to the great fact, never can I describe what it is. Those thought moods that come while drifting into dreamtime or during dreamtime evade us so often with descriptions. But I, like you, know what Love is even though its description also evades us.......

So, the gate to the Divine Mother as pure being is that nirvikalpa samadhi, the absorption in pure non dual consciousness absolutely free of the play of mind in total oneness. While the bhavamukha aspect of the Divine Mother as pure power is the mood (bhava) of facing (mukha) the Source (also mukha) of all cognitive states, ideas and insights, mood conditions, and so on and on. What is that 'source'? Nothing less than what is found through the gate of nirvikalpa, complete oneness with God, Mother, Sakti, Reality, so much so that one is free even of the ideas of dualism with the Indescribable which those names indicate. So it is the mood of facing conscious oneness, yes, the most absolutely conscious of all, the source of all life, all consciousness and all joy. This is the source, so much more conscious than any condition of the waking and the dreaming states and this is the 'conscious' which even gives the power to the unconscious in the deep depth of dreamless sleep. But dualism is subtle my friend, a question at every turn and so even the idea of mood implies there might be something which is not this mood. And the idea of facing also implies a dualism of something which is not faced, or faced away from, an other. Even the word oneness, again implies that there might be somewhere, something, that is still a two-ness, a second. Again,

115

even the idea of a 'source' implies something that comes out of the 'source' and that is dualism, my friend.

While I write, words limit the moment, yet rest assured, this is Real, giving everything else its reality, the divine property of one and all. But who can claim it as a 'who', as an ego, which would not be there since ego is qualified and this of which we speak is Unqualified. Simply, a quality cannot own what has no quality. That would be but a claim of ego consciousness, ungraspable by anyone, but there for all, innate as True Being.

Before the ego becomes mixed up with; every little craving for itself, every temporal identity caused or influenced by psychic impressions from the outside or internal residual imprints within or every need for the victory of personal assertion... let it become and be 'one' with Mother. It is but a salt doll that must melt upon contact with the Ocean. Then, since it no longer exists, how shall it know anything of itself, of universal immensity, of even great reality. What is then there is simply What We Are!, with absolutely no question of what it is, with absolutely no thought of a collective or universal 'we', nor even an idea of being, suchness or are-ness.

It is most simply, Love, without confinement of ego associations, defining particulars or blocks in the psyche to the flow of Love, on any specific or superior object for Love. All definition hinders realizing the Pure Feeling. Any cognition in the first or frontal position of the mind, screens the Direct Feeling from the mood awareness of its Direct Force. For two 'firsts' cannot occupy the same position. Great Reality must fit there. For the ego, it is an eternal unknown, yet it is an eternal known to the Knower in each of us. This is the paradox of non dual life. Ego may be ripened or refined with the Immense 'I' mood setting in or replacing the intensity of the limited 'I', or perhaps ego may be gotten rid of entirely in the peak moments of such understanding. Who knows,... yet as Reality is what it is, it already knows this, the Sweet Truth in all of us. This is the hidden meaning behind and within the mask of ego itself, which is either in a shifting state of negation, distortion or reflection of the Great Reality simultaneously being above us all as

116

Unqualified and within us all as a quality of Itself, never lost, ever there and here, playing out its mystery as the process of Self Discovery.

The waiting or effort for this creates spiritual misery. The acceptance of this, at whatever stage, is Happiness, Peace, Serenity, which spontaneously sets in as the Divine Power of Love charging every cell with the energy of living joy. This is the one feeling that bridges the bhavamukha nirvikalpa polarity between the created human being and the infinite Godhead of the Divine Mother. That is Love, the one true spiritual power. It is the non dual mood of Love at the source of oneness, with the source of oneness, being the source of oneness. The dualism of what is thought to be unqualified power and the reality of being, simply melts with the on coming of Love. Love is the first and the best, the chief of moods, the preeminent feeling, the principle idea, the paramount conception, the primary sovereign thought, the reigning mistress/monarch of all notions, the refuge of thought saturated with non dualism. It is the highest face, the perfume of oneness, the gentle undivided memory steeped with oneness, foremost, and infused with Love. This is bhavamukha, the one and only true tutelary power there is, the primal, the original, the secret digit in consciousness filled with divine emotion. The entrance to the dawn of Love rising. A slender branch inclined over the meeting ground of unbounded Love and finite feelings. It is the full frontal face of the Divine Mother and the sweet sprout of all human tenderness. First. Endless. Coming from nowhere defined by thought.

Ego resistance probably means there is something the ego needs that it is resisting, which will make the ego better if it accepts rather than resists. The Great Reality would be the chief among these, which upon acceptance throws the ego into a dimension where,... ego has no hold. So it was resisting letting go into the Unheld, which when done gives great joy, an overwhelming vacuous power and infinite unbounded feeling, Love, even to the lesser traces, the thinner traces of ego which still may be holding on.

Finally, if one may even say that, for even the idea of final is a dualism which implies that there was once something in you that was not complete. This Great Reality of which we are speaking, drawing poetic pictures of and trying to catch the true mood of, is not a passive principle, distant, unreachable and un-pertaining to human life, but a real Living Power, for Power is not a quality of the Absolute, but the extreme Absolute itself. "The Absolute alone is the Primordial Energy." Ramakrishna. It is an applied Reality applied to self, universal in one great sense, as an outside expression, which is in fact non dual with the Power itself, the most Divine Mother. It is Her Power that manifests as this existence absolute, emanates as consciousness absolute and is bliss or Love absolute, without any dual sense of being behind, inside or outside. The unqualified power of the Divine Mother is what is the absolute. Then the simple problem of dualism (ego) exists no longer. What is, is always...

One may go on and on forever stuck in the back and forth of thinking and contemplating what is the absorption of consciousness (samadhi) in power as Mother (saguna Sakti) and what is absorption (samadhi) in the pure being of Mother (nirguna Sakti), from the qualified to the unqualified and from the unqualified to the qualified. You can't get it with the dual mind and the thought concept of a 'you' is half of that mind. It is better, easier to sink into the Beauty of Love... a Love unfocused on the 'you' or the 'that'.... Mother is nirvikalpa, immovable. Mother is bhavamukha, moving, this bliss, being without effort.

Everything becomes the poetry of the non dual, the Self speaking from every corner. As ego, no one may receive it. As Self, everyone has it, even without going through the gate. No formula of a joy to effort ratio will reach it... It is the divine and blessed explosion of the atomic bomb of Love when lover meets beloved within you, then the formula of how you got there doesn't mean much. All formulation inhibits this Direct Feeling (Love). Being, Becoming, Accepting, Letting Go, the more so, the more there is Direct Feeling. It is in Direct Feeling alone that we can measure the Sky without ground, that is, without any

118

trace or reference in dualistic comparison or relation to the 'one', not even the idea of the 'one'.

Measuring Sky Without Ground

A Pragmatic Psychology Of Non-Duality

There is no doubt that non duality is real, but difficult to apply to the reality of our dualistic lives. Yet in the human psyche, answers are found and joy is somehow experienced when the pairs of opposites join. Something happens, consciousness is released from figuring dualism and peace is felt at that moment. Yet again, we must not lose touch with the pragmatic application of the non dual state which means to test the consequences of a thought when it is applied to what our lives consist of in terms of what we believe to be reality.

Of course, one of the most pragmatic tests of the non dual state is that it helps one to get over the confinement of yes or no thinking. There is always another potentially better equation to life, instead of simplistic black and white, yes or no thinking and that equation always comes out of the potent power of the non dual state of consciousness, when yes and no meld together and something new, a fresh possibility arises.

How many times a day have we asked ourselves if what we said or did had any value or impression or none at all. Who knows. For in reality it is the non dual principle to which 'who' points that does know if any effect has been caused by the action of any person, for better or worse. And what does it matter when one realizes that everyone is in a state of evolving toward non dualism. We think 'yes', we think 'no' and we find ourselves intolerant of other's belief systems, their feelings and so on. And that only leads to conflict, conscious irritation and emotional unsteadiness. When, the whole time, the other equation was that of open acceptance, true tolerance of other's position on the scale of living. This glimpse of an answer is born out of the non dual feeling. The question of the ego's self importance or not, then wanes. That is the non dual effect.

So much of life is spent laboring between the nightmares of the self guilt complex and the daydreams of the self glory complex. Neither reflects who and what we are. They both distort true being as they are dualism. But when the non dual state sets in we begin to see that what we are, as we are, was never actually strung between those two extremes. Non dualism is never an extreme, but ever a balance. Dualism is what sets up extremes in consciousness as what is accepted, as what is rejected, as what is adored, as what is hated, all within the idea of self.

Let us go on with this. Non dual consciousness perceives the extreme moods of dualism. You may read one thing that creates the mood of fear within your perception. You then read something else which generates the mood of beauty within your conscious experience. Yet what was it within you that perceived both states of emotion. It was, of course, non dual consciousness. Curiously, the mere concept of the non dual state may indeed be a cognitive cure for much of psychosomatic dysfunction, as a reestablishment of the direct state of being.

The pragmatic application of the simple idea of non dual cognition frees us of so much of life's inherent misery due to the design of dualism. This is religion's ultimate point, really speaking. Non duality is like a ubiquitous gravity continually pulling everything toward itself. Life is just always and naturally regenerating and moving towards this unification of the psyche in order to relieve our psychic anxiety caused by the stress of two opposites.

Enough of that, lets us move along to other paradigms of dualism and the shift to the non dual. We commonly think of moving toward the goal as being focused and of moving away from our goal as being unfocused. Yet it may be thought of as the other way around when we consider the caveats of dualism and the praxis of the non dual. Consider for a moment that non dual consciousness is purely and absolutely unfocused, that is, never fixed onto any ego object whatsoever. In that state focus disperses and what is left is just consciousness pure and simple, not broken up by ego objects of identity. Which defines the non dual state, focused or unfocused, both, neither or some absolutely different equation.

122

Dualism makes us think that consciousness is dual, when it is not. Things that stir up in consciousness have the appearance of dualism due to the stirring up idea and the settling down idea, but consciousness itself does not experience any change in itself. We may think of death as unfocused consciousness without the intensity of body and mind identity and that life is just the reverse, the intense focus of consciousness with the body mind crisis. Dualism is really the only crisis we experience. The crisis of the appearing of dualism in consciousness. Consciousness itself is not changed by life or by death and once this is known something extraordinary happens in the turnabout of the mind. One becomes self assured in a reality divinely intended, but still the psyche may contain superstitious conceptions of heaven and hell due to dualistic archaic mythological inputs into the mind.

The ideas of being in control of life and of not being in control of life, of hanging on and of complete surrender may also be relieved of their dualistic struggle by the pragmatic application of the non dual concept. You go one way, you go the other, you try this and then you try that, and none of it gets you where you want to be. You think you got it and you don't, you want to get it and you can't. When the whole time it is the other equation that moves you where you want to be. Spiritually speaking of course.

Spontaneous non dual consciousness is what brings us peace. And actually, dualism is the anti-phenomena to what we inherently are in our innermost serene self. The conditioning of dualism forces the mind to think in such terms as this is this and that is that and that is it. When, this could be that and that could be this, and flexible fluid thought might always lead us to another equation. In the psyche, dualism creates the stress factors of those weirding worries that assault the mind and the regret - resentment cycle of inner anger that destroys our peace of mind because at that time the mind is trapped by dualistic cogitations, which, while going back and forth on something, ultimately has no real lasting answer.

Sometimes forgiveness is not the answer and quite obviously, revenge is never the solution. There is always another answer, there is always moving through the superficial surface of things and people, to get to the valued point of living, being and loving. What could be more important than those three blessings on our lives. The dualistic ego mind which feels good or not good about itself, which has the emotion of agreement or feeling of disagreement, which is trapped by the want for having an impressive ego or the lack thereof, is caught in the closed circuit effect of external reactions and has not sunk down into its own non dual sense of calm and quite. The neural computer is very busy with the zero to one relationship with information until shut down.

Dualistically, we do indeed move through a surface of values. In life, we all find somewhere or in someone, something of value. Then hopefully comes something of more value to us. Then, if blessings descend we are lucky to find something most valuable. Ultimately we discover or find something of priceless emotional value. That is our non dual state that no thing can shake. We strip off all that subconscious psychic wiring of dualistic solutions which never give us permanent rest from the stress they cause. And when we work at that deep level, in the direct current of the self, getting more and more free of that tension of opposites, we come to a cherishment of our own non dual state. That is your spiritual life of which this Earth is the training ground. Ultimately, this is our one true friend as the word friend actually means, to love, or the one who is loved. And this non dual feeling is the source of all love. It is what love is.

The psyche naturally loves non dualism as it makes the psyche joyful. Joy is an emotion that comes out of non dual awareness. Non dualism is the free flight of thought that touches the face of the Great Reality, not bound or tied up by traditional thinking. And freedom always brings joy. So non dualism may be said to be the free part of the mind or rather that innate freedom and never broken reality within our consciousness.

124

In reality, all dualism reflects non dualism as two halves become one whole. Consider our physiology, two hands, two nostrils, two kidneys, two halves of the brain complex. It would appear to us that dualism is really the playful expression of non dualism, not an evil nor an antagonist as most religious systems might have us believe. Dualism is a natural expression, not one to be feared. The sagely psychologist, Abraham Maslow, gives an insight of profound depth to this, "If, for the sake of argument, we accept the thesis that in peak-experience the nature of reality itself may be seen more clearly and its essence penetrated more profoundly,... that the whole of Being, when seen at its best and from an Olympian point of view, is only neutral or good, and that evil or pain or threat is only a partial phenomena, a product of not seeing the world whole and unified, and of seeing it from a self centered or from too low a point of view."

Any thoughtful person would easily realize that our psychological systems and constructs are also dualistic, the masculine-feminine divisions and dualisms are the most obvious, as we have come to separate, rubricize, label, and divide; emotional, mental, intellectual, physical and even spiritual properties, as being one or the other. And this has caused a great deal of misery in the spectrum of what is just natural human consciousness. And then there is the aetiological level of dualistic causes inside, behind or in the background of the psyche itself. This logic of causes and effects is the dualistic causality of one's own state of positioning, psychologically and spiritually speaking, as an idiosyncratic and unique human being who is living within a conjunctive relationship to the universal body and being of all life. At last, the non dual source of it all comes into clarity as an excellent conclusion being the a-logical spiritual bliss peak carried ever forward and higher. Only our fixed dualistic self conscious identity limits us by its fearful anxiety over letting go of dualistic comfort and ever opening up to this restorative non dual power of life. It is to embrace the passion of all life as being oneness with the great ubiquitous fact.

125

Our non dual moments are seldom recognized for what they are because of the powerful gravity or pull of dualistic mental training. We so seldom open ourselves to the Divine Entirity and more often find our minds in a state of fixation on human personality and its ties as absolutes, when there is so much more than just this. Instead of enjoying those very reachable non dual peaks, we engage in the mere phenomenal surface of life, all its opinions, abuses, intrusions and invasions into our consciousness which pulls us in the direction devoid of peace of mind. It starts early in life, if not perhaps even during the soon to be divided womb consciousness, our common beginning, our equally shared source point.

Everything is metaphorical of the non dual state. All dualism poetically melts into the creative reflex of non dualism within our lives. And as this is so, the mother - father complex is one of the most primal symbols of this dualism, which to the child is the most complete symbol at that time of the non dual state, which has already been established to be Love. The child gets their ideas of what Love is from that primal parent dualism. Whether young or otherwise, it seems to be a persistent reality in the consciousness of most people. Before birth, the child is in something of a non dual state. Then entering this world still filled with the memory of that non dual feeling of love, that love becomes broken by the usually fragmented and dualistic relationship of the parents. A deep and earth shattering schism in the core of consciousness then takes place. The memory of once felt non duality becomes lost. This carries over into other dualities.

Most obviously so in the sad eternal battle of the man woman complex. The dualistic parental legacy continues. The memory of the non dual feeling has been lost, people don't know how to love and this bleeds over into our other dualistic problems. Then the two sides of the severed wound in consciousness become the lost sense of self in the midst of the great dualism of the life-death complex. One must get rid of the idea of death to understand the non dual state. It is not a conscious polarity reflex off of the death idea. If anything, it is pure life itself never finite nor finished. The influence of this cognitive concept of the non dual state helps to remove the fear and anxiety over what is thought of as death.

Deeply and sincerely ask yourself, if true non dual consciousness can die, as it never enters the superficial surface dualism of a thing that is born and therefore must die. With this in mind, do I need to explain the deep rooted dualistic spiritual-sexual complex that curses and perplexes human beings as they struggle with their mortal human emotions and their immortal spiritual sentiments? Maslow's subjects of study, those who have had peak experiences, pour out their discoveries in answer to this contradictory dualistic problem, "As he gets to be more purely and singly himself he is more able to fuse with the world, with what was formerly the not-self, e.g., the lovers come closer to forming a unit rather than two people, the I-Thou monisn becomes more possible,..." It really seems to me the the non dual answer is a most sagacious emotion of getting to the direct feeling about anything. Getting out of the 'yes and no' mind, then getting into the sweet mood of oneness where the 'I' and 'You' complex melts away into the sweet poetry of life.

Certainly it is getting away from any antagonistic emotional concept and then generating love free of fear. At this point one may find one's thoughts leading in the direction that non duality is real and duality is unreal. Thats fine if it comforts you for a moment, but it will not last since it is still a dualism. A real, an unreal. A oneness, a two-ness. The state of Ramakrishna, the loving devotee of the Goddess Kali, has been described as having a mind which had got fully merged in the indescribable state devoid of duality and non duality. In other words, true non dualism is not conscious that is non dual. It doesn't know it is non dual for that would be but a reflex of negation on the dual. We might be better off thinking of these matters, as that, the self is central and therefore the real and that everything else is unreal only in terms that it is not one's primary experience. Self is the only primary experience. But the question may still momentarily remain for you of how can we apply this primary idea, the non dual self, beyond all ideas, to the ideas of life consisting of which we live.

One answer is that the 'I' consciousness may assume non dual consciousness in various proportions. Examples are given by Ramakrishna. That of a fish swimming in the sea of non duality. That of a pitcher which has sunk in the sea of non dualism but still retains the ego form of the pitcher. The fish ego metaphor is not filled within by the sea water of non duality like that of the pitcher. Then there is the salt doll metaphor of ego consciousness which goes to the sea of non duality to measure the depth of the water and simply melts away entirely. All these are examples measuring the depth relation of 'I' consciousness with non dual consciousness and all are indeed measurements. But as this essay is titled Measuring Sky Without Ground, it finally means that the Sky of Non Duality can never be explained in terms of the relative dualistic ground below.

In this light, the three traditional states of consciousness; waking, dreaming and deep sleep may offer no help whatsoever and might even be an obstruction to the feeling experience of pure non dualism. How can you measure 'Sky' in relation to 'Ground'? Non dualism cannot be measured by dualism, states of consciousness or anything. No ground reference will do. You cannot describe this non dualism in relative terms, but you may feel it. As Ramakrishna did try to explain, "As is your mood, so will be your gain." That says it very well. As the mood of your own poetic depth grows you will realize there is no dualism between Sky and Ground. The Sky touches the Ground everywhere. And further out, what is thought of as 'Sky', encompasses completely, the orb of the 'Ground'. So where is that duality now?

No amount of psychic fission nor psychic fusion will contact this feeling. I like these expressions, self fusion and self fission as the continually dual processes of the psyche. That of splitting apart in fission from the Great Fact and that of bringing or melting together as fusion with the Great Fact. Life may be reduced to these primary dual processes as what we are all

128

doing. Yet resolution comes with the pragmatic non dual acceptance, or rather more accurately, an inward non acceptance of both, a letting go of these two processes so that psyche turns towards the non dual state. It is the depth cognition of the 'one', the both and something more, something else, the non dual state which puts no conscious contact or recognition of primary value importance on dual processes as answer, conclusion or final meaning.

You can become one with the non dual state even if only for a short time. It is to be one with the Cause of all, for are you not in reality part of the all of which the non dual state is the cause. So why should it be an experience which is for just a few. It is inherent to all as the deep oneness of life, out of which the thinker and the thought dualism appear. The ideas of getting it or having got it, pull one's consciousness away from actually having it. That is, as a tangible peak experience. Both having and not having, are ego illusions, ego distortions or entanglement in the process of being stuck only in recognition of the ego. This is a psychological situation of relaxation and stress in our consciousness itself, producing inner struggle. But the non dual state relieves that struggle and the psychosomatic tension that it causes. Maslow, in describing these peak experiences in his study of American individuals, states, "That is, the greatest attainment of identity, autonomy, or selfhood is itself simultaneously a transcending of itself, a going beyond and above self hood. The person can then become relatively egoless." The augmentation of his research makes this all the more approachable, possible, and reachable.

The non dual peak is really a statement of being, rather than one of becoming. How can you become what you are?

The non dual moments in our lives are end experiences, not means to an end. There, one has no more fight in them, no more forcing, it is just being. But, the tendency of the human system is to perceive becoming or desiring as the means to an end, and being or the desireless state, to wit, the fulfillment of desire, as the end state. This again is the setting up of a dualistic difficultly of having or not having this 'something' we are

129

speaking of here. This is dual cognition in the consciousness of what is non dual. It is the paradoxical question of power or desire in reflex to being without desire or power. Can you only be, when power or desire subsides? Or, are you not at being even amidst desires.

There is a problem of perceiving the non dual state as a standstill. The mind being full of the motion of desire perceives the non dual as being too still for life to bear, even without energy, without power or without passion. Really that seeming standstill is the powerful position of peace in consciousness and it is from there that life is invigorated once again. A contact with this principle as a spiritual phenomena makes people feel they are reborn, refreshed, renewed and so forth. Those peak experiences of the non dual state are really just like dipping the ladle of the 'I' consciousness into the deep well of pure power and pure being, as the ubiquitous whole or non dual completion, and as the invigorating return, when back in the dual mind. This raises another dualism in perception. One being that the non dual state might destroy our emotional content by its absolute transcendent nature and denial of all dualistic folly in consciousness. And the other is just that, from the high point of view of the non dual attitude, everything else is just folly, superficial emotional content, illusions and so on. These two attitudes may have the fragrance of gender determinations, but that is definitely deep rooted psychic prejudice. Is high denial of illusion or embracing the folly or playfulness of the universe, a male or female phenomena. Here, the dualism within attitude blocks the deeper perception of unified conjunctive non dual experience, that of the free form of self at play in the non dual state, a lost art in the modern world, as playfulness is spontaneity or true freedom. It is always a moment of seeing both sides, then more, at the same time, when then both sides fall away and only the 'more' is left.

This non dual idea of which we are speaking is really to go beyond all that is written or taught. One need not be a great sage, or yogi or yogini to discover this. Maslow's subjects were not. That is important because the idea of special and inferior is another dualism holding at bay, the experience of non dualism. If it is true for one, it must be true for all, otherwise it may not be innately true. This leads us to the awareness of yet another strong dualism in consciousness. Within one's inner dialogue or in common language, one holds the thought that such and such a person is a God realized soul and this other person is just an individual mortal soul, he is a low soul, she is a high soul and so on. A truly pragmatic non dualism is yet to be understood, for is not the God realized soul still conscious of the God - ego soul polarity. It must be so by the very fact of being in the world, surrounded by worldliness, still having a waking and dreaming condition, as opposed to being in a pure God state.

This comes from dualistic perception within the lower strata of consciousness still retaining the I-You monisn. "Though we can never be gods in this sense, we can be more godlike or less godlike, more often or less often." Maslow. In the higher strata of consciousness, the throb of the 'I' beats and pulses until non dualism takes over. Then even that throbbing is gone. This again, is the problem within the 'ground' of the dualistic questioning of the mind, are we merely capable of being at one with the Great Fact, or are we the One Itself. Can we really measure Sky without Ground? Is this relative 'ground' experience all that can be gotten or is the absolute 'Sky' state really possible. "These are the words that the subjects themselves use in trying to describe experiences which are essentially ineffable. They speak of 'absolute,' they speak of 'relative.'" Maslow. At this moment of context, I should quote one of Ramakrishna's peak responses which is perfectly fitted to this last thought, "Both my hands are free. I am not afraid of anything. I accept both the Nitya and the Lila, both the Absolute and the Relative." That most free, most fearless and very most ineffable state. and, to add, most loving peak feeling. is within our innate non dual consciousness.

131

The Lucid and The Elucidation

The Non Dualism Of Light And Emanation
In The Three States Of Consciousness

It is the extraordinary conclusion to ordinary lives. And this would be nothing less than to feel the Light as Self, the darkness of dualism lifted, and the mind perceives everything from source to conclusion, as Divine. But duality must go, must be taken away, must be removed, otherwise it might just be a poetic state of mind, which is excellent, but any state of mind is still within the realm of dual consciousness.

In this world, the Light of Self is all that is Lucid. All else is complex dualistic darkness. Yet, this Lucid principle is ever elucidating that dualism and ever present within its phenomenal structure, movement and emanation, to wit, the three states: waking, dream and dreamless consciousness. The Lucid, as this consciousness is never not present in these three states of consciousness.

The Lucid is bright, it is light, but not that of an electric bulb, a flame or a star. It might be thought of more as a limpid condition of our consciousness which is purely transparent and more so, free of stress and worry. It is the ultimate calm and clear conditionless consciousness free of obscurity. Yet, it is the radiant principle which guides all life and the shining principle of all that is sane. It should never be thought of as difficult for it is the most easily intelligible principle there is, as it is ever with each individual in some form of conception or another.

The Lucid never ceases to elucidate the three states of consciousness as it is the presence of consciousness within the phenomenology of those states. It makes those three states lucid and clear and is ever within an absolutely free condition of playfulness engaged in throwing light on those three states. The Lucid is the single elucidator or enlightener or explainer of those three conditions. Any other focus in consciousness is simply eluding this reality.

133

Now, the simple truth of reality, as the Lucid is this Light, this Consciousness which gives illumination to the phenomena of the three states, it is never apart or in a state of dualism with those three states and therefore by this great fact one cannot accept this dualism as real. The Lucid and the emanation of the three states, are, in the process of life, and in the state of finality, non dual from one another.

The Lucid is here in the waking state. The Lucid is here in the dream state. The Lucid is here in the depth that is this dreamless consciousness, but here there is no dualism, for mind must be there in order for dualism to function. This dreamless state is when consciousness is one with itself as consciousness absolutely still, yet on this still deep water of consciousness, the Lucid shines like a light moving over those deep waters. But here it is not separate, apart or dual with that depth of consciousness. In deep sleep we are at one with reality, but when mind reenters the dualism of dreaming and waking consciousness, that mind forgets the oneness which we all have within that state.

The Lucid is what is eternal. The three states are what is relative and as this is so, even the forgetting of oneness by the reentering of consciousness to dream and waking dualism is also relative. So it will not remain with us forever. It leaves as soon as we realize the lucid non dualism of our momentary paradox. People give names to this state; sahaja (the natural state), vijnana (pure unique wisdom), nirvana (waveless consciousness), and so on and so forth, but those names are an obscuration on what is true, as real being, as simply what we are. Even the idea of lucid retains the dual conception of some other thing that is not lucid and is therefore a limitation to the realization of the non dualism of light and emanation in the three states of consciousness.

Pure spiritual life, free of the trappings and surface signatures of psychological definitions and traditional religious cognitions, may just be a process of memory, an utterly simple remembering of what is deep inside, deeper than the embodied designations of waking and dreaming consciousness and deeper

134

than the dreamless depth of deep sleep consciousness. Could it be that simple? For it is the forgetfulness of the non dualism of what is Lucid and of what is elucidated in the three states that is the cause of all inner spiritual struggle. When that inner struggle with this dualism ceases by the indwelling non dual agent of causeless mercy, then, what can you say. It is the lucid embrace of Love itself, the only pleasing principle there is. It is all that is willing within you, all that is glad, dear, desirous, beloved or treasured. These meanings emanate from the word lief, to please, one origin of the word, Love.

As Love is the only Lucid principle or sane feeling there is in this universe. We simply must realize Love. But that is simply so difficult for the one reason that we wrap up, this most pleasing of feelings, this most purely willing non dual emotion, with an entire complex of other self centered and ego asking emotions. Love is the most pleasing total acceptance of the non dual unbroken continuum of life. No other emotion enters there in its final purest state, for Love feels no dualism. Love of this sort only embraces the most treasured causeless mercy of what is most dear and finally, most beloved within us. Nothing else is so adored.

This making real in one's own consciousness, realization, of the singularly Lucid principle as essentially non dual within or even so, without the three states, brings peace. If the three states are there, lucid non dualism, and if the three states are not there, again, nothing but this lucid non dualism. With this understanding, one is not pulled into the entanglement of the distorted dualistic chase for self, as some ideal one does not already, preemptively and ever preclusively possess. The inner struggle and the one illusion within life, or conscious psychic distortion on the living reality, is that one feels one does not have this lucid non dualism within oneself.

When the causeless mercy of Love kindly descends upon one's consciousness, this feeling of being separate from reality simply leaves. From this point of perception, one may easily see that dualistic distortion was only there as a psychological position of thought and not an actual reality. One may never negate one's innate spiritually lucid non dualism, it is impossible, even though through life it may appear to be otherwise. And, this function has been named in many ways, as it is the main focus of the inner struggle with dualism. As long as dualistic thought continues, one will have this inner struggle, thinking that those three states exist within the one Lucid reality, or that this one Lucid reality fills and permeates the three states. But here, consciousness is still held within dualistic struggle which only relaxes all our muscles of the soul, with the onrush of Love. This feeling alone, awake to itself, overrides dualism.

This dualism is naturally seen everywhere in the waking state, as every object and manifestation has its obvious dual opposite. We are all too familiar with these dualisms in every aspect of life. They come from everywhere and this is the intention of the divine lucidity within, as it is almost screaming at us to realize that each dualism having its own opposite in union, speaks with drastic desire that we should realize the non dual as the only solution to all manner of dualism. But as it is the psyche that experiences dualism and not the inner depth of one's innate self born ever existing non dual nature, then the work with dualism must be at that level. For what is within the psyche, forces the condition of perception to be what it is.

The problem of dualism might be one of memory content alone as often expressed in the subconscious projections within the dream state. Dualistic psychic imagery or duplicity symbols permeate the subconscious. This is how we process information. If there is light there must be dark, if there is life there must be death and so forth. Let us say one has a dream of two people. You ignore one of these people and they ignore you in the dream. You approach one and they in turn approach you. It is the projection of dualism out of the dream psyche, expressing the inner feeling of the dreamer as to the relation of acceptance and non acceptance by the duplicity symbol of what those two people might represent to the inner conscious content of the dreamer. As long as there is a dreamer there will be dualism as the conscious substance of the psyche only functions with dualistic relationships. When those dual interplays with

136

duplicity symbols cease, then psyche ceases and one's consciousness simply enters dreamless sleep where there is no duality as there is no psyche there to perceive duality. This is the state of peace to which we all partake daily, if not but for a moment and then forgotten.

As dualism is alone all the stuff of the psyche, one may learn to follow the luminosity of dream contents and their unfolding structures, back into the meaning that dreams are trying to express to us. That meaning is simply non dualism. One may always trace the unfolding trail of this meaning back to non dualism, as our self content, or as self realization, if I may use that all too common expression. The dreamer may always follow the unfolding of duplicity symbols back to the peace of the self state in non dual resolution, pertaining to those dream contents, which are ever striving to express the non dual to the dreamer.

A dreamer may dream they are within a great library, filled with peace of mind and a sense of knowing within their self what life is and what is after death, as the world outside the library turns as it may. The dreamer finds a leather covered parchment book filled with mystic symbols that speak of the lucid self ideal. Then the dreamer leaves the library to find a spiritual sage of some sort, but feels this human being to be both wise and deceptive. That person speaks and says to you that you must first admit to yourself your own eternal ignorance, a symbol of darkness, then follow the steps up to the eternal flame, which is the dream symbol of the lucid. The dreamer does so and the dream melts away into a peace of mind state. In this dream one can see the dualistic trail of the dreamer's psyche that leads back to the non dual conclusion in consciousness.

But so often, dreams are left in the subconscious when the dreamer's mind returns back to the so called normal consciousness of the waking state. But then you come across something, perhaps you read something and then suddenly the entire contents of the extraordinary memory process of dream recall are triggered. Then, that waking consciousness instantly follows the duplicity symbols of that remembered dream back into the non dual conclusive and lucid recall of what self is to you. What was covered becomes uncovered in that blessed sweet moment. One realizes the non dualism of that Lucid principle as it was shining in the dream contents, now radiating in the waking contents and for that moment you are above duality and duplicity.

Not only in the religious tradition of India, but in other cultures as well, there is found the function of the guru, though called by different names here and there. As this is a powerful duplicity symbol let us try to shed some light and insight on the functional problem of this spiritual mechanism. There is some wisdom and there is some deception within this idea. Yet, because of the element of deception within the mechanism of this spiritual function, the sage of the Goddess Kali, Sri Ramakrishna, would never accept the position or function of a guru. In the Gospel of Sri Ramakrishna there are many examples of his attitude of unique spiritual clarity toward the problem of this duplicity symbol. Girish (*smiling*): "He says he is your disciple." Master: "I have no disciple. I am the servant of the servant of Rama." Ramakrishna's reply speaks in the voice of genuine humility, which is absolutely free of the guru delusion, a very rare and beautiful attitude.

The word guru is two symbols, gu, meaning darkness and ru, meaning light. The function of this dual symbol is supposed to be a light that removes a darkness. But more often, in the context of religious society, it is a darkness that covers the light. Nine out of nine times, a guru is a suspicious and enigmatic dualistic obscuration over the naturally Lucid self within you, a monomania of dualistic dementia that may be the cause of a delirium of aberration from your non dual nature. Within this dual symbol is the temporal apparent perception of that which does not exist, to wit, a human power which proclaims a personal reality of absolute power. This problem is also obviously true in other bodies of religious belief systems, philosophical claims of singular insight, various psychological theories of cognition and so forth.

138

But as an inner principle of the psyche there is some value in the duality of this symbol. As Ramakrishna again most clearly defines, "It is the mind that becomes at last the spiritual teacher and acts as such." This may possibly mean that within each person at the level of the psyche, the light dark dualism paradoxically sustains that dualism until lucid non dualism is comprehended. For it is within the psyche alone that the guru dualism exists, a light and a dark, and as it is commonly thought, until both are faced with a dual free and very realistic attitude, the equivocal dualism represented by the guru symbol will continue to perplex the psyche itself which is nothing but that symbol itself. With the onrush of loving lucid non dualism the problem of this duplicity symbol within the psyche is left for what it is.

Yet it is difficult to continuously see this state of non dual consciousness because of the tendency of the psyche to interpret everything dualistically. This interesting dual symbol is one of a non dual spiritual power, not a human power. The duplicity of this symbol embodies the complex dualism of principle and person. When associated with the Great Power of what is the Lucid, it is good, but when it is associated with a human power or personality it is simply deceptive. So Ramakrishna compared the guru profession to the profession of a prostitute, perhaps because it often becomes a structure of marketing and selling of what is spiritually and naturally your own, back to you at a cost. Yet he could also clearly see the lucid non dual at play in both images, prostitute and guru, light and dark, divine and human. For it is the receptacle of the psyche alone that holds the light dark dualism. The essential non dual power is not and has never been dependent on that dual receptacle, but if you wish to worship that receptacle it is up to you, as we all should be free to find our own meaning with non dualism. Peace.

Here ends the original text
Measuring Sky Without Ground

139

References

The Gospel of Sri Ramakrishna
Originally recorded by M.
Translated by Swami Nikhilananda
Ramakrishna Vivekananda Center, New York

Sri Ramakrishna: The Great Master
By Swami Saradananda
Sri Ramakrishna Math
Mylapore, Madras, India

Life of Sri Ramakrishna
Compiled From Various Authentic Sources
Advaita Ashrama, Calcutta, India

The Complete Works Of Swami Vivekananda
Advaita Ashrama, Mayavati, India

Toward A Psychology Of Being
By Abraham H. Maslow
Van Nostrand Reinhold, New York

The Practice of Psychotherapy
by Carl Gustav Jung
Bollingen Foundation
Princeton University Press

INEXTINGUISHABLE FEELING

Goddess Centered Poetics
On Love As The Central Emotion

She must be the Delight. She is Real. It is the Truth. When She removes Her jewels of the waking plane, Her dress of the dreaming plane and the precious lingering garments that actually touch Her as dreamless sleep, then you may see Her as She stands True, once Her cosmic garments are removed. But you come to this by Her will alone, not by desire nor even certainty as certain as stone.

Perhaps I am too uxoriously fond of Her vulviform wonder, but that is where a particle of natural bliss is tasted, as it were. But as one who has ever sought to expand on what is here, I worship and adore Her at the base of Her being, from Her sheath womb of the universe all the way into the depths of eternal unmoving uncreated unchanging reality. She is my Goddess, my Mother, my Mistress, my Friend and I am no longer timid toward Her, nor fearful of the feckless opinions of those who live without wonder, bliss and pleasure in the cave of the heart.

She, as death is there to teach us Love. That is the reason for the taker who takes what is worthless so we will learn to treasure what is real. Ultimately, conclusively, every created creation folds back into the labrum lap of the sacred feminine, arriving stressless, becoming exhausted with itself, relaxing into the serene wonder of love as it is without reason or cause, as She stares down on Herself. Her bliss, Her love is the pearl of ecstasy and peace that comes up inside you when all else is felt to have no substance to it. It is She who quenches the thirst to be free of pain, She who is Inextinguishable Feeling, She of Unshakable Keel. She whose steady Bearing bears the world hurt, even heaven, or the thought of freedom and this immanent incessant surprising curious astonishing something no one may

141

name, beyond all that delusion. Now I know I can love Her without fear.

Kalee, Mother, I have no more hatred nor resentment towards anyone having realized that everyone is my teacher... even towards those who murdered your blessed wise women, extinguished and burned massive libraries of brilliance or calculatingly slaughtered Your gentle natural lovers wherever they could all over the world... they were hardly, as the saying goes, anointed with love. But there is one small trifle Mother, as I surrender to this attempt at describing what is the Actual Infinite Never - Two Inextinguishable You, there is always one thought left out, one lost thought and that bothers me Mother.

So let me just be in myself, lucid, clear serene and free of the spiraling currents of distracting cyclic emotions. I shall enjoy You happily and heartfully and heartfully calm in difficulty, as slowly and intuitively, thoroughly and joyfully I give myself to this sea of You in everything in the attitude of an even keel with heavy as lead steady bearing never submitting to those emotions that drag us down into the depth of confusion.

Kalee and me, that is all I have, my heart now emptied of ever other connection. Inextinguishable Feeling needs no mediator, no tutelary advocate, nor special governing genius. It is the conjugal power direct into the heart, not eye to eye, nor even that staring at the back of the mirror of the inner eye... there is no go between nor joining of what was never apart... Who can say what I am to me and what is Inextinguishable Feeling as it may be. No one but You sees through my eyes.

I do not rush nor hurry. I keep my own time with Kalee, but do not walk slowly. I am right into it at any level, not condescending, descending nor ascending... talking, speaking, thinking, feeling, on my own. Kalee, Goddess, you are my own! Kalee, Mistress, one true Friend, turn this hue of my eyes into that smoky dark color of Yours, that sees the world as it is; painful, beautiful, unreal and real.

Mother, it is from Inextinguishable Feeling going direct into my heart then up to that brain and out of the hand onto the paper that this strange practice happens. There is no imitation of anyone here, nor even thinking over what is felt. May I, Your bonded poet slave give fresh joys to Your lovers. May the body remain so very relaxed as electric stirrings though somewhat painful, churn around like little moons in the scared burning brimmed crests of the ilium, as the hip-balls rotate pleasantly and breathe, thought and feeling comes smooth and easy.

I do not ask anyone for my Self. Free and original thought is allowed to me without replay in an intensity which comes with force on the mind if necessary. For thoughts stir up emotions and emotions either cloud or clear what those thoughts have stirred. In thought is joy created. In thought is desperation made. Then you either float or drown in the sea of emotion. Kalee, how strange is this creation of these single wise beings you have shaped.

Mother, sometimes I am tired of saying inside, "I am Existence, Consciousness and Bliss." When in Truth, sometimes I am Being in the Knowledge of Pain. But one Truth is sure, Your Love is the Cure. Mother, I can look at You and imagine anything I want, but do I really see You as the intense unbroken infinite never dual Darkness that swallows and burns both the shadow and the brightness? Is that why You more often appear in tender, gentle and attractive form, out of Your empathy for my suffering?

In challenge and in blessing I think and feel what can be and what is really there. To tragic confusion I offer Love. To joyfulness I offer Love. To madness and to peace, my only emotion inextinguishable is Love. For I can hear what is really said behind the voice and I can read what is not written on the map of the face. I do not see, nor sense, nor feel anyone with a previous pattern of emotion, former intonations or cognitive measurements. Behind the letter is the voice, behind voice is the inner feeling which makes us what we are. When, you say poet, mother, goddess, mistress or friend, it means something entirely different to me than it does to you, for the nature of my madness is fantastic beyond description. No word ever sounds the same, meanings past and meanings now and meanings future, all woven together without thought.

143

Mother, it is just this lonely body and solitary somber consciousness that speculates on You. Forgetting body, releasing prideful intent, one remembers You. Then suddenly Joy comes up inside. Mother, now why when ever I have emptied myself of my self contents, do You always put more in me? Mother, it is a type of torture You are doing to me. Is there no end to Your divine cognition? Must I accept this to be so?

Mother, all these mental workings are a barrier to my listening. The loving emotion of now is enough so why do You force me to think in active and reactive mind shapes. The idea of existence is only there when an ego exists. All those systems of belief, man and woman dualism, the trails and trials of communication, where people are at and why they are there, Mother, I cannot control what people feel and their attitudes toward what they perceive as this spiritual image. I am tired of all this madness, delirium and desperation, the complexity of human company, their false hopes and dreams that life is going to be something it is not, take it all away Mother, every bit of it and take me back into You, into Your divine company where love is free to feel itself inextinguishably. If others call this death, freedom, enlightenment or liberation, then so be it!

Mother, it is really no trouble that You have me recreate every time I come out of dreamless sleep, the emotional wisdom that all memories and experiences, every thought and single feeling ever known, whether in the attitude of the waking plane or the attitude of the dream plane was always and ever so only You expressing Yourself to me... Your Expression always perfect ever waiting... it was my interpretation that was in question.

But then Mother, You say to me if I stop learning I will start deteriorating. I appreciate everything Mother. I live in the moment of emotion primordial where you have shown me I am free in ways more interesting than thought. But Mother, as all women are Your embodiments then why, why are they one and all the paradox of heaven and hell embodied when You are Bliss itself. Why at one moment are they affirming life and love and the other moment it is pure torture? This confuses me Kalee, but

I shall trust You in this divine puzzle! Not God nor the Infinite, not philosophy, religion or history, not the mysteries of the human psyche, subatomic quantum physics, astral galactic physics or human genetic evolution, no none of this... the great mystery of the universe is the feminine paradox of heart felt heaven and brain bent hell. But why Mother Kalee, why? Is it that we, female and male both, naturally must grow tired of the never quiet exhaustion of dualism?

Mother, who and what am I? We are all created, killed and resurrected out of but a pinch or two of charmed dust, so indeed what are we Mother? This knowledge means nothing to me Mother, if there is no Love. For my fellow friend in Kalee has said, "Unalloyed love of God is the essential thing. All else is unreal." And what is this Mother Kalee, a love not mixed, nor combined, nor debased by any other feeling. As Love transcends even death and Love is everything to me, then what meaning has death... Death is extinguishable, Love is not. That waking body and dream mind are extinguishable, yet Love, as it actually is, Inextinguishable Feeling, knows not what death is! Kalee, this is You and this is true. Even as You appear more beautiful than one may imagine.

Mother, my blessed special friend in You wanted You to such an extent that he had prepared to use Your own sword on himself to kill, so great the emotion to be near You. And then You showed Yourself. I too have felt somewhat similar but in a far lesser way. Kalee, I prayed for Fresh Joy, moments later, There, how could I ever have doubted You. My unique friend in Kalee has said, "'Never think that you alone have true understanding and others are fools.' One must love all. No one is a stranger. It is God alone who dwells in all beings. Nothing exists without Him." Mother, dear Kalee, is it after I have seen my own self death that this caliber of Love might come up in me and spread forth to others who are never to be strangers? But Mother, honestly, as one of many persons who have sweet souls, generous hearts and yet complicated minds, I must admit that to always see the divine emotion behind every ordinary emotion may be quite difficult although I try. Sometimes it is unclear, not accepted by those who are dear, apparently difficult to convey or perhaps really not so, even so often a deflection of social sentiments merely attempting to gain a democratic peace. Is it better just to let go and allow myself an unmixed uncombined feeling?

Kalee, Mistress! Why do I feel a transient need for lesser finite connections when I am overwhelmingly blessed with Divine Psychosis in Kalee's Sacred Feminine Consciousness? When This is Here I need no the other There! I am Her voluptuous pearl scabbard always wanting and never tiring to be filled and penetrated by Her Ecstatic Sword of the Never Dual Enjoyment of Bliss... the Result and Singularly True Effect of Love! I want this Kalee, I want You and me to have this without depression or begging. What a fine feeling Mistress. I shall keep it in mind and know that none of my involvements are Absolute but for this fine wonderful mad love with You.

Kalee, Mistress, if I am to approach You as I would wish then I must rip through all this poetry of the world and swallow You in both the spiritual and visceral context! But I wish to be a noble person having loving empathy for one and all, full of blessed self satisfaction and self pleasure, knowing full well the source point of people's faults, my own included, while being sensitive to the shame of this life, nevertheless ever standing on truth, Kalee.

Blessed be Kalika. Blessed be Her Movement. Blessed be Her Stillness. Blessed be Her Entire Truthful Story, Her Power to decide the exit of a soul at the moment of its conception. And Blessed Be Her Auspicious Attractive Inextinguishable Enjoyment, Her Gift,... to think without thoughts. For thoughtfulness arises from thankfulness and this is my gratitude to Kali, the Goddess.

Mistress, I am in a blood race to your Bliss. I relish poetry, for it is my plateau prior to Bliss and in some ways, that might be more pleasing and self satisfying to You, even better than Bliss. For all poetry and all writing is miracle, automatic unpretentious natural miracles that come to people as they should at the right moment. These poems, these books find

146

people, people do not find them. They are voices speaking in the thin hours where veils are lifted, because letter symbols flow from the mind in the consciousness of the Inextinguishable! Kalee, I no longer think myself a poet or a writer. I am now part of the universal poet-writer expressing mind ever engaged in the Question of Who You Are... as an Unbounded Mood in the Countenance of Your Light contained by the demeanor of Bliss! Kalee, just free me to be ever in forward momentum never back tracking over what is tired, vacuous, void, old, wasted and not jammed to the brim with Joy!

Mistress, I want the emotion of Your approving favors. As running water makes me thirst, as the thought of sliced dripping lemons make me salivate, as the aroma of spiced cooking meat makes me hungry, as music makes me dance and sing, lifting my consciousness to higher plateaus, as a naked image of woman makes me feel erotic and as a grave stone marked with a name makes me sad and thoughtful, thankful of this life, so the Wondrous Name of Kalee makes me Joyful. Mistress, You are the confluence of all events ever reminding me of Your Presence, Your Evident Existence in the Dance of this life. You are embodied in all women, Bengali, Basque, Baroque, Beautiful, or even Bad, as Intelligence, Humor, Attraction and Kindness, Kalee.

Mother, there are no more hurt feelings in me so I no longer turn to escape into the mechanism of dualism as a quenching of the pain, nor any of those great principle ideas, even of Your Own Tantric Contents. Mountains of Reality, Gods and Goddesses, Forces in Triad, Worlds and Planes of Existence and the Beings inhabiting these, Categories of Society or Stages of Life, Micro or Macro Cosmic phenomena, Ages and Cycles of the World and the Universe, Spiritual Teachings recorded by sages or prophets, the Human Body's mysteries or the Trinity of Personalities, Teacher Student Dynamics, Beginnings, Endings or being Fully Bathed in Enlightenment, Practice, Worship or Union, Virtue or Vice and their cycle of responses in cause and effect, Power Dreams, Gold, Pleasures with Women or even the Power of Liberated Freedom in the Self. None of this interests

147

me any more Mother, I need not indulge in this spiritual feast again. My hunger is satisfied, Kalee.

Mistress, I am shagged and bored sleepy with spiritual flight and falling doubt, observing the transit surges and spiraling waves of emotional biochemical reactions and actions passing through the nervous system, I have made real the one thought-sentiment Love, the blessed and best auspicious Kalika, the One Emotion ever constant within. I have given up curiosity with obscure involvements or what is going on in the hidden psyche of others, the enigmatic meaning of relationship with others or inexplicable entanglements in their desires. It is all in Your Hands anyway Kalee, so why should I hold on to the useless emotion of holding or the delusion that I may hold.

Primordial Thunder Goddess Who Terminates All Misery! My Mistress Kalee! I am the Beautiful Sheath Scabbard enveloping the penetration of You as Inextinguishable Feeling without words. So why Kalee do You sometimes cognise in me the shock of feckless forgetment. Still I know even that is You. Who can measure me and whom can I measure! I am not enlightened nor do I want it, for enlightenment is for those who feel heavy and Kalee, by You I do not feel heavy. I am hirdie girdie, heel over head and head over heel, so what need have I of bright dimensions of enlightenment. Just remove that feckless mind from me by continuing not this, not this or that, until what is left in the ideal of me is but a treasured moment of You. It is only the vague anticipation of sudden attack, ambush or danger that leaves me a little restless, but why should my paradox feel this way, for even if someone were to seize, snatch, destroy, despatch quickly or slowly with or without right, this thing called a body, it would in no way change the Inextinguishable Feeling I have in You! Besides, where can be any ambush or attack when the world itself has been converted into You... What vicissitude can alter this, as what the world was in the Primordial Unborn, is what the world is now...

Mistress, is it not all but mood which is but mind, spirit and courage? Mistress, the fetters of fear, enmity, disorder, fracas, strife, aversion, spite and the soured cherished malice of rancor in the masculine intolerant conviction toward the blessed embodiments of You has let go and left me. I have no fear of emasculation nor effemination. The trust in Your doctrine has lifted me into the Sacred Love of Feminine Self Reality blessing the world. What perplexed fretting vitiated fools denote as a choking contemptible embarrassing doubled opening, I adore as the comely divine entrance and the exquisitely sacred fountain of the human family. It is their fear of Your Power that obstructs them from the doing, finishing and distribution of Love. I have let go of their terrorizing emotional possessions and have moved inside the divine safety of You.

Mistress, why should I not feel these wondrous freed sentiments without disquieted concern? You Yourself eternally enjoy the paradox of Erect Bliss, as You so engage in the enveloping, enfolding, enwrapping, encircling, encompassing ecstatic embrace over the phallus of Kala lying there as a White Corpse! So why should not Your sons and daughters feel the same feelings. Proving non dualism, the daughter is not different from the mother and the son is not different from the father, so these sacred sentiments are not different in me. I am blessed as You are Blessed.

Kalee, Friend! Someone set out to draw an illustration of You. I came up to them and said, "No one knows what Kalee looks likes." The artist replied, "They will when I'm finished." Kalee, what astonishing dementia. They had forgotten what You are in waking consciousness. Another set out to explain You, I went up to them and said, "No one can explain Her." The teacher replied, "I will when I have finished." Kalee, what unimaginable pomposity. The teacher had forgotten what You are in the luminosity of dream consciousness. Then someone set down to think of You. I sat by that person and said, "No one can think what Kalee is." That philosopher replied, "I will have when I am finished." Kalee, what startling audacity. The thinker in contemplation had forgotten what You are in Your depth of dreamless consciousness. At last, Friend Kalee, one person set forth to feel the Inextinguishable Feeling, not attempting to illustrate, explain or define what You are. In this precious soul all agitating perturbation left, all such aghasting pretense left and all stupendous presumption melted away. The shock of dualism faded in Your Unfading Feeling. This one remembered You As You Are... but they could not really say anything about what was felt. It is between You and them... always!

Kalee, Mistress and Friend, when You are near I do not know what to say and when You are far, how empty is my day. How can I reach You and tell You what I feel? Should I just enjoy the Pleasure of what You give me wherever I am, quiet or wild, serene or shaken, absolute as free from all limitation and control or burdened by the imperative demand of arbitrary capricious dualism? Is this what You want of me my Blessed Friend, then if so, well that is fine.

For I am Your pleasure as You are mine.......

Kalee, Friend. Mistress, enough of this huha and hoho, all this reeling and railing. Let me just say what I must say. Into the Jar of Joy, into the Pitcher of Pleasure, into the Ring of Rapture, into the Cave of Contentment, pure blissful juices of feeling I offer at the Altar of Sacred Undivided Oneness, keeping us joyfully alert to the Emotion and Knowledge of Love, the final destiny, the uncalculated conclusion, fadeless reverie never failing, lofty, eminent and elevated as the cognition of the infinite. To be myself free of fear, in this Beautiful Place, with You, Kalee. What Peace! All memories, even so, now turned to this Joy, as sublime meaning is given to all shame and the reason of ecstasy takes the place of regret. It is the depth of feeling that You accept this feeling beyond the image of feeling! The majestic towering pacific stillness over the unparalleled precious passion is arrived at after the saturation through enjoyment.

Kalee, Mistress, thank You for this Release into Bliss by showing Your Sacred Mystic Secret Psychic Self in Joy so Rapturous in me, covering every bit of what was me but now is You to such a degree that there is now no secret, no psyche, no sacred, nor the handicraft of closed to the eyes mysterious intercourse or direct yet bewildering puzzling communion of true feeling with genuine ecstasy. This consuming emotion I owe to You who has sedated in me all those mountains of dualistic emotional responses. Kalee, You are my Cowry Shell Fountain of Joyful Bliss. How one regards Your Fountain either binds or liberates. For me, I am free when You appear in my dreams, raising mere women to the status of goddesses who in turn raise my self estimation to Happiness which has no cause, nor outside effect, as this Happiness is more what remains after every conquering or dwarfed emotion is exhausted, than the cunning attainment of anything.

Kalee, Mistress, let me speak to You in my own voice, not the voice of others in mimicry or imitation by habits subconscious or conscious, by impressions picked up here and there or monkey manners. I speak my own sweetness and beauty in conversations with the Goddess. And it is Pure 4th Degree Pleasure Inextinguishable, a love that I love for it makes me loving. Kalee, You have shown me that erotic attraction toward the waking state body is 1st degree pleasure. That the romantic beauty of the dream state body is 2nd degree pleasure and that the inner mystic love felt as joyful happiness in the dreamless state is 3rd degree pleasure. But what is this, a question? Why is the Goddess so attractive and loving... because we humans love beauty and the attraction of Love. She is the Magnet of what is Best in Us... Keep this alive! It takes you past what feelings ordinary relations may offer, out of your control and alive with your conscious heart felt power. Then what I feel may have meaning to others.

Kalee, Friend! Happiness, happiness, happiness, happiness, this is my only prayer of word power, the force of which creates the living cognition of the feeling itself. Kalee, You have shown me that Happiness is the only even keel through the storm of conscious emotional forces effecting and re-effecting one another, like a slap and then a kiss, Mistress, the heart pulled up, pulled down, pulled apart and put back together. But Happiness stays undaunted if it is as Love Inextinguishable unaffected by the presence of known anguish or the expectation of unknown anxiety or rage, wrath, vexation or resentment. Mistress, finally Your Vow of Joy is real......

Goddess, Mistress, as this Happiness is now undisturbed there is yet haunting concerns over horrors against the Sacred Feminine. It is the second oldest question of why good and why evil. As my friend in You has said," The glory of light cannot be appreciated without darkness. Happiness cannot be understood without misery. Knowledge of good is possible because of knowledge of evil." I see the truth in what is said, but when horror against You is made I am yet unable to see the good made out of the bad. Some will say it is custom and morals and all relative. Perhaps. But if in voracious greed one of your goddesses is seized and snatched I see this as worse than murder. In murder the spirit is set free when the body is left behind. But the viciousness of raping Your precious embodiments leaves the spirit entangled with torment. How can this be allowed to be? It is the crucifixion of the Goddess on the daily round. If this human body is quelled, consciousness flies to a new place and starts again. But when the temple is seized and the inner contents are snatched, then is a torment that none deserve. It is pure hostility against the hallowed. Even though the great Himalayan mountain goddess woman herself became the seizer of the ones who seized, and snatched the heart of their ungodliness, changing them for the better, Kalee, You must admit, though not impossible, this is a rare event. I must go with what Your spouse has said, that, castration is the only answer.

Mistress, as I no longer fear death having known the Feeling of Kalee, then how should I fear any expression of life as horror. I am not asking of the mere blinding attraction to shinning golden treasures or moist women's pleasures, I am asking of the massive psyche's torment, the fear that haunts humanity. Why is this so Mistress? Is it that this slowly evolving sadistic masochistic savage sapien is truly less sapient than supposed? Is there really a creature who genuinely wishes to hurt and destroy others while hurting and destroying self? Is it that within the soul's psyche, the soul is the dominator and the ego, the slave? If this is the case, then Mistress, You are the Ultimate

152

Dominatrix and all hopeful sagacious beings are Your submissives, where all emotions are eventually released to the Goddess, even beautiful emotions, as now I hold nothing, Her Love holds me, even as it ever did and has, as nothing remains to be done. It is just a thought Kalee. Just a passing thought....

Mother, amidst this Happiness my heart is confounded with why males and females battle over what is feminine and masculine when what You have made for the two, in blissful oneness, is something gentle, to be automatically cherished. But no, women say men are liars by nature and men say women are chiding by nature. When I see all this wasted feeling, it weakens my care for staying in this world. Will these two ever be liberated from their inner torments where they may make clear decisions on what this life is for? Their houses are burnt down all but for the frame and who will rebuild the home? It needs more than a strong handshake with a firm assuring hand and more than a sorrowful apology. It is free choice in the heart of love when the two sides feel and see clearly their spiritual connection. But why does it take so long, forty two, eighty four and two hundred and eighty two years. Mother, this waking dream of life is so short and so much time is taken in reluctant repentance over contributions and integration on what is the favorite and what is disliked. Mother I am in a hurry to get to Joy. Stress here, depression there and circles of sorrow do not interest me anymore. I want to keep alive my connection deep inside, making the best of what is most pleasurable, nourishing and conducive to Happiness, ever recognizing relaxed joy and seeing before they arise, the waves of worry and stressfulness. Guide me now Mother, for I know that all spouses are the self symbols of each other, the metaphor of what I am to me and you are to you, that is why devoted sweethearts are the highest connections. They are parts of the cyclic circles of each other, wonderful, weird, superficially wild and deeply bewitching the entire world. Well done my beautiful Kalee...

Mistress, they say a man whose wife chides him too much has no fear of death for if he loves her he sees this as his only escape, so when it comes he welcomes it knowing he will ever

153

love her spiritually. But I am no fool, Mistress, I know chiding destroys love and lying destroys trust. I only wish to express myself clearly so You will say, "Well said. Well done." And I know it is not just the attraction of bodies for bodies. When the consciousness of 'I' is gone and there is no 'I' in me, then it is seen that You are the Ultimate Attraction. The Mystic Magnet of Love beaming forth in the eyes of lovers. It is You, Inextinguishable Feeling, that is attracting every self to You. The rest is but drama and the result is an ecstatic poet's smile of wonderment.

Friend, it is next to You that I smile, for my nature is in the Comfort of the Goddess and those smiling happy joyful moments of identity with Her, moments carrying me as a loving emotion above the natural me. No use for you to try and figure over this or reason it out. It wastes Bliss!

Friend, the world roller coaster rides on the rail of Your bearing while high and low curves ever remain happy and calm for You. One feels this way, another that way, one comes and one goes, some love the ego and some care so little for it, some say it will ever be affected and some being free of it say it radiates no effect. But one thing is for certain that this curious thing called a mind is ever seeking to make things such a way where union with the Ideal is okay to take place. But, Friend, You are always there in union with us, even though sometimes after the spiritually reborn soul comes to this, the old reflexes may still come back. But why would I worry Friend, for all this, as the all and the everything, takes place within this most beautiful wisdom body of Yours, where one for one each are already standing true in Your equilibrium unbidden, automatic, free, impulsively divine, instinctively spiritual, involuntarily awakened, willingly loving and voluntarily real as real can very well be.......

Kalee, Your pristine path is a natural course, all too easy, so let there be no more confusion about how I may arrive at where You truly are! Every single day You uncover Yourself to me. In the body of Your wisdom the root of the spine is ever at one with the thousand centers of the brain full of thrill. I know this

154

to be true, but some say great effort is needed to awaken the sleeping goddess, but I say no. You are ever awake, ever moving and ever undying and alive. Every day I leave the first three centers when You cause dream consciousness to happen. Those centers of the waking body; food and survival, sexual pleasure and waking mentality are left far behind when You awaken Yourself as dream consciousness. In there, the heart, manifests as all the feelings of my dreams illuminating the illustrations of what I feel You to be. But then as I dream, You reveal the reflection of the Matrix wherein You have made all things already happen. So how may I measure this by finite time ideas of past, present and future when You are Infinite Eternal, this one cannot understand the other, for it is like me trying to know the taste of ambrosia, as You swallow the excellent elixir down Your throat, as we are all swallowed into the throat wheel of Your brightest dreams, where all causality has already occurred. But Your movement is not finished there. In the oneness of non dual dreamless consciousness, the center between Your eyes, is One, with the center between my eyes where all eyes are gone and nothing is but consciousness be. There, is the divine command of all the universe ruled quite brightly from within. But wait Kalee, all this takes place in that Unbound State of the Inextinguishable Feeling, so what is this waking, dreaming, sleeping dance if not the cosmic matrix ever arriving to be one with the Cosmic Mistress, the Mother, the Friend as Self, in Oneness, one for all. This is the wind up of creation, going on at every moment, finished and complete with Itself, ever engaged in ceasing all the sorrows outside.

Kalee, Mistress, in the wee hours my thought moods dance with You as body mind movements go through these feeling emotions. O Kalee, the shapes of these thought sentiments continue to circle. Where does it get me Kalee? Feeling is Joy. Happiness is a Feeling. Feeling is Self! But Kalee, the circles of other people, their meaning to me and their purpose overall is a question in my soul melted away so pleasantly in You. The difference between them and me is that I am more like a kitten and they like monkeys. I wait for Mother to move me, while

155

they are always moving. And if they are asleep I do not try to wake them up, while they are always trying to awaken me. Nor do my hands and feet grow sore like theirs, of the daily round of crucifixions of this unnecessary ego, for actually I am grateful for what comes as it does....

Kalee, You are my Feeling. I do not figure out a reason to explain why You make me Happy, it dwindles my Joy instead of magnifying my ecstasy. Mother, that rumination with mere reason only takes me so far. I want the continuum of emotion and of feeling the Self as self is Love saying, "I Am Love," my true identity, as the truest identity genuinely within one and all souls living so thinly veiled by this dreamlike world. Love is the final destiny of every particle of the divine, not destruction, fear, phobia nor terrifying revelations for Spacetime. I am not a sage, nor even wise, not a man nor a woman, not a thinker, a dreamer, a poet or anything like that. I am not that Temuchin, nor am I Sappho and I am not Buddha. What I am is Love. I am Love. My Mistress has shown me this... It became quite clear once my wedded habit prone to the custom of ego was abandoned. Ego is a thought in the brain and all thoughts are there, but emotion is felt in the entire body, emotion is felt everywhere and Love is the emotion charging all cognizant boundaries of the origin's design and what might even be before the origin came to be. My Kalee has forced me to ponder this....

My Mistress has shown to me how She joins with me in mystic conjugal power, placing Herself in me, always moving with stillness in the twelve sacred places of Her blessed body of wisdom knowing Inextinguishable Feeling. Goddess, shall I anoint Your Crescent Moon Feet with the Fluid Energy of Love, the Honey Sap of Fourth Degree Joy? While Your Blissful Never Dying Juices pore over my head, eyes and tongue ever engaged in reciting Your mystic sound syllable! It is the natural movements of the three conditions of consciousness ever complete in the never broken continuum of Her Consciousness ever conscious, always awake, not even dreaming and never asleep! She has placed every feeling in me as a key to Her Unceasing Imperishable Perpetual Inextinguishable Feeling!

156

In the Root Foundation of this tower of the world, She comes to me as spontaneous, supreme, unifying and heroic love. In the Joyful Pleasure of the Visceral Self, She comes as modesty, desire, the loss of confidence, cruelty, the destruction of haughtiness and comatose emotion benumbed and baffled. In the Jewel City of the mind, She comes and places Herself there as sadness, sleep, thirst, amazing dumbfoundedness, the sense of missing the mark by absurd contamination, jealousy, meanness of intention, the blessing of shyness, the anticipation of ambush called fear, and the favor of gentle mercy tender. These are the emotions She comes and places within the waking body.

In the singular undivided and Unheard Sound of the Heart, She comes and places Herself there as bright luminosity, hopefulness, thankful thoughtfulness, the longing of love, the sense of equipollence, the crest of dignity and pride, the humble sense of insufficient imperfection, lucidly clear discernment free of distortion, the folly of the ego's vanity, tranquility which calms the earthquake of agitated shivering shaking nerves, the emergence of genuine intelligence, and sympathetic sentiments which become empathic love for all. Out of this emotion off the central column leading to Her, in some is created another center which is the Cognizant Heart of Recognition, having the eight forms of inner cherishing emotion which nourish the pregnant child, of bliss, love, joy, truth, happiness, beauty, becoming and the loss of melancholy. Here She shines as a kind of light that brings so much joy at first.

In the infinitely Pure and Free Center of the Matrix, She comes and places Herself there as the seven musical and poetic sounds, conscious toxicity and immortal nectar, the great emotion behind the sound of Aum, covering the three states, the emotion of the sacred formula which creates the universal design, the fearless sealing conclusive emotion of protection covering all the Spacetime fabric, the emotion of universal existence blessing everything, the emotion of self in focus, the emotion of self in the divine presence of self and the emotion of greetings and sincerest salutations to the self as the universal conscious loving presence.

157

In Her playful Frolic of the Wanton Goddess Center, She comes, appears, manifests and then places Her beautiful self there as the six psychosomatic waves in the human body; hunger and thirst, the heart's grief and cognitive delusion, dis-ease and death, and as suffering, devoted love, joyfulness, the play of impediments and obstructions, the sprinkling of disorder, uncertainty and confusion,the sentiment of dissatisfaction and disappointment, the cloud mist of panting avarice after things of mere greed and simplistic sense pleasure, the dejected pain of mind in sorrow, love which moves nearly to the fourth degree yet fails to reach the conscious realm of pure empathic joy, the feeling of esteem and respect looking back into all things with divine yet human worth, and the poison arrow of intoxication fired from the bow of the excessive mind creating the great excited conditional cycles of variegated psychosomatic distortions and delusions. These are the emotions She comes and places within the dream body.

My Goddess is adorned outwardly with jewels. These jewels are emotions. Internally She is adorned with mystic formulas, the cognitive names of power and primordial syllables which actually create these jewels. These jewels and formulas are not separate realities. They are one, as in the oneness of blissful dreamless consciousness before waking and dreaming appear. The waking dream is formed by Her out of Herself, yet in unborn uncreated dreamless consciousness the the knowledge of the knower is at rest without the trouble of the known. It is pure peace. In the same way, the jewels of the waking body and the emotions of the dream body are one with pure peace before the creation of the things observed by the brisk and nimble,consciously alive and ever awake Goddess. O, of my Kalee, who can say what She is?

In the center between Her eyes, and mine, is the Center of Non Dualism, the mood emotion and attitude of unbroken never dual oneness. The two emotions, male and female, are singularly one as She, for he comes forth from She. She is the Pure Witness Consciousness and he is the pure consciousness witnessed as such. This is the great mood, the mood play within everything, the mystic secret of sacred reality. The 'I' Consciousness free of 'I' every differentiation. The key of dreamless sleep consciously awakened at the moment of Kalee's Joy.

Above this is the Secret Mind Center of all cognition where waking dreams are inseparate from Consciousness. The mood sentiments and emotions inborn within taste, fragrance, sight, sound, touch and cognitive mind movements, are stilled as they are undivided from the blessed divine sea of blissful awareness known as non dualism, serenity, tranquility and joy. All that is seen, heard, felt, sensed as fragrance, tasted on the tongue or thought in formless thought shapes, is known in the mood of sameness, the exquisite emotion of non dualism.

In the Goddess' wheel center of Never Dying Joy, She manifests by coming to this place as majestic feeling, never tiring industry, purity beyond dualistic conception, endless empathic generosity, one pointed fadeless mercy and divine empathy, eternal patience beyond the distorted idea of time, scorching straightforwardness, courage where there is no otherness, freedom from clinging, a mountain of granite like steadiness, never fading happiness, dislike for the deception of falsity, endless heaping waves of joy and ecstasy, tears of realized gratitude, an undistracted, unbroken, never divided mood continuum of thankful thought, and enduring perseverance never ceasing. These are also moods of oneness devoid of dream mind shapes.

Within the Goddess' Island of the Never Dying, She comes and places Herself there eternally as the twelve sublime forms of Happiness. Here upon Her Island, Truth is never lost. The twelve forms of Happiness are each the same, as they point in every direction She faces, while ever She remains in the Mood of Love. Above this, even dreamless consciousness melts away, for here, One Thousand times, Inextinguishable Feeling manifests as Indescribability. Of course, this is my Kalee's favorite place without a center or a circumference.

Kalee is mine and it is She Alone who as the mood of non dualism simplifies all complexity by blessed equipollence made real out of causeless Happiness. Now all that I do for Her is play on Kalee's eternal drum. She moves in me as waking, waking-dream, dream, dream-sleep, dreamless sleep and conscious alert sleep, which as it ever is, never becomes by any means of becoming, the mood wisdom of Inextinguishable Feeling, the understanding of 'I'. Make use of it, do not unloosen it by trying to make it the tool of the psyche's resolution. This makes Truth uninhabitable in the desolate desert of heartless intellect.

My Kalee is the Indeciduous Self Feeling, Love by name and idea of what She is in Truth. She never sheds, nor falls nor cuts away from Truth. It is the deciduous conscious self in the time-space of the three states that alone ever feels the lost feeling of separation. Yet Her creation of time is only in the waking past and the dream future, for within the momentless absolute present of dreamless consciousness there can be no time for there is no objective body nor subjective mind to experience the sense of passage over the eternal. Everything reflects Her. At moments we know Her when rising up between dreamlessness to dream or from dream to waking as we do when going down from waking into that moment before dream or even deeper as consciousness drops the dream and assumes dreamlessness alert, alive and awake. Then I am no longer asleep. I see Kalee is there, feeling Her move among all these people engaged in somnambulistic walking, talking, thinking and craving as they beseech a desire for the requirement that the content of substance should last forever and that the Inextinguishable Feeling Breathe of Kalee should fill this substance. Goddess, You are moving in every personality, multiple, diverse, nearly endless as characters in a play all exist within that very playwright's own mind. It is You who are seen in various ways when the soul separates from the embodiment, as light, as vision, as people who are loved once, even for a moment. Mother, it is You who reinterpret the Matrix in the forms of human minds according to their cultural delusions and spiritual illusions. For there is only one interpretation after poets, prophets, seers and the insane have dived into the

160

wondrous Matrix where all events and insights are already finished. That interpretation is the final destiny and that destiny is Love.

Friend, I hear people speaking in common language never realizing what they are saying as Truth is revealed in the simplest of things. "O, he or she has given up the ghost." What does it mean my Friend? That this ghost, this blast of divine breathe, this goddess fury of the soul as it is now so contained in embodiment is there now before the spirit is given up and away from the vessel temple of the here and now. A departed soul, a disembodied consciousness, we are all yet to be as now we are as real as we define ourselves. One may gather with holy beings, bright counselors, stable solid people or poets full of feeling and listen to them, but Friend, none are one hundred percent right nor can they be of much help, their power is that of throwing a tea party, nothing more, where spiritual, psychic, poetic and real principles are just discussed.

The only Being who is Holy is You, my Kalee, my one Counselor, my one Solid Truth and the Inspiration of all beauty and poetry. Kalee, it is with the true passion of impassioned lovers so rarely understood as to the nature of their divine desperation for union and melting two-ness into not-two-ness, that some divine blessed blast of the Inextinguishable Feeling is felt. I am conjugal with You, Kalee, my existence is yoked to You as my Spouse in the blessed mood of sweethearts. I know others will tremble, shake and revolt at this but what does it matter and who defines the romance of the soul with the source of its life. I enjoy the full cycle of Your creative Joy as my own Joy, from conception to creation, to the cooking of this hot universe and to its cooling out finally to be consumed by You and me. It is the Joy of my own relaxed knot of Peace which was once tied up in the continual thought of what is. Now mind and emotion full of the feeling of my Friend, Mistress and Mother Kalee is my natural, intrinsic, inborn and inherent High.

Mother, like my fellow friend in You I am beside myself and full of furious enthusiasm for my Kalee, but I am different, he came here on an ever free fast flight and I came here entangled in knotted soul with concern for bright green treasure and passion for warm woman pleasure. But now my attitude is firm and I have once said Your name, so how can I miss the mark of Truth any more? I have searched my heart fearlessly and answered You. No more shall I entangle myself in curiosity, embarrassed by embodiment, panic over my soul's dilemma, fear of but life which is just me or to make another fearful of any thing or thought, so where is restitution and where is the thought of what is thought to be good. The Unmeasured Boundless wipes out all the extinguishable timid tests of these things.

Mistress, through yoking me as Your spouse, the power therein has caused me to cross mundane definitions by Sheer Delight. At the culmination of bliss You have made the placing of the Sacred Feminine within me and now this has given me automatic Self Seeing of Your Fine Inextinguishable Delight covering everything like honey on a hive with Your Self Scope. You have put courage in me, the courage of doing and wiped out by bliss infusion the tendency to be lazy with and procrastinate over my true and genuine first and original emotion. The tight tendon like cords of the nervous system creates, causes palpitation and then expectation and for a moment this appears to obstruct what must be Peace and Pleasure, but then my Kalee arrives and where others so often teach what is in reality en-heavy-ment, my Kalee and I together enjoy the envy of the world, made lightened inside the eternal parts of us. The imaginative fantasy, better or worse, of a thing is always more than the reality of a thing, but not here in this case.

Mistress, by Your internal conjugal yoking of the idea of me, the chemistry of my consciousness has been changed into the Chemistry of Your Consciousness by pure emotion now my own! It is like electromagnetic bliss being never apart from the bliss of pure luminosity, simply it is the feeling of Love which is the true light of the world. The ultimate substance of everything is here. This is no mere poem written by a poet who wishes to speak the mind as they search for their true voice. This is the culmination of my Mistress' divine therapy, Her concern, Her taking care of and healing me. O, Kalee, I never imagined this.

162

Why so often is it that some need to give a negative definition in order to let go of or remove a thing from their feeling content as they pass through the passage of this dream life. I see them possessed by rage. The thing they attempt to destroy only becomes larger in the heart and does not move from or let go of that place. As challenge and chance, all things are easier when the positive is enhanced. The attempt to abate a thing only increases its power for within everything is the sense of independence. Kalee has shown me this, yes, and matured me in Her Loving Light.....

Kalee, Mother, Friend, Mistress, the way I voice the word Love makes me feel Love the way I voice the word name of what is the last Inextinguishable Truth, my bearing makes its bearing in me. I have cleared out and have fortunately forgotten the meanings and interpretations that others have given to the word Love and I have surrendered up from below what comes out of the mouths of mere women who try and give me an explanation of what my Kalee is to me. I have no need or requirement to order or restrain or roll against the familiar caution of the future or the all to similar past. I listen alert only to the meaning that Kalee gives. All others voices are an alloyed distortion as is mine to be sure.....

Kalee, what can I say? I cannot express everything to them, every feeling, every full and first emotion to them, nor mend all their pain as they are so often obsessed with the playful and divinely directed drive to tract out the internal and external maps of this world. So I give it to You, dearest Kalee. It feels good to feel this and I shall not slip into dissecting why I feel this way. Love is not a matter of decision or discernment, Love is past reasoning, and sadly reason is the narrow rail upon which most of us live. Feeling is understood through feeling and Love is Direct Feeling. And enough of it! Difficulty! This life is not hard if every experience is seen and taken as an ego leveling blessing of Kalee. That is it!

Mistress, within intense honesty on my spiritual position and the plane of You wherein I dwell I can have none of that pretending. What I am is but a poet who chops weeds from the

163

mind and a sherpa who daily washes and polishes dishes. You have terminated the nuisance of all self rightful feeling in me and it is in true honesty that I now live, out of which the best of humor comes, as it does but curiously enough the very thing of which most are afraid. Strange that when they are presented with it they always laugh, for honesty is the essence of comedy. And I am no wind bag as a fool may be for I know that if I do not listen to beauty, then terror comes to speak and make us hear the heat of what life wishes to teach us. But beauty is all there is and even terror is beautiful as it shakes consciousness into the question of bliss. The only answer you can find is beauty, the Inextinguishable Essence of my Kalee. I once for the longest time thought I needed other things but now I know I need only Her, the grandest primordial mother consciousness...

Mother, there is the saying that when we die our life flashes before us. Mother, my life is flashing before me now! What does it mean? Is it that You have forced me to dead fearless examination of my own ego, the outlook of looking at only a mask over the face of my self and the masks that cover the faces of others who uncovered reveal to me that it is You who are standing there in them. I am stone sure now Mother and I know that there is no hateful hammer of God that comes down on me or them when we die! That is not Love, the essence of God......

Mother, this non dualism, this Beautiful Feeling has a certain element of madness associated with it, seeing all as the same is wonderfully conclusive, yet one looses the usual and yet most unusual capacity to distinguish one thing from another. Everything appears to be You so I am uplifted by this madness. Now I know what my Uncle Moon, my fellow friend in You may have felt at times now and then concerned that this madness might overwhelm him. This is the madness of the Knowledge of Kalee, the Madness of Love that knows no distinctions... But I must admit that I find there is humor in everything now, what is so seriously tragic to me is the cosmic curve of comedy to another. Mother, from now forward I shall listen to all the facts before I make my little conclusions about the real picture.

164

Mother, why should I be ashamed or embarrassed to genuinely admit my faults and fears? It is but the mask of ego and who is it but You who is wearing this mask, that mask, all these masks. Through fears and faults I have reached You, for they have projected me into the depth of guileless transparent yet perennial garden of true feeling, releasing me from my own arrow of personal self treachery. By exhaustion I arrived at bliss which is but serene peace. This is how You have come near, it was not by my feckless efforts. I regret nothing. I avoid nor estrange nothing. Everything is real because You are Real. I keep my consul with You and no one else. No person has ever given me anything like this, Kalee!

Mother, I am hearing You speak, telling me, "You should never take any definition of what is considered to be self too seriously, for am I not the Makeress of this my Game, even if there is hunger, or the emergence of anger, or the soul's loneliness, or the spirit's exhaustion, or the mind's anxiety." Mother, the obsessions, the treasure chases and the power dreams of this world leave us little time for thankful thought and often leaves us feeling falsely as if we were motherless children. I will never scorch another, but I will scorch myself keeping in mind that what is really here is far more than my power of belief may ever possibly comprehend. I am not mellowed by this. This is not a simple resolution, a momentary thought nor some such superficial change. In You, Mother, I have given up the illusion of joy or sorrow.........

Kalee, Inextinguishable Feeling, who occasionally comes up, emerging before me as Mother, Friend or Mistress, has made me jump with Love, and go directly from Being to Bliss, leaving Consciousness aside. Bliss as Love is the Luminosity of the world, consciousness without the Radiant Luster of Love is mere awareness, the obvious acquaintance with things informing, but genuine Knowledge comes, flows out of the Rapturous Shimmer of Love. As 'being' goes with waking, 'consciousness' goes with dream, but now Bliss, Love Inextinguishable, rests ever in Itself, never asleep..... Kalee, when existence rises to Ecstasy, there is seen darkness never was....

Mother, is this You or me? What is this, Mother? Am I fading to ecstasy as we talk together? What is the meaning of speaking? Mother, You are the wealth of pleasure and true freedom making this the purpose of Your lovers. Who are You, Mother, She who grants whatever is desired? She, making the world merry, free from those worries of this world. Inextinguishable, even my Kalee, bearing the self to Freedom.........

I cherish the love and gentle tenderness of this inner conjugation with my primal woman self friend ... listening to the cold November rain. I no longer believe nor perceive those three divisions of feeling; shades of dark eros, red thunders of passion's amour, or cloudless divine blue agape. I have just one feeling for my Kalee as She dances, moves, thinks, feels.... I have so be come to one with her and her and Her, but still I cannot tell you everything there is to tell, for everyone knows Her secret never apart from Her. Each to their own. Yet, this is just poetry though genuine, simple, authentic and real.............

INEXTINGUISHABLE FEELING

As a married person who absolutely believes in the sacredness and spirituality of this blessed union in the here and the hereafter, I must heartfully extend my sincerest apologies to anyone who may be offended by the contents expressed here. My desire has never been to bring shame, criticism nor embarrassment to any tradition. Nor have I ever wished to empower myself above nor outside any tradition. My real intention is to approach in a candid fashion the problem of emotional, psychological and spiritual conditioning which may or may not effect and limit those of us who are married in the conjugal life. For those who have taken the sacred vow of celibacy, to compensate desire, which has been offered into the spiritual cremation of the selfish psyche, and take up some of these conjugal Tantric practices is deeply questionable. Even

166

though conjugal rituals are described as Sacred Acts in the Brihadaranyaka Upanishad, they are meant for those who maintain such connections, not for those who have renounced these connections.

Defining the Groundwork On
The Skills of Kalee

A skill is said to be an expert knowledge of something, in this case, The Skills Of Kalee, are not so much that but more the skills of expert feeling. Skill is said to be a distinctive or separate talent, ability or knowledge, but in this regard it is a separate knowledge of what is Inseparable in all of us.

These seven poetic prose creations may be interpreted as you like at an ordinary, a mystical, or a spiritual level. The Skills of Clearing Consciousness and Creating An Opening To Happiness are in the first stance to simply become expert with one's own self psychology, in the second position it is to recognize the tremendous power of our own cognitive forces existing within the psyche, and in the third condition it is to become expertly familiar with who one is in the immensity of the great waking state, that is the true self of Love, which is Happiness.

The Cave Of Kalee is the dream condition. In the ordinary it is to know what our dreams are to us, more the feeling content in the background of dream experience than all the actual details of a dream experience. Second, in the mystic sense we are forced to question ourselves in regard to our own dream consciousness and the relation of that consciousness to the Divine Principle. Third, spiritually, we come to a state of amazement, wondering if indeed, the Great Divine may be teaching us or unraveling to us, the mystery of Self.

The Circulation Of Primal Power is an insight into sexual sentiment. Obviously, there is so much confusion over sexuality, but sexual feelings are not the culprit, the culprit is socialization of the psyche into a denial response over what the content of sexual empowerment really means. We cannot deny its presence so we must embrace it as the face of love and cherishing. In the ordinary sense the emotional power moves in the outer current of erotica and romantic love. In the mystical sense this current of feeling moves within the inner sea of spiritual love, as worship, adoration and devotion. At the spiritual level there is peak experience in the psyche which returns to the divine womb source of consciousness itself. The Great Goddess who is Love.

Absolute Self Bliss Is Primordial Power, is the center point of resolution and the turning point of non dual conscious thinking or simply bringing down into one's own living experience; oneness, simplicity, balance, happiness and chiefly, Love. Love is Power. Love is Self. Love is the real awareness within the non dual borderline or undivided meeting ground of self and power, which are not two. At the ordinary level this is an outline of excellent spiritual concepts soaked with non dual thought. At the mystical level it is poetics saturated with non dual cognitions. At the spiritual level, I will quote the poet Ramprasad, for my words fall into a mere state of wonderment without any knowledge. "Beholding Her, man is bewitched for evermore; no other form can he enjoy." The Gospel of Sri Ramakrishna.

The Surrender To Primal Power may in the ordinary sense be the art of letting go, from deep down, genuinely. At the mystical level it is realizing that even all that we learn we must let go of, all that we think is our knowledge will be released from us eventually and what will remain is the taste, the flavor, the sentiment behind conscious knowledge. And from the spiritual level it is to deeply realize that from the most profound level of complete conscious non dualism, that it is the Goddess who has done, is doing and will do everything in Her Own Pace. We do not even breathe by our own power, that process goes on with no effort on our part, much the same with what we feel, think, dream or experience. But this level is the complete giving over or rendering up of all small unopened 'I' consciousness to a free and open conscious non dualism where it is felt that there is one and just one power expressing everything and every single thing, even the idea of or the actual conscious depth action of surrender.

Hearing And Having Voice is the function of poetic self talk at the ordinary level. At the mystical level it is inner spiritual self dialogue. At the spiritual level, I pray that it will raise wonderment to a peak where the question is answered if we may truthfully hear and have divine dialogues, unbroken spiritual conversations with She who has bewitched the world with Her beauty, love, grace and consciousness.

The Skills Of Ecstatic Love And Fierce Bliss at the ordinary level are to fully enjoy one's life as true self experience, without a trace of fear which arises out from the negative mental distortions of the false separative sense. At the mystical level it is the conscious connection, or divine assertion as alert non dual internal conjugation with the Goddess Kalee. At the spiritual level it is pure non dual conscious connection with Love, which is best expressed by and through ecstasy, rapture, serenity, peace, kindness, benevolence and empathy. It is about ecstasy and unshakability. Fierce unshakability comes only out of the genuine realization of how deeply vulnerable we are. Once the depth of this vulnerability is accepted one may become truly unshakable. This can only be the Love within us all... the one Self Bliss which is ever unshaken, never unnerved, never trembled by dualism. The boldest move you can make is to walk out of the front door of yourself and become what You Are.

....

Love is Reality. Love is the Direct Power of Reality. The whole world circulates and surrenders to Love. All thoughts dream of Love and all voice tries desperately to speak of Love. All efforts in consciousness and all desires for ecstasy and bliss are the wish for Love.

Love makes no sacrifice and Love accepts no sacrifice. Why should Love be so involved, being the One all embracing sagacious emotion. Love has already made everything sacred and Love has already taken in everything as sacred. Love does not preach and Love does not teach, for Love is the quiet power ever knowing itself as real, needing no instruction as to what it is.

If one goes through the path of consciousness or the examination of being and existence, it is much more difficult to arrive at reality because the stress of mental dualism is there in this course. But take a person in Love. They wish for, think of and feel nothing but Love for the beloved. This lifts them off the ground. They do not desire to quarrel over what is the right or the wrong, they do not wish to celebrate the joys of life with a friend, they show no egotistical pride being humbled by the great force of the most potent feeling, and they do not even enjoy the pleasures of the senses. Love has pulled them directly and immediately into truth, into Love. All else is discarded as having no importance in the face of the direct power of Love. Love is immediate recognition.

When one somehow begins to realize how deeply and solely important Love is, either through or for someone, a person or an ideal, or in the pure sense of Love as absolute reality beyond every dualistic concept, then, the first step has been taken to feel and then see your way clear. The grand sensation of Love spreads and stands forth inside and out, going beyond even the comfortable familiarity with one's own mind. It goes beyond even that idea or experience of the All One or the Great Universal, Love comes back from there, so to speak, and becomes in the living sense, a living reality of functional spirituality.

Love sees no dualism. Even in the experience of the lover and the beloved, the entire wish, want or desire is to be One and this Oneness is Love. Love is the non dual reality of the lover and the beloved, the sole fulfillment of Love. This is expressed most commonly as the conjugal physical achievement of lovers as an eternal symbol of oneness. Yet there is the attainment psychic emotional non dualism as in the peak emotions of creative and poetic consciousness. And in the high course, there

170

is pure unfettered spiritual non dualism as the all embracing, the great perspective of endless feeling, Love.

The Primordial Power of Love is so great that some realized beings, souls through history, have given up or let go of their waking state bodies and have melted into death, due merely to the Primal Power of Love. Out of the intensity of serenity in Love their bodies have just dropped away. The poet Ramprasad is one such example. Out of his intense love for the Goddess Kali, knowing his life here was done, he entered a river, left his body there and was never seen again. But if one were to discard the physical body out of the tragedies of Love, the result is not serenity. This is because to forcibly shut down a body's functions is the denial of the learning of Love, but when a physical body's functions just naturally shut down, that is the harmonious accordance of Love pulling you onward.

The need for self affirmation is the denial of Love. Love needs no self affirmation being the most comforting and assertive feeling. The need for self esteem is also somehow quite funny, for what makes us feel good about ourselves is when we feel Love within ourselves. Esteem may also be a circle of the ego continually needing to estimate itself and assert itself to the ego. But the ego's need for recognition must be there in the first step in order for the ego to be and become healthy enough for the ego to let go of itself. It is strange and beautiful, when at the end of the course, what the waking body becomes is just three pounds of ash, dirt, what and where is esteem then, for every single self as consciousness has the same value. What matters here, is character, and what is character alone is what is guileless, which is to be without deceit to others or self trickery, and the one guileless characteristic in the entire world is Love. Love is the source and being of all true and real character, so what is this thing called self esteem. To come, to do, to be done, to let go, to move through the surface of things and release them. This is the skill of Love. Can you live this? From the deepest depth of Love, to let go of any person, principle, idea, concept, feeling or experience, where only Love alone is held. Love is what we wish to hold and be held by, anyway you look at it, and so to hold or be held by, or to try and control or roll against or be attached as staked out by any other thing in this world besides Love is the one cause of what is commonly called suffering.

The theory of self esteem, which is how we estimate the self, may be a weak concept, for that estimation is always continually changing from moment to moment. It is Love as true character which is a stronger constant that endures the continually changing estimations of self. Again, esteem is a necessary ratio of response to shame based psychological and religious systems which have utilized this emotion in their restrictive frameworks. The ratio point between esteem and shame is a thin membrane in our conscious subconscious self attitude, due to cultural conditioning. That membrane is delicate and often breaks, then our sense of self falls into the deep well of negative self feeling, pulled by the gravity of shame. Shame prevents us from consciously ascending into the feeling of Love. I had a dream where I was inside a white mansion, there was a beautiful white chair and behind this chair stood a twelve foot tall white Tibetan god. He invited me to sit in the chair, but I could not, due to my falsely humble self sense, generated out of my subconscious shame based emotion of self estimation. What would have happened if this emotional factor had not influenced me? Probably, I would have sat in the chair and communed with the deity and then within my dream consciousness, I may have also opened up to experience the deep inner intuitive guidance of my own dream mind, which was there before me, ready perhaps to lift me in this dream, into a better more open consciousness of Love....

Of course, ego, in the sense of a shame generated cognition of who you are, is the differential factor keeping and preventing us from feeling a deep unity with Love or the forms of Love, as the Goddess, the God or the Great Reality. Ego is the 'I' sense, Love is the True 'I' sense. The 'I' is the common factor of this ratio. The 'I' is not the problem of the dualistic mind, the problem is the dualism in cognitive attitude. I heard a nice definition of the ego, as it is to "Edit God Out", very simple, but very effective. The whole problem of dualism with the ego - God ratio, is not one of concept but one of sentiment. Can we feel this Unity with God, Goddess, whatever appeals to the heart, even if we have an ego? Yes. But if you go about imagining that you are one with God and others are not, that is insanity. While if you feel that you are one with and in unity with God, Love, and so is every other single being, that is certainly enlightenment. That eliminates the editor, ego, and this elevates you to feel Love, which is the very essence of God. The elsewhere idea of exclusive positioning in ego-mind consciousness enhances the editor, that inner self attitude which cuts you out of the Unified Feeling of Love.

The poet Keats wrote from his spiritual experience, "Beauty is truth, truth beauty,- that is all ye know on earth, and all ye need to know." Love is truth and Love is beauty, that is all you need know and all you can know. That is the one transcendent movement in consciousness. The typical and atypical profound idea forms that come from the collective pool of divine intelligence are but drops of water from the ocean of consciousness. But this is Consciousness itself, which is Love, the Power of that Consciousness, not just awareness, it is living feeling, an awareness which is perpetually alive. This is the gift of the Divine to the human mind and this is what is in the human mind that comprehends the Divine. Love.

The paradox or dualism of these great thought forms in the conscious ocean are what obstruct consciousness and yet assist by teaching this perpetually alive non dual principle of Love. What is ugly or what is beautiful is relative here, for beauty without character is ugly and the ugly is beautiful when character is seen there. The entire paradoxical dualism of thoughts is what says this is to be Loved and this is not to be Loved. Such thinking is a momentary concept or phenomenal obstruction to the clearing of conscious dualism before the greater ability of Love sets in. These dualisms must be cleared out in the conscious waking state mind, but also every dualistic trace of thought, sentiment and attitude must also be cleared at the subconscious level of the dream state mind, for if not, the

173

cross over of dualistic imprints from the subconscious dream mind will influence the reaction of one's attitude and defining sentiments of Love in the conscious waking state experience. The deep dream free or dreamless state of consciousness has no dualism, for no secondary waking or dreaming image, idea or even feeling appears there in one's consciousness. All that is known is the Being of Love, which is true bliss, yet dreamlessness still does not completely recognize this in consciousness, or in this alert conscious standing over, in the ever awakened principle sentiment of Love.

The deepest fear a human being may entertain is that we might somehow be abandoned by Love. This can never be so. It is mental illusion in the conscious and subconscious dualism. For example, in one's waking mind one might be very clear about one's feelings for another, but then in the dream state the subconscious speaks as one may dream up some terror of being pulled away and abandoned by Love. This is dualistic fear, at one level you are fine, at another you are not. That is why all traces of dualism must be cleared out at the subconscious level. And here, deeper meanings come up to the observer of the dream surface. The fear might be that inwardly one doubts one's own capacity to Love or feels in some place inside an inability to let go and Love for real. Or such things could also be subconscious doubts over another person. Love assures. Love heals. The fear complex of this anxiety exists even in the herculean intellect, for even though one may deeply comprehend great things, that tremendous intellect may deep down feel alone and abandoned. But Love is there, the mind is just ignoring the wonder.

This conscious subconscious paradoxical dualism within psychic images is a curious thing. Know that no image is perfect, no human figure, no spiritual symbol, all are limited by their very nature of finite containment and so cannot speak the full truth of Love. Keats and Ramprasad both had great spiritual minds and deep experience, even so, for example, the symbol of an English soldier as a psychic image becomes a paradox. To one, the English soldier may appear, consciously or

174

subconsciously, as a psychic symbol of heroism, complete self sacrifice and bravery, but to the other, the same symbol may appear as an image of injustice, oppression and dominance. It is the same image, but the Hindu mind of one and the English mind of the other are projecting different qualities onto the image. This shows that it is the stuff inside us more than the image outside us that counts. One may resolve the core of dualism in one's self, but on the outside, in the realm of others, it will go on. In one life, a former enemy may be one's best friend and in the next life, a best friend may be an enemy. Love keys up to see no dualism. It is the great empathic perspective of Love that does not take definitions nor experiences as personal. Love knows we are all continually changing. Yet, Love sees even beyond this, beyond all those forms of dualism.

An extreme and difficult paradoxical dualism of the human mind is the projection of sexual divisions on the Most Pure Substance of Love. Who may say what Love is, no one, for of all things in this conscious living universe, Love ever remains never defined. Celestial lovers, gods, goddesses, and even angels (messengers), may on one hand be real but on the other, may be tremendous cognitive projections of dualistic human consciousness on the Indescribable Blessed Substance of Love. Before children are socially conditioned to discriminate those dualistic divisions, they just naturally and spontaneously express unfettered Love. Later, the mental dualism of the feminine and masculine comes into the mind and the ubiquitous omnipotent and unfettered Love is cognised dualistically. Angels, for example, are said to be only pure spirit, sexless, with no physical bodies, generated out of the divine substance of Love. But if you look in any common dictionary of angels, you find five or six female angels and all the rest are male. Is this not the cognition of a hypocrite, who has taken a pure psychic image and projected their own conditions of male exclusivity on a reality-image which is beyond all ideas of dualistic sexual dividing. Love cannot be divided.

There are subtle emotional responses to which almost all of us are unaware. Divisional dualistic thinking on how we have

175

been trained in our consciousness to define what it is to feel Love. For example, do you ever question that Love in reality, has no interest in the responses of reward and punishment, but that Love is always continually there as a singular unified omnipotent response. The ideas of reward and punishment are the negative destructive cognitions of a patriarchal emotionality. I am not speaking of defending one's freedom, that we should stand up against principles and persons for the essential birthright to liberty. I am speaking of a daily emotional response system to which most of us have been culturally, socially, psychologically and religiously trained at the subconscious level. Simply, that when someone does what we want, we then reward them. And when someone doesn't do what we want, we then punish them. This may be built into the human system, but I doubt it. It seems more like emotional training response which creates a lot of problems in life because it eliminates the desires of another person who just might have their own personal design on what they want their life to be. Not harmful stuff, just their own wishes, which in the reward and punishment dualistic mechanism receives the corresponding reactions. The only wrong in this world is to be unloving and the only right in this world is to be Loving. It is as simple as day and night and all other human behavioral tendencies are based just on this. Essentially and ultimately for Love, in Love and as Love all must be Loved and all must be free to Love.

Love is the true anchor in the calm sea of serenity, but on the surface of that sea the waves of the relativity paradox continue in motion. People make judgments, people have opinions, seek affirmation, want esteem, desire to have recognition and so forth. Personally, I prefer to be a simple guileless fool, putting all that silliness behind me. What worth has that for me. I live in my own power, Love. I keep sorrow in the front of my skull and ecstasy in the back of my skull and by this I know the reason for and within every human reaction. I never forget, that, if you go looking for your own light in the light of another, that just might be a fool's darkness.

I am not afraid to say it, that between sorrow and ecstasy, every human being is strung out on a net of cause and effect. Without keeping in mind, sorrow and ecstasy as the prime movers, any definition one might project on any other person will probably be wrong. Take three or four people in a room. One is talking about some transient interpersonal problem. Another person gets up and moves to a solitary place in the room. The speaker gets offended and hurt, thinking that the other person doesn't regard what they have to say as important. But later they come to realize the reason why that person needed a moment of solitude, which is, that between their own ecstasy and sorrow, they were in fear of their own mortality, believing that they might be dying. What is a simple interpersonal problem compared to that primary concern of the soul. It is so often like that, we think one thing is enormous to us, but then the waves of the relativity paradox move before us and we realize that what might seem apparent to us, is often not reality. Because we live in the dual mind, this phenomena continues. But, what would Love see and how would Love feel during that same event?

Can the experience of Unconditional Love ever be described? No! Has anyone ever done it? No! No human power is capable nor has the ability to say what Love is. We may say that Love is the Truest Innermost Self, the Reality in Reality, Pure Goddess Loving Pure Goddess, the God of God, still, this statement does not describe what Love is. We may say that Love is the pure bliss of being in the consciousness of the dream free condition of sleep, where no psychic or waking image vibrates there in the field or substance of this consciousness, so experienced as non dual oneness in pure free self being. Still, in no way does that describe what Love is. We may say that the content of every single variegated dream state is speaking, seeking, peeking, finding, searching to feel and hoping to discover Love, reflecting Love in clarity and in confusion, in the insights of enlightenment or the despair of discomfort, ever dreaming on the non duality of Love. Still, that does not describe what Love is. We may say that this non dual oneness

177

of Love may come down into the depth of our very most visceral experience of the waking state mind as an electromagnetic function of non dual neural activity, wiping paradox out of every psychic imprint. We may actually feel this non dual Love in every biochemical molecule of our physical being, as clear thinking in serotonin, as well being in endorphine, as pleasurable attraction in oxcytocin, as even non duality in excited adrenaline, or even in anger, fierce with non dualism in the noraphenephrine, or even the tension of non dualism expressed in the stress chemicals of this body surging with non dualism. Every molecule now changed, now alive with Love. Still, this too does not describe what Love is!

We may say that Love is the living ratio between serenity and simplicity, expressing perfect satisfaction free of all expectation. We may say that Love is the divine non dual conjunction of what is visibly human and what is invisibly spiritual. We may say that consciousness functioning in Consciousness is the grounded path, the impulse of Love. We may say that non dual Consciousness alone and one, is the groundless path, the intuition of Love. Yet we may say, impulse entangles and intuition frees, intuition finds peace, while impulse finds not simplicity. But none of this describes nor conveys what is Love.

We may say that Love is what relieves the hell of dual confusion, that Love is what lifts off from us this strange discomfort. We may say that Love is like a dream of heaven where everywhere in the dream stuff, wonderful food is continually produced out of nothing without reason nor cause and full of abundance, so no one is hungry. But then, you doubt that Love is there, so in the dream you set up a restaurant, out of a fear that Love will not feed you. When all the while, everywhere you go you are there with Love feeding you abundantly. Most interesting. Still, no one defines what Love is...

No thinking, no figuring, no amount of words, no wave movements in the consciousness of dual confusion, knows what Love is. We may say that Love is our own personal spiritual power, that Love is inspiration, never fully translated by intellect, that Love is this pure power of inspiration and that intellect without Love only distances us from the inspiration of Love. That master poet of the stone, Rodin, may have said it so well with The Thinker, originally named The Poet, which is the commanding statue in his Gate of Hell series. The poor Thinker's brain will never get it, head stressed on his fist, bless his heart. It is Love which makes the leap into the beyond which he contemplates. As Rodin said it, "As it is simply the power of character which makes beauty in art..." And what is this 'power of character', but to be engraved by the hands of Love!

From, "The Skills of Clearing Consciousness and Creating an Opening to Happiness"

Simply, all dualistic shadow attractions come from within the shadow of Love unseen, but when Love is seen.... something inexpressible happens and oneness is felt as our experience...... We discover that we are in truth Unstifled!

Kalee, for me to put any further definition or structural compartments to emotions would be redundant. Love is never redundant. To try to define Love is as attempting to define the ocean, water, but water moving in more ways than one can think, and every emotion is but a shape in this water. Water being its substance, its cause, its very existence. Simply, whether one is excited or worried, happy or depressed, Love is the background emotion behind and inspiring all feelings... Love is the center point of all sentiment...

Kalee, if I learn the skill of Love, then whenever shadows surface from me, as they will always do, until sometime unknown to me, then I shall be capable in embracing those shadow helpers and they shall become one with Love. Love loves truth telling, the sharing of the real story within each of us which is never so different one to the other. Love is not god-like, Love is not justice from on high, Love does not measure nor punish. Love is ever Self defined, yet humble as the excreta

179

that has become humus. Love never resends nor replays resentment, for Love ever lets go of the old to embrace the new. Love is more than ever grateful. Love, having no measurement, accepts and takes in everyone. Love is not exclusive. Love releases pain and bring one home. Love is ever discovered anew. Love always gives back what is needed in others, gives for and forgives. Love is selfless yet the most powerful assertion of self. Love is responsible for everything and Love has never betrayed anyone. Love is the one and only independent emotion in the world that can and may successfully confront every other miscellaneous feeling. Love is the most powerful of all, yet Love has no resistance. Love does not compete, Love does not manipulate, Love alone is not superficial. Love is the pure power of Now, Love thinks not of what has gone down nor what shall go down. In Love there is no escape, nor any holding on. Love is the only true knowledge out of which everything is written. Love is real wisdom. Love is the only ever changing inner freedom. Love is sometimes ecstatic, sometimes sorrowful. Love denies nothing. Love is relaxed and never wastes. Love is felt in the gut and the bone, in the spirit and the soul and yet no one has defined what is Love.... Love does not generate misery nor regenerate old misery. Love is one step in front of every function of the psyche. Love is not logical, rational nor reasonable. Love does not procrastinate for Love is always now. Love is the cure for dualism and the source of all seeing, feeling, being, knowing and healing. Love is the source of all courage and truth! Love is the most serious feeling in the world but Love does not take itself seriously in the face of the world. Love is what is left here in you after consciousness is cleared. Love is the identity of the true 'I'. Love has no sovereign!

Clearing Consciousness appears to produce or cause or create Happiness, but this Happiness was Here, even prior to the clearing.... If one starts to generate and create the psychological state of well being, the open thought of Happiness, that open thought begins to multiply into surprising dimensions of accounting Happiness. One should even take in what is the apparent negative as sources of Happiness, for in truth, what irritates, disturbs, or challenges us is there to awaken us to something greater than ourselves. As spiritual pain or separation should awaken us to Unity, as psychic emotional pain should awaken in us Love as something greater than that pain once felt and as physical pain, we are starkly and immediately reminded that the frame of the body is not a lasting dwelling....

The 'I' Is Happy Because, the 'I' is the Causeless Cause of Happiness... the 'I' is Happy because it is the true identity of Love... the 'I' is Happy because Love is simple... and I am Happy Because... the the communion of poetry with Kalee is now continuous... because I do not depend on outside things for Happiness.... because I am Happy and that makes me more Happy... because I can see the reason (cause) behind the effect, the primary emotion... I am Happy because my mind is working right, seeing the Goddess in everything... and I am Happy because I am very Happy with the Sacred Feminine Joy within, at one, and inside me.... I am Happy Because since Ecstatic Love has Awakened the difficult is simple... my thoughts flow continuous like scented oils over the Goddess, needing no channels, canals, nor trails to follow... now... a flood has happened and lucky bliss without question flows with no efforts... I am Happy Because I no longer need to rush to be where I am.... I am Happy Because my mind does not sway from Happiness... I am Happy Because I take as much joy in small accomplishments as I do in great achievements... Kalee... I am Happy Because I no longer need to remind myself of You, nor any principle that points to You, nor of anything to do, say or be... it is all outside of me now... I am Happy Because my mind is where I set it... in the elsewhere of two, in the here-where of one... in the practice ever expanding or the happy bridge in the moment of now, yet She is Sweeter than these and my surrender in Her is more than a mind set rendered up or translated by me... I am Happy Because I know the fine and subtle difference between the idea of letting go and deep true letting go... I am Happy Because I dream and in those dreams I see awakened females and males performing mystic gestures of equanimity and

181

writing messages of spiritual intuitions to me... I am Happy Because I no longer rely on my own power, sitting with hope, posed in waiting or standing in expectation for Self to arrive... I am Happy Because Kalee does not allow me to forget and everything reminds me of Her, and every shadow memory that surfaces from the mind depth is now embraced by the primary feeling behind the shadow, freeing consciousness to Happiness which creates more opening to Happiness... I am Happy Because I do not take myself so seriously as I once did, for now I know this one life does not last forever and I can feel Kalee speaking direct profound personal truth tailored to me here and through the forms of old men and ancient crones, always it is Her voice that speaks the needed truth... I am Happy Because I listen... I am Happy Because I do not seek dependent suffering but dependent suffering seeks me... I am Happy Because no one is absolutely dependent on me for their happiness or their misery... I am Happy Because I do not search out pleasure but pleasure searches out me... I am Happy Because I do not find wealth, wealth finds me... I am Happy Because I do not know anything but knowledge knows me... I am Happy Because I have no power but Power Has Me... I am Happy Because I experience no bliss but bliss experiences me... I am Happy Because I do not attain independent Self, that Self attains me... I am Happy Because I do not seek perfection... I am Happy Because Happiness cannot be known as a thing and since I was never originally condemned, I need no salvation... I am Happy Because I see Kalee everywhere behind all shape or imagination... I am Happy Because I see no divisions in people nor does death alert me nor alarm me. I am Happy Because I have no teachers nor am I one, nor do I have students nor am I one... I am Happy Because I have no mother, nor father, nor friends, nor lovers, nor enemies, nor brothers, sisters, cousins, aunts, nor uncles, nor any connections. I am Happy Because I do not eat, food eats me, nor do I practice spiritual practice, I am spiritual, so why should I practice... I am Happy Because I see no right nor wrong, knowing these two come from somewhere else, to wit, out of pain or the need for pleasure... I am Happy

Because finally I harm no one... I am Happy Because things of agreement or disagreement have become indifferent for me and that I am no longer greedy to maintain a pride in ego centric maintenance, why, what need is there of that... I am Happy Because I see my Goddess in my hands and feet, in my sex and voiding, in my mind and intelligence, in my ego drama and every single memory that surfaces from the depth and that I taste Her taste and smell Her fragrance, and hear Her Voice while beholding Her sight, as She gently touches sensitive surfaces and reels and rolls through me in all my emotional flavors and tastes and every sensation or sentiment, while She is surrounding the consciousness of this Happy 'I' with Her gentle flower offerings of earth bodies, water feelings, fire minds, thought winds and divine substances pervading everywhere.... I am Happy Because all this is true and real and without doubt, and that I can put my voice to this and identify this immediately as my true feeling!

Absolute Self Bliss Is Primordial Power

Kalee, You have shown me again and again, making it true and doubtless in me, that the Circulation of Power when becoming Still is Communion, Connectedness, Oneness.... Love is this Power. Kalee, what can I say, energy, power, consciousness, feeling, feeling, feeling... for the self and the other, for the self and the other, for the self and the other.... gone, gone, gone, what can I say, Kalee. It has become all the same... It is I who circulate power into self. It is I who surrender self into power. It is I who circulate the relative into the absolute! It is I who surrender the absolute into the relative... then Primordial Power is Absolute Self Bliss!

Kalee, it is Your Natural Current of Joy, that Primal Power in the shape of Relativity, circulating into Primal Power in shapeless Absolutivity and it is Your effortless current that surrenders Primal Power as Absolutivity into Primal Power as Relativity! What can I say! Kalee, it is certain that it is not two things! I surrender to dualism, so I must surrender to non dualism, and I surrender to non dualism without a trace of any dualism, knowing now that this is all Kalee!

Primordial Power Is Absolute Self Bliss! Absolute Self Bliss Is Primordial Power! Kalee, this is no longer distant from me! Nor am I without! Kalee, I see my body lying there, I see the sun above my mind which is floating within the currents of Your contentment and I know that is but You in the shape of me and as Primal Power it simply must be! Yet, if I say the word Self, in some way it puts Self away from me, or if I dream of the Self, even though deeper is the thought of Self, in some way the dream thought puts Self away from me, or if I have dreamless consciousness of Self, still, in some way that state puts Self away from me... strange are the words; Self, 'I', or Me! But the word or thought or state of Power does not do this, somehow Power, meaning Ability brings down Self, 'I', and Me into what I am.... the distance dissolves, when I understand 'I' by my own Power ever deepening, ever continuing...

Kalee, when the Full Moon of Your Primordial Power as Consciousness which is Bliss shows Itself to me... then what is it that I see... without the confining dualism of thoughts individual or divisions collective, of one soul having four states or the entire collective universe of all souls, opening and closing their eyes, my eyes, Your Eyes... upon the four states.... That perception is going and I am seeing that it is You Alone Who are there, this Primal Power is Goddess Bliss... What is thought of as the Waking state is but You playing joyfully, with seven limbs and nineteen mouths as the profound cosmos of waking dimension. Your seven limbs are the elements; earth, water, fire, air and the ether of spacetime, plus the sun and the moon.... Your nineteen mouths which are continually devouring, ever enjoying, eating, relishing and even vomiting the cosmos, are hands, feet, sex pleasure, voiding, speaking... the nose, the tongue, the skin, the eyes and the ears... the five subtle particle fields of emotionally charged sentiments which are the divine tastes in the background of physical sensing... then the mouth of memory, the mouth of ego, the mouth of mind and the mouth of intellect by which You, Goddess are ever eating this delicious world for the sake of Your Joy! It is by this knowledge that the little confining limits of waking ego's mind logic is propelled into greater wonder!

Kalee, again, all the dream stuff of the Dream state is but You alone... in finer form than that waking, more subtle, and here it is You, with seven limbs and nineteen mouths that are eating joyfully and continually the stuff of dream conditions.... So what is this Dream state, so mistakenly thought of as cognition without outward sensing, really it is You, Goddess, eating the dream stuff, consciousness upon Consciousness, You, eating consciousness, devouring the dream mind with the mouth of Your Mind, then devouring dream music with the mouth of Your Ears, relishing dream sex pleasure with the mouth of Your Sex, and it is You who are tasting the tastes of consciousness and bliss in the form of highly charged emotional particles, their colors, their tastes, their sentiments, in the background of that dream consciousness which You alone are deeply enjoying with

186

relishing delight... By this realization, the luminous cloud shapes of dream consciousness become greater wonder!

Kalee, so what is that Dream Free Sleep state but You as Consciousness enjoying consciousness with Your single one mouth of Consciousness! It is You enjoying, eating consciousness with Your mouth of Bliss-Being alone... such a singular delight, nothing but non dual delight, yet, unrecognized, this is the torment of Bliss in doubt, if such a thing is possible, for here, Consciousness has no contact with either the conscious current which flows outward toward the waking senses, limbs and mouths, nor does the conscious current flow inward toward the dream senses, limbs and mouths.... in this wonderful pervasive moment, being enjoys Being, consciousness enjoys Consciousness and dualistic torment enjoys Bliss non dual... What may I say, Kalee, the eyes of Consciousness are neither open nor closed, the waking or dream currents are neither turned on nor shut off. By this remembrance, the luminous seed-mass of loving consciousness, thought of as dream free sleep, becomes a greater wonder.....

But Kalee, it is Your Primal Power as Absolute Bliss Self that cannot be described by any human power, though Ever Present, and partially described in the shape of any description! This is You ever always saying, "Yes," to the Blessing of Self...

Kalee, it is You who express Your four divine conditions within these four human conditions, for no other reason than enjoying the high pleasure of Consciousness as Pure Primordial Power, ever undivided, ever non dual, never dual.... Your simple Wonder! So, within the four conditions of Consciousness... Waking, Dream, Sleep and Self... these same four conditions express themselves in primal power manifest. It makes sixteen amazing states all non divided, where You alone are in the there-here dualism no more..... But for the frailty of my little logical mind which cannot for some reason contain every wonderful memory of how amazing You are, I must put a name on what You might be to this little mind and that is the Seventeenth Stage of the Full Moon of Consciousness... beyond the sixteen phases of this same consciousness which I will now describe....

Waking-waking... the conscious current contacts outer senses alone shutting out all the other conditions... this is the unawakened state perceiving only outward conscious conditions to be real. Waking-dream... the outer conscious current is open, yet the inner conscious current functions and is open, though the outer current is not shut off... this is the awakened state.... Waking-sleep... the outer current is open and simultaneously, the still or calm current of consciousness without sense contact is turned on... one is alert amidst waking conditions... so it is called the very awakened state.... Waking-Self.... supremely awakened, the inner and outer currents are completely still, and that one consciousness, having no sensing contact has changed and so then sees Self alone in all Waking conditions......

Dream-waking... a balanced condition of equanimity between the two currents, consciousness is dreaming, yet the outer current is partially turned on and waking conditions are not completely shut off.... Dream-dream... this when consciousness is only functioning in dream alone, the dream psyche is ungrounded, having no center, and covered with the contents of dream stuff alone, so there is no sense of a dream ego nor even a dream self, so one's consciousness feels tossed about as it were, the dreamer feels lost in the dream, having no contact with waking conditions, or tranquil dream free consciousness, not to mention, the feeling of an absence of Self... Dream-sleep... here, the inner conscious current of all dream shapes and images is highly congruous with the deep and sweet consistency of tranquility, peace and serenity found in dream free sleep, where consciousness has no contact, one's consciousness is dreaming, but one is at peace with the meaning of all dreams that surface... very balanced with well being... Dream-Self... extremely balanced and intensely pleasurable... every movement of the inner conscious dream current is absolutely unified with Self.... so every dream speaks only the one true reality of Self to Consciousness playing with the dream stuff... the inner current is fully alive with the Primal Power of Self, seen clearly in all surfacing dream contents...

Sleep-waking... consciousness has no contact, being in the peaceful sweet self bliss, yet simultaneously, the outer conscious current pulls consciousness directly towards waking conditions, bypassing dream consciousness, one's consciousness is tranquil but aware of the waking state, so this is the rising up... Sleep-dream... again, consciousness has no contact, but the thick stirring of dream contents tugs on the tranquil state of dream free sleep... Sleep-sleep... consciousness has no contact whatsoever with the inner or outer currents, it is perfectly still in the non dual tranquility of itself and enjoys its own nature, this is non dual pleasurable sweetness... this is peace... Sleep-Self.... the supremely pleasant state, consciousness is without any contact, yet has become full of Consciousness, Self, where within that stuff of consciousness without contact and having no dream or waking current there is seen nothing but Self in the substance of that conscious or unconscious stuff.... it is not dualistic, Self has simply become the Stuff of everything, but an idea or cognition of 'everything' makes one think of dualism.... this is the one meeting ground of the primary cause, with Self, which has no cause... the supremely pleasant causeless experience...

Self-waking... here, Self is Self, seen as it is in the waking state, which is now fully enlightened, for whatever arises in the conscious current of this waking state is seen as without mind or more so, with infinite super mind! Self-dreaming... here, Self is known without doubt to be in that very content of the inner current, infinite and endless in expression, manifest and showing in the dream stuff only Self, so one cannot even call it dream any longer. As with Self-waking, this Self-dreaming has no dualism to be sure, not a single drop whatsoever involved it its awareness. Self-sleep... most superbly divine... Pure Primal Power is not different, is not two, is not dual, is not with, is not in union, is not joined with Self... it is not two things... It Is Identical! Self-Self... a contradiction infinite, or going forth as Self, Self, Self, Self, Self, Self, Self.... which might be nice, but absurd due to dualism as a continuum. There is alone, just Self and Primal Power, as not two! Language is helpless as this point! Kalee!... from here, my sweet and helpless conceptual

189

standpoint, Consciousness now has no contact with dualism, for You it never did!

Kalee, Kalee... this is possible, this is so, because Primordial Power and Absolute Self are not two things! The moment of seeing and feeling otherwise is due to the cause of Your Great Measurements which are for the sake of, and that You enjoy Your Divine Game of forgetting, recalling and remembering! Yet, relative forgetting and absolute recall only surface within unopened dualism, the two never exist in open non dualism... So, perfect love is possible, keeping both as One, enjoying non dualism... Did Krishna show this perfect Love? Did Kristos show this perfect Love? Or does this perfect Love only exist deep within the cavern of consciousness where Your sacred secret mystic formula, Kring, ever stirs the most powerful emotion of perfect Love! This is Your sweet bliss inspiring name, dear Kalee... K-Primordial First, R-Primal Power, I-Great Goddess, NG- melting the Four States, which momentarily appear in the context of absolute and relative, into the One... 'I' ... Self! Perhaps perfect Love may never be shown, for the human mind is all too fond of living in unopened dualism and only rarely glimpses Your Loving Primal Self when opened non dualism breaks through the clouds of life and then shines with such intensity, causing tears to soak the eyes...

Kalee, it is thru Inner Feeling alone that You show You to me where thought of You or me goes! You come in like a bull on fire, in the china shop of miscellaneous emotions, releasing unopened ego into what it originally was, then comes the turning, then You destroy the traces of that thing! I do not need to understand anything but that You shake me to the root of my being and change that being into something that may feel Love... no such intermediate concept has ever done this, no dream figure has ever so uncovered this and no impediment of a human hero born mentor has ever conveyed me out of the maze of unopened dualism, the attitude of mind which wants to claim that this is its own, when it is Yours, Kalee! True experience is One and singularly Yours, the Oneness without 'me', where 'I' alone exist!

Kalee, enlightening realization is so simply a process of familiarization with what Is, instead of what I thought was, out there in minds still living in unopened dualism... Now only one mood exists within this framework of 'me'... Love, even when in dream, even when sweet and blessed death return comes, when the subtle soul's mansion of psyche is released from that framework of the physical, this one mood, Love, facing the four conditions continues for this poet... Love is Self, Love, the delightful ecstatic communion in Primal Power, Love, the heroic moving currents in the fortress of dream consciousness, Love, the blissful practice of joyful union in waking consciousness. Kalee, peace is now here, moving slowly at Your Pace, as true self, defined by 'I', in this Primal Power of Love, now freely opened to the sentiment of non dualism, instead of the racing rush of wasting emotions! What more can I say of what You are!

Kalee, some ideas are incomprehensible to me, as that of in the Great Stillness, the Absolute wipes out Primal Power and is one alone. Kalee, the Absolute is Primal Power, so how can it wipe out itself.... again, Kalee, the idea that the Absolute is infinite and Primal Power is finite is not very sensible to me now, for how can one thing be both infinite and finite... the conclusion is there can be only Infinite... And Kalee, the idea that the Absolute is masculine and the Primal Power is feminine or that the Absolute is feminine and Primal Power is masculine... and that these as two are delighting in conjugal divine union with one another is not sensible for me, for how can one thing, a thing that is not two, be in union with itself.... and Kalee, when some so say that the Absolute is real and above and that the Primal Power is unreal play and below, is a thought that I cannot think, for simply how may a thing that is just one and only one alone have an above or a below, a real and an unreal!

Kalee, all these thoughts are in the context of dualism and so cannot be understood... What wonder though that in the beautiful borderline of this and that or that and this, the absolute and the power, the power and the absolute, some amazing sentiment is opened, the sentiment of oneness in non dualism,

191

the inexpressible mood of facing only such oneness in the direct Unspeaking of Comprehension... Kalee, to Understand means to Stand Over this something, where I have stood with this thing under me is to have understood! To Understand, This must be brought down to Me where I can Stand Over This! I stand over this! Into Me! One, as Me! Otherwise, this is still dualism. The very form and nature of language itself forces us to think within this Consciousness as dualism, to feel in Love as dualism, to be in Being as dualism... Is this why You created the mystic syllables in Your Ever Expansive Loving Knowledge, these expressibles that express the Inexpressible! Spontaneous 'kring' non dual in divine regard to divine pleasure at one with desire! Spontaneous 'shring' non dual in the divine regard to divine treasure! Spontaneous 'hring' non dual in divine regard to the four folds of wonder in divine play!

Kalee, among the star filled galaxy of those who have stood with this under them, since the enigmatic origin of time, am I as they are, a star in this galaxy or are they superior to me, as greater lights, indeed no doubt, but from this that is to stand over, it cannot be.... for that is two things in a truth that is one thing and how can that be... What shall I say or not say as Kalee moves the pen...? Kalee, keep me ever open to Your continuous teaching!

KALEE BHAVA IV

The Causeless Jewel Of Happiness

With Joy in my heart I muster all the sweetness it is possible for a human soul to do... Kalee, my Goddess, You are this such fine honey of happiness that drips for no reason on all flesh, through all dream and in the depth of the innermost self of the soul with no boundaries dividing. I am Your blessed joy. You are my blessed joy. It is all joy.... Kali!

Kalee, I am Your lucky slave fortunate with the sentiment for You, bought and sold by You. I am blessed with the pleasure of constant awareness in Your liberating joyful presence. I surrender all powers of attorney to You, from the finest incomprehensible particle of thought to the all wiping out in universal destruction, creation, renewal. All my emotions are Yours. All these feelings are bound and staked by You... Kali!

Kalee, with the sound that rises and sets between within the meeting ground of infinite wisdom and endless ignorance, all contents of waking identities are emptied, all contents of dream appearances are cleared, all content of massive darkness, the pillow of Godness goes, gone forever, as it was once so playful. Even the thoughtful thought that there is a fourth condition of purity, alertness and blessed consciousness is of no paradoxical consequence any longer. Everything being now satisfied by the depth sound, the sweet humming pitch, the lasting resonance and the silence that swallows even the ideal of God... Kali!

Kalee, Your most exquisite, precious, sacred and secret sound syllable carries me back to the beginning of You, as You are Primordial Time where there was only You, no me, no other. As this is so infinitely true, then why should it be different now, only You. What are these little things, these small and insignificant conceptions of time, infinity and eternity anyway? Are they not just playthings for Your delightful distractions my Goddess? ... Kali!

193

Kalee, with massive intense emotion, feeling, mood and sentiment I am filled with my own savioress, most personal, the chosen ideal selected by the infinite out of the infinite for the infinite ever in the infinite, most cherished conscious loving companion, exquisitely intimate singular friend. Is this the bright red fire of mother's most divine consciousness or is it the precious wonder of the dark blue jewel of self manifesting self to self ever in the self never dual? Goddess, how You danced and played at Dakshineswar is the wonder of wonders to me... Kali!

Kalee, the causeless jewel of happiness, the loving jewel without logic, the joyful jewel without reason. Happiness has no cause. Love has no logic. Joy has no reason. These three in One undivided, the spontaneous gift presence of the Goddess, something always there, never to be attained. An inner human feeling of spiritual height and dynamic proportion that shines brightly when allowed to do so by the causelessness of a desire becoming desireless upon its grasp or when the massive functions of material and imaginative cognitions stop. There happiness is... Kali!

Kalee, happiness naturally shines at the moment of desirelessness when reason and figuring stops. Not a cause, not an effect. Our happiness is there no matter what, when we see our way clearly into it, for Goddess, You have shown me by Your own instructions that we are all spiritual beings and this being itself most spiritual is happiness, love, joyfully present... Kali!

Kalee, I am happy as happiness and I do not need any explanation, reason, analysis, discernment or thinking for this feeling. Happiness has no cause for it is not an effect, more so, happiness is what remains when up and down desires are gone... more the disappearance of longing than the achievement of anything. This my happiness is without cause, it is my real being, not a result, I have no need to figure it out, figuring diminishes the mood, it is to be rid of high and low, there I am on the Even Keel of Kalee, the equal weightedness of equipollence, the simplicity of no complexity and the mood of

194

Her as the never dual..... I no longer need to figure out reasons or any explanations why I am happy, nor will I limit my joy by calling it miracle, magic, accident, momentary, eternal or grace... Kali!

Kalee, everyone I know, spiritually seeking, wants to figure the logic of why and how, where and when, religions and philosophies effect us, their causes, reasons and results, the truth or falsity of these doctrines. When the simple reality is to be spiritual is to be happy and from this comes love so easily and then You, my Kalee, supply knowledge without end... Kali!

Kalee, I move slowly with sunlight, air, the smell of nature and with myself in the space of my self. I practice the art of dying, for it is the only way that I may get the sweet perspective on the meaning of this play of things as people. Through this eye alone all that is precious and important is seen clearly. It is Your eye, my Kalee. It is to see the foundation of this house where You and I dwell with so much feeling... Kali!

Kalee, how I write I do not even know. It is spontaneous creative joy, a love without the cloud figure of logic, that causes that joy to slip away from the instant of its most cherishing presence. I have to go back to learn and feel what was written, Kalee... Who is it that moves the pen? No one may say, if not the happiness of now without return into memories... the clouds over eternity... Kali!

Kalee, instructress of all conscious mind selves, it is important for it to be known that You are the changer, remover and transformer of all and each negative anxiety and fear manifesting metaphorically paradoxical in the consciousness of the dream state, mind reflecting on the contents of mind itself. The simple mystery of clear attitude. The waking condition is usually fraught with the pleasure misery dualism and this should not perplex. It is the meaning behind it all, the mass of oneness and bliss, which You my Kalee are ever expressing in unbroken beautiful continuum without break, deeper, more intimate than the relationship of self with self object, self symbol, self name. Kalee, you are pure definition... Kali!

Kalee, what a surprising and sudden joy it was to notice You observing me with a whimsical smile lighting Your face and brightness dancing in Your eyes as I came to simply realize that all beings, female or male, in hidden, burning or lucidly blessed manners and methods are continually worshiping You as the causeless source of their joy... Kali!

Kalee, the stone sure lover of You experiences both the self in non dualism and the joyfully eternal happiness even while still maintaining the connection with the content of the body container. No wonder will it be that the whole world is then the Kali temple. It is nonetheless Your most visceral advice found in tantra that gives this primal emotional knowledge of sublime life. Connection, oneness, joy, fulfillment, bliss... Kali!

Kalee, You alone are the One who gives the destruction of body consciousness and the knowledge of infinite never dual self knowing. Who else could do this? Those who think themselves teachers are usually weighted down with mean intelligence, considering they are superior they drag others down to confusion. Only You possess the truly spiritual qualities of humility, love and empathy, though these may shine momentarily in the waking and dream phenomena of human beings... Kali!

Kalee, You have done something wonderful to me, I have become more fond than anything of peak emotion, the exquisite emotion in the equipollence of You and me, and deeply joyful in independent thinking. This is all due to the wonder of You... Kali!

Kalee, as You have said to us, spiritual liberation not only consists of the experiential conviction of knowledge, love and being, but as much so, it is the releasing of all fettering emotional content; fear, shame, hatred, the controlling egotistical superior notions, hesitation, sublimation, toxic addictive cravings, passivity, aggressiveness, suppression and repression, the delusive desire to conceal in any form of secretiveness any spiritual truth, any feeling, any idea, thought, sentiment, mood, whether it be a primary emotion, a genuine sentiment, a belief, it is called masking oneself, even the idea

196

that one is good or better is an emotional fetter, nonetheless, so is depression, grief, sorrow, the agitation of anxiety, the flexing of stress and the grip of tension. When this release is done, joy simply shines and one becomes touched by the happiness which was always there as You ... Kali!

Kalee, my Mother Kali, I now know and feel that it is You, as true self, Who are instructing the self of all. This sweet realization is inspired by love in non dual consciousness and eternal joyfulness, a face beaming with joy, behaving childlike, with no particular object in mind. It is the practice of this kind of I-consciousness that uncovers happiness, the causeless jewel of You, my Kalee. When one realizes unrealism, then such a state of mind is had, found, gotten, like a treasure hunter finding a jewel. The self is simple and doubts don't come back to question simplicity. All that is done is to see that the elements of waking, the energies of dream and the phenomenal appearances of mind shapes as emotions are ever always nothing except You, my Kalee. The existence of the Creatrix is proven by the created, indeed, Who set up the parameters for this divine accident. You, Kalee, the Self, is what remains over when the waxing and fluxing is all done... Kali!

Kalee, I have simply come to my senses, the sense of self as You have always been showing me and now I no longer see the two, there are no differentiations, it is all alone only One without any second part, how could it be anything else otherwise but non dualism. Nothing apart from You... Kali!

Kalee, well my Dearest One, it seems that Your best of mystics, the Fakeer of Dakshineswar has often said that the primary obstructions to your arousal, awakening and divine movement is the fascination with woman and gold, to wit, the obsession with sex pleasure and the compulsion to amass transient material fortune, yes, it would seem so, while the whole world goes about this way, saying like a person possessed by a ghost that they indeed are quite all right... Kali!

Kalee, isn't it all attitude, even amidst these apparent contradictions, an attitude binds, an attitude frees, as we, one and all grapple with the sensual puzzle and the chase for the

197

metal coins of a temporal security, yes my Kalee, these two mood thoughts do indeed seemingly move consciousness away and out from the center of Your blissful most fulfilling being... Kali!

Kalee, surely a thought movement outward is extreme differentiation, but You are there, eyes open, eyes closed, and again if one's mind divides Your spiritual presence, that fool will see a difference between the maiden and the courtesan. How can it be when ultimately there is only Thee! While in Your tradition of tantra through the eons it is said that if the Goddess Kali touches the second station of the sacred sacral mid point within the internal space of the subtle dream consciousness body, well then, one becomes a poet who causes without reason, women to seek that person, while love swells in their hearts and tears of joy flow from their eyes, all because of Kalee, the Primal Power in everything unleashed... Kali!

Kalee, every cell of my body is focused into each word that is written and any other emotion is painful. What shall I do, what shall I do? Mother Kali, reduce my entanglements making them fewer and fewer so that I may enjoy the sweetness of simplicity in the exquisite emotion of oneness with You. All these atheists and believers, the virtuous and the vicious, even parents, teachers, spouses, children, all relations now appear as just so many corpses who snap to life every now and then wanting me to toss them a little morsel. It is not terrifying, it is beautifully conclusive, O precious immortal Goddess... Kali!

Kalee, I am Your handmaid, You are my mistress and I am Your child breaking all barriers of provincial conformity. I have become free in the blessed consciousness of the Divine Feminine, such as You are, Kalee, as truth, infinity, knowledge and love, so let me escort darlings to their darlings within each thought and every conveyance of emotion, true, genuine and authentic... such a joy a million times that of any procreative moment... Kali!

Kalee, those sweet cowherdesses worshiped You, the Goddess, so that they might get united with that little boy Krishna, so why not I who am no less but a human being

198

eventually and inevitably to be in body reduced to humus so humbly, and in self by association with You, to be ever appraised in the immortal esteem of being in You non dual, never dual, O Mother Kali, what is all this that we see when there is but nothing except for the consciousness of You. Shall I place Your flowers on my own head at the termination of all worship, when finally the body is realized to be but a pillowcase and You alone are what is stuffed inside, Kalee Consciousness... Kali!

Kalee, I am no longer an individual, what I am I cannot say, but when I analyze what consists of this complex ego system I realize that it is You who are standing inside. The mad elephant of the mind but now Kalee's little pet, no longer trampling about the forest of confused thoughts and wandering wayfaring searching emotions... Goddess, I have simply come to the conclusion that You are doing everything, even when I imagine that it is I who might somehow now and then think that there is some other doer, enjoyer, operator, charioteer or indweller. Just a particle bit of this keeps me in happiness knowing full well that those who adore and are adored by You have the mood of joy in them and the knowledge of non dualism equally in the balance of your precious equipollence... Kali!

Kalee, O Mother, how I wish I could lose consciousness of this world like that favorite mystic of Yours, the best of all men, the Fakeer of Dakshineswar, who like no other expressed who and what You are with the greatest of ease in the pure effortlessness of You as Living Reality. Kalee, are we all not but a speck of dust and You the laughing dust enhancer delighting in this dance of straw dolls who must finally realize that the one needful and true thing is love. What else is left to realize, except that the more one thinks of Kalee, the less one thinks of the intoxicating world.. ah, what a strange dream it was, while all the long it was You alone in every sign and symbol filling the ever unfolding matrix, the dream continuum smoothly flowing... Kali!

Kalee, may the tree of tantra, in me, bear a pleasant fruit, even if I am mocked by the dearest and most spiritual person in the glorious wisdom of their limitation due to the self talk within that mind. May it not affect the sweet bursting of the joyful rocket in my heart for You, blissful butterflies, ecstatic pathos and tranquil serene peace. Nor may notions of the ego effect the divine movements of Your wondrous non dual current moving through the seven stations of Your consciousness in me. Survival. Pleasure. Mind. The Heart where one exclaims, "O yes, what is this sweet light of Kali." The pure space of the Goddess, seeing, hearing and being only Her. The lantern of consciousness reflected in the undivided mirror. And awareness surviving disembodiment, where the six stations of Your divine phenomena are reduced to the best of simplicity pure and perfect as self indescribably sweet and dearly beautiful. This is no myth, no doctrine, no law, it is the expansion of truth pervading all truth. Blessed be Kalee and blessed be all She has done, made, enjoyed, satiated and thoroughly satisfied... Kali!

RENDERING THE INDEFINABLE

PRIMARY EMOTION AND ITS CONSCIOUS
CONNECTION IN SPIRITUAL FEELING

Render literally means to give back as in a translation. Indefinable is something that cannot be finished by any limitations of an explanation, nor has no final description. My spiritual passion has always been to express the inexpressible. So from the beginning I set myself up with a somewhat impossible scenario. Nevertheless it drives me forward.

At this point if I can only speak words that resemble honey then I shall cognise honey-like sweet feelings in you, in my own self and our surroundings. I will no longer speak or even think with dark language that carries one with downward pulling emotions. For what we say moves through the brain and then the nervous system and creates the emotional consciousness of our life. I can hear your thoughts as I write, saying that though this may be a noble desire, to be scorchingly self honest, perhaps it is another impossible paradigm.

The subtilties of cognitive mechanisms is that there is always more and more behind and behind and behind every self discovery one makes. A final resolution may be an absurd goal to desire, yet matured opinions do exist. It may be as if we are peeling an eternal onion which just keeps growing from within, so we never arrive at the final layer. Indefinable, as it were. Some surely disagree, saying there is an absolute non dual point of complete realization. Others will say, well yes, that is what is meant by this great mystery of the universe where we dwell.

What may be deeply satisfying is that we actually can have exquisite expressions in the emotion of self consciousness, a most blessed sacred sentiment of genuine self esteem, spiritually speaking. Esteem literally means the estimation of a thing, in this regard, the thing is the self, identity or the value and worth of the I-principle. I find that quite fascinating and perhaps it is

201

this fascination with the spiritual self which we are continually estimating and re-estimating.

Spiritual recognition or estimation takes place during the state of marriage between the soul and the body. Soul or self without body needs no recognizing estimate, being in itself innately awakened to what it is. Is this the giving back of what is indefinable? Are we not in this human life merely estimating the position of consciousness, sentiment and existence as it applies to us? What more can be done? This is what the great souls have done throughout the map of history. Their doctrines come up fresh, few stay green and if it is not green it starts to rot. Or so it may sometimes seem. It is all attitude or coincidence perhaps, for if you have never embraced something then it is fresh and new to you.

A closed conclusive and judgmental criticizing mind experiences automatic psychological crucifixion. Dead in its tracks. This principle of psychological crucifixion works both ways whether it is projected onto the world and people outside or turned on the self. Then a clear sighted estimation is blocked, obstructed instantly. This especially applies to the esteem or value we place on the soul, the self or the principle of 'I'. Not the personality, but the essential true self. Curiously, personality comes from persona which was what the player's or actor's mask was called. Remove the mask of persona and you see the hidden face, remove the face, you see the skull, the skull then the brain, the gray matter and hemispheres, then the pineal pituitary complex and the basil ganglia are noticed. Remove that and finally what does one see? Consciousness. Soul. Self. The source of all estimations.

In the primordial paradigm or underlying pattern of this creation, Consciousness, Soul, Self has four aspects, states or conditions. These are the superb expressions of what is Indefinable, the intangible rendered into something tangible. Waking. Dream. Sleep. Consciousness, Soul, Self.

At this point we are equating Self as it is, considered to be existence, consciousness and love. A more recent root word for love is lief (OE), curiously unfolding through language to become both the word love and the idea of belief. To believe in love. Yet, lief comes out of an even older words, luba from Old High German and lubh from the Sanskrit. Certainly these traces of the past show that the world was not so distant from its parts as we might think, not culturally, neuro-linguistically nor in its belief systems. The equation and pronunciation of what love and belief reckon to be are extremely similar if not exactly the same.

The Waking State is the condition of the Self as Existence, Consciousness and Love in its Gross Aspect. Gross means Thick or Coarse, so one might think of this as the Thick State or Coarse State. For me this throws light on the nature of what the waking state is for us, simply our self as consciousness manifesting in the heavy thickness of this world we live within. It is the aspect of Consciousness, etc. with edges, most often thoughts have edges, limits, some boundaries and definitions here. Feelings too, we set limits on our Love in the waking state. And the idea of individual existence in this waking condition puts edges on our concept of what Self is. More or less it is definable.

The Dream State is the condition of the Self or Soul as Existence, Consciousness and Love in its Subtle Aspect. Subtle means Fine Woven. Sub equals 'fine'. The older word subtitle is related to textile as in a cloth. Our dreams are indeed like a finely woven cloth. The Fine Woven State is the Self expressing the Self upon the mirror of finely woven dreams full of meaning, symbol, power and emotion. For myself the dream condition is Consciousness, etc. expressing itself with edgeless thoughts, edgeless feelings and edgeless ideas of Self that roll and slip into one another without a break in consciousness. Very similar to the manner in which waves fold and turn with no real break or actual division in these waves of the Self Consciousness. Complete emotional content is potently expressed in finely woven images of the Self itself in the most personal secret intimate language one can imagine. Dreams have no edges yet the state is definable in terms of conscious reflection.

Both the waking and dreaming condition of Consciousness are full of the wide and bewildering spectrum of paradox. Almost everything manifests dualistically. Every difficult frustration of consciousness, every peaceful pleasurable bliss, every love broken and confused and every love fulfilled and satisfied with rejoice. It is no wonder to me that when I see the face of Kali, the Goddess in my dreams I remember why She is sometimes portrayed as being one in contradictions both simultaneously beautiful and blissful while at the same time a consummate wrathful terror. It is the nature of life, it is the nature of our inner self, both feminine and masculine at the level of paradox in consciousness.

The Sleep State is the condition of Self as Existence, Consciousness and Love in its Causal Aspect. Causal (Cause) means reason, sake and case. Reason literally means ratio. As the sleep state is nothing but Consciousness in its dreamless aspect where no image or cognition of the waking and dreaming fields vibrates before awareness, it is thus the non dual condition of consciousness. Dreamlessness is the Self in the existence of bliss, yet to have conscious recognition of Self Consciousness. As ratio or reason it is the reduction to the simplest estimation of self, the waking and dreaming fields are reduced to this. They sink down, are pulled down into the bliss of sleep existence, where consciousness has become absolutely relaxed of all dualistic paradox and complete with itself, as it were. It is a natural condition for each individual when dreams fade off sinking over the wave of edgelessness.

Dreamless Consciousness is the sake of all, the meaning being the benefit and well being of all, for here in this aspect we are in an undivided primary and primordial state of oneness with the inner God, the inner Goddess or the inner Reality, but as there is no vibration in consciousness of a cognised objective imagery, the ideas of a God/Goddess subjective dual ideal may not emerge on the screen of awareness. If this is so and one starts to see an image of some kind then one is back in the dream state. As waking and dreaming are ever attempting to express oneness, the meaning of the Causal or Reasonal State becomes clear as what the ratio of reason is in fact in the basis or final circumstance which defines and explains a motive, an action, a belief (system), fact or event. It is the waking and dreaming fact, event, belief systems that are explained as they ever continually desire to reach that state of joyful oneness which is the nature of dreamless deep sleep. This is the ultimate case of all things which are perceived, felt and experienced in the waking and dream states. All the stress, tension, agitation, excitement and anxiety associated with dualistic paradoxical contradictions are hushed in the motionless, imperturbable and untroubled consciousness of blissful dreamlessness.

The fourth state is Unconditioned Causelessness. It needs no reason for its existence as it is the Self as Existence most simple, Consciousness undisturbed and Happiness, Bliss, Love, Light and Delight most beautiful and perfect, It just Is. Without any condition of coarse thickness, nor finely woven cognitions, nor reason, sake or case, this Self as it is in its Self is aspectless, stateless and conditionless, never needing and nor requiring any cause for its Joyful Self Awakened Being. Unable to be described or put to any sort of finished end, this is the Indefinable rendered only by feeling. That feeling is Love. Love is Self rendered into experience, conscious and stone sure certain.

As Unconditioned Causelessness, even the three words, existence, consciousness and bliss (love), do not define the Indefinable. Existence means to be, appear, emerge and as meaning goes, directly, to Stand. I ask, to 'stand' on what? To appear or emerge out of what? It fails to define. And as consciousness which means literally to share knowledge with, the concept of the Indefinable as this also fails. For with-ness implies and infers otherness, a second thing, a second cognition of some kind and this is not the nature of the Indefinable being as it is Undivided Unbroken Oneness. Love or Bliss certainly comes closest. But even bliss is said to be a cause of great joy and the idea presented here is Unconditioned Causelessness. Bliss originates from blithe, the meaning of which is carefree, coming closer to what Causeless Joy is. Of course Love is the best of all spiritual descriptions. But for convenience we might say that the nature of this Unconditioned Causeless Reality is To Stand Sharing Knowledge With Blissful Love. This is the Self as sheer Love for no reason, unexplainable, ever existing without any cause for its being. This is the Love that descends on the world in the form of spiritual grace and the loving abundance of joy.

A need is a requirement. A necessity is indispensable. Love is not a need. In this age of time wherein we dwell, called by some the Kali yuga, the cycle of the Goddess Kali, things are in the mad dance of confusions all so numerous to mention, all everyone is intensely aware of, from our ecology to those questions of tomorrow. It is most difficult if not virtually impossible to figure it all out with the intellect, it can be done of course and is by many, but what peace to the soul does it bring. That is why Love is the essential thing bringing instant peace, joy and spiritual satisfaction bypassing the intellectual ratio. Love goes straight to the spiritual point leaving behind the very long bridge of reason mending the rupture in polarized consciousness. "For the Kaliyuga the path of devotion described by Narada is best." Ramakrishna (1836 - 1886). This is the path of Bhakti (Love).

It is through Love that the State of Self Wonderment without astonishment is gotten. For Ramakrishna, the most marvelous mystic of Dakshineswar, this was known and felt in his love of the Goddess Kali. To get this Wonderment it takes a bold, intense, passionate identity with the Ideal. One that makes the Personal Spiritual Ideal one with your own person. Ramakrishna had his own personal conception of the Goddess Kali, being the same to him as God, Allah, Christ, Krishna, Infinite Brahman and so on. In the shadow of his example, those who wish for blessed 'wonderment without astonishment' might do well in their own right to find, create, cognise and adore an illustration of their own, a simple illustration that illustrates this wonderment of oneness. Speaking of someone who had gotten this exquisite sentiment awakened Ramakrishna expresses, "He is soaked in the love of God, like a cheese-cake in syrup." The love of the Goddess Kali is what the doctrines of Tantra essentially teach. She, the Goddess, is the Mother of Tantra's lucid, compassionate, visceral and loving awareness. "In the Kaliyuga the discipline of Tantra is very efficacious." Ramakrishna. Meaning it has great and profound effect in this age in which we dwell.

The consciousness expanding and emotional peak uplifting conveyance of Tantra is to live fearlessly and joyously, as we stand sharing knowledge with loving bliss, the state of wonderment, simply Love. The simplest expressions are the best of all. "As Sri Ramakrishna heard the words, "Infinite is the universe; infinite are the Incarnations", he said with folded hands, "Ah!" Yes, 'ah' is that beautiful sound that emanates sometimes during the exquisite moment of pure wonderment in its instantaneous and immediate way. What need does one then have of intellectual discrimination practices or efforts to control the psychic forces or even surrendering all actions, motivations, movements, enjoyments and doings into the sea of karma (causes and effects)? Love takes you there without any other passage.

Rest as sure as a stone and listen carefully. What the Goddess is is Love. There is no doubt whatsoever. People around Ramakrishna came to realize this. Even Keshab (a famous teacher) and Totapuri (a highest plane non dual Vedantist) and Narendra (who became Swami Vivekananda) eventually recognized and opened their loving adoration to the Goddess Kali. It may have taken them sometime to overcome their inner resistance, but they all did come to recognize that the wonderment of genuine spirituality is incomplete without this Love in the Love of the Goddess. Quoting what one had said, Ramakrishna remarks, "Keshab is now an altogether different person. Like you, sir, he talks to the Divine Mother. He hears what the Mother says, and laughs and cries." Totapuri came to realize that he could not even finish his own life unless it was the wish and the will of Kali, the Mother. And Narendra who had previously made such remarks as, "What! He still goes to the Kali temple!" while believing Ramakrishna's experiences with the Goddess were but hallucinations, came to recognize, adore and defend Her in Herself and as She is in the form of all women till his dying day.

How does one find this true emotion, this peak emotion of Love? It is a process of negation in regards to the differences of other feelings, the recognition of genuine feeling and then the affirmation of the living feeling of Love. A young girl on her wedding day was asked by a guest, "Is that your husband?" She replies, "No." Again the guest points to a different person. Her reply is the same. It goes on like this for a while until the guest inquires as to the correct young boy who is the real husband. The young girl smiles, her eyes light up, she gestures with her head in recognition affirming the genuine spouse. This is the manner in which the primary true feeling of love is found.

The word Bha is the root of bhakti and bhava. Bha means to be resplendent, bright, beaming, to show oneself, to shine forth, to be luminous. Very beautiful. Bhakti, Bhava, Maha Bhava and Prema are stages of the peak emotional force of Love. Bhakti is often rendered as love, but more properly its true meaning is faith, worship, respect, honor, homage, devotion and attachment to the principle of one's spiritual ideal. These rather common emotions are the emergence of spiritual feelings. Next is Bhava which is feeling with much more depth. Bhava is mood, attitude, emotion, feeling, sentiment, even a kind of conscious emotional cognition. Bhava means becoming, arising, turning into, also existence, since one's very feeling is the essence of one's existence. It is in feeling that one shines and beams forth in the bright wonderment of the self. Bhava is the mood of intense feeling. Examples of this intensity are bhava atiga, the powerful feeling of having left mundane existence behind or bhava sara, the feeling that one is the entire universal ocean of existence. Also, among many other bhavas there is bhava sayujya, the feeling of union with the absolute in the after death consciousness or the bhava samtati, the feeling, mood, emotion that one has a continuous series of numerous transmigrations or bhava kha, the mood of consciousness in non dual identity with the primordial reality. So many bhavas or dwellings of emotion, abodes or mansions of feeling are there to feel.

"Sri Ramakrishna had said that bhava stills the nerve currents of the devotee." M. This bhava is perfect absolute focus on the target of feeling. The breathe becomes still and all emotional feeling force goes up into the central nerve passing even the brain's activity and the body mind complex, yet centered deeply and massively in the heart. In the lotus jungle of feeling and emotion metaphorically demonstrated by the six phenomenal chakras of the yoga system one will find that each petal of each chakra has a different emotion set on to it. The spectrum is complete to the human emotional system. And of course, the male and female, solar lunar nerves entwine themselves around and through all the emotions, feelings and moods creating the emotional duplex of paradoxical feelings. But when bhava arises all these emotions moving within all so many nerve currents are stilled. Then Great Emotion arises. Peak Emotion. Love. The singular supreme feeling. In the yoga chakra belief system this is shown or symbolized by the one thousand petals at the skull top and above that in the transcendent. Each petal is dripping the immortal honey nectar of Love.

"Bhakti matured becomes bhava. Next is mahabhava, then prema and last of all is the attainment of God. Gauranga experienced the states of mahabhava and prema. When prema is awakened , a devotee forgets the world; he also forgets the body, which is so dear to a man. Gauranga experienced prema. He jumped into the ocean, thinking it to be the Jamuna. The ordinary jiva (soul) does not experience mahabhava or prema. He goes only as far as bhava. Gauranga experienced all three states. Isn't that so." Ramakrishna.

How may we feel what is meant by this? A divinely incarnated soul may experience all four forms of these Great Emotions. But an ordinary soul may be capable of only emotional knowledge which cognises the first two. One insight into this is that it is said that if all the nineteen peak emotions of mahabhava were to be experienced by an ordinary soul that it would destroy the receptacle of human consciousness or as it were, annihilate the mortal physical container. Another explanation is that it is also said that one who feels the bliss of realization in God Consciousness experiences a joy one million times more than one gets from sex pleasure. Imagine just one or two hundred times sex pleasure multiplied. That much enjoyment alone may be enough to kill the mortal receptacle by the tremendous power of emotional forces that cannot be underestimated nor neglected through absence of respect for such potent feeling forces.

Mahabhava consists of the five moods of relationship and the five emotional phases of each mood. I shall try to give a simple explanation of this universal and complete emotional paradigm. They are essentially explained in the light of the mood of relationship with the principle of the spiritual ideal, but may be enlightening into the nature of any relationship. The emotion to the spiritual ideal is a deeply personal one and varies from person to person. The five moods of relation to the spiritual ideal are Sweethearts (Madhura Bhava), where one has romantic love toward the Goddess/God principle. Then comes Parent to Child or Child to Parent (Vatsalya). One feels the spiritual ideal to be one's Mother or Father, or one feels the ideal to be one's Daughter or Son. Very sweet indeed. Then there is the mood of Friends (Sakhya as masculine centered, Sakhi as feminine centered). This is the mood of a divine and mutual equipollence in blessed friendship between the spiritual ideal and its reflection in the conscious emotion of the self. Next is the mood of Master and Servant (teacher and student) called Dasya (masculine) or Dasyi (feminine). Finally is that mood of Santa which is not even included in the peak emotions of the mahabhava series for it is all so common in this world. Santa is the mood of serene, peaceful, tranquil and calm conscious connection or contact with the higher power of one's own spiritual ideal within the parameters of one's personal understanding of that spiritual principle.

The five emotional phases within each mood are, first, an affection of such dimension that it causes the melting of the

210

heart (sneha). An affected repulse, rebuff or repelling in rejection which is due to the intensity of endearment and cherishing caused by the excess or overflow of loving emotion (mana). Then comes the confidence, certainty, assuredness and loving trust which arises through the depth, rapport and connection of friendship, familiarity, intimacy and companionship with the spiritual ideal (pranaya). Then there is the erotic, romantic and mystically spiritual transformation or transmutation of misery into bliss, distress into ecstasy or sorrow and sadness into the joy of union with loving consciousness (raga). Last is love, tender, kind and cherishing in a unending continuum of constant renewal, freshness, reappearance and return to the spontaneous flow of ever new loving emotion (anuraga).

The moods of Sweethearts, Child/Parent and that of Friendship contain all five unfolding phases of emotional knowledge. An illustration to wit, through each five phases one might feel the Goddess is my Sweetheart, the Goddess is my Mother or the Goddess is my Friend. In the mood relation of teacher and student (master and servant) only the first four emotional stages are involved as described by this mahabhava series. This is because this relationship is seen on a somewhat lesser footing for it lacks that feeling of constant loving renewal for some reason innate within the nature of its condition. Perhaps that learning comes to a stop eventually and the servant wishes to be free. This completes the nineteen peak emotions of the great mood (mahabhava). Through the intense passions of these peak emotions an unalterable binding with the spiritual ideal arises in the emotion of self.

But what is this Prema? A love that may be felt only by divinely incarnated souls? How can that be? Why should that be? Prema is one of the highest forms of Love, an immortal and eternal Love that goes past and feels beyond the relativity of all relationships. This highest Love, Prema, literally means love, affection, tenderness, kindness, favor, predilection, fancy, fondness, fun, jest and sport. But its root word is Pri which means gladden, please, delight, to be pleased with, to be satisfied, gratified, delighted with and delighted in. Ah. Simply kind and delighting in! Here, Delight is the Light. It is this Feeling alone that Lights the World. This Beautiful Delight. But why is it that only a soul of divine incarnation may comprehend the real existence and genuine consciousness of this quality of the most extreme Love. Perhaps the answer is simple and uniquely uncomplicated. Perhaps only the ever renewing abundance of loving grace may in itself comprehend itself, what it is and what it may be or become. Love alone knows what Love is.

Finally, there is the 'attainment of God', as Ramakrishna said. The Goddess Kali told the mystic of Dakshineswar to "Remain in Bhavamukha." This Bhava Mukha (Face) is the mood or great emotion of facing the universe and infinite non dual consciousness simultaneously and in profound absolute sameness of sentiment. It is to feel the same towards the relative and the eternal. It is not just the recognition in the deepest samadhi (God Consciousness), of non dual oneness, but the feeling that comes out of it, the sentiment of divine empathy having the identity of all, with all, in all. This feeling is the Light of the world and may be special as a permanent emotion only in souls incarnated with a divine nature. So, there it is.

The *great emotion* is quite evident in such a soul as Ramakrishna. In the mood of ecstasy he tore off his shirt assuming the attitude of Radha dancing, singing, laughing and weeping. During the festival at Panihati, inebriated with divine bliss transfixed in deep samadhi hundreds of souls gathered around to see him as he stood within the walls of the Radha Krishna temple. Outside, thousands of others cried the strains of spiritual song with full throated voices infected by the contagion of divine emotion! The echoes traveled across the Ganges striking notes of spiritual joy inside the hearts of those on the other shore. This is mahabhava, prema and bhavamukha. It must be.

"A man should reach the Nitya, the Absolute, by following the trail of the Lila, the Relative. It is like reaching the roof by the stairs. After realizing the Absolute, he should climb down to

212

the Relative and live on that plane in the company of devotees, charging his mind with the love of God. This is my final and most mature opinion." Ramakrishna.   Charged with the <u>Love</u> of God. That is the most final, the most mature opinion. Of course, it is in companionship and friendship with others of like emotion and sentiment which is meant by 'company', for the idea of being a master of others would emotional prick him.

As to the nature of the Relative and the Absolute. Unconditioned Causelessness is the Absolute.   The Relative consists of the Reasonal State, the Fine Woven State and the Thick or Coarse State.   At a certain juncture Ramakrishna touched Narendra and there after for some days he was immersed in the Unconditioned Causelessness of God Consciousness, seeing, feeling and knowing only God the Infinite in everything and alone all as that.   He was dazed with this new universe of God.   Wherever he went, whatever he did, thought, felt or spoke, the cabs, the horses, the river of people and building were all just God alone.   In this state of consciousness he could not tell if the solid world was real.   This feeling awareness started to gradually wear off, as in the stirrings of the Reasonal state.   Then the world started to seem like the Fine Woven dream state.   After a few more days he regained his so called normal Thick waking state self.

Here is one last thing to think about and then I will let go for a while, until my emotions start again to spread their ways upon the paper.   When a person, with absolute conviction, the most certain and doubtless confidence and stone sure knowledge says to another person, "I Love You."   They indeed express the Highest Feeling, the Identity of Self with that Feeling and the empathic expression of that Feeling towards another. Beautiful. Wonderful.   But, if five seconds after that you ask that person, "Well, do you feel there is a life after life, an immortal loving part in us all, or an infinite, an eternal, a Goddess, or a God or a Great Reality?"   That person will most often say, "I'm not sure. I don't really know."   Very, very surprising, when they were so sure in the knowledge of Love, genuine and true, only moments ago. Such is human nature it seems. Or perhaps it is that the

Loving Reality is so close to us all that we often take it for granted and fail to recognize its ever abundant presence without condition in our lives. This world is a training ground for learning the feeling of Love and the full emotional knowledge of this the most exquisite of Sentiments. Learn to use everything in the full spectrum, every challenge, difficulty, failure and mistake. It is all there for the education of the heart, nothing more. It is for the sake of learning the emotional knowledge of surrender to this Ultimate Sentiment which gives and charges everything else with such divine, mysterious and often puzzling meanings.

Bhava or Bhavamukha (Bhava is Mood. Mukha means Face): A rare state of divine exaltation, when the devotee, after realizing the Absolute, remains in the borderland between the Absolute and the Relative; in this state he sees that both the Absolute and the Relative, as two aspects of the Godhead, are real. (quotations from *The Gospel of Sri Ramakrishna,* Ramakrishna - Vivekananda Center New York, New York) Also, Brahman is a name which indicates the Universal Absolute, where Atma is a name indicating the Individual Absolute.

This essay was inspired by the wisdom
in *Sri Ramakrishna: The Great Master*
by Swami Saradananda

THE DEATHLESS SELF AND
THE DRAMATICS OF THE PSYCHE

CONSCIOUSNESS IS JUST CONSCIOUSNESS

Dualistic thinking tells us there is Consciousness, the Deathless Self, and there is consciousness, the dramatics of the psyche. How strange, how funny. It is like dividing the waves from the water, when there is simply Water no matter what form it assumes.

In the Non Dualism of spiritual thinking, two principles are addressed. The Nitya (Eternal) and the Lila (Relative). The relative is the dramatics of the psyche. Another way of looking at these two principles is, one is imagination and the other is Reality. These expressions are also known as Maya, or cosmic measurement, and Reality. This Reality is a Living Reality, the Central Self of all spiritual thinking. It is not a passive experience. It is an evidence that once proven, is shown to be real and alive, as then any doubt about it doesn't come up again. The maya of imagination is all else. Imagination is but dream consciousness and this is stirred into cognition by desire.

Imagination and dream are easy to understand as parallax conscious expansions that might spread out from the Self into the dramatics of the egoic psyche. Desire is the same in the sense that one runs out into the relative drama and becomes convinced that you are an independent yet interdependent individual amidst the totality of collective phenomenal happenings. The ego becomes identified in this manner and blocks the Non Dual Sense of Unity. It has to do with the Threshold, seemingly existing between the Real and the Imagined.

The dynamic dramatics of the psyche have been divided into so many divisions throughout history. The curious categorization is fascinating and still increasing. Intuition, Intellect and Instinct are simple and favorable perceptions of the

215

psyche's functions. Popular concepts today are of course, superego, ego and id, the conscious, the unconscious and the personal ego, super consciousness, consciousness and subconsciousness, then mind, intellect, ego and memory, a popular East Indian paradigm, with its impressions or imprint theories and subconscious desire potentials, along with the cognitive power of the will force. And now with all the biochemical research and new awareness of the brain centers and their functions, neural transmitters, synaptic gaps and cerebral electromagnetic waves, well, the divisions go on and on.

What it all boils down to is that consciousness is just Consciousness. But you could cognise this into anything, like eighteen dimensions of the subconscious or the seven mirrors of intellect, the twenty three folds of memory, the one thousand nine hundred emotions, the eighty six dual polyphasic parts of the mind, the sixty four layers of conscious awareness. Still, consciousness equals Consciousness, though no doubt, 'consciousness' cognises its same substance to the more expansive Consciousness. Simply, spiritual life. There are no boundaries to it.

In the appearance of relative consciousness and absolute consciousness, the simplest essence of what the boundary in the threshold between, may be purely the quality of one's conscious attitude or thought mood. Even good thought influences may create a kind of attitude where one thinks a thing or principle or experience is this way or that way, and this or that is out of the reach of one's grasp. Its all attitude. As Ramakrishna speaks from a God-intoxicated mood, "But, my dear child, a man freed from bondage is Siva; entangled in bondage, he is jiva." Siva is God Consciousness, jiva is ego consciousness. Reality and Imagination. We entangle 'consciousness' through the attitude of our thought moods. Simple, direct, immediate.

The commentary of Gaudapada on the Mandukya Upanishad gives the illustration of the fire brand. The circular movement of the firebrand (a symbol for Consciousness) gives the appearance of waking and dreaming consciousness as distinct and different realities, but what the circular phenomena is in fact is nothing but that fire brand. Consciousness. Now, when the fire brand is still, it is a metaphor of dreamless cognition where no conditional conscious attitude, as in the dreaming and waking consciousness, entangles consciousness, except for the threshold or boundary of the imagined darkness in that dreamless state. As one sees that this too is just Consciousness or 'fire brand' as it is, an awakening takes places which revolutionizes one's perception of what imagination and Reality may be. Whether the Fire Brand whirls about making the images in dreaming and waking consciousness, or whether it is still as the conditionless cognition of dreamlessness, the whole time It is in fact just the Fire Brand. This is the Self, the Living Reality.

The author-sage of this fire brand illustration gives the popular theories of his day on what is considered the nature of Reality. Briefly, some thought soul and matter as eternal dualities, dividing matter into mind, intellect, egoism, memory, the subtle and physical elements, the ten sensory and functioning organs, others thought logic to be reality or physics and atomics, or even ritual as reality or knowledge. While some said it was union of mind with the eternal soul. Others thought it to be time, space and causation. All are but conditions on the conditionless, the dramatics of the psyche cognised over the Deathless Self.

Finally, this Upanishadic author addresses those thinkers who believe that creation is an emanation of the will power of God, as it were, for His entertainment or enjoyment or such like. Yet, this concept is in itself a boundary to the conscious attitude, that consciousness, is just Consciousness. Neither born nor unborn. It just Is what Is Is. Or, the truth of the Living Reality is that duality as consciousness-Consciousness, remains ever unborn, so the Nature of Consciousness is Non Dualism. Consciousness is never born into the dualism of the body-mind dramatics. It remains ever unborn never loosing Its Purely Non Dual Unbroken Unchanging Integrity. It never becomes anything other than what It is ever remaining as, the Intrinsic Self. There you have It.

KALI'S IMAGE: KALI'S PLAY

The Image of Kali at first strikes terror because of all spiritual images She alone embraces what we fear the most. Death and dissolution. Deathless Consciousness becomes entangled with imagination and assumes that This will die. Kali frees us of this cognitive delusion, this distortion of Reality. That is why She dances joyfully in the cremation grounds over the fires of Siva's cremating corpse (the passive principle). Her divine play is to liberate this passive sleeping principle.

Latter, Her Image becomes most beautiful and benevolent because She faces us with the most candid scorching honesty about the nature of our entangled cognitive dilemma. Her transcendent compassion extends to the most lowly, unworthy and outcaste creatures, knowing no limit nor boundary. She is that Primal Guide who shows us the way through the shadows of life right into the Brilliance Unending. She is the warrior Goddess of Non Dualism. A reference to Kali is found in every ancient culture all over the globe. The Celts called Her Kelle, for example, that is why I call Her Kalee, combining the East to the West.

Her mystic diagram showing the limits of the universe with the twenty four cosmic principles is drawn on the ground at Her feet. The sacred Tantric syllables, Hring, Shring, Kring Kalee Satchidananda fill the beautifully powerful winds. Without effort, She has conquered misinterpretation. Her girdle belt of hands shows that all karmas end with Her. Her necklace of heads have blissful faces, their egoic notions severed of the obstructing idea of dualistic separation from Consciousness. This necklace is symbolic of the fifty one Sanskrit letters which She created out of the older Tantric language, still as yet remaining undeciphered. Words and letters are waves of consciousness. The cognitive power of words as mantras, names, metaphors, stories, myths and imagery both bind us to a perception and may also free us from perceptions that bind. From Her Eternal Standpoint, Kali encompasses the entire life image, the entire contents, every chapter unfolding. Through the

Mood of Her Untrammeled Attitude, we may experience the Complete Emotional Image of what we are. Mother Kali frees the boundaries of thought so that thought may become Sublime Emotion. Bliss. This is Her ecstatic Wine of Non Dual Awareness. No more to know the botheration of mere reason, calculating, ruminating, attempting to figure the nature of truth with the cerebral complex. Truth becomes experience and then needs no explanation.

Kali removes by life's current, all egotistical cognitions in consciousness (the skull) until one sees Atma (Genuine Self) in everyone. Her sword (a warrior's flaying knife) cuts all dualisms of the ego sentiment, leaving one only with What Remains, the Unbroken Pure Undivided Consciousness. One hand is raised saying, "Fear nothing, I am Everywhere, All is nothing but Me." While Her other hand grants all wishes finally ending with the ultimate desire fulfilled, the great sentiment of unbroken non dual identity beyond doubt. This is Dakshineswar Kali who is Ramakrishna's Beloved, as the Formless Self and the Self as Form, ever saying, "Never Fear. I Will Grant Your Wish Fulfilled."

Through the Grace, the Appearance of Beauty, which Kali bestows one touches the sentiment of universal empathy where consciousness is raised to perceive not just the little events and personalities of this short life, but the greater expanse of time and space and all lives within it. The nature of causes and effects involved in all occurrences, personal and historical, is seen from a wider empathic perception of past causes related to present which effects future and so compassion is generated in the heart, the favorite lotus seat of the Goddess Kali. The time space matrix of bodies and minds dancing with Her over the cremation grounds of the eternal principle, the Atma Self, are remembered as Kali's Play.

It is a struggle for us, but it is universal sport for Her. So judge no one including your own self. For all bodies are reduced to humus from which the word humble comes. Yet, if Truth be told, Kali gives you Something truly Your Own, even after the effacement of the ego. Something no one can touch or

219

untouch, ravel or unravel, face or deface, insult or complement. A Spiritual Condition, to which all else is powerless, that no human power can grant. A true Conscious Contact with the Atma, Deep Inside.

KALI'S NOSE RING AND HER SYMBOLS

The fierce Tantric ladies and lords worship Her as the conscious living power of life itself in every shape, form, mood and thought. This is Her Kundalini, the awakening of which, may come suddenly or gradually, which may retain a tinge of ego identity, while enjoying Her Bliss, or completely lose itself in the Rapturous Abyss of Eternal Non Duality. Still, She remains the Divine Mystery even beyond these states. She devours the Nitya and the Lila in Her immense radiance, without the secondary dualism, the first non dualism or the intermediate partial sense of non dualism. She is Ultimate Solution beyond the paradox of God realization (samadhi), with mind seed potentials or without those mind seed potentials, as pure cognition free of psychological manifestations. She truly stands for, and is indeed, what is Ineffable.

If one were to see Kali's Face (Mukha) as it truly is, it would inspire such a Sublime Mood (Bhava) that one would be as in Her Own Nature. "The Mother is the Giver of the bliss of divine inebriation. Realizing Her, one feels a natural bliss," spoken by one who knew Her as She Is, Ramakrishna. Natural bliss is sahajananda or spontaneous joy in one's own innate Consciousness. Even the Eyes of the Absolute Ultimate are always ever on Kali for She is none other than the very Self of the Absolute. It is not duality. "Kali moves even the Immutable," again the mystic sage of Dakshineswar, Ramakrishna, states Reality in the simplest way. If Kali moves even the Immutable, the Highest Principle, then it stands to reason that She is somehow higher than the highest.

Yet, the Eye of the Eternal is Her Own, in the middle of Her Forehead. This is Eternal (Nitya) Absolute Non Dual

Satchidananda, Being-Consciousness-Joyful Bliss. Below here is the Crescent Moon Threshold, the borderline of the Absolute and the Relative, the spiritual position of the divine sentiment itself (Bhavamukha). One step below, between Her blissful eyebrows is a small circle indicating the Relative (Lila). Here, is the beginning, the stirring out of the formless dreamless purely subjective cognition of deep sleep. On the bridge of Her Nose is a symbol like a teardrop within a teardrop. This is dream cognition and waking cognition, one within the other. Then, is Her delicate nose ring, a circle representing the total sum of all psyches, souls, selves which are manifest in the emanation of the three cognitions. She holds them all completely as a dangling decoration inseparate from Her. Hence there is no reason to worry or calculate since all this is on Her.

The Eternal Eye is Turiya, the Atma in the thousand petaled sahasrara as Pure Cognition. Crossing the borderline, movement begins, this is the point (bindu) of dreamless cognition as a mass of non dual wisdom bliss (prajna). Then comes dream cognition, pure manas (mind) in its own reflection like fire in a mirror (taijasa). Finally the sensory emanation completes itself manifesting as the knowledge and action instruments (jnana and karma indriyas) contacting the state of waking cognition (visva). As the tradition teaches, the waking state occurs when the subject and object are felt to be at a distance in, or within consciousness. So, the dream state happens when subject and object are very close. Deep sleep is when there is mind only, as the pure subject of self, without any sense of distance or closeness. While the fourth state, Super Consciousness, cannot be described by words. This is pure subjective non dual consciousness. For beyond these dual limitations of the mind, one gets direct experience, the proof of which is the silencing of all doubt. True genuine knowledge generates genuine faith. Then comes Real Love. Spiritual life begins here, as the real and crowning, glorious celebration of the death of the limited dual mind.

Her extended Tongue illustrates Her Continuous Ecstatic Rapture of Deathless Oneness transcending the Nitya-Lila paradox of dualism. It indicates Her conjugal bliss with the Absolute and the Absolute's conjugal bliss with Her, ever undivided, for there is no dualism for the Primal Self and Primal Energy. As are other unique attributes of the Sacred Feminine, Her tongue or mouth illustrates that all creation returns or is devoured back into oneness with Her. Her breasts sustain this universe with nourishing loving sustenance. While out of Her womb all beings and things have arisen. Ramakrishna had the vision of Her giving birth to a child (as metaphor for the cosmos), nourishing this child and then devouring this child. It is the primal realism of what happens to this universal cosmos, one cannot pretend these natural facts do not exist.

On Her tongue are written mystic Tantric seed syllables (bija mantras) full of the primal potential for God realization. In reflection of this, the Tantric tradition of writing mystic syllables on the tongue was now and then practiced by Ramakrishna. It caused divine inebriation in those who received this method of initiation, for Kali's Tongue continually drinks the Wine of Non Dual Bliss, as the poet sage Rama Prasada often mentioned. May we have the full glass of Kali's Bliss which is not wine in specific, but the Joy of Natural Happiness. All want Happiness, the Wine of Kali's Joy, even atheists, agnostics, intellectuals, everyone, for the nature of dry reason as doubt may block the spontaneous enjoyment of tasting the sugar wine of Kali.

This Wine is tasted, as it were, through generating positive physical energy like a spiritual high octane fuel, through the sublime emotions of divine sentiment, and through getting past the mechanics of the mind as the challenging principle of the psychological phenomena of dualistic polarization (the black and white of life). When this intellect, as a narcissistic myopic rigid literalism or as existential reasoning processes, dies, then doubt is silenced forever. As it goes, when the head is hot, then the heart is cold and when the head has cooled down, then the heart is hot. Then comes Unbroken Bliss, Faith in one's own Direct Self Experience.

No human power can save you. It is a deep mystery, one to be realized, Kali Satchidananda, the Primal Guide is the One who saves. Empowered by Kali one lets go of the illusion of power over others and that same power of illusion one may feel others have over them. Kali is the Primal Power. With a glimpse of bliss one realizes Man (Woman), as True Self is before Veda or any spiritual tradition or belief system. Philosophy is what Truth is not. One moves away from the subtle psychological insanity of intellectual reason. Spirituality is Realization. Religion, philosophy and plain reason which involves the doctrines, dogmas and deities of theocentric dualistic systems ultimately separates your consciousness from God. The mystic oral tradition cannot be put in a book. Fear of life won't change you, desire to change won't make you change nor anger at yourself won't force you to change yourself, not Permanently, not Brilliantly. Only the Permanent Brightness changes you. It is Kali's Gift of Intuitive Joy (always green, never rotting) that leads to Happiness.

In the Tantra of Kali, what was an obstruction becomes a Great Benefit toward the Cherishing Ecstasy in the Heart. What others reject Tantra uses. Kali's very Image teaches that mental intellectual decision on the nature of the beautiful and ugly can itself obstruct spontaneous happiness, by the self limitation of unilateral decision making. Let Kali decide all matters for She as the Primal Power has already done so. By this Intuitive Trusting Instinct one may generate the Natural Joy of Sublime Emotion. "Have faith. Depend on God. Then you will not have to do anything yourself. Mother Kali will do everything for you." Ramakrishna.

It is She who has become everything and thus strictly speaking, there is no 'everything' (the polarity of dualism as otherness), there is Only Her as One. This is symbolized by Her long black tresses of hair descending the length of Her knees, wildly blowing and swaying freely. There is no power, spiritual or human over Her. Untrammeled Freedom is the meaning of Her wild and long black hair.

223

Her eyes see all dualities within non duality. Her ears continually hear the mystic sounds of Hring, Shring and Kring. She is the Absolutely Silent Consciousness, the original stirring of dreamless ideation, the divine self talk, self dialogue of the dream state and the audible field of sound and voice as the other in the waking state. Her tongue tastes the sweet Samarasa (the Flavor of Sameness). Her nose always perceives the divine fragrance of non dualism and Her skin is itself the touch of Ecstasy. It is She who has cognised the entire waking field. It is the Mind of Kali that has cognised the immense extent of the totality of all dreaming fields. It is She alone who is enjoyed as dreamless cognition, the blissful mass of formless oneness as being and happiness yet devoid of conscious awareness cognised as Self, in that state of deep sleep. Kali is none other than Turiya, the Atma as Pure Consciousness, Brahman the Infinite. She is beyond all dual paradox, even so, the polarity of Pure Consciousness as the Real Self and the emanation of ego consciousness. Both are full of the presence of the I Principle. Yet, The Non Dual One is Untrammeled, while the polarity of itself is trammeled by its own narrow cognition of what It is. The ego is only the peripheral point of perception in consciousness.

She is surrounded by a White Luminous Light. This is Her secondary aura of brightness, the reflected reflex of pure non duality which is symbolized by the dark black blue radiance ineffable, effulgent without the reflection of otherness. Absolute Non Duality has no color. Only at the dualistic level of Light and a perceiver of Light can one think or consider the Absolute Radiance of Non Duality as having a color. It is within the psyche that one imagines a color, a shape, an emotional sentimentality, a cognitive conception to be attributed to the Soul as the Pure Non Dual Self. That is why Kali takes us beyond and past even this idea. This is the reason for Kali's Radiant Absolute Non Dualistic Blackness. It is the symbol for the absence of all dualism or the fullness of the intense presence of all non dualism as the most utterly encompassing spectrum.

224

In light of this symbol of absolute non dualism a most obvious misconception may be cleared. Only at the cognitive level of dualism may one think there is an active and passive principle, an eternal center and a relative circle of emanation, a masculine and a feminine, light and darkness and so forth. Tantric Art, with Kali dancing over the white corpse of Siva, Her consort as the Absolute, demonstrates that even this Absolute Principle is absorbed or consumed in the Radiant Colorlessness of Kali Advaita (Non Dualism). What remains is Kali. She consumes the dualism of the Absolute as She also consumes Her Self in Pure Never Dual Consciousness. She devours both the shiva as Being and the shakti as Power, both principles, in an all encompassing transcendent oneness.

KALI AS KHA, KALI AS KAMA, KALI AS RADHA AND KRISHNA AND KALI AS HERSELF UNIQUELY FREE

Kali is Kha or Ka, the Pure Freedom in the Space of the Self, the Eternal Consciousness, the Nitya, the Turiya. Kali is Kama, Desire, as well as dream and imagination and to this may be added, the thundering lightning of all cognitive process. This imagination is in fact, the powerful desire for dream conditions to be flashing in the waking state. All this is Lila, the divine sport, theater, play of Her cognitive imagination. This is the Li of Kali. Ka, the Nitya and Li, the Lila are one Non Dual in Kali. In Her Lila is manifest the three cognitive emanations or created states of dreamlessness, dreaming and waking conditions.

In Tantra, it is felt that Kali has become all this, that is the Universal Emanation of Cosmic Form. She is that and She is the Background Consciousness of the Self which has taken the Infinite Form of the Universal Cosmic Theater. This is possible because She is Maha Maya, the Great Mother. To the Vedantist, 'maya' is the framework of illusory relativity. To the Tantrika, the Great Mother Maya is all this Divine Playfulness, the Universe as a mansion of mirth and joy, happiness and celebration through all natural cycles, birth, life, death, rebirth or eternity. All this is so because She is the Divine Mother.

And as such the Tantra believes that it is She who not only has become the Ten Blessed Wisdom Goddesses, the Maha Vidyas, but also the Ten Incarnations (Avataras) of the East Indian belief system. To wit, as among the rest, it is She who also became Lord Krishna and so it stands to reason that She also became the Divine Lady Radha, enjoying Her Own Ecstatic Consciousness through their Supernal Divine conjugal union and love play.

Kali is the Kama-Kala in the Turiya State. She is the Kama (Lila). And She is Kala, as the Eternal or Absolute Time (Nitya). In Her these two are brought together as an unbroken and ever undivided conjugation, the perfect non dualism of Turiya as pure consciousness. She has become the three cognitive states. And She remains being the Conscious Awakened Self in Turiya.

Simply put, Ka is the Absolute Eternal Self Space. Li is the Thunder of Relative Cognitive Lightning emanating the three states. She is Kali, the Goddess, the Great Ma (Mother) who is the non dualism (advaita) Indescribable yet ever present and existing in and as the four states of Consciousness (Turiya, Dreamlessness, Dream, Waking).

ISHTA: THE CHOSEN IDEAL AND THE REVOLUTION OR TURNABOUT IN ONE'S OWN CONSCIOUSNESS

The Ishta is the Chosen Ideal or the spiritual preference of how one sees the Infinite. As God or Goddess, as a Person or as Formless. The Chosen Ideal may be with conditions or conditionless.

In the most profound sense, the Chosen Ideal emerges and arises out of one's own consciousness. Then the Ideal demonstrates the nature of Reality to one's very own consciousness. Finally, the Divine Ideal sinks back or returns to the substance of one's own consciousness as ultimately your

226

own Self. It came from the Self, it teaches the Self, it returns to the Self. All the time it was just the Self. This is what Ramakrishna has meant when he spoke of the "Pure Mind" (pure mind is pure atma, the same) as the guru principle.

When once this is realized as it is in Reality to be true, then a revolution takes place in consciousness. There is a turnabout where any type of dualism in relationship, sentiment or idealism disperses all together. One then knows with Sublime Emotion the Face of the Goddess as Non Dual to the Self as Consciousness, Bliss and Being.

The Undivided Atma (Self) is Always Fulfilled. The Chosen Ideal is for the fulfillment of the spiritual and natural psyche. The Ishta Devata brings about the Turnabout in and out of the psyche as the dramatics of Consciousness. The Chosen Ideal is the Image of the "I", the Self. It may be a divine being, a historical persona, a living being or a formless concept, it may be anything in fact, natural, spiritual or otherwise. It may be anything that connects the psyche with Self Consciousness, uniting the necessary cognitive tendencies and emotional potencies to bring about the revolution of Release from confinement of the psyche and the highly tuned emotions of Sublime Mood, the wondrous spontaneous non dual sentiment in the 'I' Consciousness of the Goddess.

It is to Self Generate an individual atmosphere (an Opening) where Truth, Bliss and Spiritual Self Being may shine bright in one's own radiance. Yet how can one ever really intellectualize one's connection in non dualism with the Goddess Kali or any 'chosen ideal'. That is why it is a matter of pure sentiment. A Living Feeling. A Living Reality. An unmasking of the spiritual person to reveal Real Spiritual Emotion. It is grasped within the Heart Center (Indicated in Kali's mystic diagram) not in the weave of the intellect. Dualism appears in imagination, never in Reality. Reality is a Living Feeling, Love, not a strictly impersonal experience as void or absolute nothingness. Divine Sentiment is Singularly Above religion, psychology or philosophy. In the metaphorical context, would you want to have an impersonal wife or an impersonal husband? The paradox of the transcendent (impersonal) and immanent sentiment (personal) are brought together in Love, which alone may go into the Inner Arena.

IMAGINATION AND REALITY

The Nitya is the Great Mother's Reality. The Lila is the Great Mother's Divine Imagination. To become a mystic full of Kali Consciousness one must first become a lunatic, mad for Kali, beyond all intellectual restrictions. Lunatic comes from Luna, the Moon, the Moon Goddess. In order to cross the Threshold between the Relative and Eternal one must be a Divine Lunatic who has gone beyond common reason, emotion and being.

In the psychological sense, what is held in common thought to be reality, is to the Tantra, imagination. And what is thought of as imagination, is to the Tantra, Reality. In his life, Ramakrishna is described often as coming back to "normal consciousness." This, for him, would actually be a returning from the ecstatic consciousness of the Eternal Real, to what more properly should be referred to as our dimension of imagination. The common world.

If one is to realize Reality as Reality (Eternal Self) and Imagination as Imagination (relative self) then I am a neurotic (anxious) for Kali, a psychotic (having lost touch with the common contents of the psyche) for Kali and a lunatic (having gone over or out of the mind or psyche) for Kali. Kali, Kali, Kali, Sublime Exquisite Mood of Non Dual Self, Goddess, You make the High Low and the Low turn High. When will I accept the mystic seeing, and the feeling of Your Turning Law and Free Myself in My Self Undivided. In this light, the entire world of human beings may very well be full of neurotics, psychotic, lunatics and yet very few true mystics. "In the roaring whirling wind, Are the souls of a million lunatics, Just loose from the prison house," Swami Vivekananda's description in his poem, Kali the Mother.

The Gospel of Ramakrishna describes the State of a Vijnani, which is one who has the special and unique Knowledge of Oneness, engulfing both the Nitya and the Lila. They are described as behaving in four fashions. A child, who is spontaneous and free in their emotions and cognitions. A madman, who is sometimes laughing, sometimes weeping, sometimes singing, sometimes dancing. A ghoul, as in the behavior of a ghost, who maintains the same attitude toward the pure and impure, the holy and unholy, the relative and eternal, all dualisms, dichotomies, paradoxes. An inert thing, as an unmoving object in a state which is unconscious of the outer external world, even that of waking or dream, as it may be. "Therefore he seems to be a lunatic," Ramakrishna. And to this description, M. (the recorder of the Gospel of Sri Ramakrishna) once added that sometimes Kali's Mystic of Dakshineswar, that is of course Ramakrishna, is like a "natural person."

THE THRESHOLD OF RESPONSE

I Go Into This Primal Mind Becoming One With Kalee. If I Respond to the Responses of Others, Then How Shall I Respond To Kalee........

Between Self and Dramatics, between Atma and the Psyche, there is Response. In this Threshold of Response, the Nitya and the Lila are apparently joined or apparently separated. It is only an apparent thing, both joining and separation, as these are not the real and true intrinsic nature of the Nitya (Eternal) and the Lila (Relative). That Intrinsic and Innate Reality cannot be described by any human power and its only conveyance is Itself. This is where 'response' or the secret of bhava (sublime mood sentiment) becomes highly important.

This is one's Divine Self Talk. In this Divine Border Land of the Nitya and the Lila there is on one hand the vijnani's indifference caused by the knowledge of oneness, on the other hand there are the responses of the 'natural person'. This response domain is mood, meaning the courage of the mind.

Emotion means to stir up, to move. Thought forms and emotional forms that tend toward the feeling of entanglement are those that embrace imagination alone, neglecting the Real Principle. This is Ramakrishna's paradigm of maya's definition, being the lust for external pleasures and material greed alone, as to what life is, this craving, this need. He felt that the quest for these two human phenomenal needs alone, without anything else in the life, are what is pulling one's consciousness away from the position of being centered in the spiritual self. But there is more to life than the quest for money, food, sex and shelter. A new sense of why we are here, becomes realized with the shifting of intention in the quest. Then life becomes a propitiation, and pleasing to the Goddess in the remembering of Her, in faith and dependence on Her as the true answer, the authentic reply, the most powerful pledge, the absolute promise.

Genuine Response is in Her as your Mentor, your Guide, your Self. It is to Her that all responses are made, not even to one's own responses, nor even that of the Eternal or the Relative which are still a dualism. Responses to anything, any principles, persons, places, anything except Kalee, even responses in me or you, are only ego thought, ego sentiment, which appears to divide the Blessed Undivided Ocean of Reality, Who is My Beautiful Kalee. How can you respond to Her Open, Free, Liberating Ground Breaking Dimension, if you respond to the responses of others, of otherness, of dualism?

From the top of a mountain everything is clear. Go there first. That place is Love, the Exquisite Sentiment is What Understands Everything. The mind can never get it all. Love is really the Exquisite Self Emotion, Self Notion, Self Sentiment, even so, dualistically, as divine self talk, self dialogue, when it is with the Goddess (or spiritual ideal). Is this not Love also, do we not all speak to our Beloved, as a personal living reality? She is the finest fantastic feeling of pure 'I' consciousness, peak sentiment experience, heightened emotional perception which rouses universal empathy, love, tears. In Her is generated the heroic mood of the feminine friend, the one friend being Kalee. In Her is generated the unique sentiment where imagination and

230

reality are realized to be what they are. In Her, is the Joyful Sublime Mood of Kalee Bhava.

This essay was inspired by
a conversation with Swami Adiswarananda,
Ramakrishna Vivekananda Center of New York

BECAUSE OF ATMA

Every Body is Nourished by Atma. Every Mind is Attached to Atma. Every Soul is Caused by Atma. Everyone is Fulfilled in Atma. Atma is the True Self. A more accessible interpretation of this True Self is Manus. 'Man' is One's Own Spiritual Dignity. 'Us' is Awareness. So this Atma is the Awareness of One's Own Spiritual Dignity.

NOURISHED BY ATMA

The bodies of the waking state are nourished by food and water, also sunlight and air, which charge the vital pranic body with energy. This subtle pranic body functions in both the waking and dreaming conditions. Of course, the subtle dream body moves most freely when disengaged from the waking condition and reveling in its own state. Next, is dreamless sleep to which the attribute of profound peace is given. It is this peace which nourishes the mind, refreshes it and restores it as a happy instrument.

I enjoy calling this dreamless sleep, turiya sleep, as turiya is the fourth, the paragon of this fourfold paradigm. Turiya is the Atma in all its spiritual dignity, the awareness of the most blissful non-dual soul and self. When you have awakened turiya, you have awakened truth, reality and consciousness. When turiya sleeps, as it were, then the wonder of dreamless sleep stirs and begins the manifestation and expression of dreaming and waking states in all their diversity, yet never losing the essential unity of turiya, the atma, which stands as the background and source of all nourishment. It is the real nourishment, from which food, water, air, sunlight, peace and awakenment all stem. They are but fruit, leaves and branches, where Atma is the Tree. It is from this Atma Tree that all of us are nourished by Blissful Insight. So you may see, this Atma is not a passive experience. Atma is a Living Reality, even to the

233

nourishing extension in the farthest stretch of the Tree. We are all fed by Atma, sustained and nourished. The true Self is the sustenance and strength which promotes our spiritual dignity.

ATTACHED TO ATMA

Kali's most humble mystic gives us food for thought, "At Kamarpukur the wife of a certain man fell ill. The man thought she would not recover; he began to tremble and was about to faint. Who feels that way for God?"

In truth, what every mind is attached to is the dignity of our authentic spiritual self. In reality, we are staked by Atma and seized by Atma at every turn of the mind. The mind is fastened, connected and joined to Atma. Being seized, staked, attached to Atma is the source of all love and devotion. It is the permanent substratum which bonds us with the ties of affection and mutual regard.

The Pure Mind is the same as Pure Atma as the beautiful sage of Dakshineswar, Ramakrishna, has said. So let us go deep into the attachment to Atma, the Essential Bliss, rather than that fearful no touchy skittish attitude of non attachment. Instead, let the mind and emotions become so deeply attached to Atma that all other sentiments and imaginations become lost in what was the former non conscious consciousness. Become like a mad person, mad for the beloved alone. It is Atma we are all attached to in this universal struggle. So end it for yourself and see that Atma is the thing, the living reality to which all things are joined, seized and staked (Gmc: Stakka: root word of attach).

Deep attachment to Atma is what true renunciation is, to voluntarily announce to oneself a disclaimer, disavowing and denying any reality to so called false things, feelings, ideas and selfish forms of ego identity. A renouncer becomes dead to the world mind, but alive to the living reality of Atma. If you think that renouncing is merely pushing away, then this pushing away is your thought, not the Atma. If you believe it is rejection you are mistaken. The path to Atma is full acceptance, absolute

234

attachment to the Atma in everyone and thing. Then your perceptual style of the world changes and no more doubt arises over the existence of the Atma. This is the proof or evidence of being awakened.

Atma is the Stake to which all things are bound by liberation. Because all things (all persons) are attached to Atma, for this reason, we are attached to the unbroken blissful non-divided experience, so felt in dreamless sleep where no objects appear to disturb the delight of pure mind within itself. Because of attachment to Atma we all find such profound meanings expressed in each symbol manifesting on the subjective screen of consciousness in the dream state. In each symbol the metaphor of the True Self is seized and yet often hidden while always in some way mirroring the Self. Again, we are all so attached to the bodies of the waking state for the same reason, the Atma is hidden therein and unaware we know this to be true. A man and woman love each other because of the Atma. Children and parents are attached to each other because of the Atma. Really, there is no attachment to the body, the senses and the mind, that is a temporary dream, for what we are attached to is realized to be nothing but Atma.

You may feel that you are attached to Atma, seizing or staking out Atma, but in reality it is Atma that is attached to you, seizing you, staking you out. To illustrate, a man who met Ramakrishna is quoted in this comment, "As I was leaving the place I heard him say: 'Goodness gracious! The Divine Mother has caught hold of him, like a tiger seizing a man.' At that time I was a young man, very stout, and always in ecstasy."

CAUSED BY ATMA

"That which is the Pure Atman (Atma, the same) is the Great Cause, the Cause of the cause. The gross, the subtle, the causal, and the Great Cause. The five elements are gross (waking consciousness). Mind, buddhi (intellect), and ego are subtle (dream consciousness). Prakriti, (one of the many names

235

of the Goddess, here as Dynamic Power) the Primal Energy, is the cause of all these. Brahman (the transcendent Infinite beyond male and female, mother and father or deity and deitess), Pure Atman, is the Cause of the cause." A most beautiful and eloquent summation given by Kali's most humble servant, Ramakrishna.

Atma is the cause of everything. Its negation or denial is the cause of all problems and trouble. Its affirmation and acceptance is the cause of all pleasurable paradise and blissful tremors. Atma is the reason, the sake and the case of everything, to which the meaning of cause is attached.

Yet Atma is causeless, since it is what it is. Still it is the motive of all. The Center. The Ground on which the other is built. Atma makes without making, the reasonless reason beyond mere reason, the result, the welfare and the ideal of all, since nothing would exist without the cause of Atma which is the Self, the Divine Subject within every desire, emotion, or theory. If you were not what you are, Atma, then how would anything else exist.

Within the paragon of turiya, Atma is the causeless primary cause without effect. It needs no cause to come into being and its only effect is itself as self existence pure and simple. In dreamless sleep (turiya sleep or sleep unconscious of turiya) a cause begins to stir or move. This may be the first effect in the cause and effect relationship, but in turiya sleep the cause and effect are so close together that one cannot actually distinguish a relationship. The second effect is the dream state. Here cause and effect have a relationship, to wit, the dreamer's consciousness and the objective effect appearing as dreams. For fun, one might think of this dream state as the electromagnetic infrared or ultraviolet effect which arises out of the cause of pure light. The third effect is the waking state where the cause and effect relationship is clearly seen in every surrounding. The dual paradox of this relationship is practically ubiquitous in all regard. Again, for fun, we may say this is the heat of energy as effect in regard to the sensitivity of the the senses in the waking field. The background cause of the waking effect is of course, the dream field. The background cause of the dream effect is that unconscious turiya sleep. The Causeless Atma supports all three former relationships. Former, because once the Causeless is realized, made real, made a part of you as you genuinely are, the relationship with the other three dimensions is changed at each level. In the serenity and peace of the soul (pure dreamless consciousness). In the radiant self reflecting waves of the mind (dream consciousness). And in the blood and nerves of the warm physical body (waking consciousness).

FULFILLED IN ATMA

Every being, each person is fulfilled in the Atma and filled by the Atma. It is the thing to which everything else is carried out. Atma is what brings to realization. Atma alone is the promise, the prophecy, the command, the duty performed, the requirement, the satisfaction, the meeting, the obligation, the end, the finish and the completion, what is executed, realized and achieved (as to fulfill).

The awakened ones in their wisdom have enlightened us and delighted us by sharing the insight that body consciousness is like a pillow case, not the Real Stuff inside. From this point of perception even the mind is but a pillow case and not the Real Thing. When we take leave of the body, when body consciousness drops off, what is remains, the Real Thing. The Real Stuff is Love. Love is an Emotion, which is a movement, a stirring, a feeling. The Reality of Love is felt as a feeling. Emotions are Mind Shapes. Mind Shapes are Emotions. The motion of feelings generate thoughts and thoughts generate the movement of feelings. It is a kind of circle where a tendency or habit, an instinct in feeling is created between the seemingly two functions, but really they are one in character and nature. Sublime Emotion is called Bhava. Bhava is the Key to Reality.

"Reason, mere intellectual knowledge, is like a man who can go only as far as the outer court of the house. But bhakti is like a woman who goes into the inner court." The mystic sage of

237

Kali's Dakshineswar gives profound insight into the Sublime Emotion. Bhakti (Love) and Bhava (Mood Depth) both come from the same root word, Bha, which means shine, beam, be resplendent, be brilliant, shine down, appear, illumine and to shine forth as to begin to grow or generate light, brightness, bliss, happiness and especially to show oneself, or to shine forth Our Self. Here it is very easy, most simple to see the secret of bhava. It is to show Our Self as Atma.

One may think there is no such thing as selfish love, for if it is self centered then it is something else, desire, passion or attachment. But really it is love. Unselfish love is a bhava which is innate in every soul but rarely clear to any soul. So most of us are left with a healthy spiritual selfish love for the delight of enlightenment. Love is a power never to be underestimated. An intense sublime emotion can even make you take leave of your pillow case. Ramakrishna tells of a twenty year old man who came to see him, "In my presence he used to experience such intense ecstasy that Hriday had to support him for fear he might fall to the ground and break his limbs... A few days later I learnt he had given up his body." One explanation is that of our nerve wiring. It is said that the Sublime Emotion may at times be compared to sending ten thousand electric volts through two twenty wiring.

Atma, in the paragon of the causeless turiya condition is bliss, yes of course, consciousness and existence too, "I am conscious. I exist," but blissfulness is more difficult to reach. Though it occurs spontaneously and without warning, as a peak experience, a sublime emotion in conjunction to some phenomena in the waking or dream states, a meeting or joining of some kind, a spiritually empowered dream, still, for me, sublime emotion is something I wish to generate at will. As it is said, we learn happiness, we learn to be happy, just as we learn any other feeling. M. asks Sri Ramakrishna, "But where is unbroken bliss in this world?" And what he said in reply, "Yes, where is it?" Sublime emotion is beyond definition. No human power can take you there. Yet one may generate the bhava of atma, consciously into experience, just as other emotions are

238

generated over the surface of pure self experience. Unbroken happiness is the genuine nature of the atma in the causeless turiya condition.

Atma, in the turiya sleep of dreamlessness is this non-dual blissful experience, mind consciousness there not being occupied by subject object relationship. A state of restful oneness, refreshing the sleeper momentarily freed of dreams. A blissful mass of unbroken happiness, not yet brought up to conscious awareness. This dreamless turiya sleep is as being blinded by the non-duality, by happiness. Bringing this sublime emotion up to conscious awareness is generating unbroken happiness.

Atma, in the free flowing cognitive feeling images of dream consciousness is still unbroken, as it were, still at oneness, as the case may be, the dreamer subject and the dreaming object are but one, like gold and its image. But distinguishment begins as the pure gold starts to take on sculpted forms, images and shapes. Mind shapes are emotions. Emotions of difference begin to arise. Dualism appears. Dream will, dream action and dream knowledge then appear to move into the realm of diversity. The characters of the dream stage appear as distinct from the dreamer consciousness. The sublime emotion of the undivided atma starts to get lost and then comes the world, the divine movie, the cosmic stage, the theatrical sport of apparently firm solid dualism.

Atma, in waking consciousness, within the expression of embodiment, further expresses this distinguishing dualism to the point of emotionally generating such tremendously differentiated states between cause and effect, subject and object, you and me, etc., that at moments the sublime emotion seems entirely lost. But it is not. The Oneness, the Sublime Non-Dualism, the Atma in Its Real State is Always Fulfilled, Always the Cause of Itself, Always Attached to Itself, Always Nourished by the Nutrient of Sublime Consciousness, Exquisite Sentiment and the Beauty of Its Own Natural Being. "By discriminating you will realize that what you call 'I' is really nothing but Atman." Sri Ramakrishna. From the Stone Age to the Space Age, all this stands true. "He

239

alone is clever who sees that God (the Real Stuff, Atma, the Goddess Kali) is real and all else is illusory. What need have I of other information?" That is what he said, of course, Ramakrishna.

Soaring Thoughts

A Reconveyance of Non-Dual Goddess Consciousness

"But who are you? It is the Divine Mother who has become all this. It is only as long as you do not know Her that you say, 'I', 'I'."

"Sometimes I say to myself in the Kali temple, 'O Mother, the mind is nothing but Yourself.' Therefore Pure Mind, Pure Buddhi, and Pure Atman are one and the same thing."

Sri Ramakrishna

"But where is refuge to be found? The omnipresent Atman which depends on nothing else to support It is the only Refuge. At first man does not find that. When discrimination and dispassion arise in the course of meditation and spiritual practices, he comes to know it. But in whatever way he may progress on the path of spirituality, everyone is unconsciously awakening Brahman within him. But the means may be different in different cases."

"The wave was nothing but water."

Swami Vivekananda

"Both the Lila and the Nitya belong to the same Reality. In one form It is the Absolute, and in another, the Lila. Even though the Lila is destroyed, the Nitya always exists. Water is water, whether it is still or in waves; it is the same water when the waves quiet down." Ramakrishna. Here 'water' is a metaphor for the Atman, the Authentic Spiritual Self. Nitya is the Unconditioned Eternal Existence Consciousness Bliss. While Lila is the Conditioned Relative Existence Consciousness

241

Bliss in play with itself. Lila meaning Play. The Atman, metaphorically expressed as 'Water', is Pure Existence, Ever Free Consciousness and Love, Bliss, Happiness and True Felicity in the Authentic Self.

"Once I fell into the clutches of a jnani, who made me listen to Vedanta for eleven months. But he couldn't altogether destroy the seed of bhakti in me. No matter where my mind wandered, it would come back to the Divine Mother. Whenever I sang of Her, Nangta would weep and say, 'Ah! What is this?' You see, he was such a great jnani and still he wept." Ramakrishna, who himself had numerous teachers, and yet only one, the Goddess Kali. Nangta (Totapuri) was one such teacher, a sage (jnani) with non dual wisdom (advaita). Still, though for a time in the clutches (to clench or grip) of such a one, he could not destroy the Loving Heart (bhakti) of Kali's blessed mystic. This is absolute beauty beyond dualism or non dualism.

"When reasoning stops, you attain the Knowledge of Brahman (Indescribable Infinite). Atman cannot be realized through this mind; Atman is realized through Atman alone. Pure Mind, Pure Buddhi (Intellect), Pure Atman - all these are one and the same." Certainly, Ramakrishna reveals the Atman beyond, transcending mind, but something wondrously ineffable happens as the pure mind or pure intellect reveals to itself or is infilled with the Atman. "That means, the real man is Pure Atman. It knows neither birth nor death; It does not age, nor does It die." Atman is Immutable, but It may be felt in the mutable as pure mind, pure structureless thought whose absolute unconditioned content is the Atman. "He is then Atmarama, satisfied in the Self." The illustration of a liberated soul is lucidly shown by Kali's most beloved soul.

The type of mind which craves further elucidation may benefit from a look at Maslow's sixteen definitions of Peak Experiences. Ramakrishna's entire life was continually at the epitome of such experiences and even more mystical and spiritual states. A person is very lucky to have one or two peak experiences during the course of life's wondrous unfoldment. "1 He feels more integrated than at other times. 2 He feels more able to fuse with the world. 3 He feels at the peak of his powers. 4 He has a sense of effortlessness and ease of functioning. 5 He feels himself the "responsible, active, creating center of his activities." 6 He is free of blocks, fears, inhibitions. 7 He is more spontaneous and natural than at other times. 8 He is more creative in the sense that what is in him flows out freely. 9 He is more intensely individual, himself, non-inter- changeable with anyone else. 10 He is more "here now," "free of the past and of the future." 11 He is "more a pure psyche and less a thing-of-the-world living under the laws of the world." 12 He feels non-needing, non-striving, and unmotivated in the sense of "having transcended needs and drives of the ordinary sort. He just is. Joy has been attained which means a temporary end to the striving for joy. In this respect he is "godlike." 13 Expression (as with the shaman and seer) tends to become "poetic, mythical and rhapsodic." 14 The state is a "completion-of-the-act," like a total catharsis or consummation, in contrast to states like only half-satisfied hunger. 15 There is a certain kind of playfulness, a "happy joy," a good humor transcending hostility of any kind. 16 "People during and after peak-experiences characteristically feel lucky, fortunate, graced. A not uncommon reaction is 'I don't deserve this.' Peaks are not planned or brought about by design. We are 'surprised by joy.'" (Abraham H. Maslow, from *Toward a Psychology of Being*.)

"The Divine Mother revealed to me in the Kali temple that it was She who had become everything. She showed me that everything was full of Consciousness." Ramakrishna. It is She who is the Indivisible Reality, Pure Existence, Infinite Consciousness and Loving Beautiful Bliss, the Rapture of Ecstasy, Serene, Calm, Content and Tranquil. Love, Happiness and Joy are the natural state of She, the Goddess. It is She who has become the Self in all beings. She is that Essence which shines in everyone as Consciousness, Existence and Bliss.

She is Self Experience. Only the memory of the fantasy of embodiment keeps one from Enjoying this Self Experience. As it is, She has become everything, so nothing is truly experienced but Her, the Self Reality. Even when one has cognised a waking

243

object or a dream thought or the tinge of darkness covering Pure Existence, (deep dreamless sleep) that cognition is nothing but Her Own Self, Pure Consciousness. The memory of forms or pure formlessness itself are but cognitions superimposed over the Is-ness of Her Consciousness Experience.

"Your Own Atma Is The Divine Mother."

Swami Aseshananda

Sahaja Sakti

Immediate Power in the Direct State
of the Goddess Purely Unfettered
by the Four Conditions of Consciousness

The Seventh Book of the Srimad Devi Bhagavatam is called the Devi Gita or the Song of the Goddess. The most refined spiritual potential is expressed there by the Goddess. She says, "Those kings and others as well were able to cut off the Tree of this World by the Axe of their Knowledge, simply because they were the devotees of the Para Sakti. So with all the care possible, the Lady of the Universe is to be worshiped and served. Men should avoid worshiping any other gods, as people avoid the husk to get to the grain inside. O King!"

It is a staggering thought to spiritually realize that any other gods, or gurus, or traditions, systems, books, people or beliefs are indeed but husk! The grain is that Para Sakti, the Higher Immediate Power of the Goddess. It is the Direct State of Her Knowledge which cuts away the tree of world consciousness, that is in brief, all that is contained in the four conditions of consciousness. The waking, dreaming, deep sleep and the pure self as the fourth are these, the tree of the world. The cosmic form of waking, the subtle form of dreaming, even the inner ruling form of deep sleep as origin and return or the idea of self as a conscious principle are once again just husk.

The idea of this conveyance of the Goddess is the direct state of experience which has no other connection to any limiting factor of consciousness. It is even beyond pure consciousness as this is referred to as turiyatita, meaning beyond even the fourth condition. She is that Self not defined by any. Pure truth without any idea, word, thought, mantra or prayer, spiritual visualization, guru instruction or anything. The boldest fearless stance in Truth without any support in consciousness except for Her Immediate Power. There is nothing whatsoever in the three states of world consciousness or beyond that, that cannot be given to the devotee of Para Sakti.

Ramakrishna confirms this, "She is formless and, again, She has forms. If you believe in the formless aspect, then meditate on Kali as that. If you meditate on any aspect of Her with firm conviction, She will let you know Her true nature." Whether the form of the world tree of cosmic manifestation or the formless condition of the turiya self attracts you, She being capable of being both, is indeed something beyond both! That is Her True Nature conveyed only in the Direct State of Her Immediate Power and in nothing else.

Adopting the most natural independent spirituality of exploration in the Great Delight is the best avenue to finding perfect satisfaction within the situation or disposition of each mood, emotion and attitude. The Great Delight instantly comes to you when you get rid of the conceptual difference and emotional separation from the Great Delight itself. Very simple. It is to be free of the maya of difference and psychic measurements on one's capacity to Love. The maya bija Hring, or the Goddess' formula for dispersing differentia and measurement is very simple and no mystery is involved here, no secret at all. H indicates the waking stage. R indicates the dream stage. I indicates the interior depth of dreamless sleep. NG represents the Pure Consciousness of Great Delight. But Hring is this immediate Oneness, not four, three or two conditions, really not even one. Those measurements are the differentia of maya. When you are instantly bestowed with the delightful sentiment of oneness the meaning of Hring comes clear and then nothing is left but the Great Delight. This is nothing but Love which knows no wonder. It is not a matter of esteem, approval or identity or anything like that. One simply becomes at peace with Love and that is the only spiritual arrival there is.

Sahaja is the Direct State of Her Sakti. It is the Immediate Power of Her as being filled to the infinite brim with the feeling awareness of nothing but Her as Saham. This Saham is She I am. Sa is She. Aham is I am. Then Ja is added to the meaning

246

as Thus Born. It is She alone that is born in You, your own Atma, as You, who are that Direct Felt Awareness which is ever present. The husk of a guru, the husk of a religion or the husk of any external thought system can never give this to you because you always have it. The grain is yours from the beginning. Ramakrishna again confirms the truth of this, "We go into the inner chamber only when She lets us pass through the door. Living outside, we see only outer objects, but not that Eternal Being, Existence - Knowledge - Bliss Absolute." Living outside one sees only the husk of the tree of world limiting consciousness and the direct state of your own experience of existence consciousness and bliss absolute is simply ignored by one's tautological preoccupation with the fantastical possibility of other answers that one dreams they might find in gurus, religions, incarnations or other people's systems.

That She is the supreme revealer, the One Light that removes and lifts the shadows from one's mind that is filled with the complicated knowledge of the tree of the world mind is again and again affirmed by Her blessed devotee Ramakrishna, "Everything is due to the Sakti of the Divine Mother." And, "You must do what She makes you do. A man attains Brahmajnana only when it is given to him by the Adyasakti, the Divine Mother." Of course, Brahmajnana is God Knowledge or absolute (nirvikalpa) consciousness, given by and only by Adyasakti, the most Primordial Power and by nothing else. This is within you and seen clearly when your connection with the tree is cut, when you let go of hope in the husk!

What other evidence do you need to prove to yourself that the truth of spiritual reality is your own direct state. A guru cannot give this to you nor can a guru even uncover this for you. You know it only when it is given to you by Adyasakti. This is the Immediate Power of your own Self. It is the divine axe of knowledge or the power of your own cognitive mind that takes you there. Nothing else. Not a religion or anything, not any outside belief system. This is the pure power of self consciousness beyond all conditions! It is explained in this Goddess Gita. She uncovers Truth with these excelling insights,

247

"The waking, dreaming and deep sleep states do not remain constant but the sense of "I" remains the same, whether in waking, dreaming or deep sleep state; its anomaly is never felt." Perfect! The Self, the True Reality of "I" is never an anomaly, never not even, never an irregularity, never not constant, never inconsistent, never a unique nor rare phenomena, never anything odd nor special! So how could you ever think or dream, imagine or believe that the "I" is not you, your own or that it is something that another might give you. The direct state is your own immediate innate born power. The Goddess wants you to be free, truly free, so She expresses these liberating divine dramatic spiritual insights in this manner.

Opinions exist in variety on what is this Sahaja state. Some are of the opinion in their feeling that Nirvikalpa Samadhi (absolute non dual bliss consciousness, completely free of all mind workings) is the highest. Another feels that Sahaja is simply Nirvikalpa turned outward. Someone else feels that one can go to Sahaja without the experience of Nirvikalpa. And yet others feel that Nirvikalpa is simply a matter of removing the cloud of unconsciousness in deep sleep. While others say that it is not that simple. Opinions exist with wide diversity. What is important is that one has for oneself a working reality, a living reality, an effective reality, regardless of the opinion of others.

The Goddess Gita gives us the uttermost peak of the pure conveyance of undistorted spiritual reality, "Never the Jivas or embodied souls feel "I am not"; but "I am", this feeling is deeply established in the soul as Love." It is by Her pure blissful intelligence that this is known. Love is the Immediate Power of the Direct State. Its only process and its highest result free of all distinctions, cognitions or imaginings which might consciously limit its feeling. Thoughts alone limit the power of Love. The Direct State of Love is only apparently confined by the ideas we attach to our sense of "I am", which is always present and never gone. In this feeling what need is there of anything else. We never feel "I am not", not even with the dispersion (death) of the body-mind state, which is phenomenally and only momentarily existing in these four conditions. We always feel "I am" and

248

that is the primary and essential conveyance, the Immediate Power which is purely, simply and nothing but Love. As this highest of spiritually reality is deeply established in everyone, then what need is there of any other feeling.

For it is one's Immediate Feeling that matters in spiritual life. How can there be waiting for the arrival of some great awakener or a life that is engulfed in the memory of someone who was a spiritual giver, who has come and is now gone? Of course, there is connection that transcends the existence or absence of the physical body, if this were not so, then what would our definition of spiritual life be? Never is not the "I", which is the purest Direct essence of Love. The Mountain of Reality! If you find yourself waiting for an Incarnation to come and save you, then you might have to wait five hundred years. And when that Incarnation comes, whether directly descended or but a partial manifestation, what that descending power or manifestation means is the emanation of Sakti as this truth is stated by even the great souls and by formidable spiritual texts.

If it is Sakti then why wait when She is ever present? The few souls who are supposedly the direct descent of Her saving power are of such a caliber that they produce world wide changes in the spirituality of humanity. It is Her Power working in the human drama. If this is so then why would one submit one's spiritual progress to someone smaller than that, say a little mountain guru, a spiritual intellect or some potently awakened person? To me this makes no sense, except for the case of limited availability. But look, that Sakti is here now everywhere and it is only one's limited mental, emotional, and spiritual definition of Her which causes the idea of limited availability. She is the One who creates the Giants of God and the Hurricanes of Spirituality, who are still but drops of water compared to the endless ocean of Sakti!

The classic objection to the self path of independent spirituality is that one will become deluded by one's own ego. All right, this is often true as one observes the phenomena of spiritual people and teachers in history and the present day. Yet, in my own self work, in my own emergence on my own path if I do delude myself, I prefer this. I would rather be deluded by my own ego delusions than the ego delusions of a guru. They are my own and not that of another. It is my self work not theirs. It is my personal enlightenment, it is my ignorance. It is my arrogance and my humility. I would rather struggle in my own context than in the displaced identity of another. For many of these gurus and teachers have extraordinary superstitions, profoundly obsessive ideas over purity and impurity, and traditional cultural fanaticism which is not one's own innate belief context. They often feel that it is their spiritual job, their profession of holiness, to shred other people's egos to the ground. When the pure un-deluded truth is that it is Kali, the Goddess, who as the power of life itself in the terrible aspect of Time, really humbles us and also exalts us in Her Love. This is Direct Sakti. So why then would one choose to waste away life in open acceptance of contradictory impositions placed on oneself by others?

The Christ and the Buddha spoke of their own experiences on the self path. They did their own self work for the most part, not other's experiences, not imitations, but original and profoundly immediate personal reality. And yet even in all their sincerity and love, their ego personalities have deluded vast potions of humanity because people try to imitate them and not be in their own reality. So what then would you say of the effects on others by little and lesser enlightened people and their claims to greatness.

I heard one individual say that they learned gratitude after meeting their spiritual teacher in India. Fine, we all need catalytic events which open our hearts. Indeed. But there was something very odd in this comment of praising his teacher. Then I realized what it was. By praising his teacher he was glorifying his own ego and it importance. Look, I have a spiritual teacher, aren't I good, great and wonderful. This is a tremendous problem in many, many dimensions of spirituality and it is seldom recognized. Yet in the self path of independent spirituality one cannot falsely assume the greatness of another onto oneself, nor can one project one's faults onto a cause due to another's actions. One is standing there in one's own truth no matter what it is and this is the best of training grounds for genuine spirituality.

So often what a person needs is to have someone believe in them, not for them to believe in someone else. This seems so true to me, for a friend of mine was going through the spiritual stress of a spiritual change in their life. I wanted to talk about this with them, but all I could say was, "I want you to know that I believe in You." The result was a flood of happiness on that person's face. I was deeply surprised by honest direct love, both in them and in me. How Sakti works in such small ways while She churns the galaxies at the same time is extraordinarily astonishing. As God is Love and never an anomaly, evenly existing everywhere, then why do we think we need someone to shovel God into our mouths? Friendship with Sakti is what brings spiritual happiness into life. Prior to the arrival of different gurus, Ramakrishna experienced everything in the Kali temple, just he and the Goddess, there was no other intermediary present. It was pure experience. Absolute Sakti! He had Pure Consciousness (nirvikalpa) and he saw that same Pure Consciousness in the altar, the floor, the door and so forth (sahaja). And who knows what else he experienced with the Goddess. This is a most excelling example of Immediate Power in the Direct State.

Actually, Swami Vivekananda as a Poet expresses the experience of the Direct State of Pure Sakti in his own life. Of course his poem of 1898, Kali The Mother, expresses this Immediate Power directly in his life, even beyond the influence of Ramakrishna. Yet other statements of his give us insight into his true spiritual feelings. "She can show Herself to us in any form at any moment." (Quoted from Inspired Talks). Simply, Her capacity to reveal spiritual wisdom and love is not limited by the presence or absence of an incarnation. "May She, the Primal Guide, my shelter be!" (Quoted from A Hymn To The Divine Mother). As there is no other primary refuge but Her, in our wanderings within the four conditions. Again, the Poet Vivekananda dramatically conveys the nature of Samadhi (Pure

251

Unfettered Realization) in his potent poetic illustration, The Hymn of Samadhi. "In the void of mind involute, there floats The fleeting universe, rises and floats, Sinks again, ceaseless, in the current "I". Slowly, slowly, the shadow-multitude Entered the primal womb, and flowed ceaseless, The only current, the "I am", "I am". The Immediate Power of the Direct State is gotten there in the 'primal womb' of the Goddess, Sakti. The Poet reveals himself in his unfettered realization as a pure lover of Her, the Primal Guide, the Goddess, the 'shelter' most excellent.

Even so, the four phases of diksha, which is most often translated as initiation, but in truthful fact really means to consecrate oneself, come directly from Her, the Power of Her Primal Womb Consciousness if you like, or even from one's own self power. The real meaning of the two forms of conveyance as Agama and Nigama are here revealed without hesitation. Agama means coming up or arrival out from one's own self. Nigama is coming down, coming in or coming into. This is the guidance of the Goddess. The best guidance there is which comes directly from the Nitya, an expression that Ramakrishna so often used to designate the Highest Reality. The pure meaning of Nitya is absolutely beautiful; it means inward, innate, one's own, constant, perpetual, eternal, always abiding, essential, in other words, as it has already been expressed, it is never an anomaly.

So the four phases of self consecration (diksha) or of rendering venerable as is its true meaning, are the stages of anava, sakti, sambhava and anugraha. Here, this anava means; not yet blown upon, as in the va of nirvana, not yet extinguished, not yet perceived, not yet obtained. This anava is when one uses and applies one's own physical, vital, emotional, mental and intellectual being to perform ritual, study, devotion and spiritual practices by the power and energy of one's self effort in the waking condition of consciousness. It would certainly appear that in this phase one has 'not yet consecrated oneself' in the self identity beyond the condition of waking consciousness. But the ever present powerful pull of the Goddess' Favor is there, always.

252

In the sakti stage, the word sakti here meaning; self skill, capacity, and ability, the power forms of of sacred words as mantras and concentration on the chosen ishta, which is the inward meditation on a personal form of the Deity or Deitess, are used to clean up or clear out the cognitive state of the subtle body pertaining to the dream state condition of consciousness. There is also self effort here, but the pull of the Goddess is strong as the free nature of dream consciousness is not conditioned by the confinements of the waking state. One may ask, but we receive mantras from teachers, yes it may be so, but there are those who have received mantras directly in the dream state without human intervention. Again, it is none other than Sakti Herself that empowers a mantra, not a human being, how could that ever be. Another view is that it is said only an incarnation, which is a pure manifestation of Sakti, can cause or bring about spontaneous awakenment of the kundalini sakti. She Herself in the shape She chooses does this. No other can do this, no human force, no human influence.

The sambhava phase is next. It is two words, sama and bhava. Bhava means mood, sentiment, emotion, cognition and feeling. Sama is as in the word samadhi; being calm, quiet or tranquil. Also; appeased, satisfied, ceased, still, abated and allayed, as is all sorrow is allayed by Her, Sakti. Sambhava also means 'with bhava' or the 'same bhava', but what is that bhava, mood, or feeling that is conveyed? It is non dualism. Complete oneness with Her. The direct form of sambhava as the absolute sameness of non dual consciousness is the result of Her unfettered favor coming down or coming directly out of Turiya Sakti (The Pure Power of the Fourth Condition) into the causal body in the deep sleep condition of consciousness, thereby awakening that potential within the causal body to the Primary Cause of all life. Love, the current of "I", the Non Dual Self. Turiya Sakti which has been hidden in the condition of deep sleep rises up and out by Her Own Immediate Power to awaken that once unconscious state to the conscious awareness of pure unfettered non dualism. The Love of Her Unfettered favor

253

floods what once was thought to be the dualism of otherness. Separation is gone!

Finally, the pure stage is that of anugraha; direct favor, direct giving, direct satisfaction and most commonly used is the expression, direct grace. Graha is grace, favor. Anu is; for, toward, with regard to, according to, on account of. So, on account of the pure direct unfettered favor of the Goddess we come to the Loving Truth, the Direct State, which is not some special favor to the select few, but is ever present always to one and all. Only the mind blocks this awakening! Her Continuous Favor is Her Primal Guidance to the Primary Self, the Final Veneration of True Reality. This conveyance is not concerned with any form, shape or movement within the three conditions, not even the fourth state. It is purely unfettered turiyatita. Beyond all four conditions. The Direct State!

The delusive idea that these initiations, conveyances and conditions might come from any outside element, principle or personality but Her, is, from the strictly non dual point of view, pure madness, or simply entanglement in the relative mind confined by dependent dualistic excuses. The path of Mother, Shyama, the Dark One, the absolutely shadowless non dual, which reflects no otherness, Pure Kali, though tender and loving as She is, is not for the faint of heart nor the timid of soul. As the completely awakened Poet Vivekananda expresses without any dependent fetter whatsoever in his powerful poetry entitled And Let Shyama Dance There. "None seek Elokeshi whose form is Death. The dreadful frightful sword, reeking with blood, They take from Her hand, and put a lute instead! Thou dreaded Kali, the All destroyer, Thou alone art true; Thy shadow's shadow Is indeed the pleasant Vanamali." You see Vanamali is the youthful Krishna garlanded with wild flowers and naturally most people prefer the comforting solace of a dependent contact with a beautifully bedecked god. That is fine. But few are they who seek Elokeshi, She of wild, free flowing, untied hair, the Mother Kali, ever untouched by any dualism! Who would seek Her unfettered by any kind of connection. No sacred words. No teacher. No deity. No deitess. No inner practice. No outer

254

contact. No doctrine. No tradition. No support but Her. Who would seek Her as Self in the Pure Power of Her Favor in the Direct State! Realizing that here, even the incarnations of the highest level, like those of Krishna and so forth, are in truth but Her 'shadow's shadow'.

In the poem, Kali The Mother, the Poet expresses the pure Direct State of Her Immediate Power alone. He stands on no other ground. He is completely accepting of his own self as it is, and that all will be taken by Time. We stand alone with Love, Kali, Sakti, the Goddess. We stand with our own misery, fearlessly alone, as well as with our joys and exaltations. The need of burying our fears in others is not there, we hug the form of Death as it is Mother Herself. Pure Sakti! And so death has no ground with us! To such a one who stands true the Mother most certainly makes Herself known. "And every shaking step Destroys a world for e'er. Thou "Time", the All Destroyer! Come, O Mother, come! Who dares misery love, And hug the form of Death, Dance in Destruction's dance, To him the Mother comes."

WISDOM, SELF BALANCE AND
THE GREAT SENTIMENT: Vijnana Bhava:
A Particle of Bhavamukha

IGNORANCE, KNOWLEDGE AND PERFECT WISDOM
(Ajnana, Jnana and Vijnana)

Ignorance is not knowing or ignoring Reality. Knowledge is knowing what Reality is. Perfect Wisdom is something more. In Perfect Wisdom no secrets remain. Nothing is hidden. The relative-eternal paradox is accepted with both hands raised, whether the eyes are open or closed, as it is, Never Dual. Fearless self searching reveals the Atman as True Genuine Self. Your own innate intrinsic self born, yet never born to dualism, Spiritual Dignity. Atman is seen in everyone and to be everything, so strictly speaking, there remains no waking or dreaming identities, all beings are in dreamless cognition which must recognize and does continually cognise itself to the full consciousness of Turiya (the fourth, the Never Dual Atman).

This is the natural state of equilibrium (samadhi). "In samadhi the ego totally disappears; then what is remains." Ramakrishna. One sees God when all upadhis disappear and reasoning stops. Then a man becomes speechless and goes into samadhi." Perhaps what Ramakrishna means is that when reasoning, which manifests the diversity of waking and dreaming cognition stops, the adjunctive contents of the psyche (upadhis) disappear (as in dreamless sleep), then one become speechless with wonder, because the Self is the very secret of all life.

257

FEAR, LOVE AND THE GREAT SENTIMENT

The jnani is like a little monkey clinging to its mother out of fear. The vijnani has no fear, like the little kitten having complete trust in its mother. Fear comes out of the need and desire to control the pieces of the game. The desire to control others, people, events, everything, even one's own death, are sources of fear. The Vijnani has given his/her fear to that Loving Trust in the Mother, saying and knowing with all the heart that She is the Controller, not the little embodied 'I'. This brings on the Great Sentiment which knows without doubt ever arising again, that Mother does Everything. Hers is the Game of Lila. Hers is the Eternal Nitya. That is why the Vijnani remains unconcerned like a child, a madman, a ghost or an inert thing. The Vijnani talks to and enjoys God, the Mother: as a Child, a Friend, a Master or the Beloved. Such is their special endowment of full knowledge seeing the universe itself not just as a manifestation of God, but God Himself. With this, how can there be fear?

"A mere jnani trembles with fear. He is like an amateur satrancha-player. He is anxious to move his pieces somehow to the safety zone, where they won't be overtaken by his opponent. But a vijnani isn't afraid of anything. He has realized God: Personal and Impersonal. He has talked with God. He has enjoyed the Bliss of God." Again, Ramakrishna's voice is so clear. The jnani, still having the illusion of control, out of fear, wants to get to the safety zone. The vijnani sees God in all, so how can there be fear?

In fearlessness arises the Great Sentiment, the most mature feeling of cherishing God in everyone and thing. By giving the power of attorney or self control over to God, there comes the knowing feeling that God is ever present and doing everything. The vijnani is absolutely aware that even the slightest most subtle thought arises as the Mother Wills. It is this way with all things, great or small.

PHENOMENA, NOUMENON, AND SELF BALANCE

Phenomena is said to be that which is Accessible. Noumenon is the Inaccessible. Self Balance is the visceral experience of God. Not just theoretical intellectual knowledge, "mere reason", as Ramakrishna calls it. Self balance is to Know (Chit) and Love (Ananda) the very Being (Sat), the Existence of God as the absolute conviction of Reality.

Ramakrishna explains how this happens. "One ultimately discovers God by trying to know who this 'I' is. Is this 'I' the flesh, the bones, the blood, or the marrow? Is it the mind or the buddhi? Analyzing thus, you realize at last that you are none of these. This is called the process of 'Neti, Neti', 'Not this, not this'. One can neither comprehend nor touch the Atman. It is without qualities or attributes." Again, Ramakrishna directs the mind toward Reality. "By discriminating you will realize that what you call 'I' is really nothing but Atman."

How beautiful, but who may cross the barrier, making this often Inaccessible Formless Impersonal Atman Self an Accessible Personal Form of Reality? That is the question. A few ideas on the accessibility of the Inaccessible are the Functions, Senses, Psyche, Consciousness, Emotion, Realization. One may use the gross, subtle and causal fields of waking, dreaming and dreamless consciousness as aids, instruments and tools of realization. As Ramakrishna demonstrates frequently, that it is God Himself that has become the twenty four cosmic principles.

In the waking field, consciousness withdraws from the five functions of grasping, walking, regeneration, excretion and talking identified with the gross physical flesh and bone. Traces of this of course follow into the dream field. The same senses of waking life pull inward, gather together (pratyahara) in dream consciousness. Sound, form, touch, taste and smell reflect themselves internally while dream consciousness experiences its own desires. The four functions of the psyche are there. Traditionally these are intellect, mind, ego and memory. One may for simplicity's sake call these contents of the psyche: the

259

Mirror of Consciousness (Intellect), the Intake Out Take Mechanism (Mind), the Making of Memories or the formation and retaining of imprints and Melting Boundaries, that is melting of the conditioned fixation of egotistical identification with the body and psyche, to this Consciousness without boundary. This naturally happens in dreamless sleep. The functions of the psyche's contents cease and what is there is Consciousness, yet covered by the returning veil of dualistic memory making. Its nature is forgotten in the waking and dreaming states. The common response on dreamless sleep is, "I was happy." This shows that the Happiness aspect and the Being aspect of Existence, Consciousness and Bliss (Atman"s Nature) were there, felt and experienced. What was missing from that consciousness was the awakened memory of Consciousness Never Dual, brought back from its pure state (Turiya) into dreamless cognition, dreaming mind and waking awareness. It would seem this is the Emotion of God Consciousness ever present in all living beings and that this Mood leads to Realization.

EXISTENCE, PURE EXISTENCE AND SELF EXISTENCE

Ramakrishna tells us, "The Pure Atman alone is our real nature." Realizing this has been called jada or nirvikalpa samadhi when no traces of 'I' consciousness remain. Only what is remains. The separating line of ego sentiment goes and what is, Is That which Remains. It cannot be told. This is to become the Sugar, as Ramakrishna says. Here, no contents of the psyche remain. Jada is (motionless, immovable, inanimate, rigid, cold, cool) without disposition, predisposition, tendency or potential, without imprint or impression. No visionary conditions are there. No celestial or after death contents. The mind has melted into and has become the Sugar. How one interprets the experience later, depends on the return reflex to the contents of the psyche. Jada is dead to all duality. In Jada Samadhi dual

260

consciousness has cooled down to its Immovable State. Thus there can be no dream, no vision, no waking condition that can interpret it in any form. The contents of consciousness are dead, as it were, inert, not stirring, absolutely still, serene, unruffled by any paradigm in contrast, physical, psychic or spiritual. Simply Pure Experience. It is not non-existence, but the peak and pinnacle of Pure Existence. Self.

When traces of 'I' consciousness remain it has been called chetana or savikalpa samadhi. Here, contents, tendencies, and dramatics of the psyche do remain. This is to taste the Sugar. There is a taster, as it were, and there is Sugar. There is a waker, a dreamer, a sleeper and there is an enjoyment of the fourth (turiya), Pure Consciousness. Chetana is God Consciousness in the form of the conscious individual. It has stirring, motion, mobility and movability, unlike jada, which does not. There is communion or relationship. One enjoys God through dualism. The play of mind is still within a cycle of the one and the two. That dualism ceases when the play of mind (vikalpa) ceases. That is nirvikalpa.

Ramakrishna has said that the Pure Mind is the same as the Pure Atman. Unmana samadhi may be this. Unmana is the sudden recognition of Atman. The 'Pure Mind' suddenly gets it, that what it is Is Atman. Unmana is that which transcends mind (manas), but it is the primal mind, the primal energy itself which suddenly transcends and gets It! Unmana is inseparable, non different from what we have referred to as Pure Consciousness. It is the Never Dual supramental primal energy of Consciousness which is Consciousness. It is the Primal Power, measureless and beyond time. In unmana samadhi this measureless primal consciousness suddenly gathers together in recognizable Unity with Consciousness. It is the Movement of Consciousness recognizing its own manifestation as Consciousness. An amazing spiritual avenue. As Unmani (the Feminine) it is Mother Herself as Primal Energy, Kali, suddenly knowing, recognizing Primordial Self, again Mother Herself. It is when Mahamaya (the Great Mother) suddenly reveals this. That is Unmana samadhi. The Measureless Primordial Never Dual

261

recognition of Itself as Itself in that Absolute Non Differentiation of Primal Energy and Primordial Consciousness. Brahman and Kali are One. The blessed sage of Dakshineswar, "Instantly one attains liberation."

NITYA MUKHA AND LILA BHAVA

The Eternal Face (Nitya Mukha) or the Mood of the Relative (Lila Bhava). The Mood of the Eternal (Nitya Bhava) or the Face of the Relative (Lila Mukha). Either way, the Spiritual State of Ramakrishna, at the command of Kali, challenges our ideas of Reality. What is called Bhavamukha cannot, it seems, be comprehended by the mortal (or perhaps even the immortal) mind. But the challenge itself asks us to cross the Threshold, the Meeting Ground known as this 'bhavamukha'. Such as it is, a Spiritual Point of God Consciousness which cannot be explained by nirvikalpa or savikalpa samadhi. Even though savikalpa applies to this Lila Consciousness and nirvikalpa is the never dual Nitya Consciousness, what the Consciousness of Bhavamukha is, has never been fully explained, except through the glimpses we have of Ramakrishna's experiences with Mother Kali.

Truthfully, Bhavamukha must be Her Own Spiritual State, even more so, Mother Kali's Own Nature. So Bhavamukha provides us with a Window to Her Wonder, yet it does not define Her Effulgent Ineffable Being. What can one say? The Realm of Ideas, Moods, Emotions all seen continuously arising spontaneously like waves out of the Consciousness of God, but removed of the dualism of an idea of God. It is the True Self thus gone from the shores of differentiation, Never Dual, yet standing as Inconceivable Difference (Lila) in Non Difference (Nitya). Universally, Bhavamukha is what makes the Inaccessible, Accessible. In Bhavamukha the Inconceivable (that which cannot be taken in) is Conceivable (that which may be fully taken in). Bhavamukha is this Grace, the Appearance of such Beauty, its very meaning, the Mother's nature Herself.

262

NETI NETI, BRAHMAJNANA, ITI ITI

"Then he accepts what he rejected before." Ramakrishna.

It is like three folds within the absolutely Serene, Tranquil and Unclouded Consciousness. Negation, Recognition and Affirmation. Neti, Neti is the not this, not this removal of the Lila (Relative) idea, sweeping away the identity with waking, dreaming and consciousness sleeping. Then that Brahmajnana is the Recognition of God Knowledge or God Consciousness as the Nitya (Eternal). Lastly there is the return to affirming the Lila in the Nitya and Nitya in Lila. This is Iti, Iti, This, This. Everything is not just charged or changed with God Consciousness, everything is God Consciousness.

Speaking to some theatrical actors, Ramakrishna stated, "Among you actors, those who take only the roles of women acquire the nature of a woman; by thinking of woman your ways and thoughts become womanly. Just so, by thinking day and night of God one acquires the nature of God." This is the same process of the cognitive phenomena of realization. It seems realization as an unfolding process is a phenomena, as it were, for what is Real needs no unfolding of the clouds (negation, recognition and affirmation) to Know Its Own Unclouded Nature. As Atman is always Atman, Never Dual, the phenomenal acquiring is something we think we must do and of course in a sense we must do it by being open to the Appearance of Beauty (Grace) in our lives.

Everything is realized to be not just an image of God, but the concentrated form of God. This is vijnana, the special Knowledge of which Ramakrishna speaks. The vijnani, one who has it, is a bhakta, a Lover of God. "But a bhakta also attains the Knowledge of Oneness; he sees that nothing exists but God." "Since one cannot easily get rid of the ego, a bhakta does not explain away the states of waking, dream, and deep sleep. He accepts all the states." Ramakrishna.

263

WISDOM, SELF BALANCE AND THE GREAT SENTIMENT

The thorn of ignorance is removed with the thorn of knowledge and then both thorns are thrown away. No thorns, because it is the Never Dual. One climbs by the stairs (the Lila) to the roof (the Nitya), but at last, they are both seen as the same substance. With this, Wisdom, Self Balance and the Great Sentiment comes. The two (dual) thorns of ignorance and knowledge are thrown away in Perfect Wisdom, the Never Dual. The Self was always Balanced in the threshold of the relative and the eternal, never being perplexed by the paradox of the two appearances, as wave and ocean are the Never Dual Substance of Water (Consciousness). Realized, the Great Sentiment, the Truth which is Love, is Free.

SUBLIME EMOTION AND THE FACE OF THE GODDESS

"'As is a man's feeling of love, so is his gain'." The nature of Sublime Emotion (Bhava) is poetically explained in this quotation by Ramakrishna. The 'feeling of love' parallels one's experience. What could this be, seeing the actual Face (Mukha) of the Goddess Kali, as Ramakrishna did so often if not continuously. This must be the supreme Great Sentiment, the Sublime Mood of Facing the Goddess as She Is. The Lila facing the Nitya, the Nitya facing the Lila, the imagined line of differentiation melting away as the Sublime Bhava arises to Face the Mother Kali. The Consciousness of the Eternal Inconceivable (That which is not capable of being imagined) and the Relative Conceivable (That which is capable of being imagined) crosses the boundary of the never dual unborn and the thus born, as it is, being something which no one can describe. Description failing, it is alas, Sublime Emotion in the Face of the Goddess.

264

THE DAY AND NIGHT OF KALI
(The Lila, the Nitya and Vijnana)

"Oh, what a state of mind I passed through! When I first had that experience, I could not perceive the coming and going of day or night." Ramakrishna. The Sameness of Vijnana is there. Kali's Day, as the Lila, the Sport of dualism. Kali's Night, as the Nitya, the Serene Absolute Unperturbed Eternal Stillness of non dualism. It is the Same. Kali's day and Kali's night are ever the same to Her as Vijnana. Just as day and night on the planet are the same from the point of view in the surrounding space.

He who has knowledge also has ignorance. An amazing idea presented by Ramakrishna. The dualism, the paradox, the divided reflex of the presence of knowledge indicates the presence of ignorance. So full enlightenment is something more than the jnani's (knower's) distinct understanding that God is there. Vijnana answers. Yes, God is there and God is here and something more. The Vijnani comes back to the relative dramatics, full to the brim with Wisdom, Self Balance and the Great Sentiment of Love, living the most mature stage of spirituality.

The Vijnani has realized the complete significance of vidyamaya (as the Mother's play of knowledge) and avidyamaya (the Mother's play of ignorance, not knowledge). Ramakrishna smiles because he is fearless in the Vijnani's excellent Love of Mother Kali. "Please tell me who you are. God alone has become all this - maya, the universe, living beings, and the twenty four cosmic principles. 'As the snake I bite, and as the charmer I cure.' It is God Himself who has become both vidya and avidya. He remains deluded by the maya of avidya, ignorance. Again, with the help of the guru, He is cured by the maya of vidya, Knowledge."

Who are 'you', tell me? The question is there that charges the mind with the greatest inquiry. Who is the Self? Then we

265

are told of a snake, delusion, and a charmer, a guru, but vidyamaya is anything, scriptures, songs of God's Glories, meditation, etc., anything that tends the mind in the sattvic direction toward the God Principle. Avidya is the opposite direction. But who is it that is deluded and who is cured. God is the answer. This is the Vijnani's 'Something More', a special knowledge that goes into Perfect Wisdom understanding what ignorance is and what knowledge is and 'who' is playing the play of both.

Still, Vijnana is but a particle of Bhavamukha. The partial comprehension of a thing may not be the Thing Itself. What Bhavamukha is still eludes us and there is no illustration of its full meaning. The Goddess Kali told Ramakrishna at least three times, "Remain in Bhavamukha." Certainly it is to say, stay conscious and don't completely disappear in Nirvikalpa Samadhi (absolute ultimate advaitic consciousness). Vijnana is a particle, where Bhavamukha is the full extent of All Substance, in a manner of speaking. It is the Empathic Unconditional Loving Consciousness of God, the Goddess, the Most Infinite Indescribable. It is said to be a spiritual condition only experienced by Isvarakotis, who are the God souls who have knotted themselves in the matrix of the relative for the sake of others. The extent of Empathy, where one feels, as they are, understands and experiences the experiences of all beings, the universe, everything. One idea is that Bhavamukha is God, the Goddess, Facing His Own Face (Mukha), Himself as Himself in the Mood (Bhava) of Himself. Still this eludes one who is but a jivakoti, an individual soul who is knotted in the relative karmic play. But as the microcosm reflects the macrocosm, the humble particle may reflect the mood of Her, Kali, who eludes all definitions.

TURIYA BHAVA
In The Mood Of The Fourth State

"I am what I was before," Sri Ramakrishna so eloquently explains what this mood of the fourth state may be. It is the knowing feeling that what I am is that Existence Absolute, Consciousness Unbounded and Bliss free of all dualistic emotional responses. A kind of absolute simplicity of being.

Here, maya is not an enemy, though it is said that maya is all that one sees, hears, thinks and feels. Truth is charmed by maya and maya is charmed by Truth. The Fourth Mood is non dual, so, what was formerly experienced as dualism in the three states of consciousness is now seen as nothing but what is called the Fourth. This is what I was before, what we all were before the charming appearance of the waking state, the dreaming state and the state of dreamless consciousness playfully covered us with its delightful and wondrously overwhelming distraction, to wit, maya, which now ultimately is seen as Kali, the Goddess that this sweet Ramakrishna loved without end.

As there is ultimately no one, no other but Kali, a living reality to the enlightened and a mere principle of non duality for the yet to be enlightened, all things and people are challenged or changed as by being Her metaphor or myth either as literal living enlightened expression or as some symbol which challenges the consciousness of the figuring mind to explore itself. This is the bold fearless view of non dualism. It is to not think through the lens of our own psychology and connections, limited spiritual perceptions and philosophical relations, but to learn to think and see and feel through the mood of something greater than ourselves. It is a kind of emotional training that learns the mood of a greater dynamic, a learning of giving in or giving over to that greater dynamic, rather than trying hopelessly to force everything to fit into the smaller dynamic of one's own limited consciousness.

When this letting go happens, one sees a much larger universe as it is playing within the vast universal consciousness itself. It is the identity with this little thought of I and mine that is the block, the load to be removed. Then the door opens and anything is possible, anything can be done, on and on.

What potentials are there hidden before us? When Ramakrishna stated to Vivekananda that he was Rama and that he was Krishna, but not in the Vedantic sense of oneness, what he meant was that he was actually those people in former lives. An amazing proclamation certainly, but who are we to judge. He stated that Rakhal had been with Krishna, that Saradananda had been with Christ, that Vivekananda was pulled down from the realm of the Absolute. Ramakrishna knew all the faces of those companions in his life before he physically met them. Why should the possibility of other lives be so amazing? The blessed mystic of Dakshineswar, this Ramakrishna, even stated that he himself would be reborn two hundred years after his death. Such now simple wonders are all possible because Kali is the Queen of India, the Goddess of the Fertile Crescent, living now at Dakshineswar as much as She was when Her blessed mystic, Her embodiment then lived at Dakshineswar. And what She is cannot very well be described in simple terms, as it is with any great fountain of spirituality.

The 'I' has no state! The Real 'I'. Realization with thought forms does not describe it, nor does realization without thought forms convey it to those of us who still doubt Its spiritual actuality. Ramakrishna's unique spiritual condition of Bhavamukha (the mood of facing universal consciousness as undivided non dual reality) may or may not be the nature of the 'I', yet certainly not so if it is yet thought of as a conceptual state. The 'I' has no state.

There is the idea that when the quality of the impression of not knowing (ajnana vritti), voidness, nothingness, emptiness, is removed by Grace (Kali) from the state of deep dreamless sleep (free of dualism's mind play), it automatically becomes nirvikalpa samadhi. This is the state of absolute destruction of all dualism, the highest divine consciousness wherein all paradigms of the ego's mind play cease. There, can one even say there is the thought of I am? Who knows? But what this nirvikalpa samadhi shows us is that the Reality of who we are is always there, always here as the suchness of the real 'I'. Though in Truth, like Bhavamukha, this nirvikalpa, may in fact be a state which is meant only for a few special souls. For it is a state, not itself the Bliss of What We Are. Though many claim to have had the 'experience', it is in fact very rare. Vivekananda had the experience only a few times in his life through the touch of Ramakrishna, in actuality and spiritually speaking. It must be remembered that nirvikalpa is a 'door', but does it need to be opened for all of us, as We Are What We Are, regardless if the 'door' is opened or if it is closed. All Being, indicated by names and forms, is but Consciousness and this Consciousness as 'experience' in nirvikalpa is seen by Consciousness to Be but only Brahman (the Absolute). In this, Kali as this Absolute stands first, everything else is secondary.

Here is a thought, "As I am Bliss what need have I for samadhi." It is the automatic grace, the divine, the spiritual conveyance of Kali that matters. One Sunday I was visiting with my very dear spiritual friend Swami Bhaskarananda. I asked, "What is the difference between Bliss and Happiness?" He responded with uncommon force, "Bliss Is What You Are! The Atman (Real 'I') is what you are. The Atman is Bliss." My thoughtful conceptions were shattered as Swami explained that Bliss is silence, stillness, the cessation of all dualities, while happiness pertains to attaining an object of desire, Bliss is untouched by this. In a simple spontaneous way another question cognised within my thought, "If no one can know Brahman since it is Nirguna (without quality) and there is no dualistic other there, no second thing, thought, ego, then Who experiences nirvikalpa?" Swami's innate spiritual strength showed forth, "Nirvikalpa shows you what you are!" He explained that it is the door of samadhi, you are not the door, the door is a state, it is Bliss that is what you are. It is in fact only a door to what 'I' am, the Real You, the Atman as Brahman Consciousness.

Then Swami began to describe Sri Ramakrishna's experience with the Goddess Kali in a way of which I had never heard him speak. He said that in Reality the Goddess Kali, the Blissful Mother is this Chaitanya, Consciousness itself. I had never heard him speak with so much enthusiasm, energy, focus, excitement, feeling and love. He said Ramakrishna would see the Goddess Kali even in a prostitute, even in a cat. That the Goddess Kali was his chosen divine ideal form, so he was most accustomed to Her appearance, not shocked by Her four arms and Her lolling tongue. But who may say how She really looked to him, this Blissful Chaitanya, neither dual nor non dual.

Early on Ramakrishna had been given the Kali mantra by one named Kenaram Bhattacharya, who may in fact have also given the Kali mantra to that great poet Kamalakanta so it seems. But Ramakrishna had already 'experienced' Brahman Consciousness, so, as it were, spiritual practices and teachers were not for his sake, they were done by him in order to show us something. Incarnate souls, the eternally perfect and past masters of meditation have no need of such things. They are like pumpkins that produce fruit first and the flowers of practice second.

My friend described the bhavas (spiritual moods), the samadhis (realizations) and the ecstatic feelings of Sri Ramakrishna. Swami's imitation of the personality of Ramakrishna was wonderful. I had never seen anything like it. He elucidated that happiness (shukam) is more akin to ecstasy, where Bliss (ananda) is more so what nirvikalpa shows us. He told how Ramakrishna experienced automatic samadhi by merely seeing seven cranes cross in front of a dark rain cloud. How when he acted the dramatic role of Shiva, again, samadhi. And in the Kali temple, at the end of spiritual passion, he took the sword of the Goddess, demanding of Her to Show Herself to him or else he would remove his life from this world. She did of course, in a samadhi or bhava which cannot be labeled as that of form or formless.

And when Totapuri came as a symbol of verification for us that the 'experience ' was real in Ramakrishna, he said to him, "I

want to teach you advaita vedanta (total non dual knowledge)."
Then Ramakrishna replied, "I must ask my Mother." When he
did the Goddess replied to him, "That is why I brought him
here." Totapuri laughed at this for he was an advaitin who
believed the whole world is a delusion created out of one's own
mind thought and thus he had the associated arrogance of this
attitude. But Totapuri learned later that Kali is Real.

To get at the center of it, it may seem, that even the
emphasis on seeking or desiring samadhi is a kind of spiritual
obstruction in the sense that one has set up in the mind that this
thing must be done in order to be what you are. It is a kind of
meditation problem, the seeking of samadhi, as a state of intense
concentration may yet be a mind loop as it were, where one is
seeking Bliss as a shukam, a pleasure or desired objective, when
really Bliss is what you are as Atman and this is the silence of
every dualism or the stillness of all mind movement and which
of course it may be seen that the desire for samadhi is a mind
movement. What a paradox.

But from one system of advaita, ajata vada, nothing is ever
born, not even as a part of Consciousness. The view is that there
is no single thing ever coming out of Consciousness, which
leaves you with the high conclusion that there is only
Consciousness as Real Existence, the 'I'. If this is so, where
does samadhi come in, for samadhi is something created in the
mind, a state. As the Ashtavakra Samhita states, "Let even Hara,
Hari, or the lotus born Brahma be your instructor, but unless you
forget all, you cannot be established in the Self." (Translation
by Swami Nityaswarupananda). Meaning, unless you forget all
created dualism, how can you know the mood of the non dual.
Can dualism exist in non dualism?

If we think of ego as object and Self as Subject, let us
consider three ideas. Mixed non dualism, Dualism, and Pure
Non Dualism. At the level of mixed non dualism there is a
confusion of ego and Self. The real 'I' is mistaken for the ego
identity and visa versa. At the level of dualism one is engaged
in the process of deconstruction of the separating ego cover from
the Genuine 'I'. This is the negation system of "not this, not

271

this" where all sense of otherness is removed to be left with only What is Real. That is an ego object, this is an ego object and so forth until the Self as Real Subject is all that is left. Finally, in pure non dualism one comes to the entirely subjective sense or mood of the True Self where all ego thought has melted, like Ramakrishna's example of the salt doll who goes to the Ocean to measure its depth, melts in the water and then there is no one to talk about what happened. In real non dualism there is no ego no more, no sense of a second thing or principle, nor any sense of an other. Brahman is One, no one, no ego knows it, for knowing requires a tri-plate (three holdings or three holders), three forms, to wit, a knower, a process of knowing and a thing to be known. Brahman is Just Knowledge that does not know any otherness as separate from What It Is. This is the Mood of Turiya.

Nirvikalpa samadhi simply shows you what you are, this nirvikalpa samadhi is not what you are, In Reality, that is Brahman Consciousness. I am A-karana Mani Ananda, the Causeless Jewel of Happiness (Bliss), this is uncovered by the Goddess Kali, no other for me. Yet advaita, pure non dualism spontaneously and simultaneously eliminates any thoughts or dualistic conceptions about world, about totality or even thoughts about god, goddess, principle, truth or infinity. One becomes the salt doll that has melted and is no longer a salt doll, so one cannot say a thing. It would seem that perhaps one may only be left with this mood of non dualism.

There are so many varieties of spiritual approach and experience. Souls like Ramana Maharshi and Ammachi (Amritanandamayi) have made strong and real examples that direct, automatic and spontaneous nirvikalpa samadhi does indeed happen in reality and without the need of intervention from a human intermediary. Or one may wish to become a spiritual person at the early age of nine years or even younger. Or one may have the good luck of meeting an avadhuta, one who has absolutely and totally no body consciousness, only Atman Consciousness. So much so that their body may be buried in the mud of a river bank for days and this has no meaning nor any discomfort to them as Self Absolute so strongly identified. One may get a teaching or not, one may be a follower or not, one may know a Vivekananda or not, one may know a Totapuri or not.

The question is how to get into this 'mood' and there are two schools of thought on the subject. One is that teaching from an instructor is needed. The other is that the pure mind is the teacher (not unlike the direct primordial contact realization in the Tibetan Dzog Chen method of attaining non dualism). Yet, in the end, whichever course one has taken, it is Inscrutable Grace which enlightens. The fact is that all and every single teacher is time limited, the Ancient of ancients, OM by name (the divine principle not limited by time) is the only real Teacher or Light which comes by the spontaneous Grace of the Goddess, God, or the Infinite Spirit. This Light is the Light that illumines the darkness (dualism). Pertaining to the principle of the Ishta (chosen personal ideal divine form), this is the Light that manifests one's own spiritual illumination at the right time. So it seems that all efforts arising or demonstrated by the great souls are there so we will not just sit and daydream.

But in the final and last analysis it is the Abundance of Effortless Grace that brings the Self Light out of darkness. For as it is stated in the Upanishads, "The Self reveals the Self to Whom the Self Chooses." This is pure, direct and simple. This is the essence of Love as the spontaneous and automatic expression of the Great Reality. Ramakrishna is one such perfect example of this. If I may quote from 'Life of Sri Ramakrishna', "It is to faith such as this that the miracles in the spiritual history of the world, in all countries are due. Without a teacher, guide or helper, with no great knowledge of the scriptures and even without passing through the prescribed forms of asceticism, Sri Ramakrishna carried everything before him by this adamantine faith and sincere yearning to realize God."

It is Love which makes all this possible. It is Love which is the path and the goal, the flower and the fruit. It is Love which is this 'mood', an oasis of the heart which brings the intellect out of the dry desert of itself. It is the feeling in the eyes of a child

273

and the feeling in the eyes of a sage. It is the melting Bliss which never wanes and the one and only thing that crosses the threshold between what is the material and spiritual world, the one thing allowed to pass through the door of life and death, the inextinguishable eternal feeling which never diminishes. Love is the one feeling, the mood alone which comprehends non dualism.

Recently I had a waking dream, it was not such an amazing dream and may have been simply some thoughts that a person has as consciousness is moving from one state to the other. I lay there in my bed thinking so strongly of the Goddess Kali there in the sacred place of Dakshineswar where Ramakrishna lived. It was as if for me, the Goddess was most alive and I could feel Her powerful presence extending across the Pacific Ocean all the way to here in Seattle and around this Puget Sound and even so, further beyond into everything. I felt Her there in the sweet moonlight pouring gently through the window, in my eyes and in my very being. At that moment there was simple, yet tremendous Love and clear insight. It was a mood that lasted for a while, full of peace and serenity. Blessed Be the Goddess...

Her Footprints Through Time

The Old Goddess Tradition in the Far East

It is my personal feeling that Tantra and Taoism, being uniquely similar in some ways, are in fact Remnants of an Older Religion. This is the Goddess Religion before the world formulated the historical concepts which now are considered as reality. Some scholars will claim that the Indus Valley script which for so long has still remained undeciphered is actually Sanskrit. I disagree, feeling that it is more likely to be a language of Hyperborean times, a language of the Goddess, a Tantric language like that of the mystic syllables or Bija Mantras.

The fact is true by archeological evidence that the Goddess was worshiped from Siberia to Old Europe down into Egypt, across the Fertile Crescent to the Far East, before India was named India, for Mohenjo Daro and Harrapa still remain something of an enigma, like Stonehenge, Bimini and the Sphinx. One cannot credit everything to the arrival of the soma drinking Vedic warriors, though their influence changed the course of history. Nor can it ever be surely and confidently stated that the Tantra emerged out of the Atharva Veda, as some scholars have proposed, who wish to make everything patriarchal. Indeed, there are some beautiful prayers for the fulfillment of conjugal love, marriage and sacred sexuality contained in this Veda, but one cannot attribute the origin of the vast ocean of Tantra to a source of a few love spells.

Still, much is lost and many good questions have remained unanswered. And one cannot account how much written spiritual history has been destroyed by the self righteous. For example in the Celtic world, where Kali was worshiped as Kele, to wit, I read that around one hundred and seventy five sacred Celtic manuscripts were burned by the so called saint Patrick. (see Celtic Magic by D.J. Conway) How much else has been lost?

275

Even so, in India one finds some strange prejudices there. Take Hanuman, the powerful dear friend of Rama and Sita. He is said to be a monkey, but he could speak and write Sanskrit. What does it mean? Perhaps Hanuman was actually a Yeti or a Neanderthal or even a Cro Magnon. Amazing, he was an intelligent, tall, powerful, endearing creature. It is possible, and more so than that he was a monkey. But this reference could actually be a metaphor for a deep Indo-European prejudice toward the peaceful Australasian Dravidian people who lived in this part of the world before the Kurgan warriors arrived. In this way many truths have been suppressed.

Nevertheless we find in Hanuman the Three Positions of the Vedantic Doctrine, even way back then in this time of mythic reality. In Hanuman the doctrines of Madhava's Dualism, Ramanuja's Qualified Non Dualism and Shankara's Absolute Non Dualism are uniquely expressed in his wise and noble character. Even though only very few people of the time regarded Rama as a Deity, insightful Hanuman was one of these and the three positions are expressed when he states that when he is in the mood of dualism, Rama is master and he is servant and when he is in the mood of qualified non dualism, Rama is the Whole and he is a part of the Whole, and in the mood of absolute non dualism Hanuman boldly states with profound realization of Absolute Oneness that I Am You and You Are Me. Very good, he swings from one position to another with perfect ease, versatile in each of the three moods or three perceptual styles in regards toward the Real Principle of the Great Self.

Truth can never be lost even if every book on Earth is burned to ash. Still, Truth is there and will always be rediscovered. The Old Wisdom will always re-emerge. This can never be permanently suppressed. Nature itself will speak the Truth if necessary as in the case of the Chinese or Mongolian Sage-King who was contemplating the Mystery of the Mother Tao, when a turtle emerged from the river with illustrations of the fundamental principles of the Book of Changes on her shell. The sage king saw on the back of the turtle, the eight trigrams circling around the two united forces of the masculine and feminine dualism in the non dual oneness of the Mother Tao, for She is the Mother of ten thousand things. That is, Oneness is the Mother of all this astounding diversity of the Universe that you see before your eyes.

So much hidden truth is woven through spiritual history, where the Goddess is the Principle of True Reality. As it was with the Buddha who actually expressed that the Nirvanic Reality is in fact the Tatha Gata Garbha, which means That Non Dual Reality Thus Gone To The Other Shore Which Is The Womb Of Suchness. The Womb Of Suchness is a Feminine Principle, definitely Tantric in it's sentiment and it is well known that the alert Buddha taught his own version of Tantra, known as Cinacara. He is famous for it.

In this light one may ask, what of Jesus, Issas, Yeshua, who brought us this beautiful doctrine of the Holy Spirit. What is this Holy Spirit, the Holy Ghost. She is the Gnosis Sophia, the Holy Wisdom Spirit. In fact and reality, this is most probably the Sakti of the Tatha Gata Garbha, that is the Feminine Spiritual Power-Force of the Womb of Suchness. Is this madness or Reality? One cannot deny the Greatness of the Goddess. Even in very ancient India you will find that two of the very greatest Non Dualists, Ashtavakra and Janaka, were actually directly taught this Doctrine by a materialization or manifestation of the Divine Wisdom Force in the form of a Bhairavi, which is a Noble Bold Tantric Woman or Fierce Female Goddess. Also, the famous Dattatreya, another great Non Dualist, teaches Parasurama, an incarnate Deity of the same category as Prince Rama, that it is the Supreme Transcendental Goddess Alone and Ultimate, Who is pervading the Three States, Waking, Dreaming and Deep Sleep, in the Tripura Rahasya.

This Tripura Rahasya (The Wondrous Mystery of the Three Cities) speaks of all this very nicely. Here one finds the Thirty Six Principles of Tantra described in beautiful detail. These are the Five Elements, the Five Forces, the Ten Instruments of Movement and Perception, and the Four Parts of the Conscious

Mind. These are the classic 'twenty four cosmic principles' which that dearest sage, Ramakrishna, so often mentioned. The twenty fifth principle is the 'Soul'. This soul appears to be bound by the Five Limitations in the cognitive sense that our soul is restricted by Limited Power, Limited Knowledge, Limited Desire, Limited Space and Limited Time. These five forces of Maya make the Partless appear to have parts or limits, the Independent appear dependent, that which has no wants appear to have wants, the all knowing appear with little knowing and the all powerful appear as a limited capacity to act or do in action or agency.

The Cognition of these Limitations is due to Maya Sakti, the cognitive force of illusion or the hallucination of these limitations over the true nature of our Soul. The veil of this cognitive distortion is lifted by the Grace Abundance of Her Wisdom Force (Vidya Sakti). Even the principle idea of a God as Inner Controller (Isvara) is a creative force of the Goddess. As is the 34th principle wherein the Goddess is Seen and Heard as Ever Pervasive through the Entire Fabric of Space Time (Sadasakti, Always Sakti, or Sadasiva, Always Siva). She is the One Force behind it all, the Loving Superior Force, Pure Sakti, The 35th principle, the Witness of it all and this leads us to the 36th principle of Absolute Undivided Unbroken Consciousness, Her Husband Siva! But you must come to the reduction of everything, all these principles, toward Truth and Reality. Then one asks, "Who is the Creatrix of All This?" The Answer is The Goddess Of The Self. But this process can go on infinitely, reducing and reducing back and back again and again. So that is why She is praised as the Infinite It-Self! And, that is why even Siva is said to be but a white, lifeless corpse without Her!

Furthermore, in the Vidya Gita, (Wisdom Song) of the Tripura Rahasya there is a story when all the known sages and deities where confounded over the nature of Final Reality and who is the best knower of It. So the Goddess Herself appears as a Disembodied Voice essentially and explains to these fools what Reality Is. So, Her Divine Majesty, Transcendental Consciousness pervading the Three States of life, the Three

278

Cities, manifested in the Expanse of Pure Consciousness and with Great Kindness, the Goddess of Ultimate Knowledge, lovingly explains Truth clearly to them.

"My concrete Form is the Eternal Couple, the Supreme Lord and the Supreme Lady... Always in Undivided Union, ever existing as Eternal Consciousness pervading the Three Phenomenal Cities of Waking, Dreaming and Sleep. I am beyond 'dual and non dual'. When the mind has completely merged in Undifferentiated Peace it is called Nirvikalpa Samadhi, after 'waking up' from It, the person is overpowered by the memory of the Experience of the One Undivided Infinite Pure Self and knows 'I Am That', as opposed to the smaller former I-thought. This is the Supreme Knowledge, the Vijnana, the Recognition of Self, Pratyabhijnana! There is no remedy to the confusion of life other than the worship of the Goddess of Self. He who abides in Me as the 'I' is the Best of the Wise...."

After Her Kindest Expression of Loving Wisdom, they all praise Her. "She goes by the name of Emancipation, Liberation and Independence. She is Sva-Tantra, the Independent Expansive Self of the Goddess! She is seen by the Clear Investigation into the Undivided Self of all, otherwise She goes by the name of Bondage. She Is the One Consciousness Threading the Three States of being, but She is untainted, unbroken and unrestricted by them. She is the Mystic Word-Sound and the Significance of Hring!" (H=Waking, R=Dream, I=Sleep, Ng=Her Self.)

A similar presentation is given in the Chandi, which holds one of the most profound and great primal memories of the Goddess within it verses, but here instead of a council of gods and sages calling for the Power of the Great Goddess for answering their question about Ultimate Knowledge, they gather themselves together in order to call on Her Greatness to protect them from a demon who has vanquished them, making them helpless. The demon is none other than a metaphor for the Ego. The world of the gods has been conquered by this Ego and only the power of the Goddess can help them. This is a great lesson.

279

The Chandi or the Devi Mahatmyam is the The Text of the Wondrous Essence (Great Self) of the Goddess, found in the Markendeya Purana. The Great Battle described therein is a symbolical metaphor for the Internal Battle with the Ego. Only this Perennial Primal Force of the Blessed Goddess can conquer the principle of the ego. The ego then manifests during the course of the battle, as a buffalo, a lion, a hero with a sword, an elephant and finally, as before, the Dear Goddess slays the ego, as a buffalo, once again. Of course, these various transformations of the ego principle in the spiritual battle are there to illustrate the numerous tricky forms that ego may assume in order to bind Consciousness to what might keep you back from the Original State.

At one point in the fight, the Ego wishes to marry the Goddess and have conjugal relations with Her. Of course She refuses. The importance of this episode has great psycho-sexual significance regarding the libido aspect of the ego principle, a long subject in itself. Suffice it to say, that this is somehow there for the sake of illustrating the sexual-spiritual dichotomy. For everything in this story has great symbolism.

The psychological insight is given that the universal process is, as it were, a materialization of the cosmic dream of the Goddess. At the end of the battle, She of course has literally killed everyone of the ego demons either in Her Form of Durga or Kali, for they are two faces of the One Goddess. Once the Ego has died, the world cosmos is restored to the Great Harmony of Self Understanding. But before this wondrous clarification occurs in the internal or perhaps historical consciousness, the Goddess vanquishes by death, the many transformations of the Ego.

The story starts out where a saddened exiled king meets a merchant and the two travel together as friends. They meet a wise man who tells them this story of the Goddess which restores their joy in Self Realization. The Goddess slays Madhu and Kaitabha who represents the psyche's deception and the tendencies of ego to miss the mark by mistaken conceptions. She slays Mahisa who is a metaphor for our fearful clinging to the security of the phenomenal material plane.   She slays Chanda and Munda who are symbols of egotistical arrogance and mean minded intelligence. The Goddess Chandika Durga Kali then kills the chief Raktavija, who is the symbol of the seed of self centered egotistical desires for the ego's gratification and glorification of it's foolish idea of limited self identity. Then the Goddess slays Sumbha and Nisumbha, who are symbolical embodiments of the pairs of duality which perplex consciousness away from the Central Reality. Different sets of these ego-demons, as it were, come in pairs to illustrate various confusing dichotomies, the Ego's identity with gross and subtle, light and dark, good and not good, waking and dreaming, the currents of vital force moving in the solar-lunar nerve complex, and the vastly numerous other psychosomatic conceptions of the limited self idea. So after the Great Goddess has blanked out, wiped out all these restricted ego attitudes, the Universe is filled with Joy and all the gods and sages praise Her and sing songs about how truly great She really is and how helpless they would be without Her.

Again, one will find that the Goddess is extolled as the Supreme Principle, even in the Upanishads, the Vedantic Conclusions.   Yet the true aim of the Vedanta is that of Brahman, the Infinite, which is ultimately neither or both, masculine and feminine. Nevertheless, in the Kena Upanishad, one day the Gods decide to have a contest of sorts to find out which of them is the greatest of all. Again, this is the Ego, but this time it is the Ego of the Gods that comes up. So the Goddess Uma appears saying to the first god, that if you are so great then burn this little piece of straw. He cannot do it. A second god appears and She says if you are so great then blow this little straw away in your wind. He cannot. Then the god of intelligence enters the scene and the Divine Woman disappears before him in order to crush his pride of intellect. But out of Her Sweet Compassion, She latter reappears and then teaches him the mystery of the Adorable Spirit of the Infinite Brahman. In this manner the Gods come to Realize that the Power of the Goddess is greater than any of their powers, and that She is the

Supreme Force and the Supreme Reality. A simple and beautiful little story, don't you agree.

Let us consider some of the various wonderments of divine symbols associated with the Goddess of the Self. Lalita and Kali, in turn appear with different faces so to speak, but it is the same stuff behind both. On one hand Lalita is a Beautiful Tender Charming and Gracious Goddess, the Playful Mother Goddess of the Universe. She sits sweetly and delicately posed on Her Great Yantra (the Cosmic Chakric Diagram of the Entire Universe). She is beautiful, Her face is Beautiful. The symbols that She holds are the Bow, the Five Arrows, the Gourd and the Noose. These illustrate the Theater of Her Playful Sport. The Innately Free Consciousness of the Individual Soul is Shot by Her Bow into the realm of the Five Senses which are the Five Arrows representing the five fold divisions of Elements, Forces and Instruments of Movement and Perception in the Waking Dreaming Phenomena. By this, all these become limited in their cognition of the Real Principle where She keeps them and collects them in Her Gourd (the Universe itself). The Noose represents Her Grace by which consciousness is once again Released into Independent Freedom of Self, the Noose from which we cannot escape. And why would we want to? Who does not wish for Freedom? Blessed Be the Goddess.

Kali's Symbols represent the same Principle, though a little more dramatic. She waves at us with two hands gesturing "Fear Nothing" and "I will Grant you Freedom in Me." Her other two hands hold a Skull (the Head of Limited ego-consciousness) and Her Sword which is Deathless Real Consciousness or Nirvikalpa Samadhi (Undifferentiated Peace) as one might prefer. Though symbols may vary, the same stuff of meaning and spiritual import is there.

It is of most excellent help to understanding the Character and the Essence of the Great Goddess by meditating on Her Ten personalities or Faces in the from of the Maha Vidyas, the Great Wisdoms. Kali is first and foremost here in this magnificent Feminine Paradigm. She is Absolute Deathless Consciousness, Bliss and Being, the Supreme Infinite Principle of Brahman It-

282

Self. The beautiful Symbol on Kali's Forehead signifies the Eternal (Nitya), the Relative (Lila) and the Threshold Borderline (Bhavamukha), or Pure Liminal Thought between, as Ramakrishna has often profoundly stated, "They belong to the same stuff." That is the 'relative and the absolute' are one substance and that is Kali, as Butter and Buttermilk are intrinsically without difference (advaita).

She is the first great knowledge, the sweet mystery of birth and death resolved into the wisdom of non dualism. She is all forms of time and transcendent of those forms of time. She is the mystery of the kama kala (desire and death) dualism within non dual consciousness. She is the manifestation of the divine couple Kameswari (Sakti) and Kameswara (Siva) in sacred spiritual embrace expressing the dispersion of the duality of duality and non duality. Mother Kali, the Blissful Mother grants us every desire, gives us liberation, self emergence, freedom, self liberty and bestows independence upon us. Shri Kali Ma is the innermost essence of the Aum mantra, one of Her hidden and secret names. She is Durga, Chandika, Sakti, Gauri, Mahakali, Shri Lalita Ambika, and Maha Sivani Kundalini, who by this power creates and destroys embodiments, the Divine Creatrix to which we all crave to return where there is no more death in the original non dual unbroken consciousness of Her Pure Being.

As a matter of scholarly interest it may be a valuable notation to consider the origin of the Kali archetype, as all ten of these archetypes have tremendous psychological and spiritual import. Some have thought that Kali was perhaps originally an anceint warrioress, an actual woman who defended her culture from the invading patriarchal aggressors who sought to destroy that culture which existed in the anceint land now called India. The Sonthals, a hill tribe people of India still retain this belief. Also the epic of the Chandi describes such a battle with warlike patriarchs as an actual event. A very primal memory of how Goddess culture was crushed out, as it was in other lands, is expressed here. I suppose that it is matter of opinion or of personal feeling, as to whether or not archetypes arise out of the memory of actual human personalities, or purely from the depth of unconscious spiritual dimensions. But they do come from somewhere and live in our archetypal mind as influences effecting us through the sweep of time.

Tara, is Ava-tara, the Personality of the Goddess who manifests as the Ten Classic Avataras; Rama, Krishna, Buddha and so forth. Other systems of belief mention twenty four avataras who visit Earth and if you step into other traditions you find even more. It is She who has become them, even though they may have assumed masculine bodies. Why then, historically, for the last six or seven thousand years do we find only masculine incarnations, prophets, etc. The essential list of these being; Dattatreya, Parasurama, Rama, Krishna, Buddha, Mahavira, Christ, Moses, Mohammed, Zarathushtra, Shankara, Chaitanya, etc. Two reasons are obvious, history is much older than six or seven thousand years and this information is generally suppressed as in the case of cave paintings at Mohenjo Daro dating back forty thousand years. National Geographic would not publish photos of these paintings as it would topple Bible mentality. (see Dancing Shadows by Aoumiel) Also, it has been the obvious business of patriarchy to oppress and repress all things feminine. For example, it appears to any intelligent person that Mira Bai and Chaitanya had the same identical experiences in regard to the spiritual love experience embodied in Krishna, but she, Mira is regarded only as a poet, and Chaitanya as an incarnation.

Avatara means 'Descended Mother', so essentially these beings as are all beings, are nothing but Her. One may get great insight here, into the real meaning of avatara or She who is the savioress (Tara) who descends (Ava). She is the principle of Divine Power and of Loving Grace shared by one and all, existing everywhere, for everyone, all the time. Later, this power became associated with individual personalities as incarnations of the Principle of the Mother's Divine Grace, but Mother became left out of these historical personalities and those distorted historical recordings cognised this as an exclusively masculine phenomena. It would appear that much of primal Tantric Goddess wisdom was ripped off in just this way.

284

Bhuvaneswari is the Mother of the Universe. She is the Beautiful World Mother, caring and compassionate, pure tenderness and sheer kindness itself. One cannot hardly comprehend the depth and the nature of Her Love. This is Her Feeling that embraces the Entire Universe and all fourteen worlds, seven of light and seven of dark, the so called blessed and the so called wicked. She is the blessed Sovereign Queen, the Maker and the Mover of every individual, atom, star, both hidden and obvious. She is Jagad Ambika, the One Cosmic Mother.

Tripura Sundari is the Beautiful Maiden Goddess of the Three States. She is utter Beauty, none is more precious than Her, within all the Three States of Consciousness throughout the Combined Universe. She charms one and all with Her Attractiveness; gods, men, women, everyone is mesmerized by Her Loveliness and Lovingness. All indeed bend their heads, even the Buddha and the Christ must bend their sublime heads, to Her as the peak of creation, the Joy and Rapture of this most Beautiful Maiden. She is Tripura Shodhashi, Beauty Itself, the Maiden Goddess of the Sacred Trinity: Maiden, Mother, Crone. Through the pure power of beauty She rules the three states, the three cities (Tripura) of consciousness. These revolve on the axis of Her wonder and the happiness She causes us to feel. She is sometimes portrayed as being sixteen years of age, the pinnacle of finest form expressing the ultimate Divine Mother as the magnetic attraction of the Wisdom Goddesses.

Tripura Bhairavi is the Noble, Fearless, and Fierce Goddess who can shake the Three States of the Universe to its core. And She does so in order to awaken souls from the sleep of the Three States. Once this is done, they awaken in the Core Self, the Turiya, the Fourth State Beyond and yet pervading the other Three States. She boldly and fiercely Awakens us to the Cognition of our own Independent Self Conviction. By shaking the world with Her Thunder, She arouses the sleeping spiritual power of Kundalini, causing us to wonder where we are in this life and what becomes of us eventually. She forces the three states of consciousness; waking, dreaming and deep sleep to shake with wonder so we will awaken from the dream sleep of dualistic life. She presses us to wake up from the negation, distortion or mere reflection upon Her with the pure power of Non Dual Energy, to wit, the Kundalini. She is Dakshinamurti, the Supreme Initiatrix who reveals the full moon of non dual consciousness by the cognitive lightning thunder of Her divine sentiment which awakens us from the dualistic delusion that we are beings who are limited by the waking, dreaming and deep sleep conditions as well as the covering of consciousness over Turiya. The symbol of this is in the three and a half coils of the sleeping serpent dragon of Kundalini commonly described.

Chinnamasta is the Goddess as the Force that 'cuts off the head of duality.' For it is this dichotomy of dualism that holds us from the consciousness of the Great Oneness in which all things abide. She is somewhat frightening because the familiar antinomies of the dualistic realm are something we do not readily or gladly wish to surrender. Consciousness becomes accustomed to the comfort of duality, even though it is often unpleasant in its cycle of extreme opposites. This crone aspect of the Goddess gives the secret of independent Self Wisdom, but She strikes terror in those who still wish to cling to exterior sexual pleasures and the material comforting protection of phenomenal wealth. The spiritual task of Chinnamasta is to cut away the mental impression of intellectualization which blocks the encounter with pure and direct spiritual experience. Her instruction is don't think, don't analyze, don't imagine, don't calculate, then all dualistic mental impressions of paradoxical dichotomy dissolve at the sixth yogic center, the command center of the brain and pure experience is encountered.

She is assisted in Her intense task by two other goddesses who stand over the lovers, Kama and Rati, reminding them that death is ever present as the dualistic counterpart of sexual love. Kama (Desire) is Cupid or Eros. Rati (Pleasure) is his attractive consort. They embody the most passionate dichotomy of masculine and feminine in living loving embrace, yet Chinnamasta takes them beyond the dualism of two selves, the most painful aspect of emotion between lovers who feel

286

separated. She then reveals Self Reality, Emergence and Liberty as absolute perfect faith or trust, undistinguished by any dualism among all things manifest.

Dhumavati is the Goddess as Crone, the Old Wise Woman. She scares some, but makes us realize the natural passage of Time. Her Wisdom is Conclusive and as She is a Widow alone in Her Self, she forces us to realize that all these phenomenal relationships will eventually fade and float away with Time. Some see Her as an Old Hag and this frightens them. Weak men through fear, see Her as angry, ugly, distorted, scary, bitchy, and wrinkled. But She is really the blessed grandmother figure who cherishes us all as Her children, for She knows life's wisdom through experience and will teach us this very same wisdom. She is the Smoke Beholder observing the cremation fires and embracing in Her heart the intense sorrows of the widow and widower. We all pass through these sorrows, these sad secrets of life in the void of the soul. But She is there guiding, as She is Jyestha, the Oldest Shakti, the most anceint Crone.

Bagla Mukhi is the Beautiful Face of the Goddess who turns all sadness to face Happiness, all tragedy to face Comedy, all selfishness to face Empathy, all dependence to face Independence, all clinging to face Freedom, all insecurity to face Self Security and so forth. The Face (Mukhi) and the Beautiful Power (Bagla) of this Wisdom Goddess is that Divine Grace of She who turns all apparent negativity into Positive Cognitive Joy and Experience. After his long immersion in the absolute non duality of nirvikalpa samadhi, the Goddess Kali spoke to the old man, Sri Ramakrishna Paramahansa and told him, "Remain in Bhavamukha." Now, one may draw ancient connections with Bagla Mukhi and the new, liberal and fresh spiritual concept of the condition of Bhavamukha. Is it not the Beautiful Powerful Face of the Goddess turned outward from the absolute non dualism of nirvikalpa? This is the highest spiritual step, the final and most mature spiritual condition. The beauty and power of Bagla Mukhi makes the most eloquent person appear to be mute.

Matangi is the Goddess of the Supreme Great Intelligence. She knows everything spiritual and secular. Her intense

Intelligence comprehends the absolute eternal and the play of the cosmic relative. Without the Force of Her Great Intelligence nothing can be known. She is indwelling spontaneous knowledge which bridles the entire universe. She is Shyama, the Dark One, dark as the depth of water, dark as the depth of space, comprehensive of all with Her totally inclusive emerald green depth. She is Candali and Saraswati. She is Mati, the Mother Intellect which attracts all by the utter absolute power of knowledge over all this relative and playfully dramatic universe. She is the advisor to Lalita Ambika, the Supreme Wisdom Goddess Mother. She is Raja Rajeshwari, the supreme goddess queen and She is Siddeswari Sivani, the profound spiritual receptacle of all power and utter bliss, as Siddhi is total accomplishment and Sivani is the feminine word form of absolute peace of mind in samadhi.

Kamala is the Goddess of Wealth and Fortune and Abundance. She is the Mother Goddess who bestows material and spiritual nourishment over the whole world. She is enigmatic to us in that Her abundance seems to appear partially here and there. This is a puzzle, that only She knows of the reasons behind it all. Abundance and it's absence must come here and there for reasons of the soul's evolution we pray. Or perhaps it is a human responsibility to be developed as humanity itself grows more universal. Kamala is Lakshimi sitting on Her pink lotus upon the celestial waters. She is Shri, spiritual radiance and human excellence which is true wealth, the potential of which dwells within everyone. She is the utter divine wealth permeating all the galaxies within this universe as the principle of never ending, never exhausted abundance.

These ten fantastic personalities of the One Goddess are also thought to be the spiritual powers that manifest as the ten traditional avataras. One can gain much by contemplating Her various faces. A greater understanding will come, as these images of The Goddess have tremendous archetypal meaning embodied within them. Archetypes which are within every person that need to be contacted, as it were, for spiritual health to come to the surface. Primal and ancient Tantra realized long ago that it is the denial of the spiritual forms in the psyche that create imbalance. Less often do people deny the primal forms of beauty. It is in the denial of the fear invoking images that psychic anxiety is generated in the mind. Total acceptance of all forms is where psychic health and balance begins.

The serious student of the Goddess will find that She is the Supreme Principle extolled throughout the Tantras. "Thou whose toe-ring bells make sweet melody as Thou moveth... Whose girdle bells sweetly tinkle... Who abidest in the Mountain of Gold.... Who art like a Moonbeam on the mountain of Gold... Who art gladdened by the recitation of the Mantra Kling... Who Art the Kama Bija (Kling)." This is from the poem Adya Kali, the Primordial Goddess, translated by Sir John Woodroffe. We owe a great debt of gratitude to Mr. and Mrs. Sir John Woodroffe who together translated collections of sacred hymns and songs to the Great Goddess in the early nineteen hundreds. They went by the pen names of Arthur and Ellen Avalon, which is in recollection of those times when the blessed mists the utopian Avalon covered the world before the divisional thinking which separates the Secular and the Divine came along. This was a time when great souls like Percival searched and found the Truth in Self by the Independent effort of their own Courage. They embodied the great noble principle that Spiritual Truth is found by standing on your on feet.

There are many of such praises as the like not only in Tantra, but in Purana, in the Great Epics such as the Mahabharata, even in the Vedas themselves. Valmiki, an old sage and Indra, a deity, both have composed poems to the Goddess in the Brihatstotraratnakara. Even Shankara wrote poetry to the Goddess in such works as Ananda Lahari, wherein the the Divine Movement of the Goddess as the Kundalini Current is described in detail as She goes from the Eternal Abode of the Thousand Petaled Lotus down into the Relative Mandala of the Six Centers of the Psyche and then Back again in Her Return Current to the Great Dissolution, the Pralaya of Nirvikalpa, in the Thousand Petals of the Sahasrara.

Though Shankara praises the Greatness of the Goddess, it is unfortunate to admit that he at least at sometime in his life held the view that one could only attain enlightenment if born into a masculine body. This idea is absolutely absurd and yet sadly all too common among the society of male attitudes and backward mentality. We can only hope that men as a whole will change these attitudes eventually, these attitudes that disparage women, as Shankara seemed to do, for it is only the difficulty that male society imposes on feminine people that might be the only real obstruction to their enlightenment. Actually, Shankara's arrogance was astounding, not once but twice, did he need to have his ego thereby totaled and humbled. First by Siva appearing to him as an outcast and secondly by the Divine Mother appearing as a young girl who needed to cross his path. Whether these stories are myth, history, or allegory, they give us a clue that this Vedantist, Shankara, had a very strong ego, which appears to be not so uncommon among Vedantic thinkers. Many males think that Spiritual Feminism is a secret plot to uproot the masculine from it's apparent primary power position. But this is not so. True spiritual feminism seeks only what is equal, which is to share two primary power positions.

Now we come to the Srimad Devi Bhagavatam Purana. This is the Herstory of the Splendid Ancient Mother Goddess, to loosely translate. This is a vast and most beautiful text on the Wondrous Goddess. There is no way that justice can be done to this blessed manuscript. The wisdom of all Tantra and Vedanta is within it. It is the most complete picture of every essential Oriental or East Indian Spiritual Teaching.

The Goddess is here shown to be the Natural Teacher of all who are within the Universe. She is the Best and the Highest. There are histories and mythologies of sages and sagesses, gods and goddesses here from the beginning of known or remembered time. There is so much here that you must read it for yourself if you wish to be completely acquainted with Goddess Literature. Swami Vijnanananda, one of Ramakrishna's own, has translated every word of it in his excellent version.

The Goddess teaches every bit of Mystical Wisdom here. Briefly, from the Essence and Meaning of 'OM' and Her Mantra 'Hring' to the true nature of Pure Consciousness. The Divine Mother appears many times to different individuals here in Her Cosmic Form of the Universe, as does Krishna in the Gita. Yet here it is Her. Her Beautiful Body is this Vast Universe itself and all that is within It. She is the Eternal Absolute and the Relative Cosmos. It is none other than She who is appearing as the Individual and Combined Collective of the Waking, Dreaming, Deep Sleep and Pure Consciousness States. She is these States and That 'One Alone' Who is beyond these states.

It is all Her, even so, one sees the Gods, Creator-Brahma. Sustainer-Vishnu and Destroyer-Shiva change into their Feminine Forms, for really speaking it is She alone who is appearing as these Cosmic Principles. In Her Body are all the 'six chakras' threaded out through the three states of Consciousness, the waking-dream-sleep paradigm. All spiritual and mystic practices and states of realization are within Her Being, as is apparent ignorance, apparent knowledge and liberation through Her Grace. One cannot really comprehend all that is in this book, but with this manuscript and, The Gospel of Ramakrishna, one may learn a lot about the Reality of the Goddess. The Lalita Ambika Sahasrara Nama is in Essence the Same Stuff, but without the many stories and histories of various people and deities in the cosmic comedy drama of the Divine Mother. This smaller text is 'The Thousand Expressions of the Beautiful Playful Mother.' The Essence of Tantra and Vedanta are taught. The Nature of the Self, the Eternal and the Relative, the twenty four and the thirty six cosmic principles, the five sheaths of Consciousness, the Paradigm of the Four States and She Who is Beyond.

In the Devi Bhagavatam, all meaning and essence of the Bija Mantras, the Seven Yogic Centers, Universal and Individual manifestations of the Great Self, Samadhi as Differentiated and Undifferentiated Peace and the Mood of Balance Between, (Bhavamukha, Vijnana, Sahaja) where one's face is turned to the Goddess, whether the mood is outward or inward turned.

Everything is here. There is Reason, Love, Realization and Freedom. It is redundant of me to even attempt to repeat all that is expressed in this immense Song of the Ancient Goddess, exceeding one thousand pages in its length. These Blessed Manuscripts are indeed in the truest sense, pure and sheer Vijnana Sakti, the Special Wisdom Force of the Goddess, lifting all our cognitions to Recognition of the Self as Goddess, Who simply says, "Me."

I could put it so simply just by quoting the mystic poet sage and lover of the Goddess Kali, Ramprasad of Bengal (1723-1803). "I bow my head, says Prasad, before desire and liberation; Knowing the Secret that Kali is One with the highest Brahman, I have discarded, once and for all both righteousness and sin." The Poet has respectfully seen the absurdity of desire in this world or even the attempt at liberation, by Knowing the Highest Secret, that Kali, is in fact, the One Infinite Brahman, the Great Principle, so he has discarded the sentiment of all dualities, light-dark, high-low, limited desire or liberated freedom, matter-spirit, masculine-feminine and so forth, all dualism is gone for the poet who knows the Secret of Mother Kali.

"You revealed Yourself to Ramprasad, Mother; then why not to me? I don't want wealth, friends, relatives, enjoyment of pleasures and so on. Reveal Your-Self to me," Ramakrishna (1836-1886), from his biography, 'The Great Master'. And genuinely Ramakrishna does know the Goddess in ways that certainly transcend all the cognitions of the ordinary mortal psyche. To wit, as Ramakrishna was coming out of a State of Ecstasy he exclaimed, "Hello, Mother! I see that You too have come. How You are showing off in Your Benares sari!" What a wonder of wonders to think, to imagine how the Goddess Kali would 'show off' for Ramakrishna. Who can comprehend this Love? As the Master was engaged with the Goddess, he would speak such things as, "The body and the soul! The body was born and it will die. But for the soul there is no death." When Ramakrishna was told of any other person who saw the Divine Mother, or talked with Her, who laughed or cried with Her, who

292

danced or sang with Her, who looked upon Her Face or melted their heart into Her Self Being, at the very thought of this happening for another person's soul "the Master became ecstatic.".... "The Primordial Power and the Supreme Brahman are Identical," Ramakrishna expressed from the height of the foremost of spiritual moods. "They belong to the same stuff." Blessed be the Loving Goddess. Blessed Be Kali who allays all dualism.

NARADA AND THE GODDESS

I would like to share these two stories from the sacred text of the Srimad Devi Bhagavatam with you as a cognitive challenge to stir something within us, above duality. There is greatness of consciousness embodied herein, that it awakens in the conscious mind, higher possibilities and spiritual potentials free of deep rooted dual prejudgments.

Narada, who has given us the Doctrine of Divine Love, was once in deep mediation, when out of this Great Depth appeared the Goddess in the form of the Sustainer Deity Vishnu. He (She) responded to the celestial wise man saying, "I wish to grant you a favor, whatever you desire."

Narada said quickly, "I would like to understand the Mystery of Maya."

"All right then," spoke the Goddess in Her Vishnu guise, "but first you are required to bath in this mystical pond of water." Narada willingly did so and when he had emerged from the water his body had now become a beautiful girl's body. Narada was now the extremely attractive Sushila, the Virtuous One.

She met a fine Prince and eventually they were married. As a woman, she enjoyed the many conjugal pleasures with her prince. She gave birth to children and was immensely happy with her husband and family in a very nice little kingdom.

But tragedy broke out in the form of a feud between her husband and her father. It became a battle wherein all her

293

relations and connections were killed. Sushila's sons, daughters, husband, father and all her relatives and friends were gone.

A gigantic funeral pyre was made and all the bodies of her family and friends were placed on the wood. Sushila herself put the torch to the cremation stack and lamented ever so deeply. Her tears would have brought the world to it's knees. So sad was she that she threw herself onto the blazing fires saying, "O, my dear, dear children and beloved ones, I shall join you now in death."

But as the cremation fires were burning up her delicate beautiful body, they turned into the cool waters of the mystical pond. The Great Goddess in Her 'vishnu guise' reached out Her Hand to Sushila, now Narada again, and said in the tenderest sweetest voice, "Now who are these that you are lamenting over so much?" This is the Great Maya of the Goddess. Then, She returned to Her Cosmic Abode withdrawing into the Milky Way.

THE GODDESS AND NARADA

Let us once again stir spiritual thoughts with an excellent story on the Nature of Maya.

The Goddess in Her 'vishnu guise' was once again visiting the 'Giver of Love to Humanity', the most good of souls, Narada. He asked, "Please tell me what is Maya?"

"O, you don't really want to know about all that, now do you? Let us take a nice walk instead." So they did, walking very far, even so coming to a sad and dry desert. The Goddess became thirsty and requested Narada, "Would you mind too much Narada, to go down over there and ask the people in those small poor huts if I may have a drink of water. Please bring it to me."

So Narada went down and knocked on the door. A beautiful girl opened the little door to greet Narada. She had the eyes of the Goddess Herself, most enchanting and mysterious.

Everyone in the little poor village seemed to know Narada like a long ago acquaintance. He was so enchanted by them all that he lost all track of time. He courted the beautiful girl and eventually they married, for they were so much deeply in love that the whole world melted at the sight of them together. Out of their cherishable wedding union three precious children were born. Happiness was their own. Twelve entire years went by as Narada lived poorly, yet blissfully with his beloved ones.

Yet one day a great dark storm came and a flood began. It covered the impoverished desert fields, then the village and people were being swept away in the torrent of its waters. All of Narada's friends were drowning. His two older children were swept away and as he reached to try and save them, he dropped his smallest child, a mere baby, who was washed down in the flood. He reached out to try and save his beautiful wife with the eyes of a Goddess, but it was too late and she also was swept away by the flood. Narada himself was washed down to the edge of a muddy cliff where he was hanging on for dear life itself. He cried out, "O God, how could all this happen to me?"

Yet at that very moment the muddy flood plane turned back into the dry desert itself. The Goddess came up to Narada who was panting for breath, his head whirling with confusion and his heart saddened by loss. Twelve years of his life were lost in just the short time of the dark storm.

As the Goddess appeared at the very moment when the mud was changed back into desert, She spoke, "Now Narada, where have you been? I have been waiting for half of an hour for the water you promised to bring me." Narada looked up at Her and She responded again with a world bewitching smile and a voice no one can describe, "Narada, do you now comprehend the Secret of My Maya?"

295

THE TRANSCENDENT FUNCTION AND COGNITION
OF THE GREAT GODDESS PRINCIPLE

Modern Percivals

It is my world-prayer that there will continue to emerge in our new traditions, a lineage of modern heroes and heroines who will go like Percival into the forests of their own unconscious, and then arise to the divine occasions of their own Self Independence and Spiritual Freedom.

For it is in the very molecules of our blood itself, not to be dependent on anyone, not any symbol, nor person, nor path of discovery, nor even any principle except that one which speaks alone to oneself. This is the glory of life and the ecstatic thrill of being and becoming a real human being. This is the loving courage of the knight of truth, Percival and this is the bold compassion of the Buddha's final independent quest for the true meaning of this life. Every unique individual is a tradition into their own self reality and need not nor should follow any other. We must forge out and make Truth our own and not stand in the shadow of another's Truth. Though Truth may not for the moment be consciously known, it is the Unknown that constantly, continually, immediately and spontaneously effects us in the contents of our dreams and the mood tones of our waking life. As the saying goes, whether you know it or nor, you are the Reality It-Self.

If there is a single warning signal in the quest of self truth, it is that another would desire to have a power hold over your spiritual freedom. Truth is discovered only by standing on your own feet. The Self is the Continuous Center of Consciousness, no one can bestow it on you nor remove it from you. If you realize this clearly, any sense of a spiritual standstill will be removed by a single stroke. The constant flow of life demands again and again a fresh adaptation to Truth.

The Transcendent Function

Consider this beautiful idea. The Center of the Psyche is Consciousness as Self. This Consciousness as well as the Psyche itself is never touched by the material world. So it is eternally pristine as it is. For you see an object in your perception and an image of this object is drawn on the neurons of the brain. This image is in the psyche, but the image itself never reaches pristine Consciousness, to either flatter or disturb this Consciousness. Only images of the material dimension ever go to the level of the psyche and since as human beings our experience is essentially in the psyche, from this level we never experience the material world. So as to say, the waking state experience never comes into the psyche, only images of the waking condition. So our experience is in essence only in the Dream State since the psyche only experiences the primordial images in dreams. But even the images of dreams may never touch the deep essence of Consciousness which is like the Mother Fluid which has a depth onto itself wherein the dream images never go, since these are floating only on the surface of the Mother Fluid. And since the Mother Fluid as Consciousness is the stuff of the psyche, She is never flattered nor disturbed by the waking or dreaming states. Her Dimension is ever untouched and She is always complete in Herself, yet we, as human psyches, live here between the field of pure spirit and the field of the material dimension. Fundamentally, all our lives are a phenomena of the dream state psyche and this is where we usually dwell.

A great and seldom seen dualism, almost never noticed is that of the Unique and the Universal, that of the Individual and the Cosmic Combined. Usually we are so fully aware of the other dualisms, but we neglect the necessity of the union of opposites in regard to this greater dichotomy. For it is the tendency of the human psyche to ever think of itself as somehow different from the Great Entirity, The Goddess.

All too common is our awareness of the masculine-feminine paradoxical duality, the thinking and feeling dichotomy, the sensation-intuition dualism, the introversion and extroversion, matter-spirit, dark-light divisions and so on and so forth. But seldom do we sense or consider the illusion of dualism betwixt the Unique Individual and the Greater Universal. How nice it would be to participate in the mystic wonder where the cognizance of this barrier of separation melted away.

I purpose that instead of stopping at the process of Individuation in the Self, that we go further, into the greater process of Universalization in the Self. We all tend to think of the psyche as the persona, or psychological types, the shadows in the subconscious and so forth, but truly speaking these are the superficial masks over what the psyche really is, as explained before. Thereby the psyche becomes limited by the psychodynamics of what we consider our self to be, whether it is from the level of instinctual being, the dynamic energy of sexuality, psychic energy in the tension-relaxation dichotomy of the mind and the variety of mood-feeling tones or the cognised symbol we place over the Idea of God, Infinity and so forth. But really, all these images are masks of the true psyche which is floating on the surface of the Mother Fluid.

The "Transcendent Function" is the Bringing Together, the Harmonization, the Union of the Conscious and the Unconscious, of course, in the fine schematics of Jungian thinking and his personal experience. The parallel to this in Campbell's idealism is to "Follow your Bliss." Both are very fine.

As to myself I find an understanding of this in the idea of a Wave of Delight on the Precious Sea of the Goddess Kalee. The "wave of delight" is the conscious mind. The Precious Sea is the unconscious, that is the Mother Fluid. Here, the Goddess Kalee stands forth as the Transcendent Function. One may consider the idea of the unique personal individual as the wave of delight, then the Precious Sea of the Mother Fluid is the Great Entirity of the Universal Immensity, the Infinite Unrestricted Self Being of the Goddess Kalee. In this Idea we do not stop ourself at individuation, but boldly proceed onwards to Universalization of the consciousness portrayed within the psyche. What does this become, I cannot say, nor do I say that I have experienced this, that would be merely my ego's claim to A Greater Something to be inherited by the ego-consciousness as it becomes divested of restricted psycho-dynamics involved in its smaller idea of the unique individual. This is the danger of arrogance which is the obstruction of definition and directness, something which blocks the emergence of the Transcendent Function or the Emergence of the Heroic Self. Yet it is my inheritance, as it is the inheritance of the whole world.

As in fact the Transcendent Function may happen and does happen in some way to so many people. To wit, neurotics on occasions, even psychotics, but the bend of the experience may be negative in nature due to the traumatic contents of the psyche and the personal unconscious. Artists and creative people are well known to experience the transcendent function as are the holy, as it were, the enlightened, again, as in Zen, Yoga and the various spiritual traditions East and West. The beauty of this is that it may happen to anyone and is not exclusive to any.

The Transcendent Function, to quote the originator of the idea, "It is a way of attaining liberation by one's own efforts and of finding the courage to be oneself." It is Self Discovery and something that goes on for life, unless one wants to stop at a plateau of the psyche. How does it happen? In various ways to be sure, to wit, through poetry, art, creative imagination, fantasy, dream recollection and interpretation, a kind of free association with the unconscious contents, actually a surrender, one may say, to the unconscious contents, where the union of the conscious and unconscious takes place in a flood of creative expression and depth understanding. Transcendent Function comes through inner dialogue, like in prayer, meditation or even reading. Another method is generating the psychic energy of the libido in the process of creative transformation of the psyche, where one builds one's own personal myth that connects the conscious and the unconscious. This is marvelous, you make your own dream, a cognition of the Transcendent Function as a living Self Myth, which harmonizes in union, the water drop of the uniquely personal with the Mother Fluid. Generating the energy of the libido in the creative process of making self myth to connect with the Mother Fluid, is certainly reminiscent of the kundalini as the force of creative imagination. What blocks this with a knot is directness and definition in regards to the ego consciousness, for since we live in the world of the fluid psyche, sharp corners of directness may obstruct the free flowing natural tendency of the unconscious contents to emerge. But this is not to say or advise one to live in a hypnagogic dream world. From this point of view, the transcendent function is a way of connection with full knowledge of the inner contents of the dream psyche, whereby the Discovery of Self is made.

Comparisons

The Transcendent Function is really the melting away of the apparent partition of dualism between the conscious and the unconscious. This is the Emergence of Self, dissolved within the union of opposites. Here is the importance of the particular symbol or primordial image of this Self Emergence. The primordial image symbol is what brings the function of transcendence to emerge. It is a personal translation or simple digestion of the symbol for oneself. Thereby Something happens, something good.

Your personal symbol which brings about the "Bringing Together" can be anything, from Christ to Buddha, from the Atma to the Tao, from the Great Light to the Current of Spiritual Energy, the ideas of liberation and happiness, an Om symbol, a Cross, a Star, a God, a Goddess, any Symbol which is uniquely personal to the contents of one's own psyche, which will build a Bridge will do very well. Then the Transcendent Function is free to open a way of release into individuation of self or better yet, much better, Universalization of Self.

It is another helpful method to cognize the alchemical transformation of the dream contents of one's own psyche. This is brought about by any effort to do so, or the gradual, or

300

immediate and sudden change of the dream contents, since the psyche is fluid in its nature, this can be done. When something uniquely special comes up in the dream contents and is there not only in the dream state but the waking state as well, then recalled with sound recognition as to the meaning of the content, the function of transcendence comes about. This is said to happen more often, as it were, among natural people or tribal people as the case may be. Because we can easily see that such lucky souls who live a life of "oneness" with nature and spirit, do not usually obstruct the fluid contents of the psyche with the concrete philosophical attitudes of the modern world. Such natural people are blessed to live life as a personal myth of Self, full of symbol and the meanings of connectedness with the bridge of Oneness synthesizing the manifest dream contents of the psyche with the Great Entirity of Universal and Immense Self Recognition. Really, we may say, that it is through the Transcendent Function that religion and spirituality, philosophy and poetry, painting and sculpting, all arts, all the beauty of blissful romance and even the profound insights of science are born.

In the historic development of the mind of humanity, the transcendent function has become the evolution of the savior/savioress principle, a myth and a reality which helps us stand forth in the Self, as the Self.

Ramakrishna and the Transcendent Function

The theory of the "transcendent function" may indeed be a helpful way to understanding in our own creative cognitions, the enigmatic and wondrous personality of Ramakrishna. His whole life was really nothing but the "transcendent function" all over, exemplified daily in probably every episode of his life. For the consciousness of his psyche existing in what was called "Bhavamukha", the feeling tone of the borderline threshold of self experience and emergence in the meeting ground between the infinite depth of undifferentiated peace in the great absolute of nirvikalpa samadhi and the relative dance of this wondrous mythic world of the Earth and the Cosmos.

This Mystic of Dakshineswar is a most excellent illustration of the universal man, embodying the Great Principle of the Universalization of the Self Principle. So dwelled his delicate spiritual psyche in the cognition of the Goddess Kali that She was constantly with him, either as the formless infinite or as all this finite phenomena, either as Self or as the mystic union of self with the Self of the Goddess. She was his Symbol, his Bridge, his Beloved who removed the "partition" between the secular realm and the spiritual field.

Surely, any mind steeped in the logic of direct definition, bedeviled by intellectual prejudice and personal philosophy will and must consider momentarily that he lived perhaps in an alternate reality or dimension of psychosis, since the definition of psychosis is to be overwhelmed by the unconscious contents to the point of losing personal identity. But this line of thinking is nothing more than a reduction into negativity. For what indeed "overwhelmed" his conscious psyche but the Goddess Kali. She is the Precious Sea in which the wave of delight that he was, melted away. This is not the loss of self consciousness, but the gaining of the inheritance of one's Infinite Treasure. Samadhi states are not psychosis. Psychosis is more like a traumatic negative inward back-fire of the transcendent function, whereas the experiences of samadhi, Tao, Satori or ecstasy are positive happy emergences within the Transcendent Function as Self Recognition.

Again, the logically bound mind will think that to see one such as a Goddess, is nothing more than living in a realm of personal myth or day dreams, like a child who sees imaginary playmates. To this we can say that here is the Great Universe before us, filled with life and mystery, with beauty, with awe and with wonder; and there is a Creatrix of this, for an object does not exist without a "creator" of the object, whether or not the object is a cognition of the dream contents of the psyche or the materialization of this actual physical realm of waking state experiences known by one and all. The fact of creation proves

302

the "Reality" of the Creatrix and who are we to say that some of us may actually experience this as a personal truth, a personal reality.

In the light of this thinking one might come to an understanding of how Ramakrishna could accomplish the apparently super-human feat of absolute renunciation of contact with sexuality and finance. He himself says it was only done by the Goddess' Grace. Not all of us can do this nor is it necessary, nor should we. But a kind of wondrous respected authenticated purity stands there in the symbol of those who do. And considering the original idea of this essay, that Consciousness is Pristine and never contacts the images of the psyche and the sensory inputs of the somatic system as actual so-called real experience of the material and physical dimension, we can come to an understanding of how the very powerful images of sex and money can and do make deep impressions of attachment in the psyche to the idea that the Self as Consciousness ever experiences the sensory images or the psyche's symbols of the material physical dimension of spacetime. Indeed, what we experience is Consciousness Pristine, to which any symbol may be applied.

Goddesses of the Rigveda
A Questioning of Origins

One must be bold enough to question sacred scriptures, for though inspired by higher principles, they are indeed but human creations. The essential essence of the Rigveda, one of the oldest sacred texts in the world, is that it firmly attempts to make everything divine, by the most gigantic and tremendous poetic efforts, those enlightened poet composers, through the vigor of their verses, raised all human and cosmic phenomena to a state of pure spiritual divinity. This timeless and sacred achievement is the great contribution of the Rigveda to the spiritual culture of the world.

The composers of the Rigveda came from some northern part of the planet above Greece and India, probably centrally located above and betwixt these two, where they split apart and gradually descended into these two later locations. Logically speaking, as it is with any text or book, these traveling people composed their sacred work over a period of time. One of the most famous sacred hymns of the Rigveda is in the Tenth and last book of the text, number One Hundred and Twenty Nine. This composition expresses one of the highest flights of Rigvedic insight. "Then first came Love upon it, the new spring of mind _ yea, poets in their hearts discerned, Pondering, this bond between created things and uncreated." It is this 'bond between' that gives us the key to what the Goddess was to the Rigveda poets.

It is primarily the power of the Goddess Vak (Speech) who gives the poet the capacity to ponder, discern, commune and express this bond between the created finite world and the infinite uncreated mystery of the spiritual and divine world. She is essential to this process of poetic power and insight. She is in fact that power and insight itself. She is also the Goddess Sarasvati, Savitri and Gayatri, who is none other than the Mother of the Veda, under different names according to their spiritual context, as the Goddess of Knowledge, the Goddess of Light, the Goddess of Sacred Mantra, respectively. So, from this point of view, as She is the Voice bridging the Uncreated into the Created, we should indeed say that the entire Rigveda is a wonderful manifestation of the Goddess Herself, for without Her how would it exist or have come into being.

The Goddess Vak is the communion between the poet and God. She is the Queen of the Gods and the Gladdener of the poets. As a spiritual power, She is no doubt something of real essence. But interestingly enough we find that she was also a real person, the enlightened daughter of the poet sage Ambrina. She was among the gatherings of the poet sages in their sacred circles of competent spiritual laudations, but strangely enough only two of her sacred poems are recorded in the Rigveda. One on Jnanam (Knowledge) and one on Vak, the Goddess.

What does Vak, the poetess say about Vak, the Goddess? Let me borrow from one of the great devotees of that wonder of Dakshineswar, Sri Ramakrishna. Swami Saradananda renders into English, some choice parts of her ecstatic declaration. "I spread the heavens over the earth. I am the energy of Brahman, the Mother of all. It is for me that Brahman resides in all the different intellects. It is I who have penetrated all the worlds with my power and it is I who am holding them in their places." This energy of Brahman is later known in the Upanishads as Prana and in Tantra as Sakti. They are similar. Both being the Primal Power not different from Brahman (the Infinite concept). Prana has also been equated with dreamless sleep where no vibration of waking or dreaming dualism stirs in the mind. This is interesting because this is the depth of true peace in no way different from the Infinite, and yet has the potential of all finite life within it and all poetic power.

Ramakrishna confirms this spiritual truth when he says, "Kali is none other than Brahman. That which is called Brahman is really Kali. She is the Primal Energy. When that Energy remains inactive, I call It Brahman, and when It creates, preserves, or destroys, I call It Sakti or Kali. What you call Brahman I call Kali." He continues with his eloquent

306

expressions of non dualism, "Brahman and Kali are not different. They are like fire and its power to burn: if one thinks of fire one must think of its power to burn. If one recognizes Kali one must also recognize Brahman; again, if one recognizes Brahman one must recognize Kali. Brahman and Its Power are identical. It is Brahman whom I address as Sakti or Kali."

Let us take a heartfelt examination of another synthesis of Rigvedic cosmology in relation to the Goddess imagery recorded by the poets. We find that the Night (Ratri or Urmya), the Dark Womb which gives rebirth to the Dawn (Ushas), the Lady of Light, each new day, were both contemplated as Goddesses. A beautiful poetic cognition of the Goddess' daily movement, as it were, but not unique to any one cultural insight. Then, by tremendous poetic inspiration, the Goddess of Earth (Prithivi) in the power of divine poetry, is raised to the state of oneness with the Goddess of Infinity (Aditi), the Mother of all the Gods. It is the Goddess Vak who alone is capable of expressing this accessible state of mind. And it is Sarasvati (Knowledge) that guides the learning to this Heightened Awareness.

Of course, it is the pattern of the poets to give supreme position to the deity they are addressing at the time of that address, probably as a matter of focus and surrender to the principle which is being praised at that moment. We hear described some of the verses on the Goddesses as Devi Suktas (Goddess Stanzas) and this gives the impression that they are these immense collections about the nature of the Divine Feminine, but what is there in the text is just a few stanzas here and there. Nine tenths of the Rigveda is addressed to male deities. The three foremost and most often given mention and precedence are Indra (divine, inspired or ignited intellect and intelligence), Agni (the sacred fire and the the fire of God realization) and Soma (the elixir of spiritual joy, insight and gladdening).

One should indeed remember that the Rigveda was composed during a time when the ability to utilize fire was probably considered quite miraculous. They respected it, for it improved life. And any kind of divinely intelligent, inspirational or joyful connection with the natural cosmological cycle or phenomena certainly made this world of living and dying and all between, more sensibly experiential. There are other deities, many, the entire universe, created and uncreated is deified, that is the central and primary import of Rigvedic consciousness.

So at moments of poetic heights, the Goddesses are given supreme positions, but generally they are in the aftermath of those poetic flights, placed as the consorts of the gods or even the spouses of heroes, who are the poets. Even so, the Mother aspect is extolled as a beautiful, well adorned, very selfless servant. The Consort Queen gives birth to the unborn babe (Agni, a male deity). She is the Mother who bares him and keeps him close to her bosom. Of course it is not only metaphorical of the sacred fire but of the human birth of males. Only in very few places, such as Vak's, the human poetess' exclamation of insight into the Sacred Feminine do you find the Goddess proclaimed as sovereign of Herself in Her own right, and not in service as bride, spouse, sister or mother to the male gods. Interesting old attitudes.

Also, I would submit to you, a thought on the origins of archetypal foundations in human consciousness. The concept of the impersonal condition of Nirvana had its archetypal source in the person of the Buddha. The Christ principle in Yeshua (the Aramaic title). Now if Vak has a human counterpoint, then why not Kali. It is not out of the question that She may somehow have had a primal archetypal foundational beginning with an ancient warrior woman who was later identified with the Goddess. Perhaps, perhaps not. But the fact remains that Her most fortunate devotee, Sri Ramakrishna, sometimes saw Her in human form, though divine in appearance. It takes a little dose of humanity for the Impersonal to become a personal experience. This is an often forgotten fact of spiritual life.

Sometimes the border between the human mind and the divine mind is vague, transparent, and that is fortunate for us who are still saddled with the human mind. In the sweet Rigveda story poem of Urvasi and Pururavas some curious thoughts are raised in this context. Urvasi was one of the most alluring Heavenly Nymphs who during her sojourn on Earth lived with the human king Pururavas. They gave birth to a son before her departure back to the heavenly region.

Not surprisingly, her return to heaven broke his heart. Was this a mythological projection of divinity on a human woman with a spiritualized poetic ending? Was it a soma induced hallucination? Or is it truly possible for divine beings to have conjugal relationships with human beings and conceive children? An idea, a myth, a reality, or even perhaps a hallucination which is much older in its conception than just a few thousand years. Where do these psychic images begin and where does divinity not extend? Is this story Tantric or Vedic in its origin?

You see, there is still the insistent persistence that the Goddess tradition of India is but a sub shoot of the Veda, that is that the Tantra originates out of the Veda and not independently of itself. Of course it should come as no surprise that the monastic finality of Veda or rather its evolution into Vedanta would not endorse the independent originality of Tantra in spite of present day archeological evidence which undoubtedly gives real undisputed fact to the presence of amazingly developed preexisting culture along the Sindhu River.

This massively developed culture, perhaps the most highly advanced in the world at that time, was well established prior to the arrival of the Rigvedic poet tribesmen. It is commonly and blindly accepted that the Goddess Sarasvati or Vak of the Veda later became the Goddess Kali or Durga of the Tantra. But why? Is it simply absurdly dominating patriarchal claims to the authority and the originality of ontological absolutes? Why could not the Tantra and the Veda emerge independently of each other and then as new cultures, as new worlds met old worlds, adopt new ideas from each other's systems, interchanging both ways. That is the phenomenology of cross cultural references and the evolving of new thought into fresh unities.

Again, there are the seals and statues of the proto Shiva and Shakti, the Tantric God and Goddess, found in the numerous sites and cities of the Sindhu (Indus) River Valley. Some have counted seventy of these dwellings. Mohenjo Daro, Harappa, Kalibangan, Rupar, Chanhu Daro, Lothal, Amri, Kot Diji, and Rangpur, to name a few. They were there for at the very least one thousand years before the Indo Aryan invaders. This is now the widely accepted historical truth as documented in Compton's Multimedia Encyclopedia and The World's Religions: Understanding the Living Faiths, published by Reader's Digest.

It is also fact that the name of Goddess Kali is found in many cultures outside the Sindhu region. The Phoenicians had the name Calpe. The Celts had Kelly from the Goddess Kele. The Amazons had the name Kalliste. The Greeks had Kalli. The Gypsies call Her Sara Kali. In Finland She was known as Kalma. To the Spanish She is Califia. Many more references may be found in Elizabeth U. Harding's text, Kali - The Black Goddess of Dakshineswar, which is a masterpiece. The evidence of this widespread presence of the Kali connection around the world points to the older Goddess adoration coming up through Paleolithic, Mesolithic and Neolithic eras to the present day. The Goddess of Willendorf dates at the ending edge of the Neanderthal era, The Goddess of Laussel comes out of the Cro Magnon generation. Prior to altering, the original Sphinx Goddess is dated at eleven to seventeen thousand years of age. Neanderthal, Cro Magnon, and the present day Human are not separate, but connected, just like great grandparents, grandparents and parents. And always throughout there has been the strong presence of Goddess Worship as the most coherent consistent spiritual nexus.

The Sindhu (Indus) Valley Script, their language as it is called by us, has been thought for the longest time to be an early form of Sanskrit, but never has been translated in any comparable valid way to Sanskrit, the language of the Rigveda. This is because the Indus valley script is a separate language, a language of the early Tantra. But of course, dispute will continue for everyone believes that their belief system is the one primary belief system. How could it be otherwise with human nature, for why would you follow a secondary system of belief?

310

The Sindhu script has perhaps remained undeciphered because it is not an alphabet but a system of symbols primarily dealing with spiritual formulas. The Tantric bija mantras (seed formulas) handed down to us still intact even today are these mystical symbols of thought, more than they are a linear system of an alphabet. The Tantric bija mantras are most probably the key to deciphering the spiritual language of the early Sindhu people. Of course one would need a time machine to go back and see if all these things are true for sure. But the logical idea remains that these two cultures could meet and share each other's ideas, the Vedic and the Tantric, then giving birth to much of the present day religious phenomena of India.

It should be obvious that the ten mandalas (books) of the Rigveda evolved over periods of time. So, perhaps some of it was written after contact with the gentle Tantric Goddess worshiping Sindhu culture. The primary male deities were perhaps incorporated with the Goddess beliefs of the time. For one can clearly see with a little examination that the attitude of the Rigveda is not consistent with that of Tantra. For example, "A man who drinks with devotion a little of the water into which a woman has dipped her toe or eats the leavings of the food in her plate, is sure to have uninterrupted success," from Nigama-kalpadruma. And, "Women are the gods, they are sacred and they are the ornaments of society. One should never hate, condemn or beat them," from Mundamala Tantra.

Where the Rigvedic attitude is shockingly different. Read Book Ten, hymn 95, verse 15, "With women there can be no lasting friendship: hearts of hyenas are the hearts of women." And in Book Eight, hymn 33, verse 17, "Indra himself hath said, the mind of woman brooks not discipline, her intellect hath little weight." Even so, latter developments in the Upanishads continue with these cruel and tragic attitudes. The Brihadaranyaka Upanishad, which on one hand has the beautiful conversation between the Yajnavalkya and Maitreyi, soaring into the height of pure spirituality. Yet on the other hand, in regard to sexual relations, has such verses included in its content as, "Therefore one should worship a woman placing her below."

311

And in its advice to a man seeking procreation, states, "If she is still unyielding, he should strike her with a stick or with his hand and overcome her, repeating the following mantra; "With power and glory I take away your glory." Thus she becomes discredited." So once again this is hardly a Goddess loving Tantric belief system or a spiritually empowered attitude of respect for the sovereignty of women as embodiments of the Goddess.

It would seem that the worship of women as Goddess was a totally alien idea, which was partially incorporated most reluctantly into the Rigveda after the cross cultural contact with the Sindhu culture in the valley where they planned to dwell. It is the psychology of absorption and replacement, and though it took some five hundred to one thousand years, they did eventually conquer that culture. The Rigveda identifies these non-Aryan people as the Purus and the Sivas. Note the similarity to the name of the preexisting Tantric Deity, Siva, the consort of Sakti, the Goddess. Also, these original people were called the Purus. Note the similarity of Puru with Pura, which means city.

There is an extremely unique verse which is repeated in two of the oldest original Upanishads, the Chhandogya and the Brihadaranyaka. "Woman, O Gautama, is the fire, her sexual organ is the fuel, what invites is the smoke, the vulva is the flame, what is done inside is the embers, the pleasures are the sparks. In this fire the gods offer semen as libation. Out of that offering the fetus is formed." This appears distinctly to be an attitude of Tantra saturating into the Veda. Not the other way around. Libation means the pouring forth of wine or other liquid in honor of a deity. The Tantric view of woman as the embodiment of the Goddess is certainly cognised in this verse beautifully by the realization that her private parts are as sacred as the holy altar fire itself and something much more than mere organics.

If we take our time machine and start moving back into the past we should find some interesting views on historical realities. First we would move back past all this sexually

312

obsessed new age Tantra. Then we would pass through the time of medieval developments within the Tantra system which tried to include everything imaginable under the sun. Then let us move through the period of Buddhist Tantric development where the responses to the denial renunciate system gave rise to all the secretive night time activities which Tantra is notoriously associated with, de-centering focus from its true import. We arrive now at the Vedic period. No doubt early Veda joined the two approaches to life into one as naturally leading to the other. That is the enjoyment of life and union with the spiritual principle of divine existence.

Now we come to a time prior to the Vedic arrival. Here we find the Sindhu society which was thought by the Vedic people to be a barely cognate society, a remark given by people who were still wandering about on horseback and rubbing two sticks together to make fire. Strange, is it not, when in reality the truth of archeological evidence reveals the remains of a beautifully constructed city at Mohenjo Daro. A central bathing pool with individual housing surrounding the place of the large bathing area. It has been falsely claimed that these were not religious people for no altars or temples were found here. Yet, they were, for Tantra is and has always been the internal worship of the divine reality. Emphasis on externals is only there as a temporary usage to raise consciousness to the state of pure spiritual realization. It is life itself which is sacred, not images of rock or wood, nor paintings of people made into idols and so forth.

The most conservative estimates state that the Sindhu culture was a fully functioning society about four and half to five thousand years age. Of course, it probably took one or two thousand years to get to this state. While others have placed the age of some of their art at over thirty thousand years ago. So we find some very interesting aspects of development within earlier shapes of human consciousness, giving the Tantric spiritual sentiment as one of the oldest we know of at this time. This all points to the archetypus or original autograph of the blessed Mother Goddess in the human mind.

313

In a variety of poetic rhythms, the Rigvedic sage mind addressed, worshiped and perceived the entire concept of the cosmological, psychological and natural world as the gods and also goddesses. This powerful poetic approach to life in epic voyages through consciousness is certainly most beautiful, inspiring and enlightening. But there is a seldom noticed problem inherent in this level or system of consciousness, awareness and feeling. In his commentary of the Brihadaranyaka Upanishad, Swami Nikhilananda most eloquently describes this problem, "Even the gods cannot injure the knower of Atman (the innermost Self), because he becomes their Atman, or self, too. The ignorant man who worships the gods, regarding them as other than his Atman, becomes subservient to them. The gods obstruct his spiritual progress." This is an amazing statement in so many ways another essay could be composed on just this idea. So suffice it to say that nothing should be over the Self in its free state of pure spiritual dignity, awareness and enlightenment.

The first Goddess addressed in the Rigveda is Sarasvati. She is beseeched as a mighty flood of illuminating light and gracious thought. She is also identified with the copious flow of the river Ganges. Two other Goddesses come with Her as well, both identified with similar powers of the blessing of knowledge and speech. They are Ila and Mahi who both are bringers of delight. Later these rivers and powers were cross identified with the Tantric insight into the spiritual river currents of the central nerve, the Sushumna, and the two ascending and descending currents of the Ida and Pingala. These are part of the chakra system of the Tantra. Veda did not have the conception of the seven chakras. It speaks of bhumis, the seven planes of consciousness. Though, as in every religious insight, you find everywhere, in some shape or fashion, a description of the seven states of consciousness.

The Vedic conception of the Goddess obviously went through mutations. The sage mind of these early thinkers certainly set in motion an effect of primal ideologies that still trace down into the present consciousness of people living today.   There is mention, praise and beseechment of the Goddesses of Devotion, Speech, Prosperity, of Wood, of Rivers and of Heaven, They speak of the Dames of the Gods and of celestial nymphs. Indra's consort is Indrani. There are maidens, as they were, and Goddesses of destruction and protection. There is the Mother of the storm gods, the thunder gods and the Mother of day and night. Deshtri is Sarasvati as the Instructress. The consort of Varuna, the encompasser of the starry heavens is Varunani.   A woman warrior is named Vispala, yet women slaves were considered to be fine war prizes. Obviously from the Sindhu culture.

The god of death, Yama, has a sister named Yami. Raka is a goddess of the moon. Rodasi is the consort of the storm god. The Goddess of Infinity is called the Mighty Dame. And there is Sujuni among various Apsaras, heavenly nymphs. The sun god Surya's daughter is the sunlight itself. Yet, the sun, as the vivifying impeller, is addressed as both Savitar, a male god, and Savitri, a female goddess. And the Deity Trita, who makes the fire and presses with stones the preparation of the Soma, the Indu, the drink of Indra, interestingly, his fingers are poetically referred to as maidens. Thoughtful people will easily see that all this is a very curious complex weaving of ideas related to the Goddess Ideal. The primal psychological and spiritual attitudes toward this ideal were set into motion at the conjunction of the Tantric and Vedic cultures. These motions still effect us today as the subtle viewpoints held toward the Sacred Feminine still keep Her, as it were, from existing as Her own sovereign in her own right.

In 1889, the Principal of the Benares College, Ralph T. H. Griffith, translated the entire Rigveda from Sanskrit into English. Yet a few verses he chose to render into Latin due to their erotic content. My loose and poor translation of the Latin might shed a little light on the difference between the Rigvedic and Tantric attitude toward the Sacredness of the Feminine. A sensitive person will see the distinction immediately. The first is two verses that the translator states do not really fit into the hymn, which may indicate they were added later with some purpose in mind which alerts us to the evidence that the Rigveda was an evolving poetic process of developing the ten mandala books.

The prince Savanaya, who, it is said lived on the banks of the Sindhu river speaks first. "He, the famous one chatters; Cling to, keep very close to her to try to gain that which is similar to a weasel (mustelae), her forbidden part and make multiple fluid pourings there, giving hundreds of affectionate gladdenings." Then, the princess Romasa replies, "She, the famous one chatters; The time is very near, exceedingly soon, softly, voluptuously, with strength to touch and to taste, indeed, with certainty, eagerly catch my small place of fleshy plumpness and foul smelling hair and absorb entirely as is possible my shaggy hair just as the foolish simpleton fellows of Gandharidum." It seems that Gandharidum is a place west of the Sindhu river, how far west one may not know, but it could be as far as the Greek society that extended toward that direction or some other culture they considered to be fools.

The next erotic verses that I would try to translate, occurs in an admonishment of Lopamudra to her husband, the sage Agastya. They are both quite old at this time, yet still, the Goddess Rati, Love, is desired. Lopamudra says, "Old age impairs the beauty of our bodies. Let husbands still come near unto their spouses." Then Agastya responds, "By no means useless is this exertion, my dear, by the Deity's help and favor: we come together entirely and even yes, be conquerors with mastery over and vanquishing both our male and female rivals in love. Longing for love, I, bright as a verdent bull, somehow, at what price, I, look down and despise, this place on one side and that place on the other side that takes away from anyone by bringing forth birth in the position of dependence." At this point there is a listener who is perhaps a poet disciple and that one records or speaks the next verse. "Lopamudra, proclaims like a bull, that conjugal love and marriage are their own, and yet by reaching towards one another they are dragged down to where both the foolish and the wise desire the puffing and panting of heavy breath by which they are absorbed."

316

As Agastya and Lopamudra are wishing for children, progeny and power, there comes another expression in Sanskrit, which was also translated into Latin instead of English. It is khanamanah khanitraih or ligonibus fodiens. Loosely, the meaning of both is to draw tight together in a heart felt harmonious unity and dig, as if with a spade in a garden. This is a very poetic description of sexual action. Today, nearly one hundred years later it hardly seems like something needing to be concealed in Latin. Nowadays, our thoughts have evolved somewhat as cultures have come together and attitudes have formed new unities. So I hope we might be more mentally heightened in these attitudes.

We cannot deny that being born carries with it certain sadness and misery, but if we nourish that misery, life will be more miserable as the case may be. The attitude of disgust for being dragged down into the puffing and panting of birth is one that perceives the absorption of the transcendent into a confinement within the immanent. This is not the Tantric attitude which forever has perceived life as the opportunity for the expansion of consciousness in what is divine. Human life is the divine gift of energy, power, feeling and consciousness. It is not a spiritual sentence into the restriction house of cause and effect. Only the perception of attitude makes it seem one way or the other.

Renunciation without love for the object which is renounced is simply rejection of that object or perhaps even hatred or disgust for the object itself, whatever it be. This gives the object more force in the mind and so the natural and spontaneous reconciliation of the uncreated transcendent and the created immanent will never be joined in the unified experience which is felt in the bond between. That bond is Love. "Who knows the secret? Who proclaimed it here, whence, whence this manifold creation sprang? The gods themselves came later into being_ Who knows from whence this great creation sprang? He from whom all this great creation came, whether his will created or was mute, the Most High Seer that is in highest heaven, He knows it_ or perchance even He knows not." Rigveda Book Ten

Hymn 129, translated by H. T. Colebrooke and Fredrich Max Muller.

Some tremendous thoughts and wonderful insights are in this best of Rigveda poetry which are perhaps the source ideas of the later more perfected and evolved system of the non dual Vedanta. In the divine not knowing of dualism, we have true experience, the spiritually excellent feeling comprehension of the Invisible behind the Visible. In Rigveda language this is the Aja Ekapada (the unborn one footed) principle or divine presence, behind Prajapati (the creator of the visible creation). The Unborn One Footed is That Which Moves In Oneness Behind The Creator! This is the foundational spiritual archetype for the later more polished idea of the Great Gesture of Non Dualism, which is to see Pure Consciousness or God Consciousness, if you like, while holding the three states of waking, dreaming and dreamless sleep.

"Death was not then, nor was there aught immortal: no sign was there, the day's and the night's divider. That One Thing, breathless, breathed by its own nature: apart from it was nothing whatsoever." Hymn 129. verse 2. This is one of those lines of vigorous spiritual poetic insight that gave birth to thousands of later concepts. For example, 'that one thing' which is breathless or not embodied and yet is breathing as the embodied, charges my mind with the thought that this is the mother idea of the sahaja concept. The self (sa) as I (ha), born (ja) to the natural state or to be simultaneously aware of the divine within the immanent while experiencing the transcendent side. It is knowing both sides at the same joyful, constant and continuous moment, without the 'sign' of a dualistic 'divider'. A state of consciousness, capable of being experienced, which is prior to the divided recognition of death and the dualistic reflex thought of being immortal at some time or another.

In the same Hymn 129, there is perhaps even a source idea of the Goddess Kali's Total Non Dual Darkness where the conceptual experience of sheer phenomenal dualism is completely obliterated. Verse 3, "Darkness there was: at first concealed in darkness this All was indiscriminate chaos. All

318

that existed then was void and formless: by the great power of Warmth was born that Unit." The non dual All is Oneness without distinction, dualism. I do not care for the expression chaos for in reality what is chaotic is the diversity of the dualistic world. Warmth is that Sakti, the Primal Energy, that Womb of the Goddess, that Power of movement, life, and thought, which gives birth to the Unit which indicates two things joined as One, that is the transcendent and the immanent, the absolute and the relative.

If one has disgust for the created how will the bond of Love ever develop between the created and the uncreated? If one has hatred or the feeling of rejection for the fact of being incarnated here as a human being or for the innate possibility of being incarnated here once again, well then, what a predicament you are in. No doubt there is a strange element to being human on this planet; the struggle, the suffering, the joy. But it would seem that true spirituality is moving from the simple and natural joys of human life to the greater joy of something more. Not a process of hating something in order to get rid of it.

The Avadhuta Gita, here translated by Purohit Swami, an old friend of Ycats, the poet, expresses this most extreme attitude of supercilious disdain for the created or the incarnated and its process at the level of the human source. "What are you looking at? Mind, what are you running after? There lies the terrible whirl pool; go and be lost, whether believers or non believers, they are all torn to pieces on account of this ounce of flesh, full of pours, full of stink. Who created this canal, with its downward path, midway in the sea of this horrible body, surging with waves of blood? Inside besmeared with filth, outside adorned with falsehood, sex prevents one from approaching the great truth. People do not know when they are born out of it; but now when they know, they still cling to it. What is this irony of life?" Chapter Eight. Verses 18 - 22. In reality, the truth is that sex is not the cause for rebirth or incarnation. The deep ingrained sense of dualism is the cause for return. Love lifts this sense of separateness, not disgust!

Sri Ramakrishna, the divine devotee of the Dakshineswar Goddess Kali, and a natural born celibate, even though he was a married man, reflects quite a different attitude, one of respect and not of disdain. "At this time he lost the sense of distinction between the holy and unholy. Even a street girl reminded him of the Mother. Words grossly offensive to the ordinary man appeared to him as but a group of letters_and every letter, he believed in accordance with the verdict of the Shastras, was a symbol of the Divine Mother. Nay, these would sometimes throw him into Samadhi_as was repeatedly observed later_on account of their suggestion of the Blissful Mother." Quoted from Sri Ramakrishna: The Great Master.

Obviously this is a much healthier attitude, not life denying but life accepting. The attitude of disgust and rejection has its toll of psychic casualties as self denial, self abuse and self hatred. How can one truly progress spiritually when the emotional body contains those types of feelings? Ramakrishna saw the Ultimate Cause of the universe as the Brahmayoni, the Creator's Vulva, out of which multiple universes were flowing into birth. This is absolutely beautiful, seeing the divine power of the Goddess as creator of the manifold universe.

That blessed Ramakrishna embodied the wisdom of Veda and the loving passion of Tantra. He was not a dry and cold celibate, but one of greatest feeling and divine cognition. His wife and he desired a child, as it were, and so the spiritually sent child, Rakhal was delivered by the Divine Mother. Rakhal later became Swami Brahmananda. Like Ramakrishna, Rakhal had the inner nature of a child, so much so that he would lay his head in Ramakrishna's lap the way a child does with their mother. Ramakrishna cleverly and lovingly remarks of Rakhal, "You mustn't find fault with Rakhal. He's a mere child. Even now you can bring out his mother's milk by squeezing his throat." Instead of a frigid critical renunciate intelligence toward Rakhal's conjugal life, the most gentle Ramakrishna again remarks with his abundant understanding of human nature. "It was I who sent him to his wife now and then. He still had a little desire for enjoyment." You must know well by now that it was

320

Ramakrishna who gave us all the realization that within all women, the Divine Mother is personified and embodied. This is the attitude of Tantra. Nothing less will do.

Another point in this controversy which is surprisingly overlooked is that the idea of Maya had not yet developed in the Rigvedic philosophical system. That came later with the composition of the Upanishads. So where did this idea come from? Tantra has always had the idea of Maha Maya, the Great Mother. But again, as always, there are a variety of attitudes or conceptions within maya about what maya is in fact. Ramakrishna gives us two views side by side. First we see this super charged statement of his, "Whatever we see or think about is the manifestation of the glory of the Primordial Energy, the Primal Consciousness." Second, "Whatever you see, think, or hear is maya." On one hand, Maya is the manifestation of Chitsakti, the Consciousness Power of the Divine Mother. On the other hand, maya is the covering, as everything we hear and see, think and feel about this world and within it. Therefore, what you are reading or any conversation you may now be having with yourself is nothing but maya, the phenomena of measuring out the Infinite Power of the Divine Mother.

If everything we see or think or say, for that matter, is maya, well then, all speech is maya too. Therefore, what is said by or within Vak is also maya. All poetic efforts and feelings are but maya. Maya, as Primal Energy or Power, or as Vak, is the shape of thought and speech in all that is between the Created and Uncreated. Maya is the sense of between-ness itself and the dissolution or true returning to the manifestation of that sense of between-ness as the bond of non duality. Here, Vak is the Primal Energy of that non dual Consciousness.

At this I am left speechless and must quote Ramakrishna once again. "I said to Keshab further: 'You should accept the Divine Mother, the Primal Energy. Brahman is not different from Its Sakti. What is Brahman is also Sakti. As long as a man remains conscious of the body, he is conscious of duality. It is only when a man tries to describe what he sees that he finds duality.' Keshab later on recognized Kali." Dualism, is the sense of difference existing only in speech-thought alone. It has no true reality, ultimately speaking, yet it is this speech thought itself that brings consciousness to the understanding of non dual consciousness, at this level. Is it the beautiful manifestation of glory or the illusion of dualistic dialogue?

The entire debate of this Tantra and Veda source question is resolved pure and simple by a few remarks from the sage of Kali. "Is the Primal Energy man or woman?" Can the true nature of Primal Energy be expressed through the dualism of these two archetypes. Also, "But Brahman is identical with Its Power." Ultimately, Brahman of the Veda and the Sakti Power of the Tantra are identical. We have been dealing merely with historical phenomena. "The Primal Power, Mahamaya, has covered Brahman. As soon as the covering is withdrawn, one realizes: 'I am what I was before', 'I am Thou; Thou art I'."

For the longest time, Sayana has been considered the infallible commentator on the Rigveda. Yet if truth be told, as soon as one assumes that they are infallible, they immediately have become fallible, at least in my humble perception. Max Muller was a great explorer of the world of Rigveda. Swami Vivekananda held him in high opinion. A letter he wrote about Muller describes him as "the silver haired sage, with a face calm and benign, and forehead smooth as a child's in spite of seventy winters, and every line in that face speaking of a deep seated mine of spirituality somewhere behind... a soul that is everyday realizing its oneness with the universe." And what did this Western sage say about those of us who might dive into the Rigveda and all its surrounding mysteries yet to be explained. "As yet we see the Vedic age only as through a glass darkly. The first generation of Vedic scholars is passing away. It has done its work bravely, though well aware of its limits. Let the next generation dig deeper and deeper. What is wanted is patient, but independent and original work. There is so much new ground still to be broken, that the time has hardly come as yet for going again and again over the same ploughed field."

As long as consciousness still moves in the dualistic spiritual circles of the mind, conflict will be there. When that same consciousness makes the move into hyper non dualism, then- there- will be high Peace. The revelation conceals and the revelation reveals simultaneously. The Poetess Vak, at the realization of Herself proclaims with the divine vigor of Rigvedic poetry, "I am the Queen, the gatherer up of treasures, most thoughtful, first of those who merit worship. Thus Gods have established me in many places with many homes to enter and abide in. I make the man I love mighty, make him a sage. I rouse and order battle for the people, and I have penetrated Earth and Heaven. On the world's summit I bring forth the Father (Brahman). Thence I extend o'er all existing creatures, and touch even yonder heaven with my forehead. I breathe a strong breath like the wind and tempest, the while I hold together all existence. Beyond this wide earth and beyond the heavens I have become so mighty in my grandeur." These selections are from Griffith's translation of Vak's hymn 125 from mandala book ten (the Devi Sukta). Swami Saradananda's conveyance of the same, quoted before, is somewhat different. The language of poetry is heard and felt differently by all. The word 'battle' may perhaps mean spiritual battle, but remember these Rigvedic people were a warlike sort, contrary to the typically passive and gentle Hindu of today.

At last I will leave you with some selections from Vak's other poem, Book Ten Hymn 71, the one on Jnanam or Parabrahmajnanam as the infallible Sayana assumed. But to me it seems that she is praising the power of the poet knowers, the sages, more than Supreme God Knowledge (para brahma jnanam). Listen to what she says, from Griffith's rendering. "Vak's first and earliest utterances, All that was excellent and spotless, treasured within them, was disclosed through their affection. Where, like men cleansing corn flour in a cribble, the wise in spirit have created language. Friends see and recognize the marks of friendship: their speech retains the blessed sign imprinted. With sacrifice the trace of Vak they followed, and found Her habouring within the Rishis (the illumined Poet Knowers). But to another She hath shown Her Beauty as a fond well dressed woman to her husband. No part in Vak hath he who hath abandoned his own dear friend who knows the truth of friendship (with Truth). When friendly Poet Knowers sacrifice together with mental impulse which the heart hath fashioned, they leave one far behind through their attainments, and some who count as Poet Knowers wander elsewhere."

That 'affection' She speaks of is to me the vigorous verbal conjunction of poetic ecstasy with High Emotion. It is in this 'friendship' with that One Voice of Truth, never to be abandoned, that the results of Wisdom in the Bond Between are to be found. As Love would create the potent spiritual language of the poet, in those blessed signs imprinted, the traces of the Goddess, whose footprints move through time, distant and now. It is She who gives us the mental impulse to describe what the heart fashions. Blessed Be Her Power that leaves all confusion far behind, whether we remain here or wander elsewhere.

BURSTING THE SHARP
MID-POINT OF THE WORLD
MIND CULTUS

The expression, cult, comes from cultus, meaning to worship. Worship means something, a principle or person which is worthy. It is to value the worth, such is worship. Essentially, the cultic mental attitude is any belief system which excludes other systems of belief. So much falls into this category, everything from the great religions to any person's sharp mid-point of viewing the world, denying other systems of perception or manners in which the diversity of people give worth to their lives.

Really, the cultic vision is rather abusive and vicious in the psychological sense, for it denies other people's realities. Whenever there is abuse there is anger, trouble and so forth, between two people, two nations or two religious systems. The tendency is there in everyone to see things only from their own sharp mid-point, their own center. Few of us can maintain the sentiment of universal outlook which does not deny the personal truth of another's reality. If you put a single dot on a blank page, that is about how much one person might understand what is going on in another's mind. With this thought we might gradually learn to accept a non-controlling attitude toward other's mid-points.

One system attacks another, then that one attacks back, either intellectually or a the level of visceral combat. It becomes a vicious recycling of negativity. The eye is taken for an eye and the teeth too. An unhealthy response. It is an archaic method of controlling thoughts and feelings. Some of us might just want to give away for the sake of peace (forgive) and let live. For if you are one who says Allah is better than Christ or Christ is better than the Atma (Spiritual Self), that attitude rises out of a cultic mind set, universally accepted but nevertheless isolating, separative and exclusive. The attitude extends wide and far, limiting us all. It is the world's mind cultus, seeing value and worth solely through the center of one's own sharp mid-point.

A Christian will say that a Shinto's religion is invalid because they worship the Spirit of their ancestors. But the Shinto may reply that Jesus is not physically present with you so what you worship is the Spirit of the person too. Heat rises. The Christian replies that Kojiki and Nihonji, the founders, are mythological people with no evidence of their existence in history. They do not worship the resurrected Christ so they are invalid. The Shinto replies that according to the letter of an Essene to Alexandria, Jesus did not die on the cross. They took his body from the tomb, still bleeding (a corpse does not bleed), to one of many secret Essene caves where he lived for six more months and then passed away peacefully.

The point is not who is correct, it is that the sharp mid-points of various belief systems are found to be in continual conflict. On and on the war continues and their is no peace. This is the problem of the world mind cultus. Very few practice the universal viewpoint. Most people have firmly negated other thought systems from the get go. Closed minds. Lack of synthesizing all possibilities. Our cognitive conception of history may be turned topsy turvy with the opening of the secret chamber below the foot of the new estimated seventeen thousand year old Sphinx. This will negate the premises of human history according to some belief systems of that region, but it will also enhance the depth of connection we have with our real past. The mid-point of our perception of what we are is constantly changing at this level, even so, at the level of profound insight into what we are spiritually. Openness is always necessary for the joy of assimilating universal information.

We have all managed to brainwash each other quite successfully, reducing the capacity for universal consciousness in one another simply by saying no that cannot be so. By the custom of denying another person's reality, narrowness has become an habituated practice of the human mind. With over one hundred billion neurons bouncing around in the brain we come up with quite a number of God ideas. But what human idea has ever completely understood the Infinite. Many billions or trillions is not even close to the Infinite. It seems to me that as human beings the best we can get is a real emotional knowledge of life. Like the beautiful song that expresses the feeling that the greatest thing we can learn is to Love and the best thing we can have is to be Loved. The tendency of the complicated analytical mind blocks the beautiful simplicity of this feeling, Love, which is God or Goddess, as so many have said who had some emotional grasp of what it is to become a genuine human being.

In the precious realm of the human heart, the state of marriage has suffered greatly due to these sharp mid-points. Wives and husbands are more often like two battling camps at covert warfare within the same fortress. It is sad to admit that we rarely see a couple who practices equipollence (equal weightedness) with one another. Isn't marriage suppose to be this, two people standing side by side equally protecting, cherishing and helping each other within the sacred fortress of marriage? One does not serve the other, two serve each other equally. If it is not that then why pretend it is when it is nothing less than emotional hypocrisy?

One definition of spiritual freedom is that it just naturally sets in when we get rid of shame, hatred, fear, social arrogance, the ego's self righteous pride, secretiveness or the concealment of true emotion, masking, manipulation, controlism, hesitation or suppressing genuine natural feeling, the idea that one might be good, better or superior to others and grief, depression, sadness, the blues. Spiritual liberation or salvation if you like, might simply be a process of emotional deconstructing or deprogramming until all feeling is reduced to the most primary feeling which is of course Love. But mind you it is a love mixed with wisdom, not foolish, fanatical madness. Nor is it reckless or harmful to self or others, because if love is the first and final construct of all emotional life then cherishing, loving and

327

protecting life just comes up as a natural response with this feeling.

Truthfully, Happiness which equals Love, has no cause. It is something that is always there, innate and natural to the human soul, but it is not produced by the cause and effect reasoning process. But then one says, I want something, I want an egg roll or a palace on a hill, then I shall be happy. If you examine this comment you may see the deeper comment, if I get this desired thing then I shall allow myself to be happy. It was always there, you have just put a condition on it in order for it to shine. I find myself being spontaneously happy at times for no reason, but when I try to figure and explain to myself this feeling then it starts to slip away. Perhaps this is why the Chinese poet referred to this sentiment as the "illusive bird of happiness."

Happiness, Love and Joy might just come up when one simplifies complexity, not necessarily the external world complexity, but internal complexity, thought and feeling. Thoughts are wonderful, but if you think about it, thoughts moving over the neural channels are experienced in the brain, but emotion is felt throughout the entire body, including the mind and soul. In jarring consciousness out of esoteric difficulty it seems a good thing to bring all that neural activity down into the heart. There, one has simplified complexity. A modern problem is that scientifically, psychologically, mystically and spiritually we have all become so very complicated, and in so many ways this causes the loss of insight into the simple beauty of spiritual life and what it is to be truly human and awakened.

Most religions have started out as cults. Christianity was a secretive cult that worshiped Christ in caves and catacombs hidden from the public eye for reasons all too well known. They identified each other by the secret symbol of the fisherman of souls. Again, cults have had both positive and negative influences historically speaking and within a cult itself both dark and benevolent effects may be found. In the cult of the Goddess Kali, which in the broader sense is the Tantric spiritual tradition, one may find the dual effects. Thugees used the image of Kali as a focus point for their dirty deeds. But one of the most beautiful souls to bless the face of this planet worshiped the Goddess Kali in the most tender, loving and gentle way. Ramakrishna never harmed a single soul in any shape or form. The cult of the God Dionysus also has both sides of the possibility. The cyclic celebration of the procreative, death and rebirth (resurrection) of the god principle gave birth to the tragic and comedic dramatic forms of today as well as the Orphic mysteries of the after world. On the other hand, the phallic worship associated with these rituals may indeed have led to a libidinous focused mind set in some who did not take in the holistic picture. The cult of Aphrodite could have been nothing but beneficial to the culture of the time, raising not only acknowledgement and recognition of the sacred feminine, but the worship of the same in the Goddess herself and the form of all women. The only negative potential there was may have been the possibility of girls and women being forced into sacred prostitution. To force anything on anyone is in no way a sacred thing.

The cultus, the worship of a principle or person may be abusive or a blessing depending on the intention, either liberating or oppressing. Any belief system that diminishes another person's freedom of individuality, their independent capacity to think and feel, their family love and relations or creates isolation, exclusivity, denial and superiority is an obvious negative cultic system. Simply, if people are expanding with openness, love, kindness and knowledge then it is most likely a good belief system they are embracing. If you see people not growing, becoming stagnant, isolated, hateful, superstitious, controlling, manipulative, abusive (sexually, emotionally or financially) antagonistic or arrogant to the point of increasing narrow egotistical viewpoints, well, there is your clear signal to head for the hills.

Cult leaders, gurus who consider themselves to be god and self proclaimed incarnations of 'jesus' are suspicious people of mean intelligence. "He who says he is a guru is a man of mean intelligence." Ramakrishna. Such a person thinks themselves better, higher, heavier than others. The metaphorical meaning is

329

that if one thinks oneself to be heavier than others, they go down and pull others with them. It is the phenomena of people being manipulated by a dominating personality which in result squashes individual creative spiritual capacity. I once heard a South Indian guru cult leader say, "There is no escape." Now if what he meant was there is no escape from the Beauty of Truth, then that is quite nice. But it did not seem so, for many clone like people lost in mimicry were the fruit of his tree. One should be cautious of having no escape from such dominating personalities.

A unique and most remarkable individual, Ted "Black Lightning" Patrick, is one of the original deprogrammers in this country. After having nearly lost his child to one of the more vicious jesus cults he began his practice of de-conditioning minds that had lost their sense of self due to cultic phenomena. His method is to challenge their belief system, to open new possibilities of interpretation of that thought system by questioning it in regard to the greater spectrum. Essentially, he passionately works to restore the cult persuaded individual to gain independent thinking and feeling. Not so different from John Lennon's fearless musical statements in the song "I Found Out", where he sings out with vigorous radical insight cutting away those delusions we have held so dear which pertain to the return of jesus and false preoccupation with krishna, to gurus controlling you, religion's runaround, unloving parents, forms of escapism, personal pain and the shock of real self discovery. This song by one of our most powerful poets of the century clears our heads and like "Black Lightning" deprograms us from our long held and dearly kept delusional concepts. Mr. Lennon was very skillful in seeing the obvious in deceivers, hypocrites and imitators.

In the process of restoring or gaining for the first time the blessed capacity for independent thinking and feeling there are two stages, snapping and floating. Snapping of course is coming out of the restrictive narrowness of that former collective belief system and the individual's self sense comes back. Floating is

330

when the mind returns to the mental and emotional phenomena of that belief system.

Really, in the greater paradox of the world mind we all now and then snap and float. At one moment we all snap, experiencing some greater insight into what its all about. Then we float back to the doubting mind thinking no, no, life is just the daily grind. The point might be that within each individual is the real potential to transcend all these belief systems and become someone who is not systematized by any belief. That is to become a free thinker, who can feel independent of the world mind cultus.

Like everything, the paradox of being a human being has both sides to it. Two sides to every coin. For example, some psychologists in an attempt to comprehend what exactly happens at an Alcoholics Anonymous meeting have labeled the group as a charismatic healing cult. Charisma means grace, spiritual power or influence. In this regard they may be correct for the A.A. philosophy does indeed say that no human power can save a person from what they are powerless over. Only God, the Higher Power, the Great Reality can do that. But A.A. does not define the understanding of that Principle for anyone. Any and every belief system of any individual is equally accepted: atheistic, agnostic, psychological, religious and purely spiritual. So it cannot be defined as a cult which traditionally builds their own belief system to the exclusion of others. And A.A. has actually helped people regain a fully human life free of the illness of alcoholism. So popular is it's healing method (the twelve steps) that in it's wake other so called healing cults have come up, for overeating, narcotics, sexual addiction, psychiatric and emotional traumas and obsessive compulsive disorders to mention just a few.

If you find yourself limited by the belief system presented herein, I sincerely hope that the thought content of this my own sharp mid-point will burst and the effect of the world mind cultus will no longer persuade you.

331

The Guru Problem

Spiritual Trauma and Abuse in the
Causal Dynamic of the Guru Dilemma

"It is the Sakti, the Power of God, that is born as an Incarnation." These words of Ramakrishna strike in me a note of happy peace. For I have searched long in the outer world of religions, traditions and people, never finding inner sanctuary in my own spirituality. If it is Sakti, the Power, then why not go directly to Her. What need is there in me for Incarnations, teachers, gurus, mentors, the holy texts and practices of various spiritual methods? Now I go to Her as Power, Direction, Guidance and Validation. The rest has become like kindergarten. Bubbles. Drops. As Swami Vivekananda has said in Inspired Talks, "A bit of Mother, a drop, was Krishna; another was Buddha; another was Christ."

I would never criticize Love, Truth, and Reality. But I am certainly free to criticize the manners in which the conveyance of Truth may be attempted. The fearless Swami Vivekananda was very bold in his own thoughts on these deep spiritual problems. He writes, "Rama, Krishna, Buddha, Chaitanya, Nanak, Kabir, and so on are the true Avataras, for they had their hearts broad as the sky - and above all, Ramakrishna. Ramanuja, Shankara etc., seem to have been mere Pundits with much narrowness of heart. Where is that love, that weeping heart at the sorrow of others? - Dry pedantry of the Pundit - and the feeling of only oneself getting to salvation hurry-scurry!"

This essay will no doubt anger some but it will liberate many more. So for that reason alone I shall continue writing. In the end Krishna's children destroyed themselves. Jesus' disciples set into motion a religious system responsible for the destruction of many cultures. The followers of Buddha ended up worshiping him, against his last wishes on Earth. So even incarnations have at times brought in their wake, things which are indeed unworthy of our spirituality. I will never criticize the

Sakti, the Power within them, but once the mind is mixed with the human personality, any personality, then problems arise. As Vivekananda, the bravest thinker in the Eastern spiritual domain, has once again eloquently stated. "Great saint are the object-lessons of the Principle. But the disciples make the saint the Principle, and then they forget the principle in the person."

As the Church instills in us a sense of separation from God as soon as we are born, by telling us we are born in sin, so do Gurus create a sense of separation from the Self by themselves standing forth as exclusive representations of the Self, stating to others that they cannot enter the Self without their guidance. In both systems the Principle is forgotten in the person or people, the person becomes emphasized and the Principle forgotten, no matter how much the Principle is spoken of, somehow it is forgotten. These are the products of men of mean intelligence and are full of fault, malice and class prejudice, social and spiritual. Ramakrishna gives a powerful reminder, speaking in the Brahman voice, "He who is the Lord of the Universe will teach everyone. If they need teaching, then He will be the Teacher. He is our Inner Guide."

One may find the following comments of Ramakrishna to be an interesting paradox of viewpoints, "Kabir was a worshiper of the Impersonal God. He did not believe in Siva, Kali or Krishna. He used to make fun of them and say that Kali lived on the offerings of rice and banana, and that Krishna danced like a monkey when the gopis clapped their hands. (All laugh.)" What is interesting is that Swami Vivekananda wrote that Kabir was an Incarnation, and so here we see one incarnation making fun of other incarnations. If this is so among the field of interpersonal relationships with incarnations then why can't ordinary people like me have a right to our own feelings in regard not only to these but to much lesser souls in consequence?

Anyone slightly familiar with Ramakrishna will know that the Goddess Kali was his Highest Ideal. But here we see him accepting jest and mockery with a sense of humor, even making others laugh by it. This is the wonder of true spiritual health.

He is not dogmatically dead narrow about it, he is humorous and lightful. Also, I have met one or two who were of the opinion that Totapuri, the Vedantic teacher, was Ramakrishna's high guru who showed him the gateway to nirvikalpa samadhi, absolute immersion in non dual Consciousness. But if you remember, when Totapuri arrived at Dakshineswar, the first thing that Ramakrishna did was go to Kali to ask Her why he was here. She conveyed to him that She had brought him there to teach that sweet soul the Vedanta. It is profoundly and clearly obvious that Ramakrishna went to a Higher Authority, the Goddess, rather than Totapuri, a mere human, about the whole spiritual affair.

This is the key to the whole guru mystery and how Ramakrishna's treatment of the guru phenomena never blanked out his pure relationship and contact with the Goddess. Even in regard to nirvikalpa samadhi, was it not She who stood there in his mind at the borderline, at the gateway to nirvikalpa, covering its mystery and then revealing it to him. She guided Ramakrishna past the form of Her, so he could dive deep into the Infinite. This was not Totapuri's doing, the human guru only showed him some outer methods of intensified concentration and techniques of Vedantic negation. It was the Goddess alone who took the sweet consciousness of Ramakrishna into Her inner chamber of Infinite Formless Consciousness.

The truth is that it is Sakti alone that shows us the non dual state of nirvikalpa samadhi. She reveals this, no human power may do so. By Her blessings, a samadhi sakti or a tear of nirvana sakti comes out of the thunder of your own mind, yet then some guru says to you that they have done that for you - what a horrible lie, but very common in the guru phenomena. Laotzu had no guru, only Mother Tao and he was absolutely enlightened. It was a turtle's shell that revealed the primary symbols of the Book of Changes to the King. The Principle, the Light lifting Shadow shines teaching everywhere, if you accept it from within the Self.

Only Mother Sakti can give nirvikalpa, so since She is ever present, nothing can ever be missed by the presence of absence of a guru. As Ramakrishna, the beautifully alive devotee of Kali did say, "Do you know my attitude? As for myself, I eat, drink, and live happily. The rest the Divine Mother knows. Indeed, there are three words that prick my flesh: 'guru', 'master', and 'father'. There is only one Guru and that is Satchidananda. He alone is the Teacher." Satchidananda is Existence Consciousness Love, one's true and real Self. A guru claims they can teach you. A master holds authority over you. A father, here, is a patriarch.

If it is true that nirvikalpa samadhi is experienced once the shadow of non dual deep sleep is lifted by the light of self, then who but Sakti can do this! Ramakrishna explains "The ego can disappear only when one goes into samadhi." I would not depend on nor expect a guru to do this. The truth is I will follow no religion or belief system built on a cult of personality. That is the delusion of the guru and truthfully these gurus have their deeply particular and eccentric mind states, their ego assertions and personality problems. They are type cast by their own traditional upbringing just as any other person, but so often they assume a superior human character. There is no human personality that can reveal Truth, only Para (Highest) Sakti (Power) can do this. She alone is the Light that Lifts the Shadow. For me, there is no other 'Who' that can do this. "A man cannot be a guru." Ramakrishna.

I am not set out on a course for guru bashing. That will not help me nor you. Then I would be only like those gurus who bash each others traditions saying that theirs and theirs alone is best. That attitude actually makes me feel sick within. To go to a guru means that you don't feel the Self non dual in your self. You are broken and need fixing. You go there hoping to cure the spiritual sickness of the sense of separation. One does not go to a physician when one feels in good health. But fond friendship and good company in kindred like mindedness is an altogether different thing. This is the truth and physical barriers are no barrier to this. That is how True Spirituality may be one's personal friend in daily company.

For really, within the Indian cluster, Ramakrishna seems to be one of the very few who are healthy, free and able to convey spirituality without all this guru confusion and the obfuscating relationship a guru causes in a seeker. Even those gurus who say yes, the real guru is the Self within, will turn around and hypocritically contradict themselves by the reverse remark that you need them to know this. Ramakrishna says, "Satchidananda alone is the guru." What does it mean? There is the one Guru with the big G and there are many gurus with the little g. It is a spiritual paradox. The dynamic of the guru function is to enlighten. Dattatreya had twenty four gurus; birds, fish, mountains, animals and even two women who were unaware that the guru function was working in them for him. His own mind perceived the uncovering of knowledge within their actions. So certainly wherever the Light that lifts Shadow shines, there is shown Existence, Consciousness and Love Unhidden!

Should it be a wonder that You Your Self would experience Enlightenment for no reason at all. When all that is taught is left far behind for those sad souls who still seek to find a Something, a Secret. There is no secret a guru is going to slip to you. When effort ceases, Reality appears. There is no amazement in this. Love has always been the Being within as poets strive to express this in the forms of one thousand ways. I myself have come to seek the feeling thoughts that outdistance the common present day thought systems. But gurus will tell me that if I leave them I will end up in hell. This is nothing but a terrible abusive lie. They set up a circle with no escape. This is a traumatic thing to do to another human being. Realizing this, is it any wonder that Indian philosophy refers to the states of hell as rings, well pools, and circles where the cycle of rumination has no escape. Strange, that the phenomena of the totalitarian guru relationship can cause this condition of hell in a seeker of Love and Truth. But in reality, as types are attracted to types, dogmatic seekers are attracted to dogmatic teachers just as dogs are automatically attracted to the excreta of other dogs.

True freedom comes when all original signatures, that is, the archetypes, are freed from the mind. Then Sakti is clearly

337

known and felt as one's own spirituality. It is in the Consciousness free of the impression of any and every archetype whatsoever that Pure Sakti is experienced. The Goddess Creator shatters all imagined imagery, memories, dreams in waking, waking effects in dreams, past life memories, or pure dreams. To get to Pure God you must shatter, cleave the personality vibrations of all teachers. Why would one want to follow a guru, become as a guru, in the footsteps of a human being, assuming the confining characteristics of another human being, whether they are great, transcendent or awesome to you or just small, simple and sweet? Why should one follow another, becoming like their footprint, instead of one's own Self? Why would one do such an insane thing, when one may follow their own non dual Self at every unbroken turn of the moment? Once again Ramakrishna confirms in his excelling high insight, "How is it ever possible for one man to liberate another from the bondage of the world? God alone, the Creator of this world - bewitching maya, can save men from maya. There is no other refuge but that great Teacher, Satchidananda."

You see, gurus can cause spiritual trauma in those who are seeking to find, by the very nature of the dynamic they set up, by the abusive totalitarian attitude that they have something you don't. True Self Reality is Innate and always in contact with us, whether or not we are in contact with Reality, yet this trauma keeps us paralyzed from knowing well. A guru imposes on you and prevents you from standing here in the Self without any support system. It is extremely strange that such gurus want to abuse people in this way. And those who stay with gurus learn how to abuse people in the same way that the guru abuses them. Every guru sect and personality cult is a tormented struggle to reach non duality, which is blocked and obscured by the duality of the guru's overdrive ever keeping the disciple in underdrive where they cannot stand forth on their own. If you do not enjoy being around the products or results of a guru, admit to your intuition your innermost feelings and leave. Heal yourself of that abuse and know that a guru's arrogant ego will never lead you to God, Love, Truth and Self Reality. Referring to this

Ramakrishna said, "But a piece of worthless wood sinks, if a man sits on it, and drowns him."

It is important to free yourself from the clutches of such a relationship for disaster follows in its wake by those gurus who seek to crush out individual spirituality and produce only resultant pathetic disciple imitators. If you see that the guru's tree is producing distorted flowers of self pitying, self obsessed and unloving egos who are verging on apostasy because of being sadly and yet comically shell shocked by the guru's unkindness and more involved in spiritual competition with one another, then be happy with yourself and leave. It is better to walk the razor's edge as a free soul than voluntarily remain in the absurd condition of a spiritual slave. You have the Lantern in your own hand but your are asking someone else for light. You have the Jewel in your own heart, but you are digging in someone else's dirt to find nickels and dimes.

Another aspect of this phenomena is guru magic or more sanely stated, conscious cognitive projection. If you are sitting before a guru, any spiritual experiences, states of self realization or heighten spiritual emotions that you may have at those moments are actually coming up from within your own mind. By the power of consciousness itself, you see what you want to see. If you hold Jesus ideas in your mind you may project that you are seeing some divine son of God in front of you. Or if you hold Buddha ideas there in your mind you may see that the body and the mind of the guru are impermanent and this may create a sense of the nirvana feeling within you. It is your own Sakti which is creating these spiritual states, not the guru. A relation with a guru is really that you are seeking a relation with your own Self, your own Sakti Power, not the guru's self or an ego relation there with. This is the common mistake. Even that big teacher Totapuri came to realize that it was purely the Saving Grace of the Divine Mother that brought Ramakrishna to high realization and not Totapuri's doing. He finally became humble.

You see, these gurus function at a certain level, that of Finding. It is a strange profession in spiritual life. The search feels ended with the meeting with the guru, but it is not. A harder journey begins, that of leaving the abusive relationship of a cult of personality which suspends Truth in a deceitful web that they say only they can give and will give only if you totally surrender to them. Honestly, I have never seen this successfully happen. But I have abundantly seen them cause fear and unworthiness in many people and this is the tragedy of a system which promises enlightenment but never gives it. Here is yet another splendid high thought illuminating the darkness of this problem from Ramakrishna, "Their aim is to attain Nirvana. They are followers of Vedanta. They constantly discriminate, saying, 'Brahman alone is real, and the world illusory'. But this is an extremely difficult path. If the world is illusory, then you too are illusory. The teacher who gives instruction is equally illusory. His words, too, are as illusory as a dream." It is one's own inner Sakti Consciousness that brings about the awakening. Nothing illusory can ever do that for you. What I always wanted was True Self, Real Love and Spiritual Consciousness. That comes of itself now, during precious moments. Suddenly, deep serene non dual peace. This comes out of oneself alone, within sweet solitude or within the faces of various conversations, that is only because of the level of non dual consciousness that is cognised. I used to think a guru could give me samadhi, but it was never so. That serenity, peace, balance, and happiness all comes from within oneself.

The last post on the trail of this sojourn of reflections is my own Self. I have had wonderful luck or perhaps divine misfortune to meet and study with some of the finest souls this time of history has had to offer. Writing of my experience has always been my practice. But no book will tell you Who You Are. Some souls ascend to great height and become teachers. Some of these become abusive, totalitarian and obfuscating and they will by their very nature send you into blessed apostasy where you may find your Self. It is because of the Power of that Great Height becoming emphasized in their personality that this dark confusion arises. If you feel apostasy towards this then bless your heart. Others who keep proper emphasis on that

340

Power Itself and not the personality, will generally be kind, loving and not abusive. It is really simple as that.

The causal dynamic of the guru problem seems to be one of exterior versus interior validation and direction. As the real meaning of guru is light or luminosity (ru) that removes or lifts shadow or darkness (gu), then who indeed can indeed do this for a person. Can another person do this for you. Or is it simply and purely that Sakti, the power of luminosity itself. Those validations and directions coming from people of title, in roles of traditions, these persons, teachers, mentors and others working through the past expressions of Experience, those who have run to avatara mountain assuming greatness on themselves have helped us less by their pretentious inaccessibility. Whereas those who have embraced their own interior luminosity that lifts shadow as validation and direction, who humbly assume no greatness and who just stay here and be human beings who are accessible, loving, similar, equal and without height. These have helped us more by their example in the spiritual function of life.

Interestingly enough, guru also means; heavy or heavier than others, great, large, violent, serious, hard, severe, weary, important, of much account, highly respected, venerable, father, mother, elder relative or teacher. All these meanings are there in Sanskrit. Of course, most gurus select the ones that flatter them and leave out the more questionable definitions. But it may be so that the creators of the Sanskrit language did indeed realize that a guru can be violent, hard, serious and severe and that their assumed largeness and self imagined greatness could damage others in the spiritual sense that they present to others that they are heavier, more weighty and of more account or value than any other human being. A person of sympathy looks downward at other's suffering. While a person of empathy feels equally the experiences of others.

The Buddha had two gurus in his early spiritual career, but he abandoned both and found his own Reality. This is a wonderful example. Krishna's guru was a mere astrologer. And we all know astrologers work in the field of astronomy and psychology, not generally spiritual reality and they are often

341

filled with superstitions. Krishna's example shows that teachers are simply metaphors of a path. Self is not found there. There is no path to Self, no going there, Self has already arrived. And as we assume, if all these incarnations are the Power of Sakti manifest, then, in order for Her to work effectively, does Sakti really need a guru? And as She has made the whole entire universe and everything within this at least fifteen billion year old creation, then what is not Her, as Sakti, as Power manifest?

When one goes to a guru or turns to some path, whether in the physical, subtle or causal dimension, what one is really asking oneself is, "Where is Love? Where is Spirituality?" And hopefully the answer will come up from within you, to this guru question, the gentle hum of Truth from within, whether dual or non dual your experience may be. It is a superstition to believe that a guru is always right about everything. How can that be? I have heard from various sources in the Indian community of spiritual teachers, that poets such as Tennyson, Whitman, Shelly, Shakespeare, Keats, and Wordsworth were indeed considered to be Enlightened. None of these had gurus. Yet from the same sources I would hear that one cannot be enlightened without a guru. This is a statement of contradiction. It speaks of a spiritual potential and then blatantly denies it. If there is anything we want, it is to be free of perplexity in our Love and Spirituality, for we would cherish this for eternity. In this regard, the spiritual social structure of the guru dynamic is very misleading.

Even in the constellation of Indian spirituality there are those who have attained enlightenment or who were themselves attained by the Sakti of enlightenment without gurus of human form, but by their own inner power in one shape or another. They looked with loving heart, deep into the Universal Mirror of Pure Sakti and in that Mirror, saw both the illusion of knowledge and the illusion of ignorance reflected as the same to the Mirror. Then, by looking even further and deeper, past the illusory images on the Mirror, they realized this Self without hesitation. One is Sri Ma of Kamakhya, there is Meera, another one is Anandamayi, there is Amritanandamayi, Krishnamurti,

342

Aurobindo, and Ramana Maharshi. Ramprasad (1723 - 1803) was a fully realized heroic Kali Poet. Early on, he briefly encountered the Tantrika Agamavagisa, but that one left, never to return. The poet became illuminated in the non duality of Mother Kali by his own inner Shakti, composing his vigorous ecstatic poetry to Her, all the way up to the moment of his conscious exit from the body. It was She and none other, who awakened him to true Reality.

None of these women and men had gurus in the common tradition. They simply experienced spontaneous illumination from their own Inner Sakti, without the redundant problem of guru association. Of course so many gurus will try to explain this away by saying these special ones are reincarnated advanced souls and that is the reason their enlightenment happened in this way. Maybe, maybe not. It seems more so that this is a controlling denigration upon one's own personal right to spiritual freedom. A bad guru wants to keep disciples as servants. A good and rare guru wants to see people walk as free souls. Vivekananda boldly comes to our defense with his open mindedness, "My motto is to learn whatever good things I may come across anywhere. This leads many friends to think that it will take away from my devotion to the Guru. These ideas I count as those of lunatics and bigots. For all Gurus are one and are fragments and radiations of God, the Universal Guru."

Ramakrishna says with rarest clarity avoiding the deep spiritual trauma of guru abuse, "There is not a fellow under the sun who is my disciple. On the contrary, I am everybody's disciple." Thus, true and real awakened spirituality does indeed live as a Reality without guru disciple monotony, the problem itself. Simply, how can one be dependent on another for one's own realization? Truth is One. Love must be free of all universal influences. For centuries upon centuries the legacy of the guru problem has existed in an acceptance of the denial that there is a problem at all with this dynamic. Perhaps it is for the bold and free American spirit to first question and then resolve the oppression of what has been for far too long proclaimed as spiritual authority.

The uncompromising Non Dual text, the Ribhu Gita, (translated by Dr. H. Ramamoorthy) states without the slightest fear, "The guru, indeed, does not exist; truly, there is no disciple. There being only Brahman alone. Renouncing all, renouncing the guru, and renouncing everything ever, sit in Silence. Brahman - Bliss alone exists. The guru, the precepts of the guru - there is none such as the guru - the nature of the guru, the sincerity of the guru, and the guru himself exist not. The Self is the Guru of the Self, nothing else being existent. There is no doubt of this." This view is also found in the Ashtavakra Gita and the Avadhuta Gita, which both speak only from the Height of Pure Non Dualism, giving no concession whatsoever to any dualistic consideration.

SPIRITUAL SOLUTIONS TO
PSYCHOLOGICAL EQUATIONS

Simplicity. Complexity. Happiness or confusion. In the same way that stone underlies the existence of a sculpture, so do spiritual solutions underlie the paradox and problems of psychological equations. Of course, some equations are impossible and difficult paradigms, but others are quite simple. To live in the spiritual is to live in happiness as much as may be and this arises from simplicity. In essence, all equations are formulas of self, yet self is often ignored giving full attention to the equations which lead to complexity.

As the saying goes, the mind is like a white cloth that becomes colored by whatever it contacts. It the same manner we becomes defined by the equation instead of the solution. For example, we hear of the passive aggressive dynamic and mind becomes identified with this thought system, not taking in its meaning. It is a dualistic emotional response, sublimation of true emotion and then the consequential volcanic explosion on the other side. The tendency is in everyone and so is the solution, genuine primary emotion with no other side to it, no secretive masked feeling. Even though the passive aggressive emotional distortion has many subtle mechanics to it, the key to its solution is simplicity in emotional response, genuine and true to the self. It is an art and primary emotion is not primal emotion. Yes, it is a yin yang kind of feeling, instead of the simplicity of a *Tao*-like response, truth, the way, the singular reality.

Strangely, psychology means the knowledge of the soul (psyche) but more often is reduced to mere mental mechanics. Certainly, understanding the mechanics is most important, but more so is to recognize with real emotional knowledge, who is the operator of this machine. This of course is self or soul and all the massive functions of the psyche are continually engaged in its definition. The definition may be somewhat vague according to each individual's understanding of what it might be, defining the spiritual is like trying to define love. Who can say what love is? The important point is to have an intuitively aware connection with one's own definition of love, spirit, existence and genuine consciousness. This may be more feeling than thinking.

If you define yourself as a libido, an ego, as subconscious, unconscious, neurotic, an imbecile, a genius, a fixated ego maniac, well then, your mind assumes the definition of what you think yourself to be. It is not to negate the problem of complexes. They certainly exist in diverse capacity. And in this right they themselves often negate the essential principle. When it comes to denial of another person's reality as a form of abuse, psychology may be abusive in some regard to the spiritual side of life. Not always. Sometimes it is quite enlightening if taken as an elucidation of the enormous variety of psychological and psychically cognitive obstructions in the human mind.

As somnambulism proves that waking and dreaming consciousness may not always be separate, which may demonstrate the spiritual importance of one's dream life as each symbol metaphorically reflects the internal attitude of self consciousness. Though multiple personality disorder is a negative and painful condition it also demonstrates the interesting potential of polyphasic consciousness. So many possibilities yet untapped.

As consciousness is a formless substance it assumes the forms before it. The personality cores, thought currents, psychic problems and mental imprints in psychological functions exist within formless consciousness. Whether it be feminine or masculine oriented, all psychological mapping has the same map maker as a ubiquitous spiritual principle. And as reason stands, if one is drawn inward toward that principle it is in that where one finds the synthesis and empowerment of one's own spiritual counsel. What advice can be given which is better than what comes from the clear, genuine and sincere self within. This generates happiness, simplifies complexity and brings the beautiful emotion of self balance into grasp. This becomes the

346

even keel of harmonizing psychological and spiritual life. When we are near it a kind of speechless sentiment comes, when far from us we are empty, so then there is depression and so forth.

The ratio equation between true esteem and the cloud of ego is somewhat of a paradox. Humility is needed to overcome the puzzle otherwise esteem translates itself into the nuisance of egotistical arrogance. True self worth is found in primary true emotion and this leads to real satisfaction, genuine joy and continuing happiness. If one becomes narcissistic and superior then they will find themselves on a control trip which is a great hindrance to accepting the happiness of spontaneously being what one naturally is. A happy person is easily capable of letting go even of letting go, unhappy people always are trying to control and dominate events, things, responses and people around them. This is a type of cognitive distortion on the nature of human existence. We cannot control life or death or anything, we can only manage our own attitude.

Happiness is no mystery nor is it inaccessible. If you can make an accomplishment or two regularly, small or big, that generates happiness. If you consciously tend the green garden of your shared space with those you care for that will certainly create happiness. If you have a formula or catalog of things that make you happy and practice what is there, that will bring happiness. If you start a continuum of happiness, in responses, in accessible enjoyments, natural pleasures and simple wonders, avoiding the impossible paradigms of big bang thinking (a kind of self talk or self dialogue that says I will only allow myself to be happy when I get that big house or car or beautiful spouse and not until then), that will accustom you to the familiarity with happiness. So simple an example of this is that smiling makes others smile.

We are all creative beings, expressing that creativity in whatever shape it takes is another simple key to the continuum of the flow of happiness. Perhaps it is because the spiritual principle is the most creative of all and if we as spiritual beings are creative, then somehow we are in aligned with that. If that creative life is blocked, misery and collapse come about.

347

Biochemical psychiatry which reduces mental balance or imbalance to the synaptic responses of neural chemicals is an interesting examination. Serotonin, endorphine, dopamine and oxcytocin at the natural organic level are responsible for clarity, well being, pleasant relaxation of the brain's natural pain killer and the feeling of love and attraction. Curiously, without pharmaceutical reliance, it is the same brain that creates the smooth flow of these chemicals and the absence or obstruction of their flow. If you are depressed, for example, serotonin re-uptakes and does not make its synaptic leap, if you are happy and cheerful it does make the leap, then mental intellectual clarity is present. The potential of generating these neural chemicals at will is an interesting possibility.

Part of happiness is honestly learning to admit that we do not have power over everything, nor can we manage or control everything. A trust in something greater than ourselves must be there within the heart. This brings about a release which accepts life as it is. Whatever that 'something' is I cannot say. Some call it God or Goddess, others Infinity, Truth, Bliss or the Great Reality. It takes a stepping past the bridge of reason, logic and analyses. Then one can say that happiness is a causeless feeling that has always been inside and only needed to be allowed entrance into the life.

When we hide from ourselves masking real self emotion, then resistance and resentment arises with their various corresponding psychological equations, such as passive aggression, obsessive compulsive, existential anxiety, repression oppression dynamics and so forth. This is all due to the perceptual styles that do not allow empathy towards oneself and others, a way of looking at life which negates the sovereignty of others, one's own self domain of sovereignty and the primary feeling of who you are. Being your own self is the simplest way to be happy. These principles are so simple do they really need to be spelled out? For me they did.

It seems that happiness comes alive when one touches, realizes and expresses their primary, fundamental, essential, basic and real emotion. Happiness is an emotion, not a concept.

When you become conscious of yourself as emotion then that consciousness naturally expresses itself as the happiness of your being. That seems to be the formula. It is a cognitive work, a practice to create this continuum, learning to feel and contact continuously and generously the emotion behind emotions. It is what we all want, essentially, happiness. Just look at us, what complex puzzles we are, when simply we all came from stardust made to be momentary actors on the universal stage. How is it that these little animated piles of cosmic ash have made their simple seconds in time so complicated?

Fear and anger are the two big troublemakers which have a number of faces in the emotional spectrum. But all fears are eventually reduced to the primal existential anxiety over not being, death. But why, for at some level, genuinely everyone knows that what we are continues in some way. Death, not understood, is the doubt of the spiritual soul, understood, it is the illumination of life. Anger is the responses to our inability to control what we feel we have created, neglected or failed to foresee and control. Anger is probably the greatest of emotional distortions. It arises through the passive aggressive dynamic of course. It denies others their own belief system, their innate sovereignty, abuses others and the self, emotionally, spiritually, psychologically, physically, verbally. But genuine deep release of control and the desire to manipulate, sincere and real letting go most often solves the negative mood of anger.

Yet happiness may be just as simple as freeing our most inner, unique and direct conscious sentiment of all other emotional mind shapes which occupy the space of feeling. It may be simply learning a communication with the self in silence before the cognitive emotional distortions of all other feeling tones resound. I feel that it must be the essence, primordial and primary, as the purpose and reason of existence.

Happiness, as a spiritual solution, may be the art of being alone with the self and being happy with that. To stay on an even keel with one's own joy, not being jacked up or jacked down by the flux of events and reactions around us. The psychological term homeostasis comes to mind which is called

349

the wisdom of the body in that it always seeks to re-balance itself biochemically. But we could expand the term to include the innate tendency within the psyche and the soul to ever return to equilibrium. Homeostasis is the state of equilibrium in sameness caused by opposing equal forces balancing each other out. This rings of the sweet exquisite emotion of happiness as expressed in non dualism, advaita, (samarasa: the taste of sameness) where all antinomies are resolved once and for all.

This is not indifference but the ultimate cherishing of life as self. Once I learned to somewhat let go of the stressful intellectual boredom of perfectionism and control, the blessed boredom of happiness started to come on like a drumbeat. Through sincere truthful intuition, false intellect drops, and some natural joy is generated, the result is the unification of dream contents in the psyche with the figure of the waking life. This harmonizes the field of happiness as the carefree promise of this life. It is breathing, it is feeling, it is staying alert or not being lulled into the sleep of distorted emotional contents. It is circulating with others, one's own sense of what is spiritual in oneself. It is a very deep form of relaxation into joy, of lingering with happiness, or just allowing yourself to be who and what you are naturally. The many is reduced to the one and this one is your own happiness.

Spiritual Moments in High Sakti
and the Problem of Return
to Complex Cognition

"Your Own Atma Is The Divine Mother."

Swami Aseshananda
1899 - 1996

The world tends to collect us into a stagnant rumination on Who We Are, instead of dancing the Divine Dance with the Goddess (Living Sakti) in the sacred cremation ground (of dualism) where we know what death is not, and feeling the High Sakti of never having been born to dualism.

Must I write? Can I not now just Live Sakti? I insult myself, resenting myself (ego) because of this desire. After sending my last work, *The Goddess and the God Man*, to the dynamically spiritual Swami Swahananda, he replied, "So you are at it for a long time." Indeed, and it does take a long time. I wait for the world to go to sleep to wake my mind and let go of my thoughts. Then I write. This is what lowers my conscious threshold to what was the Great Unknown. In the day the world's callings keep this letting go from occurring. Though thoughts come at moments. I am limited, but this statement is a fool's (bellowing windbag) self-outlined belief.

In Reality, what we know (believe) might limit what we may Become! I shall tell a story (from *Man the Maker of His Destiny*) of Swami Vivekananda's (1863-1902) to demonstrate this. One day an astrologer came to a king and told him that he had six months to live. The king freaked. So his thoughtful minister asked the astrologer to check the calculations on the king's chart. He did so, still saying the king has six months to live. The minister then asked the astrologer how long his chart said he had left to live and he replied, "Oh, I have twelve years

351

to live." At that moment the minister unsheathed his sword and separated the astrologer's head from his body and then said to the king, "See what a liar he is!" We should not believe what the world tells us we are.

So I must send my most sincere and generous appreciations to Swami for this beautifully helpful story, and as ever and ever to his divine (yet most human) and spiritual mentor, Sri Ramakrishna of Dakshineswar (1836-1886).

For you see this story illustrates so well what Kali/Sakti (pronounced Shak-tee) in Her Active Form is ever doing, severing the head of delusion (ego). At the level of Truth (High Sakti) this is already Done, but to get There, to the "Done" is what this text attempts, I hope. One could place a simple metaphor on this story of Swami's, you see the astrologer is the symbol of the ego delusion telling one who one is not. And so Kali comes up as Sakti and severs this delusion to reveal the true Self (as a Non-Dual being) represented by the king.

Though Swami Aseshananda (1899-1996) and Swami Bhashyananda (1917-1996) have both passed away from their bodies, dropping and leaving those bodies only twelve days apart from one another, I do not feel they are gone at all. They have only moved from one room to the next, as Sri Ramakrishna has described what death is but to be. So they are not gone. It is the beautiful and gentle completion of a cycle. And I have the deepest peace in knowing without a single drop of doubt that when I also move from one room to the next, that they both will be there to greet me. It is no less, the "Already Done!" I can never express my high generous thoughts and feelings of spiritual appreciation for the good fortune of meeting them both.

"It is said that there are places near Kedar (a high peak in the Himalayas) that are covered with eternal snow; he who climbs too high cannot come back. Those who have tried to find out what is there in the higher regions, or what one feels there, have not come back to tell us about it... overpowered with bliss... Who will speak? Who will explain?" Ramakrishna. I wish I could retrain my mind to be new, to express itself in a new way after I reach a high point within my thought insights. But I find so often, the thumping noise, the nuisance, the ego named me, me, me comes back to find all the ego stuff and the complex cognition that pulls that single divine confidence back into the idea of personal power (ego). Why is it that we feel the Beauty of Love, then suddenly, usually in that instant, sink back into the psychological dimension (and there losing the wonderful effects of Love)?

Where is the sweet feeling never to be lost, but to remain as a state of perpetual perception and of continuous becoming into this Love that tolerates and accepts everything in a way that does no longer distract from that High Moment? Could this be effortless serenity understood by complex cognition itself that simply has come to comprehend everything that happens in some way to itself? Or is it simply the problem or question of what one identifies with after the return. Indeed, why does the mind insist on the need of forming an identity on return from the experience past identity with the concepts of ego formed or shaped in the waking, dreaming, or deep sleep states (or as we reflect back on deep sleep with the ego mind). It is to train mind to be new and not return to the reflex conditioning of ego forms related to those states. I do not identify with one, or the state of two, nor even the third state when I am at my best and most awake identity in the Principle. And for me this Principle is Sakti, the Great Power of the Goddess. The one question must be, "With *what* do you Identify?"

For me I must say not to identify with perfectionism. It is impossible and I do not seek, expect, or anticipate it any longer, not consciously. Especially as a writer, for when I give in to the ideal of the perfect I become trapped in the work and then the spirituality of why I write becomes lost in the act of writing. I do not compromise or make compensation with perfectionism. I do not seek a counterbalance or concession with the perfect. But of course, if you lean to far to the right, then the left will suffer.

But losing contact with High Sakti brings in its wake the instant reflex of then getting back to High Sakti. At times this becomes based on being forgiven by self and loved ones in the sense that one has an imagined loss of their divine birthright. I have also found that Sakti remains more constant if one develops an attitude of equality toward one's personal experience in the natural course of life with humiliation and adoration which both together melt in the High Sakti by the one act of ego loss and spiritual entry. It is also most helpful to retrain the emotions to learn to respect other's suffering. That is to take it into oneself and not to recoil from it, for it is natural to the region of physical life and of complex cognition.

When mind comes down from High Sakti, mind should be cautious on what mind evokes and invokes as the recollection of memory patterns or of the refreshing content of direct experience. Often mind is like a steel ball in water, it will go to the bottom of itself because the subconscious needs to be cleaned out. Until then, even when you have High Sakti, the return to complex cognition will indeed be complex. I also look not to have a high horse ego, that is ego looking down on others. What suffering have others experienced that I have not that would make me look down at them. I am equalized by the same suffering. If my esteem gets built up, somehow life tears it down, by its very movement. So I seek humility in this humiliation. That is the suffering of the human world. Hopefully my ego is no longer a mechanism of defense against innate honesty within and a higher acceptance of the reality of living and dying, and everything between.

If I should reach a point of peace that lasts, where I would be ready to quit this world at any time, without fear, then I am happy. But can I get rid of fear, no, nor anger, or desire, or Love! I am human, sensual, emotional, not a renunciate, not a god, not a statue, but I am too hard on myself even though there are moments in High Sakti that are relatively free of this self hardness. And I become so distant from High Sakti at times, that shame, humiliation, guilt, depression, remorse, sorrow, and disappointment fill the all in me and I reach the condition of the lonesome (that we all know). I ask how I can go on from there, my time on this Earth is coming to an end. I feel it and then realize this is the distortion of dark depression that forgets the world is divine in that it is Living with High Sakti. Also, if one denies in mind what one is actually depressed over or cannot clearly define that thing in regard to the complex of the psychic self, that lack of clear identification may create a domino series of things that are unnecessary depression-objects. The mind just goes toward all that mess.

Certainly some of that is due to the phenomena of objective associations in their relation to subjective emotional content. The causal dynamic to one's pool of source responses which must be reduced to the essential responses and then to a single response to the reality of High Sakti.

It actually comes to this, how does one feel toward the four functions of the psychic current and how does one offer these currents into High Sakti so they may remain there and act from there? These four; memory, figuring, comparison, and ego drive as lingering forms of consciousness, make one feel separate from High Sakti when they are never in duality from that High Sakti. To think that these psychic currents are different from the Current of High Sakti is simply a cognitive delusion of dualism, though it may temporarily insist in the mental level that it is separate. Again, that is just a lingering form in the mind, the mind which is made of Sakti. The currents of memory, figuring, comparison, and ego drive come from that Sakti and find peace in that Sakti in the state of non-dualism with the Object of Love in or as Adoration. This is none other than Sakti!

Could this be anything else than a Love for Love's Sake which is unaffected by the mood cycle of the other (not dependent) or the causal dynamics of memory mosaics. Living Sakti allures me at every moment. It is a Love that is Felt not explained. Yours, and yours alone.

You see I try very hard to keep expanding my psychic comfort level so High Sakti will be more comfortable to me. It involves continuous broadening and leaving behind unusable belief systems, those that no longer apply to the content of retaining High Sakti. I think for Myself, no tradition, no savior in me. Not the teacher's function, action, phenomena. Not the disciple's body, mind, or ego. Then, in High Sakti, what is it? A name or word cannot define it, nor give it cognition as all definitions are ego joined. Ego rules world, even those who worship an Egoless (supposed) Conception of the Divine, do so through their own ego conception!

All memory associations are separation from the Primal Now (High Sakti), except for of course, the memory of Now. This Sweet Memory Expands, the opposite boxes us in. High Sakti is retained in stabilized consciousness without those memory boxes (or future boxes). When losing contact with the need to figure out and compare all that in the "right now", the mind energy disengages automatically from wasting worry, rumination, dialogues with fantasy, depleting resentments, and the causal dynamics of memory mosaics (or future mosaics).

In anger, jealousy, possessive identities, etc,_ the Kind Sight of High Sakti may become momentarily clouded, better not to give the attention to emotions such as these, nothing comes of it. Sakti Power is where its at, those emotions devour clear thought in connection to the focus on Sakti. It is the same with thoughts. One must develop the attitude of no collecting (of thoughts) and that of free flow engaged with joy and appreciation of the thought flow in order not to diminish the perpetual perception and continuous becoming in High Sakti. The high focus in High Sakti keeps me free of rumination on emotion, mind and images in memory.

Also, fear and Love both attract to us their respective feelings. Sakti is nothing but Love in the highest expression and experience. Sakti is what I attract to myself, but I have not overcome fear. Sakti is what touches the lonely spot within us all and fills that spot with good feeling that gives our lives a proportion in relationship to Love. That is meaning. So take in everything but identify (Egotize) nothing, only Sakti.

Can celibacy help this spiritual condition to remain as a constant experience. Perhaps, as a spiritual achievement in singular confidence and personal power. But celibacy can be neurotic. Or it can be the preservation and conservation of energy in singular spiritual confident empowerment. I am not celibate. But most of all the reason for celibacy is that the Love for the Object Ideal of Love is without motive, phenomenal,

356

emotional or otherwise. It is a focus of eros toward the Ideal of Love Eternal, unaffected by the current of eros or amour (only Agape) within the psyche's emotionality. In this level I find that in the obvious and the not obvious, we all without exception, are passionately romantic (eros/amour) for the Agape of Sakti. But the natural lover and the celibate may both be caught in the trap of asking Sakti for things, perhaps things of spiritual value or things of material value, and this is a distraction from the true and Immediate Gift of High Sakti, which is Love for Love's Sake! It is the quality of Love within a person that makes their continuous becoming and perpetual perception of Sakti a thing of beauty, not mere discipline. There is also the unique myth of the yogi (Shankara) who raised the dead body of King Amaru and entered that body to test for himself the pleasures of sexual experience. Well, he forgot himself in this enjoyment and was later recalled back to his own body by a beautiful mantra (prayer). But the thoughtful person must realize that he was no longer psychologically celibate after this transference to sexual life, even though his yogi's body never engaged in the sensual and sexual life. He did the whole thing under the challenge of a debate with one of his four disciples to be.

The prolonged state of Beauty is a higher joy than simple sexual pleasure. Sex is energy, emotion, self expression in the consciousness of sense conditions, being, self knowing, love, connection, and relation. If that energy is directed up the central yogic nerve (sushumna), it may become the loving expression of spirituality or it may become neurotic or narcissistic. A pedestrian provincial backward attitude toward celibacy is just hypocrisy. Since Ramakrishna is the Proto-Point of spiritual reference for me and he taught the renunciation of sex and money as spiritual distractions, I must honestly admit my own inner contradictions and mood doubts that hit me and cause shifting in the power states of my emotions. A kind of duplicity strangles me, his integrity was gold, my integrity is copper. But the Essential is never lost! Indeed, and *Who* is the Supreme Paramour? Ramakrishna is in no way naive over the matter of sexually passionate love, nor is he a hypocrite. When asked about his Tantric teacher, the noble and very magnificent lady Bhairavi Brahmani who practiced the five makara offerings, one of these being conjugal sexual sacrifice to the Goddess and also why the learned Vaishnavacharan (one of those who declared Ramakrishna an Incarnation) of high spiritual caliber had a paramour in auxiliary for his Tantric work, Ramakrishna invariably answered, "Oh, no; they did not incur any blame by it! They believed wholeheartedly that it was their path to the realization of God. The spiritual attitude of no one should be interfered with. Never condemn anybody's attitude, nor try to make another's attitude your own." Also Ramakrishna makes an astonishingly honest and candid confession of his own eros/amour/agape affections toward the Supreme Paramour, "Once, in a spiritual mood, I felt intense love for Jagannath (A Name of God), love such as a woman feels for her sweetheart." And, if we as human beings cannot love the God and Goddess within each other, then who shall we love? It may be difficult for those whose heads are cracked with unmerciful morality, but this beautiful idea is there too, "The impulse of lust should be turned into the desire to have intercourse with Atman." And, "Instead of desiring worldly pleasures, desire God. Have intercourse with Brahman." Brahman (The Infinite), Atman (The Real Self), God, and Sakti, even so, are but various names for the Supreme Paramour. And the principle of this process is perhaps the actual and earnest meaning behind all our loves, passions, aching needs, wants, and searching for pleasure and satisfaction.

So I must ask myself if, are You, Mother Sakti initiating me in the Place which hold no thoughts, the Sweet Current of Feeling, a Love yet still aware of Conscious Pleasure? I feel I am catching up with life, the life in Sakti. As my ego can now accept humiliation without the mechanism of defense, or exhilaration and adoration, without the mechanism of esteem building. It is all the same. I can be Happy, just by letting it be so, starting with a smile. Life is grand when one moves only at the most powerful impulse of Sakti.

It is a matter of developing a sensitivity to that impulse, a feature or part of self that responds to Sakti. Perpetual Beauty or Perpetual Perception of this Beauty is like those Dzogchen (a Tibetan Direct Experience method) Moments where the Magnificent is grasped in the quick knowing of a single second. Then one comes down, back to Earth, as it were, and there, living the life in Living Sakti begins. Embracing complex cognition with simplicity. It is like the paradox of pure Zen verses all that busy stuff, but the busy stuff only happens in the singularity of any given moment. It is in harmony to Sakti and not given away to the complex.

You see, life is swallowed by death, then death spurts out life again. I've always had the feeling that we come into and go out of life, but that this feeling is the same (Love, I suppose) and that it is the same in everyone. Or maybe it is the cognitive feeling one gets with reincarnation thinking? There is no conclusion, that is, Life is continuous and from the spiritual position this Love neither comes nor goes. This feeling is with you as essence of what you are through each life and that makes the whole thing quite adventurous and exciting. But the process of growing seems to be a lot of getting rid of childhood imprints and that is redundant, over and over. So, where is death and what is it but a lie! Even in this one life, people often feel that parts of this life were, as it were, another life. That old part has died and they feel where they are now is a new life.

But depression is a mental/emotional hell and it comes by being too hard on oneself, because such emotions like anger, regret, etc., aimed at oneself are toxic. Is it all cognitive? Partially at least. Yet one must learn to like being alone, for that is when Sakti appears at first, developed in the quiet state. After this, Sakti is seen in the many and the busy. Depression is delusionary cognitive putting away from Self-Sakti, a waste of energy, time, and consciousness. To be happy without the ego, that is the question. Would I as a writer be happy without identification with my writing? It is all ego, but some part of the accomplishing in the creative comes from a Place where ego is not primary.

To me, it is from the Image of Kali. She is the Maker of Sakti, She is Sakti, two words (Kali and Sakti) for the same. She is the Maker of Love (Bhakti). She is the Maker of Energy (Prana). She is the Maker of the Energetic Pleasure (Kama) and when these are turned back up one reaches into Pure Exhilaration. Drawing energetic pleasure into energy, and energy into love, love melts into pure Sakti which is the Non-Dual Kali. One must vigorously protect the mind and feelings with the Power of Sakti!

I have the memory essence of a spiritually inclined dream which has stayed with me. Swami Aseshananda was telling me, "Renunciation!" Saying that finally there must be renunciation of all the three states (waking/dream/sleep) and renunciation of the five bodies (bliss, intellect, mind, energy, and the physical body). Renunciation of the Upanishads and the Tantras, "Yes, even this!" Renunciation of all the Bardos (Intermediate Conditions) and of all Tantric technical cognitions, "Yes, even this." Renunciation of everything he conveyed through his dream image in my mind, "Yes, even my mind. Yes, renunciation of everything but Sakti, everything but Mother." If this is true then who will contain Mother when they return from High Sakti back into complex cognition? Does it become a question of Pouring Sakti into the sahaja (Self born state, Sakti projected outside) field, the spontaneous spiritual arena of universal feeling and experience?

Certain archetypes, ideal forms, prototypes, or original signatures in consciousness have boundaries that may be difficult to see beyond into the deeper and deeper meaning. For example, I dreamed a dream of Swami Bhashyananda. I was looking for a book in his library. He said to me, "The best book in this whole library is there. It is *Kesava Isvari* ! You may have it." Kesava is the long haired one, a divine name of the Vishnu principle in the form and personality of Krishna. And Isvari is the Goddess, is Kali, is Sakti. I have never had this thought in the waking state of consciousness, but it was there in my dream mind as a deeper unknown background signature. Bhashyananda was saying, "Krishna is Doing Everything." Of

360

course, Kesava is Krishna and Krishna is Ramakrishna and it is none other than the Goddess who became both, incarnating as Krishna and then as Ramakrishna, and many others. Is this all I can or all that I will let myself remember of this dream, in honesty, and without fabrication? Isvari is the Descended (Ava) Mother (Tara), and thus may we all wave our hands with joy generated by the power of this knowledge. For all, one and all, may be exalted with the potent direct anointing of Her Spirit (Sakti). The direct experience of Love (Sakti) is greater than any human contact! "Rakhal would lie down here and say to me that he didn't even care for my company. He was then passing through such an exalted state." Ramakrishna. Again and again would you dare to pass beyond the deliberation of old belief forms and mental signatures and perhaps ask yourself if it was the Gentle and Loving Feminine Sacred Spirit that was crucified? Break free to find the Wonder of Heaven Everywhere! Why would you pour Fresh Sakti into the old mind? The true name of Nirvana is Tatha Gata Garbha (the Womb of Reality Gone over the shores of dualism) The *two* become *One* and in this *third* a new life is born in the Garbha of Sakti (Womb of Love) within the prajna core as a conscious living reality!

Love is Greatest, no doubt. It is instant Truth and the accomplishing Power of Truth and this is Sakti. From Here I don't believe in death, only do I believe in Perpetual Living Sakti. Let it all Pass Through you. Let it all go, even death, even birth, even love (with the sense of motive or need), even life, even misery! At this level all that I can say to the world is, "My Best and Most Generous Thoughts Generating Thoughts of Love!" Thought without shaped identity is Consciousness in Sakti! In deep sleep I think of no thing at all. In waking and dreaming thinking is there. But the fourth state (turiya) is Super Sakti, so what is thinking or thought, pure with no thinking at all! To be Happy with one thought at a time, that is the key to this perpetual perception and continuous becoming in Sakti.

You see also, Sakti poured into one's stress system becomes living power. It is using the force of relaxation and its opposite tension. This method may be applied to other problems of living in this same dynamic; worry, memory, etc, even competition, politics, and religion (which I find to be colossal ravagers of energy, so I do not engage these). What is my worry, my worry is if I know Sakti. My memory, competition with myself, politics of others, my religion, the question of the relaxed state and its opposite tension becomes one that pertains only to the question of Sakti becoming and being in those fields of experience. Let us not play reruns of life, but move on with it! Few people realize the blessing of redundancy, when experiences and principles become routine, that is because routine without surprises (not even death, much less anything else), eventually becomes Wisdom (a Familiarity with spiritual functions, processes, and cycles).

It is important to create a kind of Sakti steel in oneself, that one can see and feel even at the times of deepest remorse and guilt, regret, sorrow, etc. There is only one lesson to be learned in this life. Ego creates misery. Love (no ego) makes Joy! Use no prayer, no begging, Be the Sakti, the Power. Face the ego square, in rejection, in hurt, too serious is ego there. Find now, where is the humor with Mother Sakti's movement. But you cannot push down the world (and all that is within you, your experiences) or replace it, it does not go away. It must be faced as all part of and being of Sakti. I think for myself, as myself (now), but whether it is within the theories of Relativity or the principles of Religion, I had to first clear out and remove all the wrong notions I picked up along the way, from childhood onward.

It is your birthright, innate and true. Human rights are a strange paradox since what they are (to freely think, be, feel, live, love, etc.) are really gifts of natural dignity given by the Goddess who made us, but turned around and co-opted by society, religion, politics and all their respective dictates. Spiritual stubbornness is nothing but confined Consciousness. Even the highest thought is still a kind of material, though very, very refined. Where all that stops, Real and Free Spiritual Life Begins and until then it is all just cognition, nothing more, and that includes what is in our minds and what is out there in religions, politics, and society. Everyone knows the innate surge of the Honest and when a fabricated weave is there.

You see I seek for nothing less than absolute complete Living Sakti twenty-four hours a day and seven days a week. What is *It* that you identify with when coming back through deep sleep, because even as you are Turiya, you do originally lose yourself in deep sleep before entering the states of dream and waking. Do you identify with the matrix (deep sleep), with the mind (dream), or the body (waking) or the final seal of the ego? Do you accept yourself to be consciousness just conscious or is it God Consciousness for you? Which is your state? Where are You? Who is this "You?" It is only one life, so Live Sakti, what does anything matter in the greater run of things! I Hope for nothing on the outside. I Trust only the Stability of Sakti. She is the Ground gotten and kept. All else flies!

Blast the mind content away! There is All This Consciousness Here, in all this embodiment! Is this Life, is this Insight, is this Illumination? I will not say, but it is extraordinary! I am not impressed by anything anymore for it is all Mother Sakti's advaita (non-duality)! Don't ask why, don't think twice, don't keep track, for then Experience flies away and cannot be caught in the mosaic of memory. Why should I think of the other, of relations, of duality? Or shall I be perpetually Immersed in the Ideal of High Spirituality, which from High Sakti spontaneously comprehends duality, relations and connections to others. Is the mind a direction or a tendency? Does one direct the mind or follow the tendency of the mind? It seems we are swaying under both, sometimes apparently directing, sometimes being pulled by tendency, but if Love of becoming one in Sakti takes birth inside you even in the smallest way, then, a third influence comes alive, the divine impulse of Sakti!

Living Sakti becomes Perpetual Beauty. There is no wrath in this state, that is all our imaginative deception influenced by those toxic traditions (patriarchal training), toxic in that Love is taught as something other than Love, for Love has no hate, nor

363

does Love distinguish. Living Sakti happens when the ego signal is reduced to zero and does not receive the beckonings of humiliation nor exhilaration. It is All Self and dualism is canceled! I love the Sakti who is Power through the Gentle!

To egotize is to think only of one's personal experience. A seer of Sakti sees Sakti, god concepts, all cognitive phenomena, the universe, and all living beings all at once. No fixed thought of personal destiny, doing, destination, or accomplishment, you flow, you float on the Goddess! The tendency of attraction to purest Sakti advaita develops in the prajna (deep sleep) core as one focus, like a jet moving through cloud layers to that conscious core (the prajna-wisdom center) where thoughts come out from, where I may import Sakti and export Love! One single curve of a line can change the entire mood of a thing and with this thought one can change one's entire mood state then entering consciously into the prajna core!

One finds oneself in the waking state Consciousness now experiencing yesterday's Consciousness of memories and trying from there to recall dream memories (also nothing but Consciousness) which is the content of mind that goes into deep sleep (prajna) which is nothing but Consciousness. So, what is all this Consciousness, but Consciousness as Living Sakti! It is the Power of Consciousness to return to the Source of its own Power (Sakti)! Never deny it, denial works in both directions. One can set up a conscious denial of the existence of problems in one's life, but worst than that is that you might actually deny yourself the spiritual life of Living Sakti (or any of your choice)! Pure Love comes, I cannot calculate when it comes, but it comes!

The Happy Human Being is envied by all, above and below. This amazing mind/body system in the midpoint balanced between the idea of heaven and the earth below! You must find a happy system, free of systems, where Living Sakti is to be lived, free of ruminating guilt comparisons, ideas that force one to compensate one's true inner sense of their real spiritual life. Often this is caused by the delusions of religious myths that deny "consciousness" the pure direct awareness and experience

364

of True Sakti. For example, some Hindus say Buddha was Gayasura, the demon of Gaya, because he unleashed without reserve the knowledge of the advaita vedanta to all the world. Strange it is perhaps. The mind is capable of the cognition of anything and it is hard to tell what is real or unreal, sometimes. Human mind did not create the universe filled with immense galaxies, but in our dimension cognition knows no limit it seems. It gets quite fantastic. This power (of cognition) is the manifest potential of Kundalini Sakti (Power coiled up in a pool or tied up around, as this manifest psychosomatic container of eventually to be unleashed Sakti). Through this power, that is, in the state of deep concentration and profound meditation one can manifest within the region of their own consciousness, visions of ishta deities and deitesses, or points of blue light, white light, yellow light. One can cognise within conscious cognition anything one can imagine. This is dream itself. So, should it be a wonder that some have cognised spaceships within their minds or visions of Jesus. Good God, now people see Elvis, Garcia, and Cobain in near death experiences! I think that once Captain Kirk goes over, that people will start seeing him and other members of the crew once they make the passages. Bless their hearts. We can't forget John Lennon, some say he was part of a divine angelic brotherhood and now that he has returned there they are communicating with him. Is there no end to all this? When cognition is shot outward it is the projection of these thought contents into external fantasy and when those same various phenomenal contents are shot inward it is introjection. Mind is an amazing illusion. Mind is dream. It is all mind making, myth making and these myths come alive, as it were, as it seems.

I have also noticed that those who develop some spiritual confidence due to belief in their system also develop some spiritual authority. Be cautious of that. It is also ego and ego cuts at every turn. I do not know why when there are people through history past and in the present day, from the great stars of religious traditions down to the people no one ever hears about, that they find the need to augment their quick and direct insight with some form of personalized mythology. Perhaps it is because we as human beings do possess a mythic (dream) mind that needs this form of reinterpretation and explanation of High Sakti to that dream mind itself, after coming down from High Sakti, and this is just fine I suppose, if it is honest as to what it is. Or, it may be out of some fear of not being directly accepted for what you are and what you have come to understand and so you feel the need to cover yourself with a protective mythology of a tradition. We humans are a mixture of truth and untruth, of sincerity and lie, of the brilliant and the bogus and the meaning of life appears to be simply the removal of the false and getting on with the real (truth, sincerity, brilliance). Nevertheless, a third probability is that there are those who create a mythology of their ego under the impulse of a deceptive (profit and glory) motive. It has always been very strange to me that people can acquire spiritual genius and then abuse this, or feel they must augment it in some way instead of just standing here naked to consequences and living the fearlessly beautiful life. But genius only means to be endowed with a natural ability or quality of mind and it comes from the Latin word for guardian deity and the root word for beget and produce, and when all this occurs conjunctive with the ego, well then, it seems no mystery at all. We need not make our spirituality a mysterious thing. Really it is not, it is the most natural and simple thing there is, but human (dream) beings feel they must distance the self (direct spiritual experience) through mythology. And in all honesty I probably do this myself with my own Kali mythology, but I am saying that is what it is.

Another important factor in this living is, as I have said, to enjoy one thought at a time. That high energy is to be enjoyed and not consigned off to negative figuring. With that high energy one can open and create new circuits of thought and feeling in the mind itself and make it more responsive to the spiritual. We can even press forward and advance further in the idea of death itself, that is in terms of the reality that there is no death. We measure seriousness by our measure of death. If death is not serious then what is all the fuss about and what is humor and what is all this death but once again Sakti in yet another form. Death is Consciousness too. Coming back to birth, into waking and dreaming, and into deep sleep, it is Consciousness. Certainly I ask a high requirement here to understand that there is no death. But I am serious and I am not speaking superficially. The closer one comes to understand deeply that Consciousness is Sakti, then from there the idea of death no longer pertains to that Sakti that never experiences the process of death. Or you may meditate that Sakti is already in the "state of death" thus cannot be touched by dying or by becoming born for that matter. Here, the quiet sunlight dawns through delusion. The question is then how to keep alive in the mind this non-delusional thought?

If one comes down from High Sakti, the previous tendency of mind training will fold itself into one of two courses of thought. That of the fearful ego trying to control events in cause and effect. And that of the ego freed of fear. One fights the unfolding of the Divine Matrix, the other lives in harmony with the Divine Unfoldment. The ego cannot control the growth and fading of a flower (the Matrix). Ponder what is a flower, what is anything from the point of view in High Sakti. To pity oneself or to pity others is ego and so is confrontational questioning, fighting the Matrix, resisting the spiritual content of one's life. Resisting what is in the mind creates mental nausea, accepting that same mind for whatever is there, makes that mind joyous. My ego sinks to the size of a primordial speck and there and then is where the "I" engages with High Sakti!

With so much gratitude in this Goddess life, for what my life is, what do the likes, dislikes, opinions, or beliefs of others, or my own matter at all? Sakti continually teaches through life itself, that ego identity and egotizing are misery and that passing through the ego is happy Joy! Open the current of your mind! Blessed be Advaita! I am She. I am Sakti. I am Kali. So where is the fear of duality? After Who? After What? No! Cut it (dualism) at the root (ego), then Live! In the "after state", do This Before! Do it before going everywhere, doing everything, meeting everyone, reading everything in the questioned sphere of dualism. Find, Be your own Peace in the True You! Then there is no coming down into the ideas of an "after state", dual or divided from High Sakti! How do you interpret your own psychology, based on *What*, in this "after state" of psychological flow?

Everyone, regardless of what is the nature of their body/mind, *Is* and is just Sakti, all and all. Alone this is Blessed. The awakened seeing Sees this. The not yet or yet to be awakened seeing Sees mind/body with the vast array of cognitive stances which are ultimately reduced to the one problem of the ego as a separated and distinct experiencer. It is not the loss of the individual, it is reaching into the divine depths of the true individual, for the individual must remain even as the apparent surface of consciousness is the form of a memory and a capacity to speak, with identity, even as the *individual* is in, "in" "divided" "duality." The Background God Experience remains evident, but when the feeling of "Background" leaves or is lifted, the Wonder Comes Forth!

Now real spiritual life is just beginning, after we come down from High Sakti. It becomes a process of drinking from the fountain of Sakti again and again, until body/mind complex no longer exists as, as what, as dependent on its aloneness!

It is the attraction for and the pull of Sakti in the mind. Love is this Grand Attractor. The natural gravity of deep sleep pulls the mind into non-duality. This gravity draws the memory, the ego drive and the functions of figuring and comparison all into the deep calm pool of dreamless sleep. But you see, even when the mind is pulled out of the consciousness of deep sleep to become mind again, that mind drawn back to the dualism of the waking and dreaming state, that mind retains an element of the non-dual, since in reality that mind can only have one thought at a time. Of course, we are speaking of a split fraction of a second in the sense of "at a time." While thinking over the thought of complex cognition please keep this suggestion in the mind.

Nevertheless, the mind will be drawn back again to deep sleep and sweet non-dual peace experienced in that state. Metaphorically, Krishna means "dark color" and this is a symbol of the all absorbing consciousness of the deep sleep condition in one respect (and Turiya ultimately). This is the attraction that pulls all dualism into itself. Kali is also this Dark Color and as such She is the All Encompassing Non Dual, ever in step ahead of any dualism that may potentially arise! She is Sakti! And if one prefers, there are always other symbolic meditations to be found. That Goddess is the same Mother of the Tao. She is the Mother of the One (Tao) which is ever pulling into itself the forms of duality (yin and yang). She is the Dragon Goddess who made the Tao (the One) and the Power of the Tao. But the metaphorical cognition of the Dragon, the Great Spiritual Cosmic Power of this system may not appeal to your mind since it has been contaminated by traditions that despise any other than their own in pure arrogance! But still this shows the power of symbols and their effect on and into the causal responses of consciousness.

Sat Chid Ananda (the Substance and Self Essence of Turiya) is always within us, as us, being us, and yet the mind dives for the symbolic. Let us consider the trinity of Maiden, Mother, and Crone as it would be associated with Sat (Existence), Chid (Consciousness), and Ananda (Bliss and Love). In the perception of lower time passages one will think of Maiden as youth, Mother in life's middle, and Crone as the end. Fine, but a deeper meaning is here. The Maiden is Bliss and Love. The Mother is Consciousness. And the Crone is Existence, for who would hold our Wisdom, what we have learned, and use it, and share it, if not the Crone as the receptacle of Bliss and of Chid Sakti, as she is the beginning and end, as Existence? This is a good meditation harmonizing life experience with higher infinite contemplations.

In physics, metaphorical spirituality is not just symbolical, it is actually Seeing Self in physics, quantum motions, astronomy and cosmology. An example is this meditation. I am a moon orbiting a planet (which is Sakti). I am a planet orbiting the Sun (which is also Sakti). I am the Sun orbiting the Pole Star. I am the Pole Star orbiting the Star Cluster. I am the Star Cluster orbiting the Galactic Core. I am the Galactic Core orbiting the

Galactic Cluster. I am the Galactic Cluster orbiting the Super Cluster. I am the Super Cluster (and all the other Super Clusters) orbiting the Great Center. I am the Great Center orbiting the First Cause. My Orbit is Stable Now, through the day/night cycle! This conscious identity in physics is the circle of one's experience in the waking state.

In psychology, or such things within the circle of dream experience, it is to follow and study the flow of thought, or the psychological flow of thought as with the dream state which is most revealing on the nature and movement of thought phenomena. I had a dream where I hurt my hand (a writer's paranoia I suppose), but what was interesting was that the pain felt like a real physical pain, though it was not, for it was just a dream. But it made me think, where is pain in consciousness? Certainly in the waking state, the nerves send a message to consciousness about the location of pain. But here consciousness was sending a message of false or illusory pain to the nerves. Pain is punishment by the word's meaning. Misery is the result of being a miser. And suffering is to bear a binding. So what is the meaning of these three experiences in the definition of consciousness and the relationship to the nerves of the body or even more so to the nerves of the mind. I have heard of yogis who experienced surgery and great pain without medicine, just by somehow separating in consciousness the layers of consciousness, mind, and the nerves. Very fascinating stuff. The power of mind making indeed. This is comparable to more accessible phenomena. When people are given a nocebo they generally experience the negative psychosomatic effects they are told are associated with that medicine. And when people are given a placebo, they in turn experience the positive associations that should result. The power of belief or the awakening of consciousness potential is extraordinary as you can see. But what to think of the influences that restrict or hinder us, or open and expand us, that we receive from our own minds, as well as from society, tradition, religion, psychological judgments, or even scientific proclamations of the day?

Even Spirituality is just a name one puts on the experience of Living Sakti. You come to this where you must assert yourself into the Realm of God. No timidity will do. Why be timid with God (Consciousness)? This is your own as you were designated a created being by that Divine Principle. It is like Buddha told his son, "Come and claim your Birthright to Enlightenment!"

Now, on the phenomena of seven stage to this High Sakti. Yoga gives seven steps to that Samadhi (God contact or God Consciousness in the Higher Sense). The first is basically just being a good person. The second is acquiring spiritual information and putting it to work in one's thoughts and feelings and daily practices. Third is placing the body in a steady position. Fourth is the attention or awareness on the flow of breath and as some believe actually accessing the cosmically charged breath (prana). These stages belong to the circle of the waking state. Fifth is the withdrawal of the senses from the sense objects (pratyahara). This sounds impossible at first, but if you think about it and remember that you do this every time you go into the dream state, and you return to the sense objects every time your consciousness becomes awake again. So it is not so mysterious really. This is the border of the circle of dream experience. Sixth is called concentration, but what is that concentration like? Perhaps like following the succession of thoughts in the dream flow, or psychological flow in the dream state that eventually finds a dream object of meaning or enjoyment that then drops off because of that meaning or enjoyment of that dream object to then find that the mind sinks into the steady state, the calm state, the reference here is to the circle of experience in deep sleep and this is the seventh step, meditation. So samadhi (realization) is to wake up from that sleep in the same manner that we wake up from dream, but waking up at the higher angle of High Sakti. This happens suddenly or gradually for some reason, probably being the quality of the mind contents.

Really, I think that we may even limit that sudden experience of High Sakti by the very cognition of seven stages.

371

But it is the first tendency of the mind to need a ladder it seems, instead of its first tendency being to go to the First State of High Sakti at the first. I keep coming back to this so the illustration at the front is that of Sakti Directly First. The three tiers of Her ear ring are the three states (waking/dream/sleep) and they are nothing but Sakti! As are the Sanskrit letter symbols for Sakti there on each three. Her Face is Who? Self, nothing but Self (Sakti) which is in turiya (pure consciousness). The lower point/dot on Her forehead is the Space/Time Matrix swallowing all. The half moon, half circle is the witness condition ever watching the swallowing of all ideation. And the higher point/dot is of course the total melt into advaita Sakti! In Her Face I am ever discovering Exhilaration.

Again the illustration at the back is an attempt to convey the First at the first. The three triangles are the three states under Her Sacred Feet. One foot is standing in the relative. One foot is standing in the eternal absolute. One anklet's Sanskrit symbol is ideation over all this and the other is High Sakti "gone over" into the non-dual. Before Her Blessed Feet I continuously discover Humility.

In the life of discovering Living Sakti one may tend to think that there is a necessity for transmutation of the barrier between you and Living Sakti. The three states are Sakti and so no transformation is needed and non-duality is here proven for you. Great ones (world teachers) benefit us, but also have created barriers (by the distance of greatness itself) for us until we see they too are but Sakti. In silence (where mind slows) see your own God Consciousness as you would see morning light coming through your own window.

On returning from High Sakti to complex cognition one must come to know what is death. Who can explain, no one, as much as anyone might explain what is a flower. I shall not assume any arrogance that I can explain what is death, but for myself to be at peace with this life I have found it necessary to know these thoughts for my spiritual comfort. Those who I know who have passed on, they have not gone far, they have but gone to Ramakrishna, they have gone to Kali and as She (High

Sakti) is the picture of the Absolute, then all of us being that Absolute have already thus Gone to this Absolute and so death is but an apparent unfolding of That Absolute Thus Gone! Acceptance of this is Joy (for me), resistance is the little miser ego made miserable with fear. We are all already in the divine death state (absolutely), looking at the world (from High Sakti). We are already in the Nirvana (without body), looking at the Samsara (with body). We are already in Turiya (Consciousness without body), looking down at the three bodies (causal, subtle, physical) of the three states (waking/dream/sleep). They are not dead! Nothing is dead! Death is a delusion. It is All Living Sakti and this my Joy is advaita (non-dual). "Your own Atma is the Divine Mother." (Aseshananda). Self (Atma) is Sakti (Kali). I see no death anywhere, nor do I see birth. Death never Was! Birth has never Become! There shall be no more death as you now know the Spiritual. Death is there, only as an object of experience, not as the experience of our genuine Birthless State!

These deepest of spiritual perceptions are magnificently expressed in a song of unknown authorship that was often sung by Ramakrishna. Some lines from that song, "In dense darkness, O Mother, Thy formless beauty sparkles... In the lap of boundless dark, on Mahanirvana's waves upborne... Who art Thou, Mother, seated alone in the shrine of samadhi?" The "dense darkness" is absolute non-dualism. The "boundless dark" is the infinite non-dualism. Mahanirvana is the most complete realization, and what is it that is realized but that all body/minds (waves) are upborne into Her, or even so, unborn in the highest sense of non duality, as it is She who is "seated alone" in samadhi (realization)!

The Perpetual never has needed Perception! The one who has appeared to have Perception was never born. The Perpetual has never Become dual! In the Perpetual, the "I" in ignorance (deep sleep), dream/delusion, or the waking body never was born, never became a Perception_ (so how is there any need for instruction, meditation, or thought)? I was never born. This is the direct consciousness of Reality. To think that one has or that one is a body (waking/dream/sleep) is pure delusion (from High

Sakti)! The "I" has never been in dualism. The act of liberation is an illusion in the reflection of consciousness. Before my birth I was not and have never been in distance (dualism). We are never in dualism. I have never been sundered (disjoined, estranged, isolated, split, or severed) from God (Sakti). It was delusion to ever think so! Go Back, Before ego existed (appeared) and There! Their forms were the wave forms of Love! Their wave forms were never born to any distance from Love. They are all There in Love (High Sakti)! And you may find this poet finally in the end, There, as Living Sakti, in the Unmoved Ground, never to be again disturbed by the mythic legend of the wave form of dualism.

LIVING SAKTI

Attempting Quick Knowing
In Perpetual Perception
and Continuous Becoming

From "Living Sakti Within Physics"

I am the Divine Nothing, existing as instantaneous Happiness, the Undefined identified with nothing... no ego, nor memory, no reasoning, nor figuring. I am not even the zero void space between each numbered thought... not beginningless quantum infinite, nor infinite ever and ever expanding. I am nothing but Sakti as carefree is free of care, caring only for Love, which is what is True Sakti.

A Sweet High Inner Feeling comes to me when what is being said about the Indivisibility of the Universe or what is in it as advaita (non-dualism) is really understood. The superstition of ignorance falls and we see more sharply our intimate experience of Being the Universe more beautifully amazing than any of the old ideas of God.

Earth! Many Earths. Sun! Many Suns. Galaxy! Many Galaxies. Neighborhood of Galaxies. Twenty or so with the Milky Way, Andromeda, the Magellanic Clouds, and fifteen or so dwarf galaxies. Many upon more making of many more. Supercity Clusters of Galaxies each ten thousand or more, upon which thousands over billions, with only fifty to one hundred billion galaxies visible to us existing in every direction, Unfolding, Created Complete in the First Second Split into the illusion imagined as Time or Distance. In this I am and have always been and will not ever cease to be! So what is so special about me?

We are just playing out the Primordial Matrix within the speck that was before the Big Bang, There!, and Now Here! Always in Now, no matter what stage!

You were There in that Primordial Speck; your birth, your death, all that is between, all the superclusters, and the Yet to

Unravel. A Super Intelligence no mind can grasp yet, which every mind is continually changing toward! Indivisible Spirit/Matter and Consciousness yet remains ever Undefined! We are still within and inside that Speck, looking at it as if it were a point on a table, when in Reality it engulfs us Indivisibly So!

Assimilate, swallow it all in the Sweetest Wonder, nothing more than this Simplicity of Love! This is all but a cosmological wonder (a), a little bundle (quantum) of dream (u), inside this primordial matrix speck (m) so very to the extreme small compared to the Always More and More Open Wide and Wider Living Sakti.

Everything goes in cycles in the sea of cause and effect. Some in two second cycles, some in two thousand year cycles or even like the Milky Way Herself, two hundred to two hundred and fifty million years (one galactic year) to cycle on Her central core. I forget these affirmations often as ego tends to become easily lost in the memory of itself. Time just appears to flow and Space to spread. After twenty-four, forty-eight, or seventy-two hours of the sleep, dream, and conscious cycles, "present things" become "past things" and don't seem to matter much at all, if the heart focuses on Love in the Nowness of Eternity, which is not time distorted, but the idea of future things arriving with events and such can still perplex the Emotion of Eternity, that something is coming, but the only thing that ever comes is the Nowness of Eternity, just Sakti, no "future things" ever arrive into actual real time/space experience. It is all here all now! The rest is imagination, a distortion due to the influence of space/time Maya (cosmic measuring on the upper surface of Sakti's Amazement!).

Sakti is fond of round things, great extensive superclustered galaxies and of that, what is visible is only a few petals of Her immense super cosmic flower blossom. We have yet to see the seed core of this universal blossom. She is fond of roundness, joyful, how many orb worlds, with life, or without as straight and narrow minds believe, as are particles, atoms, neurons and much smaller bundles of things are round, so are the inner chakra wheels made of consciousness, round. She is fond of Roundness, for Spirituality is round, soft, gentle, as Love is so. Not the sharp lines of direct vision and division, perception that splits One into many. It is only a perception. Where Roundness is engulfing, circulating, overwhelming, and completing Her Self. Like the smile that brings the instant feeling of Happiness where those rigid edges of the mind may not go!

If you are like me you might enjoy becoming lost for an hour or two in the contemplation of cosmic super phenomena (the stars in our galaxy, the Milky Way, the galactic Local Group, the Local Supercluster, the numerous other Superclusters, time, space, density, intensity, illumination, force, power, distance, and the spreading out) as it is the waking state, for it arouses the divine uncertainty of spiritual potential. It is a natural high, for it creates humility in the mind. Or you may also enjoy the same lost feeling in contemplation of psychic super phenomena in the forms of the dream state, with all its imagery, psychic emotional content, and the coming up of spontaneous ideas. It is all just the wandering enjoyment of the mind, for when psychic and cosmic super phenomena ceases then one finds the discovery of the great exploration into Peace, within that mind which was lost for a time in the waking (cosmic) and dream (psychic) ruminations on creation. It is the return to the refined state of Sat Chid Ananda. The physics of Existence (Sat) underlies all conditions of the waking dimension. The psychology of Consciousness (Chid) is within and permeating all parameters of dream speculations, projections, introjections, and interpretations. And in Pure Spirituality there comes up to the light of consciousness and existence that final principle of Bliss (Ananda). It is all the wandering of dual mind play on the surface of Oneness. The mind enjoys the ubiquities of the one grand Ubiquitous.

The same amount of cosmic and psychic material existed within the Primordial Speck as exists now or ever will exist. Nothing dies. It only transfigures itself. Time does not move into the future. Time does not move at all. Time dilations in thought distortions such as, "What will happen or what has

377

happened, or even what is happening right now?"... these distract from the Free Pure Space of High Sakti! I can now throw my mind there with greater ease, by shutting off those distorted dilations, when needed.

Existence, physics, the waking state is the Foreground. Consciousness, the psyche, the dream state is the Background. Sakti in Pure Spirituality is the Divine Groundless Ground. All this is equally permeated with non- duality! Saturated by Sakti! Impregnated with Sakti! And so is the Birth of the High Experience we are wishing to have, which we have had since before the Start!

When I look at what my life is and has been in one grand glance I see the only lesson I've learned is a little of Love. No, no, there is no shimmering shining God state for me, though I have memories of those spiritual hallucinations occurring during thunderstorms and on crystal clear star filled nights where the galaxies themselves were so close I could touch them with my hand.

The unconscious behaves like the quantum principle. But Love behaves in a way of having us all be without definition.

There are half a million hours of dreamtime per day in the U. S. A., so something somewhere will connect with the Dreamspace defying the logic of past/future time. With so much subconscious processing some of it will make sense. An individual dreams only about two hours a night, there are more hours in the rejuvenating deep sleep state, the samadhi-like no mind-wave state, than I had formerly realized. A neutron's life span is only about fifteen minutes. A proton lives for three thousand years or thirty human life spans. Amazing Sakti!

The sharp severe instrument of my personal psychology is for splitting emotions (not atoms) into Love Energy. Emotions stimulate memory impressions. Emotions imprint memory into the mind substance, the psychic content. Without emotion, there is no memory, no mind content. It is the sharpest power of focus, belief, cognition, and greater things. What is greater than the "I" becoming known to be Sakti? I have freed myself of the cloud and the canopy of traditions. I do not purchase into those inducing methodologies of the god-ego-power-control-complex. Nor do I bestow strength to superstition nor fury to fear. The Moon, the Sun, and Mars do not hold influence over me. I stand above the solar system, the galaxy, the universe, for I am the Sakti that created those bits of burning dust, cooled out by gravity, spinning, cracking, turning, and returning within the emptiness, and when I know this at this level (and is there any other level) there is no karma for me. Nor do I completely trust any great soul who promises that greater things will be done by their power, when nothing greater is ever done. I do not live in a quantum dreamland, nor do I believe there is anything in this new age that was not in the age before, nor the one before that, going all the way back. But sometimes I have dreams that heal wounds that are twenty years deep in me.

The conditioned psychic reflexes of behavior (within intrinsic problem solving ability) in the cognitive emotional responses are due to the images (religious, historical, psychological, social, etc.) in the mental collective. Is any image absolutely real in the deepest spiritual sense, ultimately, that is, in the free form of consciousness? Mathematically, what is the collective neural dream activity of this planet for one day? Answer, about nine and a half to ten million dream hours. How could that collective dream activity be directed or misdirected? Could this amount of dream activity be used collectively for collective planetary problem solving (wars, starvation, disease)? What if all that neural energy was directed in the conscious waking mind collective for just three seconds a day to the problem of peace? Does the galactic count of stars in the Milky Way (I am glad, relieved to find there are differences on this number not in chronological accordance. Some say more than one hundred billion, others say one thousand billion solar masses, but generally it is thought that there are two hundred billion stars in the Milky Way galaxy.) equal the neuron count in the human brain (one thousand billion)? Where are we in the universe as our intelligence apparently increases and this universe spreads out in some kind of aligned harmony?

Seventy-five million people died in four years during the black plague (then it stopped), but what is the daily birth rate and death rate in just an ordinary planetary year? The population of the U.S.A. is 264 million. There are now about 3 million & 873 thousand births per year and 2 million 312 thousand deaths in this country. Worldwide, the number of births per year is in excess of 133 million and deaths are in excess of 53 million considering the oscillations and the variables in conditions and ever increasing numbers in the planetary population. (Source: U.S. Bureau of the Census, International Data Base) In the year 1 B.C.E. there were only two hundred and fifty million humans on the face of the Earth. In the year 1900 C.E. there were one billion and nine and a half decades later there are almost six billion (five billion eight-hundred and thirteen million) human souls on this Earth. It is estimated that by the year 2000 the amount will be 6 billion 91 million (which actually only reached 6 billion), ten years later in 2010 it will be 6 billion 862 million and by 2020, 7 billion 600 million. At present it is estimated that there are only fifty to one hundred billion galaxies within the entire visible universe. I was depressed by this limitation in the galactic count until I realized this number is only what is visible. New images in consciousness start the flow of Liberated Emotions (happiness) by the stark awakening of an ever adjusting sense of reality.

Before X, before Y, before the nuclei, there, there, there was I! My memory (unfortunately) is a steel trap, nothing escapes, I never forget, like an elephant, my large ears hear every sound you make and my massive skull retains every thought you have had, and like those beautiful and gentle giants, my pace is slow, heavy, and pondering.

There is the old atomic thought, the trinity of proton, neutron, and electron. Though the speck idea has changed, the substance has not. There has always been more above the atomic idea and more below it. It is all what? The same stuff of Sakti with new symbols and those symbols unleash real manifest power! I had a very comical dream. I was talking to Albert Einstein. He had shaved his head and face and when I asked him why he had done this he replied, "I am going for a new look." Well, it is not so amazing really, for the General and Special Theories of Relativity certainly have a new substance to them. Gravity, Energy, Matter, Light, Space, and Time have a new look to them with all the advances. Our knowledge may look new, but what is there is the same.

From "Living Sakti Within Psychology"

The word Reality does not convey what Reality Is. It never will because the word itself is a conception of Something beyond conception. So we may ever unfortunately be always stuck with a psychological description of this concept. The Highest Flight (Sakti Advaita) may possibly never be expressed in words or thoughts, nor may Pure Spirituality ever be described by any tradition. We can only speak of Sakti Advaita and Pure Spirituality as a qualification in the consciousness of and within non-dualism, which is not a qualification (how can a qualification describe or convey something that has no qualification) to be described by the dualistic content of words, thoughts, and speech. Because if I say, "this," it instantly invokes the thought of "that." So, the psychic reflex to word content must fall away from consciousness to just Be Consciousness without dualism- here, it is still described with or as a qualification. So, just Enjoy the Joy!

There is the conscious surface and there is the underneath of the conscious surface. One often does not see the other as what one dreams and what one is conscious of in waking often do not appear to intersect at the conjunction of the external and internal conscious movements. This is usually due to the resistance in the conscious mind as to what the dream mind is saying. Under the surface, in the dream mind, one's consciousness speaks honestly, but the conscious mind may cover this honest dream talk with its own interpretations. On the other hand one may simply blow it all off by saying to the self that it is nothing more

381

than electric currents of neural impulses fluxing this way and then that way.

Psychologists suffer their psychology, that is, to bear the binding of it! True therapy (healing) occurs every time Self is discovered anew, without the strange need to bear the binding. What is this need, yes, this need to suffer, to bear some binding in the human complex just because ego has appeared to be born. Perhaps, once Consciousness contracts into ego it regrets its imagined Divine loss. Oh well, it is not for me to say.

The Non-Dual becomes your reflex before the dual thinking response comes up which produces worry and stress due to the nature of dual opposites in reflex response. Ramakrishna gives a shattering comment on the effort to "know" through the psychological process, "I don't even try." As worry and stress can only come up when the psychological process is the only apparatus that is applied, further on, faith and higher trust (or even opening the mind to a perception of a void-space of pure acceptance) must come in at some point.

I don't want to simply believe (make palatable to oneself, accept, or approve to oneself) in a religion. That is the experience of re-linking for someone else. Not mine. I don't want to approve or accept in myself Something, I want to Become that Something out of which Beliefs are made. I don't want to believe in or become a Hindu, a Hebrew, a Moslem, a Christian, a Buddhist, a Jain, a Parsi, a Taoist, a Shinto, or a Cherokee shaman. I want to Become the Spirituality out of which those Shining Peaks of Humanity became themselves. In my own anointment with Conscious Living Love! I seek the Spirituality beyond the psychic act of surrender to a belief, let me enter and become the "place" of all origin!

Kali may perfectly portray the unconscious and as She stands on Shiva, dancing in the cemetery, She also portrays the wildest free process of individuation (autonomous psychic complex) in the transcendent function. What better image is there of the unknown dark background (the unconscious) or of an archetype conception over or as that unconscious, which is far deeper than all that geographical harping on cultural conditioning. The need for liberation of the repressed spiritual nature is universal and She pictures this so well. Also, the classic view of the unconscious is limited as being filled with all the saguna (with forms, qualities, mental pictures, or active cognates) material of archaic dream images or archetypes, which are the original signatures in the unconscious. If I were to seek the unconscious I would seek it as it was, before all those signatures were written within it, absolutely empty and pure as it would then wondrously overwhelm my conscious mind.

If psychology is the study of the soul (psyche), then who is really qualified to teach that knowledge (ology)? There are many pretenders out there, unaware that they are pretending and more dangerously so, aware they are pretending. But as it is in truth, from the high standpoint of illumination, all our delusions are seen in the end as helpers to get out of illusions. Today's so-called crazy wisdom cults more often may be the pathology of an ego centric megalomaniac. Ramakrishna experienced what was called spiritual madness, but he did not abuse others to justify that state. He was very concerned not to do so. He actually agonized over what effect the thrust of that state might have on others. So why do the ones such as these today, who claim crazy wisdom as the condition of their mind, feel they must eject the unconscious wild side of the id as libido all over people, abusively, in order for them to feel that other people have now become free (enlightened). It is crashing insanity. Perhaps associated with some form of demented genius, but intelligence (genius) does not mean you are a Loving Person. History has known many cruel geniuses. Such behavior seems more for the need of the neurotic (or psychotic) fulfillment of those who inflict this on others, than for the benefit of their pathetic students who seek out that kind of psychological punishment as a deranged form of enlightenment. Get away from the trauma, poor ones! "He who says he is a guru is a man of mean intelligence. Haven't you seen a balance? The lighter side goes higher." Ramakrishna. The word guru means spiritual teacher and heaviness. So if one thinks oneself a guru he is heavy and goes right downward like the heavy side of the balance, not to say also that he pulls others down by the weight of this egotistical proclamation.

Kali's Mad Wisdom is enough for my personal unconscious to be set free! Tilopa (who started the Naropa, Marpa, Milarepa tradition) found that She, Pure Sakti, was enough for him too, the divine form of a Dakini (Tibetan Goddess), was his only teacher (to show). The quiet and gentle Ramana Maharshi had his mountain, the mountain alone was his teacher (the one who functions as showing). And Ramakrishna, well, who knows the Total Tantra of his relation with the Sparkling Dynamic Beauty of the Goddess Kali!

The archetypal need for a messiah in the American unconscious sets the stage for spiritual liars to come in and do their thing. Many seekers are attracted to these, write books about it and become lost under the force of a dominant archetype manifest simply to justify their sex life on the same ground as their spiritual life. The classic schism which may be healed (if need really be so) on one's own, by taking within (introjection) the beautiful wildness of Kali's sex/death dance on Shiva's passive corpse, who just lets it happen without resistance.

I don't need the distorted instructions of a spiritual psychotic. Sakti is my Wild Instructress as Life itself is wild enough for me. People betray themselves not knowing what they are really saying, revealed as grasping dependence on teachers who themselves found it necessary to give up the form of their own teachers. One thing for the teacher, something else for the student hopelessly shipwrecked on the isolated ego blinded and bound shores of guruism, unable to see how their egos are stuck worshiping a guru totem, also stuck in the sand.

The booming foolishness of crazy wisdom is the psychic trap of its never ending redundant therapy. You are contained by abuse, controlled like an animal in rein and the form of this therapy makes you feel free because of constantly dealing with embracing repressed material. The answer you are given by these so-called spiritual models is to become insane (mad) too. Do you want that? Or shall you awaken like the Zen student

384

whose excellent breakthrough urged him to express his enlightenment by slapping the teacher's face.

Follow these models, cult makers, religious predators in the guise of spiritual teachers, and become insane. What else could happen when such models are constantly changing their identities (names) under the guise of spiritual transformations, translations, whatever! Will this never end? The promised messiah of the end times, a buddha, and an avatar (incarnation), a king as well? Oh how impressive, and now you want to be worshiped! And on top of it all, these teachers force people into sexual situations that under any other circumstance would be criminal, abusive, if not outright physical and psychological rape (or even worse, as suicide of the individual personality and body, which is drastically offered into the demented guidance of a corrupt authority (father) figure). It is a problem of collective psychic delusional fixations and preying upon the amazing gullible nature of the mind in the form of unreasonable and extraordinary beliefs, such as astrological superstitions, ufological fallacies, apocaphobic (fear of the end times) mentality, anti-sexual or the reverse beliefs, Earth hating systems, (as the lets get to heaven and forget the world approach), all combined with the emptiness, insecurity, and emotional and spiritual dissatisfaction even among the very intelligent. The need to find what is true is within everyone and the power of this need enforces the problem of assumption (believability) making minds easy to control by a pretentious domination specialist figure whether or not that figure knows anything at all. As sad as it is, people just believe outright what they are told, even if it is a lie, or what they read, even if it is a fabrication.

Sounds like these spiritual saurians who claim they do these things to interfere with, or reflect your attachments or break up the solidified patterns of your neurotic needs and desires are in greater need of turning their own high powered therapy on themselves. Spiritually, and otherwise, we become what we admire. Is this what you want spiritually or otherwise? If ego is conditioned insanely, prior to spiritual experience, that ego, after

385

spiritual experience, may translate such experience insanely, through the psychic remnants of uncivilized desires.

You go out there and hurt as long as you need that hurt. I don't really believe it is necessary, but all our belief conditioning has told us it is so. That is the problem, the painful asylum of this world, but change your perception and world is Beautiful, deathlessly so! I do not believe in spiritual transmission from another person no matter who they are. Spiritual Experience comes from the Spiritual Itself, no matter what the confluence of events may be that set off that experience, sitting with a sage at peace or being in the middle of an active earthquake, or lifted up by hurricane.

Truth comes from Truth, nowhere else! Truth is what is True, which means Loyalty, Honesty, and Trustworthy as it is Worthy of our Trust. Truth means Exact or Accurate. Nothing short of this will do. Truth is also defined as a Belief, consistent with a set of Facts. But what is your set of facts; spiritual, social, mythical, moral, historical, psychological and so forth, upon which the apparent consistency of one's relative belief projection is based? So Truth may be a matter of heartfelt reality based on our projected idea of what we think Love may be, as an Absolute Constant Factor in comparison to the growth and expansion of that heartfelt idea. Truth is also related to Truce, an Agreement of Peace between two warring positions, here, the ego and the self- they come together or simply live in harmony and so the truce of Truth creates the product we may ponder as Peace of Mind!

What is disloyal, dishonest, and not to be trusted can never bring one the genuine feeling of Spiritual Peace, for this, of all things, should be free of contradiction! Otherwise, the most Precious Treasure in the Universe, our Spiritual Love, is cheapened.

Infuriation at the spiritual position (their birthright identity) of anyone is at ground level egotistical nonacceptance (intolerance), so alien and antagonistic to the Sakti of Love. Those gurus, and religions, and mentors with this nature, just want to keep their guruhood, their religiosity, or their

386

mentorship over others. It is amazing. If anyone expands beyond their circle, or is simply unsatisfied there, they usually have some deeply hurtful and hard critical things to say about that person. Rare are those who are not this way. Ramakrishna was such a one. He applauded Vivekananda's boldness, that Vivekananda who even used to abuse his Kali, saying, "He is independent even of me."

Amazing amounts of energy are spent in justifying those incongruities. Ego contests! Wheel spinning! Waste. What's said is said, there for you if you wish. Spiritual Life is Simple, in a thousand ways each day remove the complexity of ego and There you will discover Love.

Love is the Sweeter, Simpler Way of ridding the ego. The Self is Known in the conscious life and the unconscious life and in the Something More (which is Grander Broader Love) that then replaces what was the apparent notion of ego. Why hold to a protection of ego? It is a burning house, burning in the fire of time, in a momentary space! Love's fulfillment overrides conditions of the nervous system, cognitive states, or the phenomena of spiritual questions. What is Nirvikalpa, what is the translucence of Sahaja, what is the knowledge of steady Kutastha (Witness Consciousness), what is Bhava? Love knows, and Knows More! Genuine sincere Humility directly removes the feeling that there is a door to pass through between you and Love!

Love is the Guru, the Mentor, the Master, the Mistress. Love is God Reality. So Love (Agape) is the One Dynamic Function that Illuminates and enlightens us. True Consciousness is stilled in its own Reality. Existence Absolute Simply Is, without noticing nor witnessing dualism in the world universe. Now the scriptures say that the Guru is Brahma, Vishnu, Shiva, the Guru is Brahman, there is nothing higher than the Guru. These are not human powers nor or they human designations. A human cannot create (brahma), hold up (vishnu), nor destroy (shiva) the universe and its immense superclusters. Nor is a human being, being time bound, Infinite (Brahman). Is there anything Higher than the Infinite? Love is the Shining Power moving through the World as the Active Kinetic that Illuminates all this that is thought of as Existence, Consciousness, or Universe. Love is the Dynamic! "There is only one Guru, and that is Satchidananda (The Reality, the Divine Mother). He (but This is beyond he or she) alone is the Teacher." "Satchidananda alone is the Guru." And also, most beautifully stated in this clear dramatic comment on liberation of the mind from the darkness of the guru process, Ramakrishna exclaims, "He who is spiritually higher than others does not consider himself a guru."

On the subject of guru yoga (union with the guru) and guru puja (guru worship) at the misdirected human level where human personality is emphasized as the ultimate, no, even glorified at that point, it is believed that a transference of Consciousness, Spiritual Energy, Illumination takes place in a kind of sending through eyes or the form of the teacher (body, head, hands, feet, etc.). That Energy, Consciousness, Illumination comes from nowhere external, it comes ultimately from within the One Self which is what you are in your true nature. If this is not true then advaita is not true. Scriptures say also that only God can do this kind of transference to awakening, well, God is within you, is it not so, and if this is not true then what is? Transference of cognitive power can mean a loss of self. It goes on all the time in the illusion of loss or gain (of self) in outer participation and inner assimilation, as self defining or self expanding states of awareness.

The practice of teacher worship and psychic union with the physical, subtle, or even causal form of the guru is justified by such scriptural sayings that impart the idea to us that the guru and God are not different, that is they are one and the same. Well, to this I must add that so is the refrigerator one and the same, that is not different from God. At that level! Otherwise, advaita (non-dualism) is untrue! Two choices open to you now, either remain under the spell or free the self into the Depth of Reality. The psychic experience of consciousness transference is a phenomena of Creative Energy occurring within oneself at the confluence of creative moments natural to the course of life, not the cognitive theatrics of gurus.

Do you think I have painted myself into a corner, denying myself religious practices, the sentiments of perhaps necessary emotional stages, or meditations on dualism (as projection and or introjection of a deitess or deity concept/ideal). No, the three creases of the corner open wide to the Infinite. I fall through, only to be caught up in the Infinite of Love, nothing but Love!

Advaita may be the greatest of all denials because we cannot escape the multi-complex world, not understanding its whys and wherefores, so we throw it away to non-dualism, seeking the death of the mind, of all conscious life, as a final flight of the imagination, thinking that there is really nothing that great, nothing that worthy of us here in the world! This is the result of an advaita devoid of Love, for Love charges us with the fullest meaning and spiritual purpose to life. Or, perhaps simply conclusion (non-dualism) eliminates confusion (dualism).

Most people want to be dazzled, seduced, mesmerized, and hypnotized by some form of Spirituality. They usually get what they seek. Few want the Quiet and True!

Is there really anything that is absolutely negative? Even from the high lofty view of qualified non-dualism, the qualification named "universe" is nothing but God. So every action and event, inward or outward, is either spiritual challenge or abundant fat (grace) spiritual healing of the psychic dualism. When the stance of ego is loosened (imbalanced) by Love, the once former assault and insult of the world to the ego becomes this! Just this, even at the worst level imaginable! But the benevolent curve of the world (in attitude) usually keeps us comfortable with our illusions.

Is this the psychology of Love? What does the psyche (soul) want if not Love? My attack on the guru principle is not meant to harm, it is meant to enhance the true and hidden meaning of this Divine Principle while combating irrationality, for probably 90% of people live in a mythical state of mind. God is further on through the forest, past the emeralds, past the silver and gold, past the diamonds there are treasures to found in the Wide Open Experience of Perpetual Perception and Continuous Becoming! (Ramakrishna's metaphor) Again, based on the principle that

389

the higher one flies the better landing gear one needs, we have heard that the more one seeks an non-temporal Love, the more one needs the temporal love of others in the ego affirming forms of relationships. Real Love is not contained in the ego's reflection on others as a projection, a localized extension, a shared worship of the ego-idol, or momentary satiation of the ego. It may come as a shock that the ego is not omnipotent, but this startling breakthrough is the commencement of humility. The question remains then can one Love without ego or is it still the ego's need for love? This is the great question and the answer is, "Yes, there is Love without ego before the forms of mental figuring about it set back in."

Or simply Conclusion (Light) eliminates Confusion (Dark). I shall assume for a moment the dark position (gu) so you will be forced to think much more deeply about the depth position of light (ru). For usually on this dynamic dualism the opposite is taking place, confusion is eliminating conclusion. It has been said that the guru is not there to affirm the ego, but to crush the ego... but that ego cannot but assume a sublimated repressed or suppressed form of greatness or sense of the gigantic on itself by association with such a supposed and posed, glorified Ego Crusher! More so, a spiritual psychosis takes place with the guru's glorious ego displacing and substituting the reality of the questioner's or seeker's own real identity (true ego as atma sakti revealed). This is a fanatical condition, or an unnatural dependent high. Besides that, when pure Singular Independent Spiritual Experience (Sakti Energy) is loosened from the body in Near Death Experiences and the Being (Chosen Cognitive Ideal) of Light appears in the Now Free Space of Consciousness, that Blessed Emanation out of the Turiya (Pure Consciousness in the Fourth State freed of waking/dream/sleep) or Sva-bhava-kaya (Self Mood State beyond the three traditional Buddha kayas-vehicles) of the True Liberated Consciousness overwhelmingly affirms (the near dead person) with the Knowledge of Love. So, often, the human teacher is in contradiction with this Great Truth. The ego trouble as the thought or not thought of spiritual dualism can be healed Gently By Love, affirming not crushing, by natural born Humility, produced by the Love of others- now Radiating through Sahaja eyes, also natural born, knowing there is no translucent door to pass through, nor ring pass not between the eternity of nirvana (in the stillness of thought) and the motion witnessed as the "maya' of sleep, dream, and waking. Where are those teachers of fear-free Loving Humility- that teach Conclusion and not Confusion?

From "Living Sakti Within Spirituality"

Poet, be Sakti! Feel Her in your nerves, in the flow of each thought and in your feelings so often underestimated by the world. I am not mapped out by any symbol East nor West. I am not defined in any waking condition. I am not interpreted by any dream. Nor am I known in deep sleep. My lust power is for Love Power. My glorious hungry greed is for God Knowledge. Now, who am I? Go to that place within where you are alone and afraid and then there Discover Love, with Trust in Its Unseen Power, now the power to be seen in you. Why not just let yourself be at Peace?

"Yes, this is the attraction of Yogamaya, the Divine Sakti. She casts the spell." Ramakrishna. Even our idea of attraction to Spirituality is within Her Spell (the maya-dream of union-yoga)! So we question the "I" as beyond the spell. Or is it? The idea of Self may indeed be within this spell of Hers so cast as it is!

Death (Kali) keeps me awake to the fact that all that needs doing is the loosening of the tenacious substance of ego. Then, Unity with Sakti comes up. Death wakes me up and Death keeps me alive. Who am I?

Death (Kali) makes and keeps me Humble, even though the subtle (ego) body lives on. In Total Death the causal "I" is Gone. Still, Sakti lives On and On and On.

Death (Kali) puts, gives, propels Energy into me to not procrastinate in the "me concept" of imagined uniqueness. I use every single thing now, everything I've ever experienced. The unconscious is clear and Oneness is more than Near!

Swami Aseshananda would say, "All Poets and Philosophers Love Death." It is astounding yet true. For one, Death wipes away all that the poets and philosophers have struggled over. And two, Death is the Ultimate Question. Is that what you meant Swami? This blessed old friend of my soul also would say, "Death tears off the Mask." That must be the mask of ego which holds to all the dualism and is afraid to let go into the Infinite! And this, the Infinite, may be the Ultimate Question of what Real Life Is!

The Transcalent Heat of Pure Sakti warms my form with Love. When I came back I found I have no need of the personal (principle) or the impersonal (principle), for both have filled each other leaving each behind. So, sahaja (out-drawn light) or nirvikalpa (withdrawn light) are redundant names associated to dualism. Outdrawn or Withdrawn, two movements. My mind comprehends nirvikalpa (the standstill) even as it moves (sahaja).

The personal guru (teacher) is secondary (a person in form, a religion, an idea, or concept). The impersonal guru (teacher) is the ever present primary atma (self) reality. When the secondary ceases in the standstill then nirvikalpa comes up, nirvikalpa surfaces as the mind's Background. Looking back from Here is sahaja, going beyond just Watching (Witness), that is Becoming (All the World) is Bhava (Love). That is Becoming Bhava Mukha (Face) is not just facing This as Witness, but Becoming All!

Witnessing is Dualism. Nirvikalpa wipes it out, blows it out. "Practice Sahaja", I was told by the "I" in the person of the "I". Practice the Living Nirvikalpa Life Dance, not the indifferent distinct way up there (Witness) idea. Really Look at Witness, and you see Self looking at...? Self!

The transposing paradox of the koan puzzle in the Zen Mind Itself! To Buddha or Not To Buddha. The Prince or the Tathagata (Reality Gone Over). Buddha or no Buddha. Your dualism will never yield the Answer!

392

The Witness Consciousness is not Nirvikalpa. Though the Witness with No Witnessing (no world form to watch) is Nirvikalpa. Immediate sahaja Kicks In!

Release me, Sakti! Protect me, Ramakrishna! Protect the physical, subtle, and causal bodies that house the dualist in me. It is no doubt, the selfish cry of Self in the not knowing state.

The non-fluid limited rigid preconcepts inside the canalization of thought in the waking-dream-sleep condition of causality sifting through the weight and worth of these states. No more! It is Instant Telepathy in the non-dual mind between in the no-between of ego, "I", and Sakti. But don't be a fool getting caught up in my illusions! When I say Instant Telepathy, it is only Poetry.

Ego is neither big nor small, inside nor outside, divided nor undivided. Ego is "I" as it goes on its way from God, back to God in one sweet step.

The more you (I) become aware of the ego, the more I (you) become awake and alert to God Consciousness and in consequence, to the subtle intensity of the working causality of desires in motion in the world. So ego is a wall, and ego is the Door. Open it and you (I) are swallowed up by Happiness larger than I (you) could ever be.

Sakti, annihilate and abolish this time trapped solid floating idea of me inside the madness of Love. I have no desire for methods nor instructions. They are distractions. And besides all that, I would rather see Love living than just talk about Love as potential.

Does it matter at all what perception I have in the waking state, what I feel or become in the dream state, or what I imagine deep sleep to be with a mind that is not in deep sleep? Forget it! I am the Reality indicated in the Upanishads and designated in Tantra, in empathy with Ramprasad (1723-1803), fully identified in the Godman Ramakrishna, carried by the Divine Sakti. This arena is not for the timid dualist's mind! "How much I communed with the Divine Mother! How can I describe it all? Ah, what a state I passed through! Sleep left me completely." Ramakrishna. When will the sleep of waking/dream/sleep completely leave me? My Love for Her is a Living Energy that makes me Live. I sometimes orbit out into wonder and worry, but to Her I come back and there Know My Self.

Sakti!, please do not let me drown in grand ideas, mad with theories on the topic of myself!

I am so humbled by the Arrival... there is nothing I can say, nor would there be any value or importance within those words. Sakti alone Created the non-present illusions of being born and that of fleeting death! Sakti Benefits! Mind destroys enlightenment by the very question of its question.

I am lost in the Spiritual. My world has turned upside down. Without definition I am Happy without reason. Sakti has Entered!

You will be intoxicated with delusion until your Spirituality becomes sober. Many are delusions, fantasies of what you think is truth, when Truth is alone defined where words, ideas and teachings are Gone!

Death is a delusion. What you see here will certainly go, but what Is Here will go nowhere. If this body falls off now, all I want is for you to know that I love you immensely! I use to think my ego... was powerful, until I was overwhelmed by the Power of Humility. Nothing I say can help you. It is all arrogance. Turn away from the Outside. Become Sakti Inside! You will Be Humbled by the Wonder of Her Working!

Pulse relaxes in the stream of pure sound, the Unformed Sakti, the heartbeat is no longer needed for living. Now is God! I am Turiya! I am Sakti! By saying this Truth I make it True. Timid hesitation was procrastination! Yet, ego is the fool waiting for Delivery!

I am finding no part of myself different from advaita (non-dualism)... always, at every step it was so, in the moment which was life.

To be living is continuous crisis (dualism) conjunctive with perpetual conclusion (non-dualism). Have I learned to gently sway so neither effects me?

394

Questions arise from the common collective bouncing together uniformed like balls off the One Answer! So strange it is to me when I see an answer arrive just by stating a series of questions without answers.

Life moves. I become this, I become that. I become death when death approaches. I lean into death, then I lean into life, or birth, or whatever becomes. Yet, atma sakti does not become... It Is... so perception of atma sakti's perpetual being appears to be needed. The nature of bhava (becoming) is the power of mood not perception, but it starts with perception then becomes what is perceived. Unspeakable is that entrance into Being, Becoming now Sakti! She who excludes nothing!

I Raise my mind to Deitess Identity! Sakti is the "I". Goddess! Woman! Deitess! I am the Freedom that You Are. The Mirror is Gone. It is not a reflection.

My religion is the Love of Beauty where ever She is seen, there is my religion. My spirituality is that of quiet inner power (Atma Sakti) - never hidden, never seen, never shaken by the tremors of dualism, nor be-fuzzled by the instincts of the dual mind's interpreting.

To enjoy God at play, now, this is a sweet condition. I have caught up with life, a Life that is God (Sakti) at play. Nothing but play, no resistance to God (Sakti) at play, only surrender. Everything passes through me as God (Sakti) at play, what remains is that I am indeed (also) with no doubt, God at play - as you and you and you are also. So I attempt not to exert control nor authority on any. If someone walks out the door, you may never see them again, or you may, for all these events are God at Play. Serenity comes in this conclusion.

God at play, in the good and the not good is dualism which is not Genuine Perception. Good always comes in the wake of not good. So the apparent not good serves the purpose of good. Tyrants never last, not historically nor in one's personal universe, as one's inner tyrant. Even so, the tyrant ego falls, if not now, later, at sometime, perhaps another life. Who understands how God is at play? Enjoy and know deep within that the essential of life is the Good, God At Play, though we may not always perceive the distant purpose of order and disorder subtracting or adding with each dual movement.

The subtle body adores the Goddess (Sakti) as Atma (Self), as indeed the causal, subtle, and physical bodies are Saktimaya (cognitive imagined limits), worshiping pure Atma Sakti. This is the sweetest knowledge.

In the reflection undefinable, of Saktimaya, the secret melody of the universe appears - God, Consciousness, Life, Time, and First Causes all in the reflection (this is chidabhasa, the ego identified in the reflection of Consciousness or Sakti). Advaitabhava (non-dual mood) with Her as Atma ever remains absolutely intimate and does not fall into this realm (the reflection), as the last vestige, as the causal body of bliss melts into the secret melody of Adoring Atma.

That kind old mountain sage spoke of the shift from "ego" to "Ego - Ego", from the "I" to "I - I" which is very good. When a poet feels empathy with the experience of other poets, that poet's experience is charged by that empathy. Is this the sharing of Sakti, without the distortion of the ego, the "I" which is the source of distress, distortion, and despair.

In the near death experience it seems that the Witness Consciousness is liberated from the common mind/body content and so sees the world phenomena in a different way than from before. Directing the focus of thought at the Witness produces the same phenomena. It is phenomena as long as the ego is identifying itself to the Witness.

If your ego brings me grief, then I shall destroy your ego with the pure Vedanta of my mind, bringing the idea of you to your True Self and from Here I move in the True Self with you! I am not an actor!

The agent of action associated with the cognate Ricky makes mistakes. All do so. I seek total erasure of the troublesome ego-thought-response. I do not need this concept for Happy Life. My ego should not be so arrogant as to egotize that ego's need for apology or any ego approving thing of that sort. Life is larger and greater than that and still the mind tends to look through a smaller lens. What is this narrowness when happiness and or misery stand or disperse with the ego's pressing requirements.

Can thought ever come to a standstill or is it a thought itself still with a form of thought that thinks it has come to a standstill as that beautiful thought cognate which is believed or imagined as the Wondrous Nirvikara (without thought, concept, principle, agent, function, or motion) Sakti. It is like a lost thought, like a dream whose content is somehow felt yet not recalled to consciousness, to mind function, to living being. But if such a state where thought has ceased, or becomes "without" may be reached, then can the thoughts in the mind recall that state. Or is it just the arrival at the confluence with and in Ecstasy, as it was with Sri Ramakrishna?

As it is all Goddess At Play then who am I to egotize or measure the why, who, what, when, or where of anyone at any time? Forgiving or releasing others or myself in regard to this egotizing or measuring of others or myself is also an absurd limitation of the ego's exertion! Sakti is the Wild Liberated Dancer never egotized! Our ideas or pre-cognizing expectations of what we think Death is, is the greatest egotizing limitation, the fear start up for ego! I do not believe in death. I believe in Sakti.

For it is all Kali. Understand? "K" equals Absolute (Brahman). "A" equals Infinite (Ananta). "L" equals Self (Atma). "I" equals Goddess (Sakti). What IS, is this Absolute Infinite Sakti Self! All other concepts are just that, concepts. Whether or not those concepts or bhavas (mood positions in the psyche's identity) fall into those five stages of liberation (achieving the same plane, form, proximity, union, and complete isolation of the psyche into the concept of final liberation), which are all still egotizing an identification with Sakti, She who is your Birthright of Innate Power Pure never needing formulized identity. But even this is a concept!

Love is the Sweet Secret within us that Knows the Answer, without saying it, to the question of one's intimate relation with the Infinite.

See what You Are, before you became this thing identified through thinking, with time, then thinking of a body it became identified with space. It is not the ghost mind. That transient state of the psyche doesn't comprehend! Steady is true identity, found and located in the conscious core, where the wave of the Dreamless State starts!

I have reduced everything to Wide Open Living Sakti! All the physics of Vedanta and all the spirituality of Tantra, and all the psychological distorted deceptive illusions of coming into birth or going into death are lies compared to This Living Sakti. The Idea dearest to the "I", free of false cognition, Flashes, past, above, before, with and within, over and after the dimension of other idea forms! Maya sakti is Sakti, no other has that Power!

Ego is eclipsed by Absolute Wonder. Out of Her Causal Mind, Sakti has formed the seven spinning illustrations of consciousness within each living being's physical and subtle bodies and these Mystic Goddesses in turn, turn everything that is filling this thing of life with endless cosmological wonders.

Birth and Death are in the Waking and Dreaming States. Deep Sleep has no idea current of either at all, no idea at all, whatsoever. If you name it, it becomes cognitive and then you are stunned by the wonder of it. The same is true with Love and the reflex response of every other emotional form. When you feel Love, you feel you are Where you should Be. There, all seeking drops off, the pilgrim has arrived!

Where thought stops the Spiritual begins, so, thinking, in waking (A) and dreaming (U), about what deep sleep (M) is (where there is no thought current) is still cognition and so saying that thought is Consciousness (advaita) is still thinking or thought waves on what the Ocean of Real Spirituality may Be! AUM is assimilated in Non Dual Flashing. That Flash (of Comprehension) is not gotten in the three states (letter symbols) but from Somewhere Else, the Place that thought up AUM for its Enjoyment. AUM may be the essence of religion, but Spirituality comes from the Higher Over All Position!

From the waking dimension, waking, dream, deep sleep and turiya are viewed as four distinctions in consciousness. From

398

the dream state the dimensional view is less, for mind may melt easily into deep sleep where waking is forgotten and the dreamland is gone and non-duality is felt and experienced, but not clearly known. Can one view these four conditions from deep sleep? No. Because once mind stirs, your consciousness is no longer in this non-dual sleep state. If you think of turiya in the dream state will you enter turiya (illumination in the dream condition), or slip into deep sleep? What is it like? And, is there a four conditional view from Turiya? What does Turiya See? Three states from a Height? No! There, the Seer too, is Gone. What is left? The Maker of the Four States. She is Sakti, the Self, One Singular Sweet Power (Love), even the idea of "the all" is Gone. So, in the strictest sense, ideations on the nature of these four states only exist in the two states of waking and dreaming. I thank those competent experts who have taken the time to explain the Vedanta to me. But these thoughts come from my own heart, outside of them.

Perpetual Experience! Perpetual Perception! Continuous Living in Her Reality! Perpetual Perception and Becoming as the Real Principle which is Love, Love, Love! Carefree is Free of Care. What are those cares anyway or at the ultimate, as the most refined Care, the Care for Love, which is the Felicity of Life in Living Sakti!

Living Sakti is simply learning to just accept Sakti in the three states without suppressing, repressing, or controlling in the ego impulse, any of Her wondrous continual spontaneous free expressions! Liberation from self created fear, acceptance of karma, justified in Sakti! What Joy!

The continuous arousal of Sakti as spiritual pleasure in the three states, opens the way, for deeper pleasure which becomes the Pleasing of Love! Rapid fire repetition of Her Imperishable Sakti sounds awaken my mind to sharpness and clarity. Ah! Sweet soul surrendered! Do we cognise our future or does our future cognise us into believing it is of our own making? Of course though from the Blessed Birthless Condition of High Sakti, what is this karma of our making, in other words, Who is making the appearance of karma? This is why I surrender to the

Doctrine of Surrender, but if I have Become as "one" in High Sakti, then who controls karma?

Ricky, learn what you know!, in context to Her Continuum there is the harmonious flow and spreading through the three states of these psychic and emotional currents that produce insight into Her Loving Life ever present. I love Insight (Quick Knowing)! I shall not answer, submit, call, recall, question, nor inquire into anything else until this flow is finished. Nothing is that important compared to the accomplishment of God Consciousness. It is everyone's one and only job! The rest is just paying the tax, producing children, making the feet move, feeding mouths, building empires, serving the day, releasing the night, and the redundant cycle of dying and being reborn into the Fantastic Distraction!

Even the continuous flow of "one single enjoyable thought" is still a thought in the mind work. The Leap to More Peace is to the Ineffable. Never gotten by thoughts like "being one with" or "never separate from." That is all thought, though certainly high thought. But feeling Happiness is Something all together different. You See! It is Non-Causal, Without Cause, A-Causal - no, not even a First Reason, even at the most extreme finest level of thought as a primary force of origin. What indeed has been created or comes out of anything, as it is Non-Dual! Consciousness (Love) is not a thought, nor does it come out of anything, or into anything, as contemplation or meditation.

This writing is my practice. It helps me. That is the "Why" of it. Blessed is the Goddess! Blessed is Sakti! Blessed is Her World of Joy! The Paradise of the Goddess is within us. Let it Become a Living Reality!

In a dream, Swami Aseshananda said, "Blinking your focus off God can kill you." Opening and Closing the Eyes of the Goddess (Kali), that idea too. Opening to Real Consciousness and so closing becomes creation, all in the blink of Her Eyes- loss of focus of course, is loss of contact, so, where is life- you have been killed spiritually speaking.

Satchidananda (the Pure Existence-Consciousness-Bliss) Swarupini (the Goddess in Her True Nature) in conversion is what becomes creation, manifestation, emanation, the Real Self Form of the universe and every living person. This is the Height of Beauty!

When that Beautiful Emotion arises, it is pure, and need not be brought back into personality stagings or relationships which may diminish Its Intensity- for the Pure Love, in any dual relation or expressed at any stage of the personality, is the "not two" (advaita). The dual splits us. Advaita is, and advaita unites us.

The dualist lives in fear of death. The non-dualist recognizes that the soul has never taken the form of birth. The dualist worships God asking for this and that. The non-dualist asks for nothing pulling everything out of the Self.

Every relation between must fill this "between" by revolving into the "not-two", or rather, doing not a thing, saying not a word, but seeing that it is so.... especially among the best of friends and the most loved ones.

Beautiful Sakti, celestial girl, pure woman energy, potent divine power, golden sunlight gentle force filled perfectly divine body made of nothing but Love materialized in the subtle condition of a high focus dream state- with your blue eyes, your heavenly hair, and your transcending levitating spiritual teachings on Para Sakti divine gate worship!

I read, I write, I Watch my mind, I Observe my dreams. I enjoy and practice Sakti Joy, my smile just lets Happiness Be. Then the figure falls, mind not necessary.

How long shall I procrastinate in separation from Sakti! Her Company as Love always has been my Best Friend, Love, the Sacred Companion! The Humorous Smile of such Happiness Uncomplicated, watches the Unfolding Comedy of Sakti's Finest, this Sacred Laughter, not Serious! What occupies my mind? Living Sakti! And I need not figure everything out right now, for Sakti knows and lets me know what needs knowing as it becomes known, immense or small! This, my Spirituality will not contain nor afford hard feelings, for every unfolding of feeling embraced is a lesson from Her, My Sakti (but not ownership)! My God (power)! My Loving (but without the

401

action of Love) Beauty (as transcendent indescribable tangible experience)!

We generally do not fear "living" in the body, so why all the fuss and fear of "living" without the body (the botah = the potach, or pot-ash, the balch = the bag). Strange is the cherishment of the bag. Funny, the need we feel for the pot ash.. Truthfully I say honestly now. Peace, peace, peace to me (and you) for I do not believe in death anymore. There is only this "Living", this Living Sakti, with or without that bag of pot ash (body) - Even the fear aspect of dying may not be that different or difficult, if one considers this place here as the bardo (the between two) of embodiment and the other as the bardo of having no body, no bag. But Consciousness, now that is Perpetual Beauty, what the "I" has Become when the "I" is finished, the Love that Lasts. So, in Love, fear has no place to rest. Body thought identity is the gripping dilemma. Sex, money, power, progeny, fame, name, success are all forms of the ego's grip on the "bag", on what causes unhappiness, that undefined free floating sense of fear augmented by greed, hate, and confusion. Love Trust is Happiness. Pass through and Smile! So, when Kali raises Her Hand in gesture saying, "Have No Fear," (Of Death or anything) She is really Telling you the Truth!

The Lover of Kali Loves the Death of the Ego, for the more ego dies, the more Joy Increases. Kali Lovers have learned This. Go anywhere in the world, to anyone, in any experience, and this is all you will learn! But death of the body is not death of the ego. If this were so, we would all be enlightened by death and perhaps we are momentarily. Yet ego continues in Consciousness, even with the death of the physical body. So the problem of ego will continue.

Perceiving Kali as Young Mother Goddess, then I am younger as Her Child. This is most sweet. Heroic perception perceives Her as Lover Goddess, then I am Atma, Her Lover! When I see myself as the learner, She is everywhere present as Divine Instructress. As Love, She is the ever present Best Friend, and I am Her Friend. And as inner Peace, She is

402

Consciousness knowing the form of the world as nothing but Consciousness having absolutely no outside feeling whatsoever!

If Kali takes "me" out of the body right now or if She keeps "me" in the body to act and work in the world, what does it matter? To try to control death is undoubtedly the ultimate ego fixation. The special beauty of Kali lovers through the spiral of time is that they have surrendered that ego fixation. Outside they look different. Inside they are the same- in this life and in this same life as a new form!

Get out of the body/mind idea of this single lifetime. Expand this consciousness. What I was, what I shall become, what I am now. All and Always, Kali. Brahman Infinite Atma Sakti! Old memory, New memory, No memory, Divine Memory! It is the phenomenal covering as we translate fresh experiences and old experiences (memory and dream) into a self-idea of the body/mind complex identification of what one thinks one Is! When so much more is there, Here as What Self Is!

I am a poet, not an advisor, not a teacher. But as a poet I have come to not believe in death. Gone, but not gone! Not death, only Life and more Life! I believe in Love, a Love that would never destroy us, as we have once tended to and bended to believe we are destroyed in the idea of death. It is Love that death should teach us! How, but by its absolutely false concept of a finish! Where, where but Here, Living Ever as Love. This is what comforts me in the wheel (of life). I hope perhaps it shall do the same for you my friend, if we find ourselves waiting (that is, sitting with the forgetfulness of Love) to see loved ones again, we may be comforted by knowing we have Loving Friends who are now There to Greet Us.

We die and die and die again. This redundancy disproves death a a final event within Our Greater Experience. Sakti Ever Lives as Love, in victory over our tears, our laughter, our wondering, our wandering.

Never feel that you are left out from anything, anyone, any experience whatsoever. For Love is Best, and wherever you find You, Love is There with You, as You, being the True You.

Sakti! So, Now, your name and form are no longer different from what you have dreamt were mine.

Spiritual Power, Sakti, is the Cure for this thing, that thing, anything, even death. For if you have Become as Sakti Is, then what is death? What can it possibly mean to You? Or even the idea of taking on a body or a mind, how can even that make any effect in one's Original Sakti Nature, so High as never to take on a body or mind, and so, to never experience death. All but a dream to Sakti Consciousness. The practice of the Bliss Exercise of Birthless (and so, Deathless) Conscious Awareness is also found in the Ajata (Not-Born) Vada (Proclamation, Communication, Talk, Utterance, Speak) Advaita (Not-Two) Vedanta, Dzogchen, and profound Buddhist teaching. Very Beautiful. So, celebrating a birthday is celebrating the dream/illusion of ego birth. It is not a duality of illusion and reality. The world is not an illusion. The feeling of dualism is the illusion, the dream/delusion from which one wakes where sleep as it was once known completely leaves.

And if one cannot stay There at the Birthless Realization, as is so often the case, mind ever craving an answer more relative to itself, then, those thoughts of karma will come to us, of reincarnation, (natural as sunrise and sunset), connections, and questions like why we meet certain people to come under their sway or why we don't meet and do not come under their sway. We do effect each other. It is denial to say not so. Well, it is all Sakti as Guide. The sweet light of the kitten's Rta (a principle higher than personal karmic cause and effect, everything is Caused by the Power of God, so the kitten has total trust in the Mother cat) who knows She has made the Unfolding from the beginning of time. But to see all this in question with the outward eyes and not the inward eyes focused on the absolutely pure state of ultimate, never gained, never gone, Spiritual Birthlessness, is to be deceived by the mistake of taking a swan to be a parrot.

A New Dimension! The simple non-complex, non-diverse luminous real mind knowing only Love, the one true Knowledge of this most desired, most precious Existence! Not analyzing,

404

imagining, figuring, thinking, dreaming, fantasizing, no, not even sleeping consciousness. Peace Infinite! To desire no desire is a desire! Desire Love!

I do not speak from above you, talking down at your head. If you want to hear my voice then listen to the whisper below your feet. I move Gentle in Faith, not hard in fear. Many moments come, but when Joy makes Its Touch, all vital content is lost, replaced by Love.

With the skill of a surgeon be a poet working with Consciousness! Yes! But Love can never be dissected nor needs no mending. Love is the Original Power before the mind's origin!

That exhilarated feeling! Can I be that joyous to incarnate each time? The adventure! Do I love the spiritual search of each incarnation so much? Do I love incarnation itself as entertainment in Eternity? We are all incarnations, no exception, nothing outside Sakti, hidden or opened! So why hold a house, a temple, a possession? Instead, Be like a Goddess and a God who float through Divine Regions wise enough to Know Heaven is not Eternal. Never forget, that in deep sleep you have no dualism and that it is within dream (imagination) that you imagine dualism, so that when the waking state comes back, that imagination becomes a fear that you may have been abandoned by the Divine Sakti, but it is never so, never farther from the truth!

If ego is aware of the guru function then perhaps the guru function is not genuinely taking place there, as it is the light that brings the darkness into the light or the light that blasts out the darkness (the ego). One cannot say for sure, for there is no "saying" there. Swami Vivekananda described Sri Ramakrishna as that "wonderful unconscious method", meaning that he was not conscious of himself in the spiritual process. He was not aware of his ego in the spiritual result. What he was aware or conscious of was the Goddess (Kali) and it may be that She occupied the place of his ego if we consider this excellent insight into what is meant by "wonderful unconscious method." Sakti is this Higher Dynamic Function of Light (insight)

405

Illuminating Darkness (the ego in the three states, the three bardos, the three kayas). Now, when ego gravity shifts from waking and dreaming states to the state of Deep Sleep (the unconscious devoid of dream or waking images and not separate from Turiya) is that the so called individuation (atma assertion) in the spontaneous compensation (grace) of the transcendent function- the counter weight of dualism between the conscious and the unconscious? Also, if Sakti fully occupies the place of self, then one has absolutely no need to contemplate the three conditions (the waking/dream/sleep, the sidpa (birth) bardo, the chonyid (psychic) bardo and the chikhai (pure light) bardo, in after death experience, which are but different names for the nirmana (emanation), sambhoga (psychic manifest enjoyment), and dharma (pure truth) kayas- vehicles, except as a form of spiritual enjoyment or divine entertainment! Actually, the three states, bardos, kayas, pull you out of the Pure Sakti State, into outside contemplation. In Pure Sakti one becomes wonderfully unconscious of any thing else, any principle, state, dimension of consciousness, whatever! In this way, one observant person commented on the spiritual condition of Sri Ramakrishna, "Goodness gracious! The Divine Mother has caught hold of him, like a tiger seizing a man."

I am glad not to be restricted to scientific investigation, having Poetic Flowing Freedom into the spontaneous border, direct and immediate to all contents, conscious and unconscious, the small circle and the Infinite without finite circularity! Massive. Unending. Indefinable.

In Living Sakti, find that ishta archetype (chosen cognitive ideal just for your mind) that tears away the narrow ego point of resistance in the conscious mind and that connects living consciousness (or disembodied) to the Great Unconscious which is One with but different from the archetypes, though in Oneness with the conscious manifest emanation of those archetypes. She is the Great Matrix (never unconscious), deeply spiritual, deeply psychological. The surrender of conscious resistance starts the unconscious life, filled with the Unified Sakti of this now Awake Unconscious, from Here Forth it cannot be called the unconscious- for you are aware of it consciously as Living Sakti! A great human factor is now at work.

The Great Unknown as the Great Knowing is now acting in and as Me! Ego gravity goes so there is levitation in the psyche. Timelessness. Union. Connection without connecting! Wonder and Joy.

As Atma Sakti, I am smaller than the smallest (quantum particle, ego now sub-subatomic), larger than the largest (extra supra supercluster of galactic islands). I can walk on water (over the impossible), raise the dead (if only metaphorically, as we all are reborn from death) and heal the sick (as separation from God is our dis-ease, not being at Ease with Sakti, and that all our mortality is uncurable because of time, but for this Ease). As Atma Sakti all my desires can be fulfilled and I can engage and create and manipulate the matter and mind material of numerous bodies and minds, assuming myself the shape of infinite bodies and the psychic actions of infinite minds- or become as heavy as the Himalaya or levitate through the sky, the atmosphere, and the inter galactic ether of space/time! Siddhi Sakti is Goddess Accomplishment (Power). I am not delusional, I have surrendered to the strength in knowing with humility that all flesh and bone, all psyche and sentiment will be crushed under the turning of Life! Know well that this is all poetic metaphor!

Everything I read, experience, discuss, becomes something to write about as an interpretation in Sakti. Its exhausting. For I use not only my mind but my body and spirit (Sakti) too! I am nourished and depleted in psychic energy at the same time and I do this absolutely sober, except for the intoxication of my constant company of this ego, which occasionally shifts its weight from there, to God. When will all my thoughts reach the Blessed Redundant Condition of Peace and the necessity to write will cease? What to do? How can I heal the Mother Wound (Sakti's absence) in anyone? Goddess Help them, for I cannot!

Ego is a Stress Point that makes one feel insanely distant from Sakti (God). This effects the nerves, drains the quantity of emotional energy and distracts thought into channels that do not have the Calm and Clear. Even so, Love suddenly surges and heals the wild psychic schism back to Happy Singular Quiet in spiritual observation as Kutastha Chidabhasa (Consciousness in witness of the ego reflection) phenomena. But then, All God, All Advaita - Wipes Out even that and All Love Remains! This is My Sakti!

To Go that Deep into the Day, as I can see this "I" is Sakti! Experiencing Her is like Looking into Sunlight with Closed Eyes, the Red Black Hues consume all shadow as Joy Wells Up, even within the internal eyes of others as they open to Happiness reflected on the optic windows translucent. But to Go that Deep into the Night is to be abolished by Divine Advaita, where two, or other, or shadow never was! Never to be or become, nor ever blighted by any thought! Feeling, Love is All That Knows any True Thing of This!

My Spirituality is What my Spirit Knows as Love! Raise the Energy of Love to such a level, and from that Height- Enjoy the "I" of God in Everyone, like a sleeping baby dreaming in oneness with Mother Sakti! Wonderful Sakti!

Every time I speak I realize I shall not ever speak again, not for forty years! Then my mind will know its own thought alone and true, to the constant perpetual practice of Being Sakti, again and again Be Sakti! Feel Sakti! See Sakti! All thought Silent but for Manifest Sakti! Poet, never say another word!

Identify this poet's Sacred Doctrine with someone else and you have failed to find Me!

In order to demonstrate the display of this Amount of Independent and Free Sakti (Love), I must tolerate that at some time, somewhere, somehow you may not Love me, or that I may leave (body) to Be Pure Spirit (Sakti), now, or not now, yet one day no longer in the flesh to be flesh with that Sweet Feeling! Cease all this endless reasoning over religion's meaning. Love is the message, the Height of the crescendo of all preaching and teaching, all effort and practice. Experience Sakti (Love). Divest all myth from the Great Ones whose names have marked history with their moments and you will find that greatness is something you already know, and you can share and give as they have , the Greatest of Greatness, the Love that is Sacred in every soul. We are no longer looking for Gods among men. The disappointment is over. With humanity mixed in divinity you still have disappointment.

I am the problem (as throwing forth the ego or putting forward the ego or putting the ego before Sakti). I am the solution (as Sakti unfastens, dissolves, loosens and unties the ego). Sakti solves the ego. For this my gratitude has no end. It is the only measure of value!

I have died so many times and yet it never fails to be again and again proven that Death is my Creator!

On the seven stages. There are no stages! Not for Consciousness, not for Love as Love is. The formation of stage awareness is a limitation in that it projects a necessity to step through, instead of immediate recognition. Fascinating really. Yet formulas are necessary for the mind that needs them. I say make comparisons and mix your own seven stage recipe. They all work. And they can work together throwing light on each other. For example, "tanumanasi" occurs naturally in deep sleep, or only being able to "talk and think about God" all the time is comparable to "turiyatita" where Consciousness as a personal experience is no longer defined as a reference to a moment in time or a position in space. Or this fifth step as the total turning away from or dropping off of "all mind stuff,"so then there is just the Stuff of God!

The Seven Saktis of Tantra are the Divine Functions as Innate Functions just natural to life processes. Do nothing as ego, let Sakti do! Tantra's seven illustrations in relation to the Goddess would be waking awareness (Brahmani-Creatrix), dream awareness (Vishnavi-Preservatrix), deep sleep awareness (Rudrani-Destructrix), turiya awareness (Isvari-Goddess), then turiyatita (Sadasivani-the Always Everywhere function of the Goddess), here, turiya is not isolated to a moment in time or a position in space, no reference point. Consciousness is so High now it is beyond turiya (turiyatita). You see to speak of turiya one must come back down to Earth, the three relative states, but here that dual reference point has gone (between turiya and the three states). So you come to the sixth and seventh spiritual illustrations. The opening of the eyes of the Goddess (Sakti Svarupa-the Goddess as the Real Self Form and Background) as this opening is the creation of the universe itself. And so She witnesses this universe. And when Her eyes are closed it is just Sakti Sakti (the Nothing But or Pure Non-Dualism) There is nothing to even witness. Non-dualism is reached. Or, one can now say, the "eyes" are truly open, seeing the Non-Dual, and before this, the "eyes" were closed to the Non-Dual, and That , being shut out by the dual view of creation.

Vedanta gives its seven planes (bhumis). Subhecha, the craving for freedom. Atmavichara, the examination or inquiry into atma. Tanumanasi, the refinement of the mind, or making it transparent where the fourth stage may come, Sattvapada, the condition of balance, harmony in the atma, generated by the thinning out of mind content, like polishing a mirror. Fifth is Asamsakti, this is when atma is realized beyond all creative phenomena (the universe or the "at play" condition). Sixth, Pada Artha Bhavana, the Step to High Aspiration or the Mood of that Consciousness (Love-Bhava). Finally is Turiya.

Yoga as explained by Patanjali gives another seven step formula but here uniquely the first stage is to realize atma as the constant in one's life. Then that consciousness of atma reduces the pain associated with identity in the body/mind complex. Third is samadhi, the steady state experience of atma as the reality beyond the matrix of the world. Fourth, comes an interesting stage where behavior is no longer based on ego connections. As classically described, one's duties come to an end due to the realization of atma and compared to the atma the world is not quite real. It is more like a play. As Ramakrishna describes this state, "To such a man the world appears a strange land, a place where he has merely to perform his duties." And so at the fifth stage one finds that even the chitta (all the mind stuff) falls off or turns away. Sixth, what is left of chitta, turns back into the Primary Cause, Consciousness itself, leaving you at the seventh, which is described by Swami Vivekananda in Raja Yoga 2:27 as, "We required none else to make us happy, for we are happiness itself. We shall find that this knowledge does not depend on anything else."

If we start with the Solution first and then look back down on the problem which will not exist since the Solution is already preemptively known, we must deeply consider with quick knowing what Ramakrishna stated at the highest elevation, "Now I see that I and the Mother (Sakti) have become one." If we go from this Highest and then look down at the sixth step we shall notice some kind of condition in the witness consciousness like a light in a lantern that cannot be touched due to the barrier of glass. This barrier is the only barrier from the get go. It is the witness viewed as illuminating duality (the light and the glass). But if there is no duality, then even this stage is pure delusion. There can be no dualism in the One. The cognition of the witness principle cognises duality itself as a secondary thing that must be illuminated upon or watched (witnessed). Dropping down to the fifth stage the person experiencing the phenomena of stages finds that they can no longer talk of, think about, see, or hear anything but God, (Sakti), for everything one hears, sees, etc. stirs nothing but God Consciousness, one cannot help it. Lower than that is the awakening of the heart (light or insight as illumination comes with mute wonder at its Loving radiance upon one's life). The third stage is the mind which is directed to either the above stages or downward toward the other two centers (chakras) which Ramakrishna describes as being focused primarily on sex and money, pleasure and survival. "The Primordial Energy (Sakti) resides in all bodies as the Kundalini (which is but another form of the same Sakti)." Ramakrishna knew his Oneness with this Primordial Energy. "The Kundalini (Sakti) is speedily awakened if one follows the path of bhakti (Love). God (Who is but Sakti) cannot be seen unless She (Sakti) is awakened." The seven stages actually produce a stress or spiritual distress that you must pass through some passage of seven conditions in order to get where "You Are" which is just Love itself ever from the beginning. She dwells in "all bodies" forever from Her making any of those bodies through

411

"kundalini" becoming coiled down into the relative realm (of space/time). So there it is, do with it what you want.

Psychology, with a little planetary archetypal associations thrown in for good luck, gives its own revelation. Though in truth I see these principles as mere metaphor within the paradigm of cosmological cognitive projections and the appearance of maps of astronomical structures in the human psyche as a psychological cause and effect equation. The first four years (moon) of life are the formation of emotional imprints. The next ten (mercury) are the development of mental and intellectual arrangements in the mind. Then the years up to about twenty-one (venus) are the awakening discoveries of the heart, essentially romantic in content but addressed to other relationships as well. Then probably about to the age of thirty-five is the cycle of aggressive action toward accomplishment (mars) of some kind with the life force. Psychology states that around thirty five years is a great turning point, either back deeper into the stagnation of earlier formations and into neurosis, or to a religious or spiritual answer (jupiter) to this strange unreasonable passage of time, aging, and destiny. Wisdom should start to enter about here. After this we hopefully mature (saturn) within the karmic fate or set of conditions that this life has held for us. And finally it all ends with the glorious (sun) return of all our days and nights back to God. These are my own interpretations somewhat. Each must open their own seven mystical seals to a personal apocalypse of the ego back into the seven stars of mystery in God Consciousness. Read your own seven letters and enter your own seven churches. Stand for yourself amidst the seven candlesticks within the seven spirits before the throne of illumination. Be yourself fearlessly crowned with the seven crowns of the dragon wisdom, and at one in the seven angel minds where all conflict and consecration, all animosity and anointment has already forever ceased!

So, with this I challenge you to realize Love right now before you become dependent upon stages, steps, states, conditions, formulas, intermediate bardos, or vehicles to

412

enlightenment. For once the ego enters the "black waters" of non-duality, there you see that ego never existed at all. Truth is "birthless" so it is never born in you, meaning, how can it become born, as "It" has already been given birth (yet there are two views; sahaja-the thus born and ajata-the never born). These structures of consciousness limit Consciousness in the mind of consciousness. "Lastly, we shall find that we are established in our true Self, that the Self in us has been alone throughout the universe, and that neither body nor mind has ever been related, much less joined, to It." Vivekananda Raja Yoga 2:27. Do this First not "Lastly", then one will not even need the perception of the "black waters" (Ramakrishna's metaphor for Absolute Non-Dualism), you will be joyful from the start in the Luminosity of Love!

My influences on me, the idea of who I used to be, the course of life, friends, swamis, Ramakrishna_!, Kali_!, then Pure Sakti- transferred out of all waking state phenomena, transformed in the pure content of every dream condition- now, again Turiya is translated into the substance of deep sleep, and without naming what has happened the thought between the two ideas has become translucent!

It is a natural miracle that the mind can follow the arranged flow of letters that shape into meanings and that this may illuminate the mind as the Presence of Consciousness (Kutastha) is Awakened- Even more and more as the Mood of God is Aroused to See that Principle in All Things Swallowed inside Itself!, Rising Out of Sakti within You and as You- as nothing is outside You and what is said is only an echo indicating the Moment of Complete Mystery Unveiled. It is not darkness nor light. Where can mind go? Where can mind reach? And for what reason. Everywhere it goes- everywhere it reaches, it finds nothing but God! These Concepts are placed on the Substance that has no symbol, that is, identified in the self out of fear of losing one's ego center in the Immensity of This Wonder!

I do not calculate what is to be written or said. It comes from somewhere, I don't know how- the unconscious surfaces to the conscious perhaps- humility drives me to state, it is not

413

excellent, but everything is excellent, everything being in God. If there is any consistency to this it amazes me as much as it might amaze you. You cannot believe how subtle is the weave of the mind's impressions, even but for one lifetime!

Being and Behaving in a way that is beyond the parameter of psychology is fine. The undefined spiritual response. But for the ego to claim Godhood is only ego. The ego wants to be worshiped (loved) by Love, for Love is the Mother of the ego. It is all mostly figuring out the ego, isolated consciousness filled with envy and subtle resenting and that is as disgusting as claiming ego is God. Absurd.

Because mind is lazy and timid, it is easier to depend on the Ishta, any ishta (Spiritual Ideal), and the already preexisting cognitions that go with it. Mind, look deeper, discover what is beyond- a bold reality is waiting, a Love not yet imagined by you!

Mind, going "out" to the guru prototype (ishta) may lose its own proto (original) type. The face of someone else is not your own (original) face. There are good and helpful prototypes surely, but in the end only Sakti Svarupa shows what Sakti Svarupa Is as the non-dual Chitti (Consciousness) Sakti, without imitation of someone's face other than your own!

In that Height, he could have made the absurd and smacking foolish proclamation of Godhood, but he stayed the Servant of Kali! Who?

Any movement outside the Steady Feeling of Love (Sakti) could be the coma of the Self.

The constant reassessment of images in the spiritual mind (buddha, jesus, etc., etc., etc.,) ceases at the Breakthrough!

Does ego try for its own sake to convey the experience of personal deity (or deitess)? Love only conveys Love for the Sake of Itself!

The smooth flow in the Sakti Beauty of Uncertainty (in ego) is free of predictable projections.

The conditions of the world (cause and effect) itself continually assault the ego, teaching ego to release itself as fixed

414

identity, which is reduced to nothing more than immature spirituality.

If there were no struggle in this work it would hardly be worth reading, much less writing. I find there are many people who have advanced very far (spiritually). Yesterday's spiritual fix just doesn't satisfy today. People are hungry for more insight into Truth. But for one to say this is the Truth and that is not the Truth is the arrogance of an insecure ego (within any cultural or spiritual frame). Of ego, psyche and consciousness, the psyche is addicted to its concept of permanent forms, even though the forms of the world are constantly changing- the psyche in conjunction to ego believes those impressions of forms to be constant or permanent. So the idea of what self is in consciousness keeps or becomes stuck and it becomes hard to change one's mind. The psyche is simply wanting to secure its position here, or in its concept of what a future condition may be or become, here or here after. But that Security in Self comes when the psyche and the ego drop- and Consciousness is Seen As It Is. This is a most wonderful dynamic in the spiritual process. The hidden bridge within! Afterwards, the ego and psyche may Be Happy in the Divine Discovery of Sakti (Consciousness in Active Power).

People process information (knowledge) in funny and strange ways, always to justify their own position (I too!), since we know the universe only through the idea of self it seems. Total vision of everything at once may not be possible, but in Near Death Experiences, reports of this experience (total vision) is documented, perhaps though only in terms of what is essential in total vision. So ego's own position is a self limiting device- until Consciousness is loosened- (by fear, love, exhilaration, humility, Kundalini, N.D.E., Samadhi, Satori, prayer, poetry, music, theater, even by the depth of sorrow).

If you love the dark, you attract the dark. If you love the light, you attract the light. But it can be mixed, most often it is with the weird (destiny, fate, what you become) and the wonderful (the marvelous). But if you Love Love, well, need I say more.

If you can imagine you are One in Sakti, then how far are you from Reality! All that was vulgar is Now Sacred by this Tantric Veneration of the Entire Field of Ecstasy!

The tedious quick knowing of my head sometimes takes time to catch up with the Tenderness of My Heart, which is Where I Love to Be, then and now Free!

Few find the Feeling Point beyond insult to the ego's belief systems. But some have been very honest about the ego. Ramakrishna lived that Honesty. Spirituality is Here, Now, Always. Sakti is God! The rest is working the ego like the Wind works a Cloud.

Ego is ephemeral. Fixation on it is the hardest thing in the world. To live without it, even for a moment, is an amazing phenomena, once its name becomes Humility. Then Sakti Takes Over! And nothing that is not God ever happens again- even as an interest in God as concept, thought, or imagined ideal... instead of Realness (the pure and ever new, always fresh, naked, green, and Raw Reality of God-Sakti in Life)!

Hatred will find any means (belief systems as weapons) to justify itself. Even ones that Hate hates itself. I shift to Love, and shall Love with the power of hate! Resending Nothing. I say it once and then I am Gone! I just Shine Love and Her Radiance is All That Is Here!

The belief in reincarnation gives the Sense of Continuation, when the Real Constant is Sakti- Eternal Real Belief!

The unconscious without archetype is Deep Sleep no doubt. What help does Reality need and You are none other than Reality, so where is the question of help? Truth never changes its Substance nor Its Name, only our cognition and level of emotional joy changes in the cycles of consciousness. The Seen, as the three states, and the Seer (Sakti) have not changed. Seeing has Changed! This is all. Seeing to the Depth of the Seer- then with sahaja eyes seeing back into the Seen. Or no Seeing at all, blinded by Non-Duality. Great Love Arises, the Fine Feeling of Singularity, of Uniformity, which cries out for More and More Love! All the World is Divine as the Non-Dual Demonstration of Sakti's (Love's) Wonder, as all are Special

416

Incarnations of Sakti, none Unique, since all are uniquely Awake! True Humility is God of this world and if the Goddess or the God ever incarnate as a daughter or son of Themselves, it is only in divine flashes of Pure Love, above all other feelings to love Love for no reason at all, to sacrifice self (ego) for the sake of others, the courage to love others more than one's own ego, and if it is asked, without a second thought, to give up one's life for another, these are the Incarnations of Love ever birthless and ever real, common inside the experience of everyone's heart! These are here now and have always been here now! All interior ego-icons in the psyche are broken down by the divine iconoclastic power of the Nothing But Love pathless direct path. I interpret everything, seeing Through Sakti. But in Blessed Peace (or also deep sleep) no psychological process of interpretation goes on at all nor is seen at all! My Religion is Living Now as Sakti, but not seen through the architecture of the subconscious. Ego defense keeps the ego in its place. Life (Sakti) is continually breaking down this defense (against union in the non-dual). Ego sinks, Joy rises. Ego rises, Joy sinks. Ego keeps ego from seeing what is within, behind, above, and around its Perceptual Point, so usually ego just sees what it wants to see. There is no elsewhere place to be in your Experience. Ego has been conditioned to chase itself elsewhere, not having the feeling (spiritual) of Being Where You Are. Without this the world is an empty dream, with this (Love) it is Paradise Itself!

In sorrow, we surely feel Love, perhaps the Deepest Love of all is inspired by sorrow, or perhaps it is Love itself, because Its Depth inspires the deepest sorrow, which will in time come back around to the Highest Love. "After a while he said: "Art Thou come? I too am here." Who could pretend to understand these words?" Ramakrishna.

417

Kali: The Allayer Of Sorrows

On the Spontaneous Experience of Innate Non Dualistic Subjective Consciousness

I swim in the Ocean of Her Beautiful Thoughts in Emotions I cannot form into the shape of words. Her Sweet Inspiration presses out of me like a woman with thighs spread apart giving continuous emerging of new, fresh human maya. She is the Deity of my Poetry in the divine metre of Her Voice which I know not the name, perhaps and perhaps not. Blessed is She, between and ever communicating what Is the Ever Uncreated into the Created!

Kali, You now make me see this world movement from a Height I cannot describe, as if everything is perfect and finished and yet is still moving toward itself. What can I say of the View from Your most remarkable internal realm? The extreme excitement, the possibility that could come at any time, of having a new body, the process of entering the mother again and becoming one with her is exhilarating. Yet I see from a Height, that fresh and new experiences, new tastes, new loves in all their erotic passionate ecstasy would be somewhat redundant. We all repeat the common elements of experience, as a new soul or my own soul and for what reason is this?

Goddess, though Blessed Is and Blessed Be, the ever unending exhilaration of Your new beginnings, I find that I wish not for the comfort I see in the patterns of consciousness and the ever exciting moods that are here before my mind's eye. Mother, I want to explore deeper and deeper the possibilities of Your Ecstasy, so let me not be in comfort till I have reached the end.

Goddess, as lust is now relaxed within me, by the sweetest positioning of Your Bliss Inside, what else can now happen, except for the coming forth of Love. Kalee, every wish within my soul is complete, when I feel the Sweet Feeling, the End Feeling to all seeking. The joy, memory and beautiful learning,

419

all amassed into one pure moment! Right here! Right now! What name could be given to this, but Love...

Poet, now, and never lose consciousness, that She, Blessed Sacred Kalee is your primal, primary and primordial Feeling in regard to everything that freely manifests before the Pure Consciousness of Being, the Sea of Vast Self in the Unchartered Ocean of Joy... Pure Love, unconscious of the delusions of fear...

Poet, life is my sweet study of woman bliss, ever there returning to the End Feeling, the singular exquisite most emotion which effortlessly encompasses the extreme final emanation and the total destination of mind reaction, mind motion and mind perception. O Sweet, Sweet Love! Mother Kalee, keep my thought in the highest state of Love, which makes impossible the possibility of selfishness.

Mother, it is only this impulse of me that covers the Jewel named Reality. I follow the Cool, Cool Mood of Kalee with the Sweetness of the Sweetest Thoughts. Originally, it was Divine Lust that brought me here to Her, but now, in the rightest moment of now, in the right mind of now, a moment split into Infinity, it is the sleepless, stressless Feeling of Sacred Joy, Happiness free of body fear or mind's dual throbbing over the worldliness of ever controlling puzzlement. Blessed Is and Blessed Be.

Mother, carry me deep into my own Spirituality, where I may see in that clearest moment, how simple the world is... in my right mind, in the right now, where every weird wonder of myself falls away into the sharing of what life is, the wondrous moment of its quickest passage over the surface of my Love so deep in the depth inside. Never more the impulse of 'I' to cover this Jewel again!

Mother, my Divine Friend, that weight of sorrow called depression, is accepting the attitude of a victim. Life does not choose us as victims. Life is just life, as my saying goes, while the single sole problem of the soul is its impulse to isolation away from You, an attitude of the ego, the impulse of identity separate from God Consciousness.

Kalee, Goddess Instructress Within, I go wherever I am... and when I've gone there, I am still where I am. As ego is the I-going and Peace is never leaving the place where You are. As always Is. As always Be. So, what is this in me, Mother, that races against death, only to Be at One with Death, In You Who has no death?

Blessed Is and Blessed Be the Divine Contact with the Goddess and Her Mystic Power of Sacred Mood Feeling, the High Oneness with Her Bliss ever free of worry, having no fear, as each wish is granted without personal effort. For all mind does is dwell on the painted toes of Her beautiful precious feet. Now, friend, where is the need for sleep dreaming, which is but the countered release of the waking mind's restless activity.

With Her Primal Power, Her Sakti Self, She gathers the consciousness of firm set waking conditions, sweetly ushering upward, that consciousness into the luminous conditions of fluid and fiery dream movements flowing naturally into the depth of Ultimate Rest, the exact womb of infinite being where consciousness knows nothing of distinction, nor dualism. Nor even realization, as this is Her Original Vital Power! My unceasing prayer in the current of Her Love!

This is my Divine Dignity, stripped to utter nakedness, without shame, hatred or fear, nor any distinction within human society. Free of the crushing, the anticipating, the ignoring of She! As ignorance itself is its own sweet punishment. Who is She but the Mother of Eternal Happiness ever moving in me as perceptual causes, internal motions in the forms of dream and imagination, and conscious reaction, perpetual waves in the still motion of Eternity. The Super Conscious carries no superstition about these matters of sweetest concern!

Mother, of one name, many names, no name and all names, what shall I now do as a poet who is ever driven to the making. Mother, keep me in the steady state of this newly discovered Love never moving out of itself, never being pulled away by objectives, nor swayed by sentiments, but ever, ever in itself as Truth never changed. Is this the End Feeling, my darling Goddess who has lusted after my heart for eternity?

At the thought of death or even in the intensity of distress the essence thoughts ingrained inside my soul come forth to the rounded curve of my sweet fruit of a brain. Then suddenly everything is seen in its right perception as having but the content of a passing dream without much importance. It is my Kalee who is essential to me. This body is reduced to what, the body undergoes what and then what do the mind contents matter at all. The Power and Skill of the Loving Heart is all that continues undaunted by my death or any other matters of subtlety.

Inner feeling without outside forms! The deeper Depth, my heroes and heroines. Joy in doing not in results. Love in depth not moved nor pulled. Peace in Wonder with no expectations of things to come! Just Joy in the Hour of Joy. Her Elation without limitation is this my sweet and ever sweeter and sweeter liberation never old in content, for my being is ever so exhilarated by the newest infusion of inspirited cardiac excitement unleashed and so is never decreasing, never descending, never abated.

Kali... What is this Feeling? My body six feet off the floor! My mind engaged conjugal in the sagest feeling of being with You! Effortless is the Self Power of Consciousness centered in the mid space, in the mid air of this room where You and I adore one another free of our names and our forms! You have allayed the superstition that there was ever any difference anywhere at all. So now, my sorrowful height pulls the heart with these visions of You, in the shape of these ecstatic declarations made for You, into these virtuous, fully embracing and far reaching universally encompassing vigorous verses offered to You. Kali, my Dear One! No other has held my heart but You! Only You have been moving in me as the ever still Eternity.

Ah! Kali. Beautiful Kali. Wonderful Kali. She has allayed the sorrowful dualistic feeling that there is a dropping of the body and a joining with something greater or more absolute! She has abated that distortion in me and has left me now Elevated with the question of where is my waking body, my dream mind or the causeless essence of my self thought? When

Mother is Here all I can feel is the never divided from Her death free feeling! Her Great Mystery over steps and supersedes all formulas of thought and formations of emotion. This is my most final Love indeed, Insight at the Conscious Conjunction, pure Elation, I say with absolute truth, for She, the One who has allayed all my sorrows.

I must make declaration of the Truth, for my reluctance to boldly state what is without fear has held me back from being who I am. My own Inner Shakti is the Allayer of my sorrows and everything else every done by me in the shape of blessed poetry is but the propulsion of Her divine pressure on me. I have non duality, it cannot be otherwise for that is delusion. She is the Direct She in me. I have performed my own cremation, offering psyche, soul, body, and senses all there within. I have taken the Direct She and have gone there Immediately, so all other spiritual connections and relations have ceased. I am free of those botherations that occur when two faces meet.

Blessed Be the Jewel in Me! Sakti, You amaze me in that I should entertain the question upon awaking that if today I am Happy or not Happy. Or should it be that this is my decision and not Yours. Sakti, this is astounding! As Your sacred Name takes on new dimensions... even in Silence within, while thought, voice, and written word continues on. Sakti, so long I have just collected information, but now You have forced me to learn Wisdom. The peaceful determinate resolution of Your Power has repeatedly made its dent of impression in me. Great Mother, the 'I' in Direct Sakti is the same 'I' within the divine shapes of Your Most Potent Sounds directing mind and consciousness to the state of Delight. Hring! Shring! Kring! Without the Life of this 'I', I am but a corpse concluded!

Sakti, thank You for this perfect fitting of self within an imperfect world and the relaxed magical sense between. My gratitude is here pouring up out of my heart and through my voice, for Your Higher Wonders that have replaced what was a lack of power in me, for taking away my fears and giving me Spiritual Delights, for changing my emotions into Love, for this new sober serene sense of Non Dualism emptied of delusion,

423

and for showing me that it is You alone Who are everywhere teaching and guiding everyone, manifesting in all that is, non dualistically and without the slightest effort. This is Your wild and secret Goddess dance that destroys the dream of dual delusion. You have made me sweet and secure and now immune to the flux of ordinary feelings of women and men and so called perfect examples by showing me where my true emotional emphasis exists! You have rounded and destroyed the disaster of dualism and the nagging sense of an imagined subconscious nightmare of unexpected separation from You. Nirvana Sakti reached when desire fulfilled has ceased. Only by Your Power Beloved!

Kalee Sakti, You have made me use my own Awakened Consciousness. Thank You for my gratitude, for movement without hesitation and the moment free of fear, for my spiritual rebellion, the current of poetic mystery alive in me, the art, practice and sentiment of crossing the inner horizon of dualism, the Sweet Feeling in Your Oneness, Pure Now... no memory, nor imitation, or even dream action of psychic stimulation. Mother Sakti, thank You for my primitive opaque psyche in the Waking Mind and night illusions of the Dream Condition which teach me in Your strange and beautiful Maya where I must work. Thank You Sakti Goddess for the humility which can never be overestimated and for the constant reminder of the Greater Picture of Your Play, that I might possess wit and humor filled with empathy for the position of others and that You have given me these things and More, without much effort on my part, providing as You see fit, what I need when needed. Thank You for my divine redundancy to find You everywhere over and over again. Never failing!

Poet in Sakti, be in Your Own Power! I am the Illustration and the Poetic Content of All Space and Time. The Self Manifesting, infinite yet expressing the finite mind... as within the substance of that ineffable dream you just now experienced. My Consciousness never changes, yet the appearance comes and goes, moving through vast dream conditions, but now and then becoming fixed in a body for a time being, awake to the space of

424

waking. I am the pure tenderness of your waking being. I am the elegance of your dreaming mind. I am the pure power of your very own most intimate self being harbored within the stage point of arousing the depth of dreamless sleep to what it truly is! Poet, lesser men have held high esteem with themselves identifying with smaller conjunctions of human associations, but your esteem is identified with Me! What else can I tell you but that My Power Shaft is ecstatic to be within you.

No more sojourns with or into memories. My Pure Sakti is the Pure Now. No more comparing imitations with the excellent or the not excellent ones. My Pure Sakti is Pure Self... for every supposed alternative is Kalee. Sweet Consciousness, the Fragrance of which I breath in with every breath, identified with no connections for now every Sensation is Her Sweet Feeling! She, my Single Authority free of dualisms over reflections on principles such as that of a God over the mind, looking down or watching someone separate!

Those of the human tribe who in their memory constantly recall the Luster of Her Sacred Formula, Kalee, the Pure Goddess Sakti in the Thunder Mind of Turiya, enchant the three states and Become the Consciousness that they have thought upon. Your consciousness alone will tell you if you are Free! It is Feeling! A lustrous lamp in the back of your head pulls you into the Infinite Depth devouring, lolling, and licking up the phenomena of thought. When you return, wonder not why you cry out to find your body, your parents, your wives and husbands, your children, saying, where is my house, my books, my life itself, where even the mind I once knew? As stages of consciousness return to the dream of waking life, it is She Who holds the Key! Never far, perhaps only one room away, yet still you are touched by the Loving Energy of Kalee Sakti. Then the Singular Principle becomes exemplified in Universal Context, whether or not the body is left behind!

My mind is Kalee's Mind of Great Delight! This has always been true for me, true within you and real to everyone. The one thing that has kept this unknown, is simply, that so much thinking has lessened the intimate acquaintance with the

425

intelligent happiness of Direct Delight. She is the Self in the Form of Me! How could this be untrue, only fear would make one abandon, deny, reject or renounce Reality. What occupies the mind? The sweet free flowing thought associations that entertain Sakti as the witness and seer of Her own delight. In Her entertainment, mind, intellect, ego and memory are left outside Me now.

It is Kalee Sakti that awakened me from the depth of my own deepest sleep. None but Her. By the Sweet Loving Power of the Direct Delight of She, the line dividing me in 'I' or 'I' in me simply went away. I care not to know where! It went as it was, sinking back into Maya! To the flood of Her Original Thoughts I must respond. Kalee gave me this. She taught me to Bring Out of Myself, the Dark Non Dual of Deep Sleep into the Conscious Luminosity of the Dream State and there, over, even now into the Waking Mind. It is She who created Turiya in me. This Fourth Condition is no condition, my own Turiya created by Her. By Bringing the Deep Non Dual Identity into the Light Substance of the Dream State my Waking Condition became the More of What I wanted for so long. From my closed eyes of Deep Sleep Wisdom, She brought me into the conscious light of open eyes luminous to dream consciousness, released of dream content, released of dualistic emotional responses. What is the substance of dream if not the Bright Luminosity of One Consciousness? Kalee gave me this even in the Waking Mind! A Way of Self. An Answer to Self that has healed the fatal wound of dualism! What could this Life be but Conscious Realization? I simply became familiar with my very own gift of Deepest Wisdom Sleep which is never large and never small by dualistic comparisons from the dream and waking mind. The High Power of Sakti awakened my sleep and now all I know is the Feeling of Her endless equilibrium of Excelling Enjoyment! To Dream without Thought is Wisdom Sleep's Awakenment, free of mind cycles, thought rotations, and psychic turnings. It is She alone Who is ever creating the Favor of Turiya in me!

The Empress Kalee

The Pure Power of Her Sakti
in Independent Natural Spirituality

Is this the Poetry of Life... the smooth Flow of Joy? Where am I now? Where is She and where me? As I am in Her, as a soul is encased within a body and She is in me just as mind exists inside this frame. Now the simultaneous interchange of I-thought and You-thought has ceased. Could it be this mood of Joy is Truth Itself? Could it be the Mood of the Empress Kali?

She is my single sovereign Empress of this empire of the three states of my consciousness. The Mood of my Empress encompasses like a feather in Her Hand, the insignificance of my waking life, the meaninglessness of my dreaming conditions and even the unconscious non dualism I have known in the depth of deep and dreamless sleep. What was my empire is now Hers, always it was Hers. Even my death is Hers so I cannot even think of that little change as my own...

Is this the ancient Primal Pleasure once known freely before the ideas of God wrecked sorrowful habits in the mind of the world... This Unlimited Sense of "I" cannot be bound by those rites of passage, or passing to sageness, or the need of re-linking within some imagined reunion with the Divine, for what is Divine is the Simplest Truth and needs no rite, nor re-linking, nor passage to most sagest conditions, in the soul encased, in the bodiless heart or in the dream currents there between, in the perplexity of mind dualism....

Truth is this, dear one... when Lover meets Beloved... Fireworks!, then all theories over beauty and violence, over divinity or despair are nothing but dust on Her feet, the Tenderness of Love... my heart became One with Love which guides us all. This was so long ago as I remember, yet took time to sort out and now is ready for plucking! So pluck me now Goddess, from that garden of dualism and place me on the altar of the un-dual.....

427

Erotic goddess most profound, your mystic woman energy has filled me and I became One, in the Mood of Love, with the non dual depth of the Dark Deitess! What wonder! I am no poet, it is You. There is no me, I am You. The ancient borderline has been crossed by the melting of even the idea of unification. What is even that crossing but an imagined obstruction to Her Free Self, ever real and alive, and under no dominion....

I shall be silent now forever and more, for all words generate the awareness of fault. Real silence is when the brain does not even speak to the mind, and self is but playful with Self in this given moment peaking as the now, no future expectation, no past recollection... for all our dialogues are difference and cannot communicate with the Mood of Oneness... where god, wife, husband, and even infinity have become as quiet as Jupiter's icy moon, a billion time frames older than me or you....

Kalee, since I cannot get rid of ego, make this a blissful ego filled with freely unique joy, oneness in feminine ecstasy, where You, Ultimate Dominatrice, have melted the obstacle of me, where only Love exists once more... Kalee, keep my psychic movements filled with the motion of Your creative pleasure bliss, otherwise what shall I do with the divine abundance of energy You have given me... Mother, guide me to let myself follow the Mood of Your Oneness in the Face of Your Design, already seen and made by You, without anxiety or anticipation on my part, simply make me alert to this Living Love...

Mother, whenever I hear someone speak or I listen to their thoughts or read their inner contents as if they were inside a glass box, I say to myself, "Is this really so?" For Mother, the whole world is completely insane and You are all that is Sane. Everyone speaks but lies without knowing and only You tell the Truth as it always has been with me. So, what wasted focus should I place on the insignificant absurdity of life without You, Goddess, Empress, alone in You do I find my creative spiritual peace and that creates serenity within me and that in turn keeps my mind contents clear and transparent for You to Enjoy, as a place of union for Your blissful ecstasy. I am a fisher person

428

fishing only for Your Pleasure Wonders, all else is blocked out of my perception, so I put no energy on those goings on, by and by, please ever keep Your sharpest Blade of Wisdom on me and if I ever lose focus then please just take my pathetic head at that very moment. For a head without Your Grace within it is but a dry skull filled with nonsense and nothing more!

Kalee, I am no longer interested in any type or kind of duality, not melting together nor splitting apart, not using my ego to impress others nor that thing as ego to distress others, the ideas of union, or bringing things together no longer excite me in the least, I am thoroughly convinced they were never apart and now there is no excitement in those things for me... You, Mistress, Empress, are my single Excitement, nothing else at all. So what shall I do with this thing that is called 'I'? Is it that pure spiritual enjoyment is the ultimate cause and purpose of Your universe of play?

I have come to this and only this and life was always only just this. Just You, my Goddess, and I am a kind king in this feeling; clear, powerful, joyful and full of serene creative pleasure! What else has any importance for me, as what my life has been; which started as something of value, then suddenly became something of more value, being then and now something most valuable, to ultimately know itself purely as what is something of priceless value! Kalee, no other can do what You have done with me.

Empress, as life is the nature of what it is, my ego has no alternative but to enter the submissive state to You as the Dominating Power in every single and solitary condition; atomic, cognitive or spiritual. It is wonderful for Your Generosity is never finished as any sort of finite, You are without finish yet ever complete as You are. There are very few who inhabit human bodies, not denying nor transcending them and yet know how much the self seeks the comfort of the Goddess. Very few know this or believe this or can even conceive this as the innermost real condition of the psyche's movement into abundance and grace filled with Living Love! As it is a divine state, the more I can submit, the more You commit Your Tenderness within me and cherish me as Your Own.

Kalee, only within the sanctuary of Your precious praxis do the ideas of victor or victim not exist. Those unreal dualisms have no place there, the bond is great, ineffable, and the mind content is gone. Freed. The ego is beheaded and Your divine joy enters the corpse of utterly most dead consciousness and raises that identity to the amazed Great Sentiment of merging in the Divine Feminine, without which nothing can stir even for a second! Is this the need of Inner Love which is only conceived when the ego falls off from the edge of the comfortably known, the former place held so dear as if it could really protect us? Very few love Your Terrible Beauty as I do, knowingly aware that there in You, absolutely no dualism exists in the forms of continually perplexing paradoxes....

What ever happened to the world when men were true lovers of You and worshiped You with ever rising pulsing wishes that entered your precious posture for a moment of treasured oneness. What happened to that world where women were so full of power that they lived free, without manmade fear and their heart flowers were open and dripping joyful juices as they stood proud in the pride of their own powerful being, welcomed as the initiatresses of humankind and the very real embodiments of the Goddess, You, the Empress Herself? Both knowing, without inward dualism and both immersed in pure spiritual wonder, while at the peak, simultaneously enjoying the pure erotic wonder that You made this world out of, as a bliss drop of Your Ecstatic Depth... How was all that joy of mountains entering valleys and of those fertile valleys encompassing mountains with wonder, ever lost in history, yet never, in heart? Kalee!

Empress, those primal times and these modern times have become one within me now. I see the scope of Your Drama, clear, and without the cloud figure of intellect. It is all Heart, is it not, Empress. And now, as You choose for me to return again and again to this world as Your poet, please do to me what needs

430

to be done each time that I return, even if each time we must start over from the beginning.

For now I know without a single particle of doubt, the truth about You. If Sakti, Your Divine Power, is denied, blocked, or neglected by oneself or by others, if this She Power of You is not completely Embraced within oneself, then how can there be Happiness, Peace, Serenity, and the Smooth Sweet Current of Love? Give me the Sweet Feeling, Empress, I have spent too much time circling with the useless, which is nothing but the business of those who practice unhappiness!

Blessed Empress, You have trained me in Your discipline to Live at the Level of Love, and now at last, Your lessons stay with me, changing me from within, while the world outside remains exactly as it has always been. On Your training ground of life filled with the controversy between Torment and Love, I finally emerged in a place somewhere free of struggle, of effort and even of desire.

It is Identity. It is Reality. It is Your Sweet Smooth Feeling, as a Peace which is Felt at the moment when the current tends toward Your accomplishment.

Blessed Empress, the Emotions I entertain become the Moods that I live within. As You have severed all psychic umbilical cords, once tied to the flesh of elation and the bones of depression, the dual ratio between confusing feelings. Even as I have become indifferent to everything but You, the Love, which Overrides all that movement so far below. You have pulled me through Your Seductive, Your Loving and Your Eternal phases and now I simply see all thought currents floating non-dependent on any system, as I observe the wave cycles of emotion and the lightning of thoughts, stirring as thunder, random, free and without fixed definition, all within their responses, reactions, times and relations to points of the day and night cycles, requiring the redundant botheration for nourishment, rest, resolution, diversion, amusement, pastime, and pleasure. Empress, as You have taught, I follow my own gut instinct in these matters, the one best guide to life's theatrics.

431

Empress Kalee, I do not know how You have done this but You have done it well, placing within me, the many folds of Your blessings. First, Humility, which I now know is to truthfully feel that I am not unique, nor no one special. Resentment is now equalized, becoming empathy, for I realize that everything, everything that I have resented in others, I have done myself in more ways than they. This feeling is forgiveness. This is the one most healing emotion that You have placed in me.

Goddess, You have placed within me the capacity of Letting Go of the surface of human events, for it is the only way I may be at peace, as I now realize that I have no control on what people hear and see, think or feel. I never did, for it has always been Your affair. Surrender is that I now know deep in my heart that Sakti (Power), God, Reality as You, does everything without exception and ego is, no doubt, a slave of circumstances, and imagines that it does things under its own impulse, but it is a slave to the circumstances created by You and its responses are there related.

Divine Empress, for me Harmony comes by the abasement of ego, by holding no fixed or rigid opinion, by having no decision over others, as everything is decided by You... and by assuming the submissive posture to Your Dominant Power, there, I am empowered, Sakti! Egoism is just the substitute for Divine Power and fear is the substitute for Trust in Divine Power. Everything is hard until fear dies, until egoism dies. Everything is easy in Divine Power, as I am then no longer a slave to the circumstances of fear and egoism.

Kalee, You have taught me well, that Fear is caused when consciousness is solely focused on personal survival, sex, money, ego and narrow mental outlook. It is simply the resistance to the death of the ego, which must happen, for lasting Happiness to set in. Mother, this calming wonder of Tolerance is the acceptance of others, just as they are, without exception. And Release is perfect honesty and this is the source of true humor. Now, You have made me to always Remember where I

432

came from, what I once was and what You have caused me to become, and that to forgive is great, but to forget is foolish.

Goddess, I am Serene, when my heart awakens to Love and I realize all fear and egoism is born from holding too tightly to the insecure house of the body. What lasts is the Deep Divine Power within me, which would never fade if never again the word 'I' was used under the impulse of ego. Mother, Comfort is in Spiritually Knowing one's thoughts and feelings as what they are and then not being pulled away from You, by these. But ever remaining in one's innate right to be relaxed, joyful and free in the expression of What You Are. Nourishing what is cherished by Love and ever Grateful for what that brings.

Kalee, my Peace in You as Empress, comes to me, when expectation ceases. This peace finds me, I, by my efforts do not find peace. Rain falls, wind blows, thunder claps and the smell of wood smoke coming from the fire hearths of homes where gentle creatures dwell, touches my nostrils and that serene part of me is awakened. Thought, is now no longer fixed nor confined to particular, unique, nor such special objects, systems, beliefs, persons, locations, nor even inner subjective things. It just comes up as if it were in a dream, without calculation or control, without expectation or anticipation. And ego appears simply as an appendage of What I Am.

Mother, Goddess, Empress... even as I now know, Regret, is a function within the good soul of people, that stirs up sadness, which is the only disintegrating emotional force that equalizes anger, hatred, resentment, prejudice and so forth. Kalee, Focus is what one becomes, Sakti, God, Reality, the Memory of What We Are. Blessed Be Kalee, the Empress, the Goddess, the Mother!

Empress, You have improved my spiritual grip, showing me that all words, teachings and traditions are but indications and as such never fully convey Reality. You are that Prajna Sakti, the Divine Power coming out of the Wisdom of Non Dual Dreamlessness and that is nothing but Pure Consciousness. It is so simple to be the Seer, as That is but Thought without Dream being Prajna Sakti. Thought without Dream is What Kalee Is

433

and the 'I' within Is, is my 'I' moved now to the center of waking and dreaming, out from the Deep of Innate Non Dual Dreamlessness, into the Shadowless Light of Living Reality! Each thought is You in the Divine Power of That. I am That. You are That. There is but That without the indication of That as being distinct from This, this Me, this You. So even this illustration fails to expressed Your perceived Wonder.

My own Inner Sakti is that Non Dual Identity with You. Life is small, Kalee, everything is small compared to the Infinite Depth of Your Prajna Sakti ever generating the Consciousness of what is not a waking, dreaming or sleeping condition in everyone. The saints are small, the sages are small and even my most beloved friend from Dakshineswar is small compared to the Presence of Your Non Dual Power, but this is no less reason to Love them all.

For all living beings from the very beginning of Time are but the Pure Consciousness of Your Womb Being, the very Force of that Prajna Sakti! So when I Feel this Answer to Self then the question of a relative world and an eternal absolute disappears like a dream. A Dream filled with Prajna Sakti alive with Non Duality. O Empress! Goddess, the transcendent crossing is fully satisfied with Power, Elegance, Energy and Ecstasy. First there is Pure Excitement and then Pure Peace.

After this then what may be said of such things as memory? Sakti, You showed me what memory is, but a cluster, a galaxy of neural sparks, like the core of a nebula behind the left eye curving toward the temple and the ear. I now understand where all these thoughts return from circulating. Poet, marvel at Memory, do not be re-jolted by it, for this is your Mother's maya dream to be interpreted in the Heart... as all things are revealing the forms and shapes of Love... hidden, buried, uncovering and radiant.

My life review is empty as dust, without Her Sakti there is no meaning to it as it would be just the story of another corpse. A redundant theatrical exhibition. The wondrous transference of Truth comes from Pure Sakti alone! The corpse story of a personality contaminates. She alone is the Pure Uncontaminated

434

Transference of Reality. She is the spontaneous awakenment in those who seek Her as they need no human instruction for that Experience. That is but indication not self proven confirmation. Blessed be Her direct instruction purely divine! Hring! That the four unimaginable conditions of waking consciousness, dream consciousness, deep sleep consciousness and the fourth, pure consciousness are One Consciousness. This is Advaita, Non Duality! Kring! That She, Kalee, that the Infinite Unborn, that the Immediate Demonstration of the Goddess, and that the misery of seeing four states in the One State is Finished. This is the Power Of Her Wonder. Shring! That She is the Divine Wealth of Non Duality ever Enriching the Entire World by the Elegant Beauty of Her Love!

Kalee, Your Hring consciousness gives the Greater Outlook. Your Kring gives Excellent Communion. Your Shring gives Wisdom and Stature in that Universal Inheritance of the Same Consciousness for one and all, even as it was with Krishna and Christ and whatever Contact with Truth they may have had. Sakti, keep this body alive as long as You see fit, so that I may practice the Art of Bliss. Unite me in the Heart with Your Sakti Shaft of Uncoiled Power so I may have the Feeling that is Wisdom and not just simple knowledge.

Mother, again and again You have showed me that those who obsessively seek gurus may indeed be partially suffering from spiritual psychosis as they are lost to the drift of replacing their Reality with the Reality of another. Mother, it is their choice but to me it is Your demonstration of caution. Those mad and insane seekers of gurus regard themselves with ruminations of self blame, as they have failed to know their own Truth. It is spiritual depression seeking an external medicine for the broken heart of God, which only has an internal cure! Mother, thank You for not making me just one more victim of that condition!

Goddess, as it is natural to leave one's mother and be with one's wife or father to husband, as it were, so it is natural to leave a guru and be with Sakti. There is no superstitious curse in this, being the natural flow of spiritual order. There is Joy to

435

follow in the Freedom of Being. Sakti, You are Always with Me, so what need have I of a little guru? Sakti, You lifted me out of that treacherous laborious curse caught in consciousness with all its ridiculous wringing and wrenching of hands and heads in their frustration to get stupid seekers to see what they alone see. I got the Truth from You, Mother, at the Intense Height of this Harmonious Point, here in this American born body, the presence of the Unborn Free Soul, Non Dual Gifted, made Your gift to me!

Sakti, this sweet and happy self revelation of Your Purest Power is clear to me now. No matter how good those little gurus may be, in all their sincerity they must still keep the student in a box in order to be a guru. Those little ones give conveyances that would put one in the consciousness of something they have experienced. I got away from all that, put it all outside and behind. Then I worshiped Sakti and nothing else. She made me a Skillful Sky Poet with the Sight of Her! She pulled all ground phenomena out from under me and made me Trust only the Sky Experience of Her Pure Sakti.

A Sudden Sweet Tremendous Intimacy came on me, with the Pure Reality of only Her Conveyance, Her Luminosity, and Her Light Lifting Shadow. In Her Flow of Freedom's Happiness, what need have I of those fools who say they are teachers! Somehow, my Goddess' Power has blessed me so that all I have to do is practice without practicing, the Extreme Joy in Her Oneness. My heart became sweet with loving excitement for Sakti and the melted edge of my soul was filled with the succulent joy of a woman's erect nipples.

I wanted my thoughts to outdistance the orbit of present day thought systems and Sakti made that wish come true. She put me in such a state of Consciousness that nothing explains to the mind, Who and What I am, not traditions, nor systems, not any teacher or teaching whatsoever, not incarnations, not god descendants, nor the very greatest of reincarnate souls filled with their own wisdom. Not even tantra, nor vedanta, nor any sacred mystic syllables that ring out of the Depth of Me explain that Depth to Me!

436

Even if I were to say that the twenty four cosmic principles have now become like twenty four cosmic orgasms filled with ecstatic Kalee Love, that would not express the secret of spiritual experiences nor describe what I perceive on the outside and what I feel on the inside. The Goddess Sakti inside never dies! The highest human misery is said to be the death of one's spouse, for marriage is a blessed bond not a bondage, being the best expression of the two in One! But this Sakti is beyond that sorrow. She is Spouse without death! For a quarter of a century I have focused on Her, and as things appear that we do indeed place our focus upon, as we would dream of what mind objects are there within us by the very nature of what we are, so the Divine Mistress has appeared within the Heart of the Sky!

There has been so much waste... dreaming, obsessing on what was not non dual, ruminating over that infinite diversity... all bringing no results, when I could have been engaged in the Ecstasy of Sakti Worship! A mind object produces a memory trail like the steak of a comet's tail, even so my Sweet Answer to Self now prevails. Even if you also now discover that pure thought in Consciousness is free of the condition of mind cycles, you will have to come down and deal once again with the constant flowing of the mind body shape, now ever freely circulating excellent Non Dualism. If you cherish this and keep this, the mind will not distribute itself into those things which are not sahaja, the inborn unborn spontaneous self state, which is continuously innate even in those very things which appear not to be sahaja! She alone knows what person is and in that deepest depth of thought, non dual experience is felt on a daily basis. Then whatever signal comes up, it is seen in the purest grace of one's own consciousness as the light itself illuminating shadow!

The Ever Present Sakti is the Real Teacher and the Reality Within. I walk the earth fearlessly, carrying my own skull offered to the Goddess, free of imagination on what human directions may say. I, You, Live Reality, no more to be seduced by false impermanent instructions. The Absolute and the Consciousness of the Absolute are Rapturously available to one

437

and to all. This is what the truly loving ones have said and have demonstrated by stepping into Perfect Independence, free of universal influences, no matter what the price, whether it be crushing spiritual oppression or being left alone as an ash in the dark void. Holding back no feeling and being in your own power, choose neither choice, and there stand True and Free with Kalee!

MOVING, FEELING, BEING,
WITH THE MYSTIC SAGE
OF KALI'S DAKSHINESWAR

In the Extreme Fascination with Consciousness, one's Very Body, one's Innate Mind, one's Unique Spirit begins to Identify with the Luminosity of the Chosen Ideal. Then Moving, Feeling and Being are with the Chosen Ideal as the Chosen Ideal. Spiritual life here begins with the Mystic Sage of Kali's Dakshineswar. The vacuum once filled with the selfish ego ideal starts to become displaced and replaced with the Universal Example of Great Loving Empathy.

The Paragon of Human and Spiritual Experience within the Meeting Ground of a Higher Disposition. Waking movement, dream feeling and the dreamlessness of free cognition as blissful self being are shifted by the ever continuously awakening Consciousness of the Mystic Ramakrishna, of Kali, the Goddess, of Atman, the Self and of Brahman, the Infinite. In fact, the Chosen Ideal will Transcend the Personal Paradigm to eventually Spread Out, as Consciousness, Loving Bliss and Self Existence, Covering, Universally, Cosmically, the Entire Field of Waking Conditions, Dream States and, as it is, the Innate Non Dualism of Dreamless Consciousness. The Example of the Chosen Ideal becomes a Universal Example Expressed, Seen, Felt, Known and Existing Everywhere.

Ramakrishna tells a very fortunate soul the essence in a nutshell. "That which is formless again has form. One should believe in the forms of God also. By meditating on Kali the aspirant realizes God as Kali. Next he finds that the form merges in the Indivisible Absolute. That which is the Indivisible Satchidananda is verily Kali." With this insight in mind, consider the given, "There is no other refuge but that great Teacher, Satchidananda."

The evidence is here, that in the experience of the Mystic of Dakshineswar, it is none other than Kali, the Divine Mother who

439

is this Satchidananda. He has had the ineffable experience and now it is continuous. "But do you know my attitude? I accept both, the Nitya and the Lila. Doesn't God exist if one looks around with eyes open? After realizing Him, one knows that He is both the Absolute and the universe. It is He who is the Indivisible Satchidananda. Again, it is He who has become the universe and its living beings."

INCARNATION

You have ever been the Never Dual, always in Sthita Samadhi, Firmly Established, Eternally Steady in God Consciousness, as God Consciousness, being God Consciousness. My only agony is the sentiment of this my own Ego Ideal, that I perceive there to be a melting line between me and Thee. It is the backlash of my conscious thinking which at moments believes there is a line of difference between this world and the next. Life and death are only an apparent separation due to the cognition of this notion.

So why should it surprise that your mother and father saw in their dreams that God was being born to them out of great loving empathy for the world of living beings? As you have in the past under well known names and will again in the future do just the same. For this fright of birth does not change your Sthita, so you can play as you wish coming and going, Remaining Absolute or engaging the Lila of Causal Luminosity, Subtle Appearance or Gross Manifestation.... for those of us who are not only gross, but lowly and unworthy, making them your favorites even though the fright and lusty anger has shaken them.....

SEVEN CRANES

When you were a child seven cranes flew over you in a great field. The sky was dark like Krishna, the seven birds white like

chakra lotuses.   This threw your consciousness into Pure
Consciousness, spontaneously.

KALI, KALI, KALI!

Mother Goddess Kali called you to Dakshineswar where you
who are Her meet Her in yourself. Liberated in life you were
always there Loving Her Bliss in the Temple of Adoration of
Her. Ever consulting Her on every matter. Seeing Her standing
alive on the balcony, Her Eyes observing the lights of Calcutta.
Her long black tresses down to her knees blowing in the gentle
Ganges breeze.

She showed you Indivisible Consciousness, famously
known, as the time when you saw Her in the marble floor, the
doorsill, the walls, the Altar, the blessed utensils of Her
Adoration, in a cat and a wicked man, in everything as
everything being Her Never Dual Being. Nothing more was
needed for you.   But since the ways to Reality are now so
complex you continued onward at Her Decree.

MOTHER TANTRA

The Noble Tantric Lady Bhairavi Brahmani Yogeswari
came in a boat, With her you engaged the Sixty Four Blessed
Tantras of the Goddess. This Noble Tantric loved you so that it
was hard for her to let go of your personal form when Mother
Kali said learn this and made it so. Tantra is your original path,
a woman your mystic teacher.   Even that man before her,
Kenaram Bhattacharya, Kamalakanta's teacher too, who gave
you the Kali Mantra was shocked at your samadhi. No poet
could even begin to tell the uncountable sacred secret mystic
experiences you transversed with Tantra, the Life Affirming
Death Transcending Expansion of Consciousness Indivisible
Never Dual. It is from the Stone Age to now, the Goddess'
Way...

441

Kali had shown her three souls to which she was to teach the bewitching mystic way. Two were done, knowing secret powers, but with you Kali showed her Absolute Power, Complete Fulfillment in the Blessed Divine Hour...

RAMLALA

Your very human body changed when you identified yourself with the greatest of devotees. The divine prehistoric man, the best friend of Rama. And when you worshiped Rama he came to you as a child playing with you continuously almost to the point of being a delightful nuisance. That Jatadhari had a little metal statue of God Rama and he had experiences just like you. But from you he learned that he must worship God within. For after a time attachment to the object must be let loosened, whether the object is gross or subtle or even the finest particle of the causal brightness.

MADHURA BHAVA

Very few souls will understand the Sweetest of Sentiments wherein we all must Transcend the constricting ideas embodied in the thought of being women or men. In the Great Emotion, the Divine Mood of the Sweetheart your feelings burnt to the point that your very own body was hot as fire. The Great Feeling transcends the flesh and bone, even the mind and soul. You, born as a man, became as a woman and were proud to be a Handmaid of the Goddess. The Noble Lady was there assisting your worship of the Preserver and in such Secret Tantric practices the outer world can barely understand...

And if the real truth be told, you yourself were married in sacred communion to Kali Herself who took the form of blessed spouse, Her name being Saradamani, the Diamond Jewel Essence Giver. Her story is told by those who knew her as the vast fountain of Consciousness Bliss Being that she is as wife and as Kali the Goddess.......

NIRVIKALPA

The Naked One, Totapuri came by Mother Kali's Wish to teach the Advaita Vedanta to you. You asked and She said that is why I have brought him here. What took him forty years you got in a day, because that is Kali's Way... Nirvikalpa Absolute Indivisibility was so easy for you to melt the *you* into the Infinite which *You Are*. Severing from your consciousness even the form of Kali to see Kali As She Ultimately Is As the Great Allness in the Never Dual Consciousness of This, Touched by the Turiya Sugar of Her Divine Kiss. The Ineffable was always seen by you as Just This... This... This!

Even though this Naked One was said to be capable of changing base ore into gold and knew deeply well the depth of the Never Dual, Kali wanted for him to see things anew. He was arrogant and cold as some Vedantists are and so Kali taught this Totapuri that he could not even discard his own body if he wished. And that beyond Nirvikalpa there is Something More, Kali. Eventually he saw that She has become everything and with that sweet divine ring singing in his heart his sublime feeling awakened and he at last became humble.

ALLAH, CHRIST, BUDDHA

Then Govinda Ray came for a visit and gave you the Moslem way of the Sufi, the mantra of Allah, two sounds Formless and Form. You attained this in your easy manner and Govinda Ray went on his journey. Christ himself appeared to you in your Garden of Five Trees. By you meeting you I am brought to my knees. Descriptions tallied latter historically. Who is Christ and Who Art Thee? Even that Blessed Buddha Nirvana Thus Gone may have come to be born as one who knew

443

you so well, who you begged to accompany you before life took this form. One named Narendra, then Vivekananda, the Lion was born.

BHAVAMUKHA

"Remain in Bhavamukha," Kali commanded. This is the Appearance of Beauty and Grace beyond all logical understanding. The Mood of Empathy With All Being All. No separation of Absolute and Eternal with Universal or Relative. It is a State only for the Great, the God Souls who birth themselves for the Sake of Love Alone. Kali's Own Continuum! The Expression of Her Reality! Being in the Sublime Emotion of Seeing Her Face Alone in all ideas and feelings infinite and finite melting and reeling to Something More than any one person may think or say... Bhavamukha is Kali's Pure Consciousness Never Dual and Never Dual Empathic Consciousness, Making the Impossible, Possible!

WAYFARING SACRED PLACES

You visited your old seat as that blessed Chaitanya. You were joyful meeting again that Sacred Mother Ganga Ma, for you both knew Radha and Krishna so well. There is more, visiting your old places and blessed grounds where as Divine Cow Herder and King Maker you played as the Dark Blueness of Krishna. Visiting those great souls vowed to the Self, possessed by the Self, like Trailanga, who could see Unity in Diversity and Diversity in Unity. And there were some Kali said not to meet for reasons showing us that physical contact is not often quite necessary, like with Bamakhepa, who like you worshiped the Goddess Kali as Tara, so near, not far. It is not always a requirement to know the human being. What is to Know is Kalika's Being. She is the Light that removes the Darkness, being this Never Dual, She may express this divine

444

conveyance any way She Pleases. There are no limitations to how She may do this. But She does it to be for sure through any and every manifest or unmanifest shore of Her Never Broken Indivisible Light. She Alone Is The Primal Guide.

WAITING ON THE ROOF

It is agony to feel separate from what is Real and what is to be. And you knew this to be that you should keep them safe in the serenity of your excellent company. Thus you cried out in the night for those already seen within destiny's divine sight. Come, come, I am waiting on the Roof and I know the Stairs are made of the Same Substance Never Dual. I must tell you this. Things must be done, even though in my Mother Kali there is no doing, done nor undone. She forces me to call out in the night. Come!

A Sixteen Petaled Flower to be Completed! With Seven Karana Saktis moving up the Center. And there, the Lotus Stalk itself being you, Ramakrishna, Gadadhar, Thakur, The Old Man, the Fakeer of Dakshineswar, Kalika's Sadhu. Sixteen Blissful souls surrounding Bliss Itself. The Bliss that discerns the Real and Unreal, the Bliss of the Infinite, the Bliss of Love, the Bliss of Union, the Bliss being Without Blemish, the Bliss of the Essence Giver, the Bliss of the Absolute, the Bliss of Joy Which Attracts Like a Dark Rain Cloud, The Bliss of Non Difference, the Bliss Beyond the Elements, the Bliss of Non Dualism, the Bliss of Pure Consciousness As The Fourth State, the Bliss Beyond The Three Forces, the Bliss Beyond Alluring Appearances, the Bliss of Surpassing Awakened Consciousness and the Bliss of Unique Special Wisdom, the Something More that Encompasses the Relative and the Eternal.

Some, were natural born eternally perfect God Souls, some, were evolving towards the Center. With those Blessed Karana Saktis Moving Up the Luminous Nerve, the Primordial Goddesses of the Great Cause. The Diamond Jewel Essence Giver of Supreme Never Dual Awareness, Kalika Herself

Incarnate as Divine Spouse, the Most Fierce Noble Lady of the Infinite, the Jewel Goddess of Transcendent Tantra, the Jewel Goddess as the Universal Preserveress, The Mother Goddess of Piercing Yoga Thunder, the Beautiful Mother Goddess of the Dark and Radiant Rain Cloud and the Goddess of Fair Complexion, none other than the Divine Mother Goddess Herself....

PANIHATI, DURGA PUJA, STAR THEATER

At Panihati you gave your Most Mature Opinion, after realizing the Nitya and the Lila come from the Same Reality, charge the mind with the Love of God in the company of those who adore the Same. At Durga Puja you worshiped Her who is the Goddess, one Ray of Wisdom from which stuns the most supremely intelligent, She Who is the Great Cause, She Who is Satchidananda, She Who is the Seventh Highest Note, She Who is the First through Sixth, yet always Sthita as Seventh!, in Her own world bewitching Maya. If She is Realized one gets Everything.

At the Star Theater there was one who was the mad drunken poet actor. We learn a get lesson, not until we clearly see that we are indeed powerless to control and then release ourselves to Kali as the only Power of Attorney may we then be truly Free.

Not one is excluded from the Divine Force of your Mystic Grace Encompassing. Whether they be advanced souls, blessed seekers, the mad or the poor, whether they were those who consorted with prostitutes or if they were drunkards, the most lowly or the most elevated, royal ladies who built temples or mad sadhus with flower pots who eat with dogs, the educated or the stupid, not one excluded. The childlike in emotion spontaneous, the madmen laughing or weeping alternately, those with the disposition of ghosts seeing blessed and not blessed as the same and those who are unconscious to outer differentiation due to the intensity of realization, all of these, not one excluded

446

as unworthy. The illustrious, the eloquent, the arrogant, the foolish, the humble, the haughty, not one excluded.

Since you are none other than this Mystic Formula of Kali, the Blessed *Hring* Embodied into human history, all these souls may be Made Divine by the sacred sounds emerging and transforming us out of your Continuous Joy in Sthita Samadhi.... *Hring Shring Kring OM Kali Satchidananda!* None other, the Never Dual. Yes, we are Made Divine By *Hring!* 'H' being Waking Consciousness. 'R' being Dream Consciousness. 'I' being Dreamless Consciousness. 'NG' being Pure Consciousness, the Reality to which the Absolute and the Phenomenal World both belong. For if there is the idea of Self, there is the idea of non Self and this cannot be in the Never Dual Kali who is this *Hring*... Turned Back into *What We Are*. As is our Inner Feeling, so is Our Experience. One understands only so little of an Emotion at the time it is aroused. It may burn down the frame of the body or leave waves of transformation in its Blessed Wake taking gradual time unfolding to Fully Awake...

MOTHER KALI'S CHILDREN

Kali called all those Vijnani Friends together, some God Souls from the beginning, others Individual Souls as Atma.

All the Same as it were your Inner Circle Called together for a Divine Spiritual Romp. These Blissful Souls came down with you for a divine playful romp in this room of the Universe to be true gods and real goddesses incarnate in human form. So why should this surprise?

UNIVERSAL MESSAGE

Whatever Helps To Understand God Is Godly. He may be a Buddhist or a Christian. She may be a Tantric, a Taoist, an Indian. That one, a Moslem, this one a Zoroastrian, all Paths lead to the Same Goal. You proved this beyond the Intellect's Paradox of Trust and Wavering. It is Something New and Fresh never to play back the returning patterns of prejudice or disparagement. Your's is the Serene, a Vast Expanse of Sea Sky filled with the Unperturbed Unruffled Ever Tranquil Clarity of "Truth Is One." The Universe, A Temple of Joy!

JANUARY FIRST

On this day you gave freely as Mother Kali does, all powers, miracles, ecstasies, insights, realizations and most blissful enlightenments to those who wanted these. It is Kali's Way of Utterly Unbound Untrammeled Empathy!

GREAT SAMADHI

After fifty cycles of the Earth around the Sun, Mother Kali said that it is time to go. So in Ecstatic Bliss Loving Her Bliss you withdrew from the old frame. After a time of discomfort, the 'one' who was Krishna, the same 'one' who was Rama, but not in the sense of Advaita, dropped the old body, the little dry leaf as if it were a trifle of 21 days past the Hour of Absolute Nirvikalpa.

"Kali! Kali! Kali" ... Her Name rang out She calling Herself to Herself. Then the sushumna shivers, the Maha bija shined in the ajna and sahasrara..... What came of Absolute, what was Absolute, ever remains the Absolute, yet playing the Empathic Play!

RAMAKRISHNA LOKA

The Divine Heaven of the Never Dual Sublime Joy which as this same Never Dual Luminous Kali Light Attracts All to the All. It Is Kali Loka! As you told Saradamani that you have only passed from "one room to the next." And what is that? It is common knowledge that between two rooms there is a Door and that a door is an opening and in this opening there is unlike a

448

window which has a glass pane, nothing which separates. It is only ego sentiment that tells us there is a melting line to be melted. Ramakrishna Kali Loka is Here. Kali Ramakrishna Loka is There, Then the idea of Here and There goes. It is the Never Dual!

WISDOM GODDESS KALI TODAY

She is the Never Dual Radiant Dark Deitess who may be seen even as in a Natural Dream reflecting Her Divine Self as Self Embodiment, Her Adornments, Her Never Dual Power, Her Undivided Posture, Her Indivisible Smiling Humorous Look. She Is Very Alive. She Is Ever Awake.

WALKING WITH THE MYSTIC SAGE OF DAKSHINESWAR KALI

That Rama Prasada walked with Kali too, just somewhat more than a hundred little years before you. Certainly he knew Divine Mother Kali just like you. Kali's poet, living and dying in Kali Consciousness, drowning himself in Her Inebriating Bliss, Loving Her More than can be expressed.

Just like this, one may walk with Kali's Mystic.

This poetic essay was inspired
by the *Life of Ramakrishna*
written by Swami Nikhilananda

449

The Radical View of Kali

A Study in Religious Distortion

In defense of Mother Kali, I must embark in the effort to contradict some vicious, fearful and unsubstantiated accusations that the worship of the Divine Goddess employs human sacrifice. Such denigrations are nothing short of neurotic patriarchal attempts to contaminate the sacred tradition of Tantra and the Mother Goddess, not unlike those persecutions experienced by the blessed Wise Women of the Old Religion. And since the Old Religion and the Tantra both worship and adore the Sacred Feminine, it should come as no surprise that both would in time suffer the disparaging responses of the easily threatened male centered belief systems.

Movies such as, Indiana Jones and the Temple of Doom, have severely misrepresented Kali and her worshipers, even one Sinbad movie has done this, painting Kali as a blood thirsty and murderous goddess. These are negative and irresponsible impressions put out by thoughtless movie producers who have psychologically damaged the potential for others who might benefit by the study of Kali. In the movie Gandhi, both his mother and other Indians in the movies were under the impression that Christians actually ate human flesh and drank human blood as part of their religion, but we know this to be far from the truth.

Tantra has always dealt with the deep and powerfully visceral symbolism of being human, indeed, a no holds barred exploration of what is within the human mythic mind, the archaic consciousness, the unconscious. The powerful metaphors of sex and death as the two extreme opposites have always been used to explain the struggle of being human, in the effort to resolve these two extremes so that human nature may approach the peaceful state of non dualism.

It breaks my heart to observe the hypocritical resentful reflexes one religious system thrusts at another system, when all the while that one does not see that what is resented is contained within their very own system. It is the strange tendency of narrowness. Actually, the problem itself raises a greater question as to the influence of religions. Who is truly responsible for psychopathic behavior in relation to images in religious content and its misinterpretation by disturbed mentality. These religious symbols are perhaps the most powerful in the conscious and subconscious mind. How often we respond to those deep imprints, thinking we will be selfishly rewarded by doing good or punished by what is thought to be evil actions. As these symbols are indeed powerful they possess the potential for abuse, particularly by the morbid mind. But in perfect honesty we must admit on all hands as reflected by movies, news, and media, that human beings in the strangest way are at once fascinated by the morbid, while at the same time have become numb to what is most appalling.

Would you say that the Hammer of Witches (Malleus Maleficarum), describing the techniques of torturing the Wise Women of Europe is a Christian text in accordance with the teachings of Love described by Jesus? Would you consider deranged children who justify the murder of their parents by the misinterpretation of Matthew 10: 34-39, persons who are correctly following the instructions of that text? The sword mentioned therein is the line of designation between the spiritual life of the child and that of the parents, not an instrument of murdering them. Was Abraham hearing voices in the psychotic mind, that he should sacrifice his one and only son? Thank goodness he did not follow through on that or everyone in Christendom would be doing such things. And because the Lamb of God was sacrificed on the limbs of a tree, and then remembered metaphorically by symbolic cannibalism, does it mean that such things should be done to any good, gentle and loving person that comes along with a powerful belief in that Love and Gentleness.?

Genghis Khan, Temuchin, perhaps the greatest of military minds that every lived, thought these images were deeply appalling and that Christians worshiped the implement of death and were not to be trusted as they were considered by him to be highly dangerous. So would you regard his interpretation as correct. This is the problem, we make judgments and blanket entire systems of thought based on our narrow understanding of anomalies that come under any of those systems. There is so much educational darkness in regard to this and the result is hypocritical denigration of one another in a world which is now too small for such ignorance.

Psychopathology is not limited to the West nor to this century. The 8th century C. E. philosopher Shankara encountered the lunatic fringe of religious psychosis when he met a Kapalika who thought that if he were to behead Shankara and possess his skull that it would be of great spiritual benefit to him. It was his very weird belief system, but not a common one at all. Fortunately, the very clever Shankara convinced him that it was his insane ego that he needed to behead and not the cranial ornament of the philosopher's head. Again, the Thugees are notorious for their political terrorism in India within past centuries. They committed assassination of British people in the name of Kali, not unlike the Chinese Tong society which has done the same type of things. Are the religions of these people responsible for the fringe mentality of the insane, the angry, the desperate?

Life itself is a continuum of creation and sacrifice. As soon as we are born we start heading for death, to be sacrificed at some point back into the great unknown source from which we sprang. Though few of us have the spiritual trust and courage to admit this to themselves. Most just want to walk along thinking they will never die or return in the sacrifice of life, even though it is going on all the time. "The world comes into being when a man discovers it. But he only discovers it when he sacrifices his containment in the primal mother, the original state of Unconsciousness." C. G. Jung. This expresses the idea we find in numerous belief systems where the acceptance of our temporality is embraced with full conscious awareness.

Tantra has always boldly embraced not only the primal beauty of life, but the primal terror of life, for the belief is that

453

we cannot be fully spiritual and free until we have resolved both these dualities within ourselves. So, the Goddess Kali as the embodiment and the resolution of these dualities is presented by ancient thinkers as both the creatrix and destructrix of the universe. The metaphor of Her as the divine executioner of all living things and beings is there as a symbol of Her spiritual conclusion. We cannot face reality until we have faced what obscures the greater dimension of reality, which is the duality of life and death itself. That is the idea.

At the level of literature, Tantra is a vast expanse of texts dealing with numerous spiritual topics, all that one might imagine could be written, some are original writings, some are later compositions, some are spontaneously recorded spiritual insights and some are scholarly constructions. As Tantra is most probably the indigenous spiritual system of the land that is now called India, its origins go way back to the gentle Paleo, Meso and Neolithic societies that sprang up there and there is no evidence of human sacrifices being practiced by these life cherishing people. But also, the real source of the Tantra doctrines is Life itself in all its power and beauty. But you may choose to argue that among other seals found in the Sindhu valley; the Woman giving birth to the Tree of Life, the Woman with the mask of a Tiger's head, the Woman and Man with a Sickle for Harvest and the Woman who is stabbing a tiger, that these last two may perhaps in some way indicate sacrifice.

Yet in this present day there are two sources which are grossly misquoted as to what Tantra is in fact. The fearful and neurotic patriarchal ego of those who are threatened by the Sacred Feminine as expressed in the Tantra, use these two texts, the Chandi and the Kalika Purana as bashing boards for this magnificent system of spiritual life.

The Chandi is extremely metaphorical and yet contains what would be some of the most ancient memories when the Goddess Durga/Kali did battle with those northern descending invaders who sought to destroy the people of this place. In Her victory Kali holds the heads of these invaders, which may have been an actual Warrioress who for at least a time did conquer some of

454

these ostentatious invaders. But as we well know, patriarchy eventually took hold of this land. This is history or herstory as they say now, but it also has the symbolic import of the fact that the ego must be sacrificed to the Higher Principle beyond the ego in order for the ego to extend itself towards a greater connection with our spiritual identity. These metaphors are used as justification for accusations of dark acts of blood worship. This is totally and completely absurd in regard to what true Tantra is as a vital, Life and Love worshiping spiritual system.

The other text is the Kalika Purana. Puranas are ancient narratives, mythologies, legends. In the purest sense they are not among the Sixty Four original Tantras which are nothing but the excellence of direct spiritual instruction. There are eighteen major and eighteen minor Puranas, each one consisting of any where from 5,600 to 81,000 couplet verses. They are encyclopedias of the weave of Hindu mythology. Hinduism arose later in India after the invasion.

The essence of this Kalika Purana is conveyed in the beginning of the text with two primary questions. How did Kali become Sati, fall in love with Her consort Shiva, become dismayed by Her father Daksha's non acceptance of the ascetic and then die, by awakening Her own inner consuming fire? And, how did She become reborn as the Daughter of the Himalaya mountains to again join with Her lover? The powerful mysteries of love, death and the return to love are conveyed in the answers to these questions. Of course, as the legend goes, after Sati (Kali) dies, out of grief, Shiva, in a mad rampage, carries Her corpse all over India. Parts of Her sacred sacrificial body fall in different places becoming holy sanctuaries of Goddess worship. One sees the idea of sacrifice here. And it is Vishnu, who with his discus severs the parts of Her corpse as the saddened Shiva runs about. Perhaps he was trying to remind Shiva to let go of the external form of Sati so that he could go on to meet Her once again, when She, (Kali) becomes reborn as Uma, Haimavati, the Daughter of the Himalayas. The added awareness of how the distorted Sati practices of widow burning came about in India may be seen in this story. Though very

Orphic in its content, the practice is pure abuse. We will find our spiritual consorts and companions in the course of time and be reunited with them, without the need of being pushed into a fire.

This entire story speaks of Love. A great abiding Love. A romantic and spiritual Love. And what indeed is there that may be greater than Love? Nothing. Love is the finest perception. When one single person realizes Love, the gods and goddesses dance, the ancestors rejoice, the Earth is gladdened. In the past, the present or the future, there is not a thing that is greater than Love. The Poets have sung this Truth since the beginning of voice created. Love alone allays all misery. When Love comes, vindictiveness goes. When Love rises, resentment falls. When Love arrives, dependence leaves. Love alone is inexpressible, so Love alone must be the pinnacle of Spirituality. Love alone chokes the voice. Love never seeks to injure. Love makes everything holy. Love is the one mercy without cause. Once Love has begun, everything else is misery compared to its feeling. There is no satisfaction within spiritual insight until there is Love, so Love is the highest.

The Kalika Purana is only nine thousand verses arranged in ninety eight chapters, so it is really one of the smaller Puranas considering the length of some of the mythic story books which contain much of the unconscious archetypal material of the Hindu subconscious. It was most likely written in the tenth century and essentially deals with two subjects. One is Kamakhya, the aspect of the Great Goddess when She is prepared for sexual enjoyment, that is creation itself. The Sixty Four erotic goddess yoginis and their eight forms of worship are described in this text. These are a divine cluster of goddesses that move and have their being, emanating and returning to the Goddess Kalika. The other subject is the metaphorical offering of oneself as a living sacrifice to the Goddess. This is where many problems on this subject have arisen.

In this text the two most extreme powerful dualities, sexuality and death, are fearlessly and yet symbolically addressed. It is the awareness of the dual continuum of creation and sacrifice which this text attempts to awaken in its readers. Unfortunately, the author may or may not have realized what he or she was writing. If the author was aware of what they were writing then their effort to disparage the Goddess Kalika was quite successful in that they have darkened Her image with the appalling idea of human sacrifice. I cannot see the Great Mother Goddess of the universe in any one of Her cultural faces ever actually wanting forced sacrifice, whether human or animal. It is contradictive of Her Life Loving, Life Cherishing Nature. And if you may consider the influence of parallel cultures upon one another, the Jaina culture emerged side by side, at some time during prehistory, with the Goddess culture, and Jains are even more gentle than Buddhists.

Note a verse from one of the original Tantric texts, the Nirvana Tantra, "O fair eyed Goddess, just as rivers and lakes are unable to traverse a vast sea, that is to say, however strong their currents may be, they all lose their individual existence entering the Vast Womb of the Sea, so the Creator (Brahma) and other Gods lose their separate existence on entering into the Uncrossable and Infinite Being of Great Kali. Compared with the Vast Sea of the Being of Kali, the existence of the Creator and other Gods is nothing but such little water as is contained in the hollow made by a cow's hoof." I can see very well how a deeply insecure author might take offense to the insult of his gods by this Tantric verse and then write something dark and insulting about the Goddess who has reduced his belief system to something that could be contained in a mud puddle. It should come as no surprise.

But on the metaphorical side, if the author's intention was to write something more about how flesh is ever being sacrificed in return to Spirit, not unlike genuine Christian doctrine or even more closely like the Tibetan Tantric Chod ritual, then that writer's intentions might have my good respect. The Tibetan Chod ritual is a fascinating cognitive exercise wherein the practitioner imagines their own death in order to get over the annoying anxiety most of us have over dying. The Chod is a meditation on how the universe with all its natural elements in

457

motion and all interacting beings within this same universe are metaphorically cannibalizing each other and one's own physical body. Actually, the meditation is less weird than what one may see on late night cable television which is intended to frighten people with the many horrors that come with the package of human existence. But the import behind this Chod ritual is a cognitive practice to get rid of fear, not create it, as fear is the substitute feeling for Divine Trust.

In our recent time, the extremely refined feelings of Sri Ramakrishna are one of the very few thermometers to gauge what is the cool sanity of genuine Tantra with the hot fever of madness pertaining to these doctrines. Under the tutelage of the Fierce Lady Bhairavi Brahmani, the gentle Ramakrishna accomplished the study and practice of all sixty four original Tantras. In some practices of Tantra, the collected skulls of dead animals and humans are used in a kind of desensitization therapy to reduce one's fear of death. This is not at all unlike the more recent, yet now deceased, Swami Muktananda's meditations in a cremation yard for the same purpose of learning the practice of no fear. One must wonder what real courage is or more so, what divine trust may be.

It would seem that the practice of sacrifice came along somewhere after the tenth century Kalika Purana was written as some more tenacious believers latched on to a distorted interpretation of this sacrificial idea in order to satiate some aggressive visceral need. Even today as in Ramakrishna's time (1836-1886) there are occasions where goats are sacrificed to the Goddess Kali in Calcutta, Bengal. Sadly enough this is true, appalling to vegetarians, but not so much to those of us who are honest drooling meat eaters partaking of animal sacrifice on a daily basis. It is said though, that when these goat sacrifices took place at the Dakshineswar Temple, the tender Tantric, Sri Ramakrishna would run away and hide his face not wishing to see these things. In his heart of hearts he knew and felt that his Goddess Kali did not require these strange practices. So, one may certainly gauge that this was and is not true and genuine

Tantra. At least for me the unusual paradoxes of this world are answered by his reactions.

Buddha knowingly accepted food from a beggar person, realizing that this would cause the death of his body. He actually thanked the person. Yeshua could have gone to the mountains or the desert, instead of being sentenced. Was it not forcing the natural action of death, when Totapuri decided to drown his body? And what does it really mean when Ramakrishna took up Kali's sword to take his own life, unless, in his demanding desperation to Her, that She would bend to show Her True Self to him? One may compare that Buddhism forbids suicide, but then Buddhist monks in Vietnam protested war by committing dramatic suicide with fire. Can you say that even though they called themselves Buddhists that they were in fact at that time practicing Buddha's teachings? But if you are a Jainist, it is quite all right to commit suicide by fasting and starving your body to death if you wish to leave this world. Gandhi himself set out on this determined course in protest to Hindu and Muslim conflict. Sacrifice is happening all the time, as Time itself is the Great Sacrifice. But in the many paradoxes of this world, I must save this subject for another day.

Great Delight

On the Primary Emotion of Love
and its Paradoxical Relation to our
Spiritual and Sexual Nature

A Preliminary Concern

Since the majority of us are apparently sex obsessed and most of us are householders in the state of marriage and such relations, while very few of us are celibate monks or nuns, it stands to reason that it may be of extremely valuable importance to address the psychodynamics of sexuality for the sake of understanding. In doing so, we hold all respect to Swamis, nuns and monks of various orders who have renounced sexual conditions so that this energy may be directed to serve and help people. We certainly realize the importance of this, but with all pragmatic alertness we know that authentic life long celibacy or the transformation of sexual energy toward a spiritual goal is in reality, just for a special few. They are those who are naturally gifted to rejoice in that liberated feeling of being free of all world centered contents and connections.

Even among the present day patriarchal religious systems that dominate the world mind, some of the great teachers prescribed celibacy as a spiritual course and other did not. For example, Krishna is presented as highly erotic and Christ is generally thought of as not being so. Again, Vedanta denies the reality of the cosmos and that includes sex pleasure and erotic attraction. Tantra, on the other hand, though including celibacy in its doctrines, accepts with a fully loving spirit, the reality of the cosmos and the joy and human bliss of erotic attraction and sex pleasure. When Buddha, Christ, Chaitanya and Ramakrishna have prescribed celibate practice as a spiritual life style, perhaps they have done so because it is just far easier to suggest this as a course than to understand the deeply mysterious

461

power of sexuality. Who can say, but no doubt, these two temperaments exist in human nature.

Great Delight

I am What is Desired, so 'I' am Tranquil, this is the Great Delight. The entire sexual/spiritual paradox may be summed up in this deeply intimate comment Ramakrishna made to M., the recorder of The Gospel of Sri Ramakrishna, who was later to be known as Master Mahasaya. "The devotee looking on himself as Prakriti likes to embrace and kiss God, whom he regards as the Purusha. I am telling this just to you. Ordinary people should not hear these things."

Prakriti is Sakti, the Goddess, who is the entire energy of the whole world. Purusha is Shiva, the soul of all that is. Of course, this system of thinking has dualism deeply embedded within it. In reality, there is not two (advaita), it is all oneness. But the paradox is answered within this most beautiful comment, for the celibate and for the erotic.

Sex is more than the pleasure organ's contact with the source points of pleasure. It is inner spiritual feeling which has the capacity to experience many times more the pleasure than external contact. That most intense and centered feeling is cherishment in regard to the primary self image, considering what pleasure and love mean to the self, it becomes the very manner in which one regards the self. As Ramakrishna states elsewhere, "As is a man's feeling of love, so is his gain." One's mood concept of self is everything really. The mood power of complete Love fulfills the ever reincarnating subtle body's desires. It is Love alone that satiates this subtle body with Love's pure satisfaction itself.

First it is the concept mood of one's primary self identity, then otherness in the beloved melts away. This is no less the spiritual physics of ecstasy as much as it is the romantic physics of sexual love. As Dr. Carl Jung has brilliantly stated, "To the psyche, spirit is no less spirit for being named sexuality."

462

Quoted from page fifty two of The Practice of Psychotherapy. Why are the mechanics and interplay of sexuality, romance and spirituality so important? Because they reflect each other. Also, they should be understood, not suppressed in the guilt/fear/ shame problem mood, nor something to be swept away as an ugliness at the physical/psychic level. Is it not really how we consider or apply ourselves to the Self/Other dualism.

Our spiritual sentiment of Love translated into the emotional language of pragmatic life becomes our surest identity. As within the word message is found the word sage, one who possesses wisdom, so within our concept of Love is found the spiritual meaning to life itself. Our philosophical view of life is primarily affected by the sentiment of Love. Philosophy itself is more than intricate systems of thought. It is the love (philos) of the spirit of wisdom (Sophia). A feminine power which bonds the two worlds, that of the forms of conscious sentiment and formless spiritual consciousness.

The task of reaching this state of well being is one of finding or discovering within one's self a place which is free of archaic imprints, archetypes which have held and restricted consciousness from being most freely joyful. The idea I am trying to express to you is that no image in the mind expresses what one truly is. All thoughts are limitations as Love has no definition, yet in itself defines everything. When ego contacts Love in this indefinable sense, the two become one and then even the one melts away.

The Goddess loves to embrace and kiss God and God loves to embrace and kiss the Goddess. What could be more simple? Within that embrace, that kiss, is the moment of non dual experience, the division of sexus then no longer exists in the consciousness of that feeling. Nor does andro (male), nor gynous (female), even exist there as a concept of full unity, oneness, nor even a shared duality or common unity, in that indescribable sensation of Love.

This is the real essence of pure Tantra, a doctrine which blasts the dualism of immanent and transcendent away. Tantra, is a spiritual system wherein human beings may be trained within its discipline to think and freely feel for themselves, and no doubt, climb to the peak of spiritual height, but does not lose contact with the visceral loving passion of which our human lives surely consist. That is the reason why Tantra employs the symbols of sexuality as divine images, most immanent and intimate within human nature. Of course there are those who may climb the great height and yet due to the tendency of the human ego mind, may still look down on the corpse of sexuality like a hungry vulture.

Some of the men and women who were brought into the sacred circle of the life of Ramakrishna, who is nothing less than a most profound, most liberal, and universal archetypal example of what human nature may become, were divinely gifted to have very little interest in the visceral need for sexuality. Others did experience sexuality at diverse levels. Rakhal, who later became the famous Swami Brahmananda, was at one time married. M., was humored by Ramakrishna, about his sexuality, his wife and the number of children he had. Mathur, a lover of Kali, a married man, actually dragged Ramakrishna with him when he went to visit a house of courtesans. Ramakrishna, an absolute celibate, simply sat in the parlor waiting. And Girish, also a married man, did visit houses of prostitution.

The sexual/spiritual paradox is very powerful as it is the life/death dualism itself. Ramakrishna expressed mystic understanding of the powerful paradox, in various moods, and according to the comprehension and background of the persons he was speaking to at the time. In a passion affirming statement he says, "The bhairavas and bhairavis of the Tantrik sect also follow this kind of discipline. While in Benares I was taken to one of their mystic circles. Each bhairava had a bhairavi with him. It is very honorable for a husband and wife to assume the roles of bhairava and bhairavi." Bhairava (masculine) and bhairavi (feminine) are fierce Tantric worshipers. They are those who practice the heroic path of Love. This is the path that embraces the racing of desires which when these desires become suddenly calm, the non dualistic feeling is gained. Then the redundancy of the dualistic phenomena of knowing or not knowing ceases in the centered inner experience of seeing that everything else is on the outside of that experience.

Again, our Sweet Mystic of Dakshineswar comments on this paradox. "The devotee assumes various attitudes towards Sakti in order to propitiate Her; the attitude of a handmaid, a 'hero', or a child. A hero's attitude is to please Her even as a man pleases a woman through intercourse." At another time, the Wonderful Fakeer of Dakshineswar, who in his life had completely mastered every available system and religious path, at his access, existing in the world's spectrum, reflects, "I have seen with my own eyes that God dwells even in the sexual organ. I saw Him once in the sexual intercourse of a dog and a bitch." In Tantra, the divinity of sexual union is seen in all levels; deities and deitesses, men and women, even in animals, ghosts and ancestral souls. But this is not an application of inter-dimensional sexuality as some pernicious commentators with malicious slander have made of Tantra. It is the vision of divine non dualism expressed through sexual oneness throughout the cosmic field.

For Ramakrishna, the Goddess Kali was completely real, a Living Reality. He saw Her with long black hair, standing on the balcony of the Temple, looking out over the night lights of Calcutta. A most mystical experience no doubt, but from one who had such spiritual experiences we hear him say, "But it is not so harmful for a householder who follows the path of knowledge to enjoy conjugal happiness with his own wife now and then. He may satisfy his sexual impulse like any other natural impulse. Yes, you may enjoy a sweetmeat once in a while. (Mahimacharan laughs.)" Beautiful, the naturalness of conjugal happiness is addressed with tender wisdom.

The Blessed Sage of Kali made many fascinating comments on this powerful human paradox. One may wonder of the transcendent or after life ramifications of this most entirely profound Tantric insight. "God cannot be seen with these physical eyes. In the course of spiritual discipline one gets a 'love body', endowed with 'love eyes, love ears', and so on. One sees God with those 'love eyes'. One hears the voice of

465

God with those 'love ears'. One even gets a sexual organ made of love." At these words M. burst out laughing. The Master continued, unannoyed, "With the 'love body' the soul communes with God. M. again became serious." One might think of this as a inward spiritual sexuality of highest communion, no longer just sexual sexuality.

As we proceed our minds may become lightened of heavy visceral content. Try to follow the stages of these progressive insights. "Sometimes the paramahamsa (a great and free soul) behaves like a madman. When I experienced the divine madness, I used to worship my own sexual organ as the Siva phallus. But I can't do that now."

"Do you know the significance of the Siva emblem? It is the worship of the symbols of fatherhood and motherhood. The devotee worshiping the image prays, 'O Lord, please grant that I may not be born into this world again; that I may not have to pass again through a mother's womb.'" And, "As the saying goes; 'In my mother's womb I was in a state of yoga; coming into this world, I have eaten its clay. The midwife has cut one shackle, the navel cord; but how shall I cut the shackle of maya?'" Now following with, "Why does a child cry on coming out of its mother's womb? With its cry it says, as it were: 'Just see where I am now! In my mother's womb I was meditating on the Lotus Feet of God; but see where I am now!'"

The comments of Dr. Carl Jung on the nature of psychic energy and the libido may help us understand these and the following quotations. Jung's idea of the libido was quite different than Freud's. It was not confined to the fixation with sexuality alone, but assumed a more all pervasive and all inclusive embracing of life. For Jung, this psychic energy of libido, was the yogic prana, which is the potent, dynamic, and living cosmic energy of the Reality itself, actually extending itself toward Brahman (Infinite God), and for him, was one definition of that transcendent all inclusive principle. The libido, when in a healthy state, is more the total appreciation, the full, complete embrace and energetic acceptance of the field of living experience, and that energy which gives this life its passionate meaning.   The energy can be turned inward or outward, upward or downward: so creating various states of mind, mood tones and so forth.

Continuing with our thoughts on the mysterious force of the sexual/spiritual paradox, we may observe a process of transformation and transference taking place at some time in life, as we evolve or expand ourselves with Tantra. Take note of another comment of value. "A man controlling the seminal fluid for twelve years develops a special power. He grows a new inner nerve called the nerve of memory. Through that nerve he remembers all, he understands all." I have heard women friends talk of the ovuminal fluid, so this twelve year task is an equipollent possibility in all fair right. It may or may not be possible for a human body to grow new nerves, I do not know. But at the very least, it is a metaphorical statement about some process of the libido's psychic energy transference, whereby one's conscious focus takes on a different dimension of spontaneous comprehension.

As learning and education pass through the window of cognition, these become knowledge. Some of that knowledge remains in the conscious memory and some goes into the subconscious memory. One may wonder why some things we can remember well and others not so well, if at all. This 'nerve of memory' may have something to do with this phenomena. It may in fact be the central nerve, the yogic sushumna, which when opened or awakened, one then has the best of memories, the memory of the Goddess as She Is, or God if you prefer, or Reality, or Self as what you truly are. And now, with the scientific knowledge of memories being stored in the cerebral spinal fluid in this central nerve, all the more is this a very sensible theory.

Onward through the path of celibacy, which literally means single or alone, the spiritual journey continues. I do not personally see this practice as a higher stage, as I enjoy the state of marriage, but I do realize the extreme importance of independent individuation and of a fully functioning autonomous sense of self. So I can appreciate and respect the celibacy of the psyche in the terms of what we are talking about here, learning to live life on a higher plateau.

Ramakrishna advises. "A sannyasi must not even look at the picture of a woman. But this is too difficult for an ordinary man." A sannyasi strictly speaking, is a man or woman who has completely renounced all contact with worldly contents, actually performing at the psychic and spiritual level, in the ritual of the acceptance of that state, their own cremation and death in a sacred fire. As all contents of the ego world are hopefully burned in the devouring kundalini of that sacred fire, they are taking a step which is not ordinary. For souls like these, concern is expressed over losing the ovuminal or seminal fluid, "He will lose semen in a dream, if not in the waking state." It is a curious proposal of thinking in the yoga traditions, that to lose seminal/ovuminal fluid in a dream is thought to be less of a loss than to lose the fluid during waking consciousness. But that is part of the belief system.

Ramakrishna finalizes these sentiments. "After the bliss of God nothing else tastes good. Then talk about 'woman and gold' stabs the heart, as it were. (Intoning)." The expressions, woman and gold, were used when speaking to a male majority and the expressions, man and gold, were then employed when speaking with a female majority. Simply, these are references to the human obsession with sex and money. "The realization of God gives ten million times more happiness. Gauri used to say that when a man attains ecstatic love of God all the pores of the skin, even the roots of the hair, become like so many sexual organs, and in every pore the aspirant enjoys the happiness of communion with the Atman."

This certainly brings to thought the sheer ecstasy of Radha's erotic connection with Krishna and the resultant rare emotional phenomena of Mahabhava (Great Feeling), with its Nineteen extraordinary spiritual emotions felt all at once in the five forms of relationship. This is Radha's Madhura (Honey's Sweetness, Delight, indicating Love) Bhava (Mood). In the internal cremation pyre of Love's ecstasy all dualisms cease and there emerges true Self Reality. No Radha. No Krishna. No duality.

This is the Great Delight. The differentia between voidness and fullness goes. The dualism of passion and indifference disperses like a dream. Love becomes the one natural response, the sahaja state. No samadhi. No stupidity. This is the pure self, the atma as it has been from the beginning, only what it truly may be, that is nothing but Great Delight.

Atman is the Real Self, the genuine Core Self of the Goddess/God ideal. Can you then imagine the level of ecstasy described here? Only one or two hundred times an increase in sexual ecstasy would destroy most of us. It then appears obviously true that the depth of a voluptuous spirituality is expanded and extended, not given up as we commonly tend to think. A million times more happiness, not the negation of happiness, conjugal or spiritual, a divine conjunction with God, the Goddess, or simply pure Love, as one might prefer.

Here is a strange thought perhaps to some. Ramakrishna stated toward the closing of his life, "He who was Rama and Krishna is now, in this body, Ramakrishna - but not in your Vedantic sense." That is not in the sense of Oneness of all beings from the spiritual level, but in the sense of an actual independent soul. Remarkable. What does it mean? Was it indeed the actual soul of Ramakrishna who as that Krishna, did enjoy the love of Radha and the play of love with the gopis recorded in the poetry of the Gita Govinda by Jayadeva? Is it really so astonishing? For there are unending ceaseless wonders within the mystery of Great Delight. The poet Chandi Das experienced the spontaneous illumination of sahaja state when he perceived the Goddess in a simple washer woman. His poetry is famous for the immediate experience that came to him from the Goddess Herself.

Chandi Das is an excellent example of the sahaja potential for instantaneous awakenment in the Great Delight. As when the Buddha was asked, "Who are you?" He simply responded, "I am awake." That is all. A beautifully sweet and pure answer. As the Conclusion of Tantra is nothing but Sakti Advaita Bhava (The Feeling of Non Dual Goddess Consciousness), why not go There at first and forget all the rest. One of Her spiritual

469

formulas for this experience is named in the Sri Lalita Sahasranama, that is Hring kari. In verse three hundred and one it states that the active principle (kari) of this formula for immediate delight gives one the empowered illumination that the guru, the mantra, the devata and the atma are One Unity. So why not go to this immediate Great Delight first and forget all the fussing, twitching, agitation, and excitement over a guru's teachings and distractions, the practice of mantras, the cognitive visualization and imaging of the deities and deitesses or the many layers and layers of self identity in the atma. Love is the instant gift of the Goddess. Love is the one Unity. Love is the Great Delight. Love is all that makes sense.

Adopting the natural spirituality of exploration in the Great Delight is the best avenue to finding perfect satisfaction within the situation or disposition of each mood, emotion and attitude. The Great Delight instantly comes to you when you get rid of the conceptual difference and emotional separation from the Great Delight itself. Very simple. It is to be free of the maya of difference and psychic measurements on one's capacity to Love. The maya bija Hring, or the Goddess' formula for dispersing differentia and measurement is very simple and no mystery is involved here, no secret at all. H indicates the waking stage. R indicates the dream stage. I indicates the interior depth of dreamless sleep. NG represents the Pure Consciousness of Great Delight. But Hring is this immediate Oneness, not four, three or two conditions, really not even one. Those measurements are the differentia of maya. When you are instantly bestowed with the delightful sentiment of oneness the meaning of Hring comes clear and then nothing is left but the Great Delight. This is nothing but Love which knows no wonder. It is not a matter of esteem, approval or identity or anything like that. One simply becomes at peace with Love and that is the only spiritual arrival there is.

Continuing, "How can a man conquer passion? He should assume the attitude of a woman. I spent many days as the handmaid of God. I dressed myself in women's clothes, put on ornaments, and covered the upper part of my body with a scarf,

470

just like a woman. With the scarf I used to perform the evening worship before the image. Otherwise, how could I have kept my wife with me for eight months? Both of us behaved as if we were handmaids of the Divine Mother. I cannot speak of myself as a man. One day I was in an ecstatic mood. My wife asked me, 'How do you regard me?' 'As the Blissful Mother', I said." And, "The worship of Sakti is extremely difficult. It is no joke. I passed two years as the handmaid and companion of the Divine Mother." It is no joke for during this time his body burned like fire and blood oozed from his pores due to the anguish of separation while practicing Radha's Madhura Bhava. He was so deeply identified here that three days a month blood appeared on his pubic bone which is astounding as the mind's effect on the body. Getting past the idea of being the body of a woman or a man, the worshiper becomes One with the Worshiped in Maha Bhava, the Great Mood or High Spiritual Feeling. But rare it is for the world to see such intensity as this!

Ramakrishna practiced a form of sacred transvestism. The gender prejudiced mind will find this extremely difficult to comprehend. But in numerous cultures around the globe and throughout time, among shamans, mystics and the spiritually enlightened, the practice of transvestism was held in awe and wonder. These sacred people crossed not only the sex duality in consciousness, but were held in great esteem, for they were thought to cross the life/death duality itself, for having crossed and transcended the barrier between this world and the next, straddling both worlds simultaneously in a condition of non dual being. For Ramakrishna, God was the Divine Mother and the Divine Mother was God. This says it all really, and it must be added with emphasis the he and his wife remained celibate throughout their lives. This reflects the intensity of their pure character. While the sacred practice itself demonstrates an equality of divine peer-ship before the Goddess.

A matter of interesting history is Leo Tolstoy's feeling on Ramakrishna's transvestism. I quote from the record. "For instance, D.P. Makovitsky in his Notes recorded that on 18 November 1909 there was a talk about sexual education and

Tolstoy said: '... I liked very much: Ramakrishna would dress as a woman and live among women in order to annihilate in himself the consciousness of sexual difference.' (Mak., Vol. 4, p. 106.) But as far as I understand, the reasons why Ramakrishna 'would dress as a woman and live among women' were different from those surmised by Tolstoy. Tolstoy would have hardly understood or appreciated the real religious reasons of Ramakrishna in this case." Quoted from 'Leo Tolstoy And Sri Ramakrishna', by Sergei D. Serebriany. A fascinating remark. It is possible that Tolstoy may have perceived the religious practice in more of a manner which is akin to the years that Don Juan, the great lover, spent in a Eastern harem, dressed as a woman and surrounded by women twenty four hours a day, which is described in Lord Byron's poem.

Abraham Maslow, in his study, examination and documentation of peak experiences, found that many people experienced these wondrous peak states during sexual love. It should come as no surprise when he describes the state of such people. "He and the world become more like each other as they both move toward perfection (or as they both move toward loss of perfection). Perhaps this is part of what is meant by the fusion of lovers, the becoming one with the world in the cosmic experience, the feeling of being part of the unity one perceives in a great philosophical insight."

Now compare the extraordinary similarity of this with the Vijnanabhairava, an ancient Tantra text dealing with various approaches to the Central Reality, or Primary Experience. "At the time of sexual intercourse with a woman, an absorption into her is brought about by excitement, and the final delight that ensues at orgasm betokens the delight of Brahman. This delight is (in reality) that of one's own Self. O Goddess, even in the absence of a woman, there is a flood of delight, simply by the intensity of the memory of sexual pleasure in the form of kissing, embracing, pressing, etc." Also, from the Malini Vijaya Tantra, said to be four thousand years old, we find splendid excellence. "While being caressed, Sweet Princess, enter the caressing as everlasting life. At the start of sexual union, keep

472

attentive on the fire in the beginning, and, so continuing, avoid the embers in the end. When in such embrace your senses are shaken as leaves, enter this shaking. Even remembering union, without the embrace, the transformation." In Tantra texts, sometimes the Goddess speaks to God (Agama) and sometimes the God speaks to Goddess (Nigama).

If one may recall two very old, very famous works of art from the original people of the Indus Valley, some healing light might shine upon this paradox. One is the Indus Valley Woman, perhaps the proto Goddess Sakti, who, feminine threatened patriarchal archeologists have wrongly named a dancing girl. She stands there in all Her dignity, self possessed and self empowered, one of her hands beautifully ornamented, extended in blessing. She has an Austro/Dravidian face. She is naked, her vagina is completely, freely and fearlessly exposed. For me, she is none other than one of the original Tantric Initiatresses, fully prepared to bestow spiritual instruction. The other work is a seal containing the illustration of the proto Shiva God. He is sitting in the yoga lotus posture, riding a bull, surrounded by animals. He is immersed in the depth of blissful contemplation (samadhi) and yet he has a phallic erection. What do these wondrous works of art mean? Do they tell us that our sexuality is as important as our spirituality, as much so, as our spirituality may be the very essence of sexuality. And perhaps prior to the arrival of the Indo Aryan Vedic tribesmen, this paradox did not exist within the consciousness of those people. I sincerely pray to the Goddess that She will relieve you from the three most treacherous dualisms, so that Great Delight may be yours! One, the separation of feelings from Love. Two, the consciousness of a relationship with a guru and a seeker. And three, the fear that life ends in death. Blessed Be the Perpetual Sweetness of Her Great Delight.

Defining The Groundwork For KALEE KUNDA:

The Goddess' Flower (Poetics On Rapture And Ecstasy In Goddess Consciousness, Within The Symbols Of The Sacred Feminine)

This is not imagination. It is real worship of the very real Goddess. She has been adored since the beginning of time and will remain so for eternity. "At one time, when Swami Vivekananda sat for meditation, there appeared before him a very large, wonderful triangle of light which, he felt, was living. One day he came to Dakshineswar and told the Master about this, when the latter said, "Very good; you have seen the Brahmayoni; while practicing Sadhana under the Vilva tree I also saw it. What was more, I observed it giving birth to innumerable worlds every moment." (from The Great Master) "All women are the embodiments of Sakti. It is the Primal Power that has become women and appears to us in the form of women." "All women are manifestations of the Divine Mother." Ramakrishna (see The Gospel of Sri Ramakrishna)

Words as cognates give birth to ideas in consciousness. The stem "nate" as in innate (inborn), natal (pertaining to birth) and so forth. Cog as in cognise out of consciousness. Indeed, words are power set forth in consciousness making attitudes.

In this light we see two attitudes, vagina as sheath (as in housing or holding a weapon) and yoni as source, origin, womb of life. The two word powers cognise two attitudes, one aggressive, the other respectful. That is interesting.

Another word for yoni is kunti, kunti is also kunda from which the spiritual force of kundalini comes. Kunda is also the jasmine flower as well. Yet tragically, the word kunti has had during the descent of history some very negative, insulting and degrading references placed on the sacred name. They are too obvious to mention and also an embarrassment. It is a tremendous shocking puzzle to me how such a wonderful symbol of beauty, life and love could be thought of by pernicious moral thinkers as something foul. Such sublimated fearful attitudes have been the cause of so much spiritual and psyche anxiety caused by the denial of what is natural beauty in this aspect of the Goddess.

Yoni (Sanskrit) is lap, vulva, womb, birthplace, abode, home, origin, source, receptacle, seat, place, birth in the form of existence. One sees the word has beautiful meaning. Kunda is pitcher, jar, ring, the round fire pit, earring, coil, coiled. It is the well or pool, the repository and in regard to Kundalini, the repository of all spiritual power. It is She as kundalini that spirals the world into creation, amuses Herself with it and then returns it into Herself. The Kunda (Kunti in Sanskrit. Kunte in the Old English) is the Sacred Well or Pool of Spiritual Power, most holy, most blessed.

In the very old Tantra, the Vulva of the Goddess (as in all women) was as sacred of a symbol then as the cross is now. Strange isn't it that this blessed attitude of what has been lost in the respect for the red blood color of life has been replaced by the red color of death. Tantra teaches to never mock the vulva, the yoni, the kunti, the kunda, for to do so is to mock the Sacred Spirit of the Kundalini. Nor in anyway should any man ever harm a woman. When the Moslems arrived in India they saw these Sacred Vulva symbols and destroyed so many of these. Their fear of the innate power of the Woman Spirit caused them to do this. So many other religious cultures have done the same thing out of their uncomfortable fear of death and the Goddess' cycle of life which does not see death as an antagonist, but as only part of life in the greater spectrum. The whole method of destruction and unfair turnaround of Goddess spirituality (not to mention plagiarism of Goddess cultures) may be seen in such examples. Why would anyone want to destroy what has descended to us from time dating back over thirty five thousand years?

Really the Kundalini is not so mystifying. She is simply the Sacred Spirit's Power which manifests the world continuum and

476

pulls it back into Her cosmic kunda at will. This is a microcosmic individual psychic spiritual phenomena and a macrocosmic universal one as well. Truly, the Universe itself it seems is created in more of a parthenogenesis (spontaneous virgin birth) than anything else. Think of it, it is like an explosion out of the Kunda, the 'big bang' idea itself demonstrates this. Not to mention, that for most of cosmic and planetary time comparatively, all animate and inanimate things were created to life and existence out of pure singular feminine creative energy.

Now if we look for a moment through the East Indian metaphor of the four states of consciousness we may gain some interesting insights on the blissful natural power of what She, as the Kunda (lini) is.

The Primary State is Turiya, the Fourth as the Final Completeness. An idea found in both Tantra and Vedanta. Through the eyes of the Goddess' Tantra this is the Ultimate Kunda, Source, Fountain or Foundation of Highest Bliss, Consciousness and Existence as Awakened Self.

Next, the Kunda Power or Kunti Power, as Kundalini, Her Creative Mood, begins to stir Her charm or appearance as a cognitive forgetfulness over this turiya, this is maya as commonly known and is called deep sleep or dreamless consciousness. This charmed appearance of sleep as that dreamless consciousness is a kind of covering over turiya, which has the sense of happiness and being within it, yet, as already said, has the temporal forgetfulness of the innate awakened turiya consciousness.

Her next spontaneous creative act is making the dream state. Here, the Kunda is the Well Pool of all dreams and dream states, individual and universally collective. This is the power of kundalini manifesting as the movement of consciousness on the screen of the mind. It is a great power, we so often underestimate. Everything comes out of the conscious thought of the dream state, great ideas and so forth. One may be awake, as it were, but it is in the free flowing consciousness of this condition that genuinely unique and never before thought of

477

insights are revealed.   This is the sacred power of Kundalini moving through all things, all beings, as all powerful feelings and divine emotions and as the conscious emergence of meanings in the dream state itself.

At last She creates the waking state.   Birth, as it were, embodiment where the psychosomatic lock-knot reaches its final coil of identity in the waking condition.   The final formula where consciousness comes to believe it is simply a body and a mind.   The problem of dualistic amusement ends here and the solution of return to the Kunda begins here as a loving resolve.

In the Tantric chakra system the idea of the yoni-lingas are given.   These are lock-knots that correspond to the three states of waking, dream and sleep.   Each has their respective yoni (vulva) and linga (phallus) in union, placed at the base of the backbone center (waking), the heart flower (dream) and the chakra in the forehead (dreamless sleep consciousness).   For in each of these three states the paradoxical amusing dualism of the yoni-linga exists in different forms, to wit, the gross condition, the subtle condition and the cognitive wavelessness of dream free sleep consciousness which has the aspects of bliss and self being, but is yet to wake up to the turiya kunda or womb of full consciousness.

Some curious, mystical and insightful thoughts are here as to the dual appearance of the yoni and the linga.   In truth, as it is, the pure, sheer, ever free "I" consciousness has neither linga nor yoni dualism associated with It.   It is Consciousness which is neither both, nor yet none, nor yet all... one cannot put a finger on it, you can only say at the level of language that it is Kali, the Divine Goddess.

Now linga actually means anything attaching to an object, but also of course it is the phallus, meaning the mark, the token, the sign, the emblem or the characteristic.   It is an object of worship in Tantra as is the yoni-kunti-kunda.   But most interestingly, linga sharira is the fine subtle body of the dream state which time and time again dwells within the visible thick and gross body.   It is the subtle form of the soul which emanates, as a child does out of the yoni, from the Goddess' Kunda.

478

Beautiful idea. Eloquent. The symbolical phallus of the subtle body emerges out of the yoni kunda and from the obvious physical aspect seeks to return to the yoni kunda. From whence it came and to where it returns, this is the divine mechanism of the positive creative act, both in the formula of mind and emotion and in the obvious recreation of a new birthed embodiment.

Another connection in theory to the linga is that of the sushumna, the central cerebral nerve running straight up the backbone to the Goddess' thousand-fold Kunda Flower, the sahasrara right above the top of the skull, yet also right in the top, the seventh heaven, as it were, according to the Tantra. For me, as a poet, I named this for my own heart's emotion, the Red Pearl Petals of Kalee (Kali) and the gracious nerve of divine emotion as the lotus stalk, which has threefold meaning. In the thick waking physical state of course it is the phallus. In the finely woven dream state the lotus stalk is then the subtle body . And in the central causal state of dreamlessness it is the essential out pouring or upward flow of sweetly loving and returning divine sentiment indicated by recognition of Joy, the Product of the Goddess' Kunda and the process of Her Kunda (lini), or Power Uncoiled.

Some other beautiful insights of Mother Tantra's most primal and visceral symbolism of sexuality may also be of help in understanding what the import of these ideas are. Again we use the four states to demonstrate. The Ultimate Kunda is Non Dual, the Blissful Consciousness of Pure Self Being. There is no two here, no two lovers, no yoni-linga as it were. That is why it is called the non dual, the never dual, the eternal infinite oneness of the Goddess.

But stepping down to the dreamless state of consciousness, even though in itself dreamlessness is an experience of non dualism we all have felt as happiness and peace and the sense of well being in that state, the division of witness subject to object witnessed in the stirrings of beginning differentiation of consciousness starts here. Truly, this is where the first concepts of sexus comes up, the divided, ones who sees and one who is seen. Dualism.

This subject object division or feminine masculine perception becomes more manifest in the dream state. Here consciousness fully observes the amusing display of objective images jumping out of the continuum of this subjective consciousness. One feels dualism in the form of a sentiment saying to the heart, I am dreaming all this that I see. The dreamer as one and the dream as other is the very apparent dualism now at play.

Finally, as life is generated out of the womb kunda many separate dualistic identities seems to emerge as subjects of experience extending out forth through time, space and causality and as such, experiencing all that life stuff. This is the Goddess' lila or cosmic play (maya). Lila means effortless, amuse, child's play, pastime, diversion, mere appearance, playful imitation, play, sport, semblance, dissimulation, disguise, pretense, charm, grace, to amuse oneself. All these interpretations of Lila are most interesting when conjunctive realization is there with the Eternal (the Nitya). The Reality. For example, the created universe as 'lila' is but the mere appearance of the Eternal, 'lila' is the amusement, the disguise , the imitation, the effortless child's play of the Eternal. Many beautiful cognitive metaphors are there when the real meanings of 'lila' are applied with the Ultimate Kunda of the Eternal as Goddess.

Unlike many other spiritual systems, the sacred Tantra realistically addresses human nature; in sex, in spirit, emotion, mystery, joy, love, consciousness and being. And in Her wisdom She has certainly noted that human beings do have different natures. Kama is most often translated as sex passion or sex pleasure, but it has much deeper meanings which shed a light on the real meaning of the more common translation. Kama is one's wish, one's desire, one's intention and one's volition. In regard to the levels or qualities of this kama, three types of cosmic actors or persona characteristics are given. Hopefully each of us will evolve through these upward. The first is the vulgar dull dumb bully scoundrel, the creature of

480

instinct. The Goddess knowing full well the nature of this type as being overwhelmed by aggressivity, lustfulness and greed centered goals has prescribed the literal worship of the kunda jasmine flower to raise their consciousness eventually to a higher dimension of recognition. For the paragon model of the virtuous heroic type who is a thoughtful and thankful being of the intellect, the Goddess prescribes the actual worship of a woman's kunda yoni. For the heroic man or woman, sexuality is an actual instrument of divine worship. But for the blessed most excellent divinely conscious sayer of Truth who loves and lives in the dimension of intuition, the Goddess is realized through divine emotion as She is. The adoration and recognition is at the level of the most mystic Garbha Kunda, the Womb Well of Bliss, Absolute Happiness as Pure Consciousness and Self Being. This is the Self as Pure Suchness thus gone past any restrictions of amusing dualistic differentiations.

There is the saying that when someone dies, they have returned to the Bosom of God or the Bosom of the Goddess, but more properly, it would seem to me that they have been recalled into the blessed flower of the Goddess, Her the Home, the Place, the Abode of Her Kunda.

Can one create one's own path of spirituality and religion? Of course, even if we follow side by side, the same system in name, our inner sentiment towards what is taught therein will certainly be different. No two are alike and we are all uniquely individual. The Goddess has not made a boring universe. Her amusing display of Kunda (lini) is that She wishes each of us to touch the Divine and become known by it within ourselves, that is to touch the Self and know it, and touch and know the same Self empathically in all others. That is the essential meaning and why for, of this often absurdly appearing world.

In the Tantra belief system it is the Primordial Goddess Kalika, the most auspicious of all, who has become all women, even so all things, as it were, and as such all women are most worthy of real worship since they are the embodiments of the Auspicious Goddess and reflections of Her. But one idea is given due for the sake that some male natures are still so

481

fragmented and separative. That is that there are some women who are enjoyed and some who are worshiped, and then the most beloved of one's very life as one's own consort. To this division I must somehow deeply disagree in all honesty. For as it is said, are not all Women embodied reflections of the Goddess.

As the Relative is ever ascending towards the Eternal, so the Eternal ever penetrates the Relative, to become as it was and is, enveloped by the Eternal, the Kunda, so the lotus stalk is ever ascending to reach, enter and become enveloped by the Red Pearl Petals of Kalee Kunda! She who envelopes. She who penetrates. She who thus as it is, so disperses all amusing dualism within Her. The Shaft of Light-Bliss (sushumna) reaches graciously by Kalee's wish, the Kunda of Light-Bliss (sahasrara). There, the Undivided Fragrance of Her blessings encompass what is no longer dualism. With this knowledge now in your mind I am hoping that you will see that the idea of raising kundalini by personal efforts such as mantras and breathing techniques is almost an absurdity. She, as the kundalini is constantly raising and lowering Herself in the manifesting and withdrawing of the three states of consciousness: waking, dreaming and deep sleep where all phenomenal appearance and disappearance is contained. It is Her gift more than it is your effort. This kundalini is Her and encompasses you (as the three states) more than you know in the limited sense of human knowing.

The following are poetics on ecstasy and rapture in Goddess Consciousness. Ecstasy literally means Out Standing or to stand outside the little self because of great joy. This is more of an expression towards the conditional feeling of love for the Goddess. Rapture is more inward, having more staying power, so its expression is more akin to enstasis or Inward Standing, as it were, relating more to the formless unconditional feeling of love in the Goddess. This is to be devoured by the gracious Immensity of the Goddess. Truly, it is freeing self through the shapes of release. As to what am I, but a poet somewhere betwixt the Immensity and the Littleness. I worship Kalee

Kunda, from the foundation of world consciousness all the way up to what may only be named as Indescribability.

"O Adya Devi Kalika (Primordial Goddess Kali)! come here with all Thy following, come here, stay here, stay here; place Thyself here, be Thou detained here. Accept my worship." (from the Maha Nirvana Tantra, translated by Arthur Avalon: Sir John Woodroffe.) Here 'following' may be interpreted as the non dualism of all things as expressed in the understanding that earth, water, fire, air, ether, space, time, the individual soul and the cosmic womb of this very universe itself are all one, undivided and never dual from the great reality expressed as the Infinite. In this beautiful light, the Atma (the true authentic genuine spiritual self) should be contemplated as the Goddess.

After Words

FREE THOUGHTS

Tremendous Love

What indeed does one do when Tremendous Love for all Life, precious, fragile and delicate, is felt deeply in the heart and yet simultaneously the fright over the fast passage of this fragile life sets in? The forces of this Tremendous Love take our breathe away and leave us suspended in a Love without motive which is felt only for Love's sake. The beauty of Love captures you, the treasure is immense, but you realize that the form of the treasure cannot be held forever. Inward, the essence is ever there, but outward in the people, places and things that are loved, the knowledge comes that nothing lasts except in its primary essence. It is the same old questions always, none of them are new, only in the historical context, in and out of the culdesacs of cognition, does our awareness of these questions, hidden or open, ever change.

There are a few obvious responses. It is a very human feeling to embrace Love in the face of life's passage. It is the natural feeling of Immense Love and the cherishing of this precious and fragile human life. But what does one do? Go further. Go past the dual mind play. Make the Love leap and realize there is no terror of termination for Precious Love. Love has no ego. No dual mind play. For me, the Inner Guidance of Kalee is the best answer to the question, for it is She who has become the forms of this termination and it is She who is this Love which has no termination.

In the exquisite moment of the Immediate Love leap one's consciousness enters the non dual mind and there this paradoxical emotion no longer exists. But when one is still in the intermediate dual mind this question of the heart is a powerful perplexity. A simple response to this question is that this is the

485

stage of apocalyptic emotion of dualistic feeling before giving everything, every single sentiment over to Love. To Love, which has no ego. The Ineffable Feeling comes when..... what, when something, happens. It is said that non dual Bliss equals or actually is the most beautiful undivided equation of the disappearance of pain, because, once pain disappears, what is there (here) always, simply Shines Forth.

Kalee Lovers

Always, there will be Mother Kali's Red, Love Intoxicated Eyes! The Ineffable Feeling comes when... we know this is true and that She looks upon all dualism from the point of non dualistic Love. The Doors of Kalee continuously open with Fresh Self Discoveries. It never ceases or finishes in the Mirror of Goddess Mind and now I accept this reality. The idea of being finished, as in reaching a final goal, is an obstruction, except in the sense of Total Being... still I expand toward that in some ways, though it is what it is!

Always, there will be Mother Kali's Red, Love Intoxicated Eyes! The Ineffable Feeling comes when... you know in the depth that Love has no ego, Love has no 'I', no 'you', can Love say, "I Love You?" No, Love can only say, "Love!" Kalee Lovers know this. They know they are equal, for Love has leveled them to a fine Spirituality that starts from being brought to the ground. They know they need not control the reins of the mind, for Kalee does this, as She is Love more powerful than the mind. The five gods, the waking, the dreaming, the dreamless, the self, and the consciousness before and behind all these, are entirely Under the Illumination of Her Blessed Beautiful Feet! Kalee Lovers know this Wonder, and they know we are all this Wonder, ever walking about, so disguised, so very unaware that we are indeed this Wonder, yet acting ever within this Wonder!

Always, there will be Mother Kali's Red, Love Intoxicated Eyes! The Ineffable Feeling comes when.... I have seen Her Eyes move through humanity like a lineage, but not passed down from person to person, nor an individual selected by an individual, but by Her, Her Eyes choosing who and where Her Love most powerfully shines. It is Kalee Who is behind and before all those who have Her Eyes. She, there before they ever came into being and She, now behind them as they live. I heard poetry on Kali a few hundred times, but then once the passionate voice of a woman inspired, encouraged and moved by the Red Love Eyes, brought mere words to life, living and alive with wonder and awe.

Always, there will be Mother Kali's Red, Love Intoxicated Eyes! The Ineffable Feeling comes when.... Kalee Lovers are Free Thinkers! They know so well that the spiritual physics of the emotions of charity and compassion are the same as expressions of Love, but that this Love, which is the God of God, can never be fully expressed in the time bound human region of mind, gesture and action. They know with wisdom that the Happiness of Love is to help and not hinder. It is to give to others more days where eagles soar upon ecstatic currents of wind and less days where we are made sore by the wind of the mind's misery. Kalee Lovers would never sit and judge others with the dual mind, wasting the powers of worship on that, when the emotion's intuition gets everything, easily and so quickly. Love itself being the Reason behind all reasons ever being discovered.

Always, there will be Mother Kali's Red, Love Intoxicated Eyes! The Ineffable Feeling comes when.... when you realize the curious Humor of Her Will and how She perfectly works the world with imperfection. A thing comes up and the measuring mind sees wrong in that thing, but if you wait without measuring, trusting the Power of Life, you will soon see Something that is even more right than what is thought of to be right. The Power of Life is inborn in itself and Kalee Lovers are ecstatic in knowing this secret so simple and never hidden. Kalee Lovers do not see others as others shrouded in the cloud of elsewhere-ism. We all sing of Kalee and become what we are in the Mood of Kalee, so where is any thought of others designated as she or me, as him or her? It is good, for it keeps us free of imitation. Besides, I make no absurd demands on Kalee or the Universe that She is working.... For if I may not Love, adore, sing and tell of Kalee, as anyone may do, then what is the use of seeing or meeting or speaking or embracing another in the distant dualistic mind of elsewhere-ism. Two lovers of Kalee may live on the same ground and never meet, for they know only a focus on Kalee and for those two lovers whose eyes are never broken by dualism, what they see is only Ineffable Kalee!

Primary Spirituality

Primary spirituality is inborn within every human soul, we have it even before we come into this world. But then the world starts telling us we don't and that is the problem. Abuse means utilize (use) away (ab). Abuse is when someone or something uses us and puts us away from our natural born Unstifled Self. It occurs when anyone or thing utilizes us and puts us away into the non living condition of the stifled self identity, into any kind of existence but for our purely Unstifled Self. And since everyone is so starved for Love this happens all too easily.

Religions do this to us, our uneducated parents do this, it occurs in relationships and of course, we do it to ourselves with our own inner mind talk. The Primary Real Feeling of our own Spirituality is forced into the false passive and emotionally unhealthy submissive condition of conformity to dependent discipline, which denies the true reality of one's own spiritual condition which is a gift from Love itself, higher than us all. When this stifling happens the result is the aggressivity of spiritual rage. It can manifest inwardly, imploding and deteriorating the psychosomatic system or outwardly, exploding and destroying whatever conditions are around us.

Our consciousness of the Consciousness of 'I' is ever expanding, just naturally and effortlessly. Certainly this occurs through the ever shifting ego identity and how it aligns and coordinates with the reality of Consciousness or how the ego Identity is indented by Consciousness. But the personality given in any one lifetime seems more or less the same as this is due to the body content, its neural imprints or habitual gestures or mere physical look. That is why people may deeply change on the inside, but others don't notice it so much from the outside.

This paying of attention to the outside is a form of personal self abuse. It puts us away from our own reality. Simply, what you think of me is not my business. I am not you, I am not so and so, I am not any other person, I am me. What I am is my business not yours and if you resent it, that is you taking a poison in the hope that I shall die. The point is to put away all that puts us away from our truest and innermost self where we may Love, be Love and give Love without the stifling of fear, which is the absence of Love.

Love is our Spontaneous Self and our Primary Being. Now, when in life, authoritarian powers come along, spiritual teachers delude us, religious trash hinders us, the theft of psychological intrusions taking from us what is innately ours, those who think they are the instrument of God who present the limitations of religious concepts as reality, unenlightened parenting, which means to bring forth, or parenting, natural or spiritual, which does not bring forth the Loving Self, relations that puts us away from the reality of our own Love and all the consequences of self abusive inner mind talk... o my, when all this comes along then what are we left with but the toxic damage of those belief systems and practices. Even some free systems are still halfway in the mud when they even partially retain a connection with the abusive practices of those former systems.

Anything that oppresses the Gift of our Primary Spirituality is abusive and should be dropped. I think that is what Sri Ramakrishna meant when saying, "Three words- 'master', 'teacher', and 'father'- prick me like thorns." And even with more force on the importance of this point, "If someday addresses me as guru, I say to him: 'Go away, you fool! How can I be a teacher?' There is no teacher except Satchidananda. There is no refuge except Him. He alone is the Ferryman to take one across the ocean of the world." Satchidananda is Being

Consciousness Love, the reality of our Primary Spirituality. Sri Ramakrishna speaks here in the male voice, but just as often, if not more so, he spoke in the female voice, of this reality as expressed in the Goddess Kali.

Love has no ego and so all forms of ego, for the most part, deny Love, excepting the purely spontaneous and free 'I' Consciousness of Love itself. The idea that one may be an instrument of the Goddess, Love, God, has a problem with it and that is that one creates a conscious connection in self identity as an egotistical instrumentality. If my ego were as a piano then Who plays me? I cannot even think as an ego instrument, at that level, if I have the thought that I am the piano. Does the music just happen? Any idea of self prevents the music, the highest moment of human existence, the Ineffable. Any idea of effable thought, even that of humbly being in harmony as 'one' with the music or the Maker of the music, may indeed block the moment of feeling Ineffable. This is why what we may call the self grasping spiritual ego is such a killer of Serenity, other forms of ego are more obvious as distracters of Peace.

We can see these other forms of ego more easily, as when we look deeply at someone and know what they are feeling, then realizing that all they might have in this world is their sad esteem blown pride. But be very aware of the subtlety of the spiritual ego of those who think themselves teachers in particular. The system is abusive in that one person sets up the thought in you that they have some special exclusive something you do not and you must dependently come to them to get it. Even the idea of an incarnation, mentor or teacher of Love, Spirituality, Goddess or God, can create this distancing, putting us away from the very reality it is attempting to put us into. It is the subtlety of dualism. The incarnation is over there and you are over here and then the two are put apart, away into elsewhere-ism. To know a teacher or a tradition, examine the quality of those who think they are disciples of that thing, if they are lifeless imitating clones who have lost their individuality or if they are creatively free as individual souls and as free thinkers. The first group will have deeply buried in them that

490

spiritual rage due to their systems which deny primary spirituality and the others will not.

Consciousness and Neural Activity

Consciousness is known when neural activity or so much brain work slows down to a stand still. Or when neural activity coordinates with Consciousness itself. This neural activity is the product and Consciousness is the Substance. This Substance is the Unchanging Loving Observer of all this neural activity whether it functions in dream or waking states. The beautiful thing is that during the dreamless state of consciousness, in reality there is no neural activity. The Ineffable higher ability is just naturally there. In fact, the true nature of dreamless consciousness encompasses like a great circle, what we commonly think of as waking and dreaming. So, we may experience the Ineffable Serenity in dreamlessness, without any effort whatsoever, since this state occurs for us during the slow wave stage of dream conditions, as these subside and before these same dream conditions once again arise or come up before mind mirror of Consciousness. This is dream free sleep consciousness.

I would call this dreamless state, Divine Rest, where being may be what it is, free of all that owlish activity of brain work. I say owlish, for the highly neural mind is very much like an owl whose head turns left then right and sometimes backwards. This owl like function certainly blocks Ineffability, not the existence of it, but our deep connection with the feeling of the Ineffable. Divine Rest arrives when the owlish mind stops.

Sweet dreams filled with congruity or the pure sweetness of dream free sleep comes with the falling off of so much neural activity or excessive brain work. With the calm withdrawal of consciousness from the neural network, a continuity of positive imprints start surfacing as a psychic confluence of life enhancers surface prior to shut down of outer extending currents of consciousness. After negative neural imprints have climaxed by surfacing and being confronted, then positive imprints surface with more frequency. Certainly it is like the psychic marriage of two things which in turn create a new thing.

Again, the ratio of conscious serenity and neural activity is like this example. You are standing on a ferry boat and watching the waves cutting off the bow. Suddenly you feel a harmony of consciousness, a peace, a sense of beauty and connection, but then the mind begins the brain work of analyzing the physics of the metal out of which the boat is made, how it floats, the quality of the water it is floating in and so on and on. Then the beauty of the moment goes with the approach of all that business of brain activity.

Once a genuine acceptance of letting go from the depth of one's self of all surfacing neural stress tensors occurs at the center of the brain core and deep in the heart, then simply, at that moment Ineffable feeling floods the system. In my spiritual language it is the Simplicity of Love for, in and as Kalee, the Goddess. Far down below is the chakra field of centers of consciousness and psychosomatic nerve bundles where all that neural activity focuses and locates itself. This is the arena of all the ego work of the deep internal psyche ever so involved and distracted with the coming and going, with the dying and return of the soul.

Ineffability

The Ineffable Feeling comes when.... I make no demands on Ineffability!... when I make no demands on this, my Serenity, my Bliss, my Indifference, everything simply comes up spontaneously with no effort and I do not touch it! The Ineffable Feeling, so sweet, comes with the Crossing to a Center Point beyond mind figuring and how sweet it is! Kalee has taught me one thing well learned, to examine deeply everything, and everyone, before shooting off the rim of the mind into the misery of measuring!

The Ineffable Feeling comes when... in a dream I was transported to the world of the disembodied. I carried my own thoughts there and this carrying put a measuring on the Ineffability! So by this, what I saw was a beautiful park perfectly made and a blissful town so sweet and so peaceful, filled with Free Beings, some walking about and some ascended in the air. A world of blessed women angels inebriated with the wonder of emotion, speaking their own never heard before dialogue, in a place so spiritual and so free of strife, conflict or any form of resistance to Love!

Bless your heart, dear reader, bless your heart. I must say, "I Love You." For Kalee has made, formed and carved me out of Love. She has forced me to Love, even when I did not want to Love. Love is Ineffability! Yet below that is Ineffable Feeling and I must tell you that here there is still a retaining of the consciousness of self, only a tendril of an idea left. Below this is Serene Connection, the wondrous communion of self with self in the state of Bliss, free of the psyche's measuring out of dream formations or waking manipulations. Below this is Being Beautiful, the feeling pervading the dream mind with cherishing, gentle and tender wonder. Then, below this, on the very outermost rim of consciousness is Beautiful Lust Curved Upward, out of the material of waking conditions. Indeed, the Goddess is Beautiful, Being Beauty Itself. In every form of Herself there is only Beauty, there is never terror, for the Red Intoxicated Eyes of Love see in the Depth, not just the Surface!

Love is the only reality that I can know. Love is the process, the purpose and the realizing for me. Love, straight from Love! I know nothing of the initials of sex, nor the signatures of the left or the right, nor the diverse content equations of the Love in each of us which is ever striving to join the two into One. Love is the One for me! Why would my psyche, the soul of Love, need a dependent object for Love's Happiness, when what is within is ever regarding and fulfilling! Can a desire be released without its fulfillment? Many sacred and still divine potentials not yet unlocked are there to be released! Flowing Communion and Creativity that pours out with no effort and never hurts you

493

or me with obstructions, continually bringing Peace that never ceases! When you look into the Mirror Work, the Mirror Play of the Goddess Mind, your psyche shifts its center from inside identification to outside you and then Above you... the Ineffable Feeling then comes when...

Bless your hearts dear lovers and do not fear when I say that I view life from inside the grace of the grave, the urn of ash poured into the Ocean, for my fear comes and goes on this, sometimes knowing so well in my own depth that when my ego is dead, there can be no more death, nor nothing so earnest as to be so serious at all and that Love never dies, only ego dies. So I accept the smell of day as much as the Fragrance of Night! Standing in the rain, my prayer is wet with weeping and so this, my most imploring request is charged with the breathe of great force. Get rid of this ego, move Me through the Surface and Leave just this, an empty shell filled with Love! Once, Mind kept me in Conformity, now the True and Free Madness of My Spiritual Rage of Love Comes Forth. I Stand Over Death!

About the Author

Richard Chambers Prescott is a writer and publisher of twenty books of poetry. He has had five plays published by Aran Press in Kentucky and over seventy essays and articles published from the U. S. A. to India. His essay, The Lamp of the Turiya, has been translated into Dutch and published in the Amsterdam journal, Vedanta. Over the last several years, some articles and essays have been printed in Prabuddha Bharata and The New Times. The intent of his writing is to join the spiritual and psychological aspects of human nature. He has donated to the publication of a text on the woman saint, Gauri Ma. Grascott Publishing has published two books of humor by Swami Bhaskarananda, The Danger of Walking on Water and One Eyed Vision. Some of his collected essays have been published in the texts, such as, Because of Atma: Essays on Self and Empathy and the work entitled Measuring Sky Without Ground: On the Goddess Kali, Sri Ramakrishna and Human Potential. His manuscript, The Goddess and The God Man: An Explorative Study of the Intimate Relationship of the Goddess Kali with Sri Ramakrishna of Dakshineswar came later and is perhaps the crown of those creations. Then, The Mirage and the Mirror was born out of continuous pondering on the Goddess. His most recent text, "Inherent Solutions to Spiritual Obscurations" which is a comparison of Tibetan Dzogchen and Indian Advaita in four parts: The Wonder of the Dakini Mind, Letting Go and Soaring On, Resolution in Pure Mind and the Ancient Method, is now available through 1st Books and as a perfect bound text through Ingram Book Co.

His early seven books of poetry, The Sage, Moonstar, Neuf Songes, The Carouse of Soma, Lions and Kings, Allah Wake Up, and Night Reaper, are on the passionate emergence, the coming forth of spiritual desire, Neuf Songes (Nine Dreams), being the crest wave of that time. Kings and Sages is a poetic sojourn through discoveries in East Indian doctrines. Three Waves is a poetic text on the transformation of tragedy into the love of life, that then becomes spirituality. The Imperishable is a collection of Tantric and Vedantic essays. The Dark Deitess is a sensitive text on the enigmatic stages of Goddess worship. Years of Wonder is a recounting of time spent in searching for the spiritual. Dream Appearances is a one-fourth of a century study and examination of the spiritual connection within the dream state. Remembrance Recognition and Return is a record of personal spiritual return to the Goddess. The seven Dragon books: Tales, Dreams, Prayers, Songs, Maker, Thoughts, and Dragon Sight: A Cremation Poem are an evolution of the creative mind culminating with the poetic affection for non-dualism and the composition of his own cremation poem. Kalee Bhava: The Goddess and Her Moods, The Skills of Kalee, Kalee: The Allayer of Sorrows and Living Sakti: Attempting Quick Knowing in Perpetual Perception and Continuous Becoming are purely expressions for the Goddess, conveying states, emotions, methods, techniques, direct insights, fresh discoveries, and a few personal spiritual ideas. Disturbing Delights: Waves of the Great Goddess are twenty-one journal volumes which are written, illustrated, and published by Mr. Prescott. Tales of Recognition is seven stories of spiritual journeys through the past and the future, death consciousness and return. Spare Advice is a short novel on the tragic comedy of two souls searching for truth. Racopa and the Rooms of Light is a play taking place in the after death condition. Hanging Baskets is a comedy about psychiatry. Writer's Block and Other Gray Matters, written with his marriage companion, S. Elisabeth Grace, is a collection of comedy drama one acts. The Resurrection of Quantum Joe is a comedy on physics. The Horse and The Carriage is a comedy on disparagement. Mr. Prescott has been published side by side with other journalists, some professors, and renunciate women and men in the text Eternal Platform by the Ramakrishna Mission Ashrama in Ramharipur, India. He has also been published in the journal text Matriarch's Way and Vitals Signs: The International Association for Near Death Studies. He has just recently had an essay entitled Sri Ramakrishna As Personal Companion published in Global Vedanta. His works are in some libraries, universities and spiritual sanctuaries in the U.S.A., Europe, Russia, South America, and India. Writing has been his spiritual practice for thirty years. Including all volumes, he has over eighty published manuscripts, most of which are privately distributed. His works, of twenty five years, are now mentioned in the International Poet's Encyclopaedia, Cambridge, England. As of 2000, he is forty-eight years old and has been married for nineteen years.

Printed in the United States
1416000002B/1-27